The Tuskegee Airmen

and Beyond

The Road to Equality

The Tuskegee Airmen
and Beyond

The Road to Equality

David G. Styles

The Tuskegee Airmen and Beyond
The Road to Equality

© Dalton Watson Fine Books Limited

ISBN 978-1-85443-258-2

Dalton Watson Fine Books
1730 Christopher Drive
Deerfield, IL 60015
U.S.A.
info@daltonwatson.com

www.daltonwatson.com

The Tuskegee Airmen and Beyond
The Road to Equality

332nd Fighter Group

99th Fighter Squadron

100th Fighter Squadron

301st Fighter Squadron

302nd Fighter Squadron

*These men fought for the freedom and liberty of the world,
yet did not have freedom and liberty for themselves...*

Other Titles by the Author

Riley 75

Sixty Years of Naval Eight / 208

As Old As The Industry – Riley (Winner of 1983 Society of Automotive Historians Cugnot Award)

Sporting Rileys – The Forgotten Champions (Winner 1989 SAH Award of Distinction)

Alfa Romeo – The Legend Revived

Seventy Five Years On – The Flying Shuftis

Alfa Romeo – The Spyder, Alfasud and Alfetta GT

Porsche, The Road, Sports and Racing Cars (with J. McNamara, M. Cotton & J. Snook)

Aston Martin & Lagonda Vee-Engined Cars

MGA – The Complete Story (Winner, International Automotive Media Conference Moto Award 1996)

Datsun Z-Series – The Complete Story (Winner IAMC Moto Award 1997)

Riley – A Centennial Celebration (Winner IAMC Silver Medal 1997)

All the Eights – Eight Decades of Naval Eight / 208

Porsche 356 – The Flat-Four Engined Cars (IAMC Silver Medal Winner 1999)

Riley – Beyond the Blue Diamond (Winner 2 x IAMC Silver Medals 1999)

Alfa Romeo – Spirit of Milan (Winner IAMC Silver Medal 2000)

Moto Guzzi – Forza in Movimento (Winner IAMC Silver Medal 2001)

Volvo 1800 – The Complete Story

Doolittle Tales

Volvo Tech for Parts People (Winner IAMC Bronze Medal 2010)

National Diploma (UK) Motor Vehicle Technology, Unit 15 (Winner IAMC Silver/Bronze Medals 2011)

National Diploma (UK) Motor Vehicle Technology Workbook, Unit 9 (Winner IAMC Silver Medal 2012)

National Diploma (UK) Motor Vehicle Technology Workbook, Unit 29 (Winner IAMC Silver Medal 2012)

Two Flights to Victory

To Marie
My Inspiration for this book.

This book examines the progress to liberty and freedom
from slavery of one sector of society, the African Americans.
They fought long and hard to secure equality in a world
that labeled them as inferior only because of the color of
their skin, segregated on the basis of race. On what grounds
can that be justified, when
homo erectus originated in the Rift Valley of Africa?
What statement does that single fact place before every one
of us? Surely that we are all members of only
one race – the Human Race...

DGS

CONTENTS

PREFACE: Lieutenant-Colonel James C. Warren USAF (ret)

This book is the result of a lot of research and careful work. It goes much deeper than just the Tuskegee Airmen, but of course, the area of most interest to me is the Tuskegee Airmen and their achievement. They are the central part of this book because of what they did and how they did it. David tells us that this was the most highly decorated fighter group in North Africa or Italy and he gives us evidence to back it up. He also tells us what many people don't know. For example, he tells us not all Tuskegee Airmen were fighter pilots that this group also includes a Medium Bomber Group. He tells us about the women who were part of the Tuskegee Airmen – the nurses, the clerks, the technicians and even a pilot. He tells us about every combat victory and lists the men who received the Distinguished Flying Cross, then tells us how many Air Medals were really won. When I'd read through this book, I told David that there wasn't much I could tell him about the Tuskegee Airmen that he didn't already know! Add to this the fact that he has trodden the path of four hundred years since the first Africans were brought to these shores, through military conflict, and I can tell you that this book fills a large gap in American military history.

JCW

Lieutenant-Colonel James C. Warren is a Tuskegee Airman. He was not a fighter pilot and so did not fly with the 332nd Fighter Group. He was trained as a navigator and was assigned to the 477th Bombardment Group, which was equipped with North American B-25 medium bombers. The 477th never went into action in World War II, as it was battle-ready too late to meet its intended assignment to the Pacific. While the 477th was located at Freeman Field, Indiana, there was an incident in which a group of African American officers challenged the discrimination that prevented them from entering the all-white Officers' Club. James Warren was one of the young officers who entered the club anyway and started what became known as the Freeman Field Mutiny. Almost 50 years later, he succeeded in getting the convictions and fines for the two who were court-martialed lifted and their records cleared.

Colonel Warren's record includes 12,000 flying hours and participation in two significant wars – the Korean War and Vietnam. His total combat missions number 123, 50 of them in Korea, flying with Jimmy Doolittle's old bombardment Group, the 17th. Jim Warren's greatest claim to fame, perhaps, is that he was the navigator of the Lockheed C-141 named "Golden Bear", which flew into North Vietnam to pick up the first group of prisoners of war to be released by the North Vietnamese in 1973.

FOREWORD: Major-General Mary J. Kight USAF (ret)

The fight for our freedom resonates throughout the theme of this book. Honorable service in defense of this great country is reflected on every page. The untold stories of personal struggle and humble strength to overcome denial are not written but understood as David captures the struggles by telling the story of many accomplishments as they relate to our country's rich heritage.

My service reflects a point in time beyond the experiences of the people who triggered change captured in David's writings. My military career is an outgrowth of those former Service Members who proved they were worthy to wear a United States Armed Forces uniform.

The Tuskegee Airmen and all of their supporters stand equally with significant historical events in our country's history. While proud of them and all Veterans, I am most thankful for their courage. I am undeniably proud of my own service and I will remain grateful for The Tuskegee Airmen contributions along with those from all Veterans embraced by this book.

David, thank you for your service to US military history and for allowing me the honor to contribute.

MJK

Major-General Mary Kight, a Californian, was commissioned into the United States Air Force in February 1974. Her first tour of duty took her to Fairchild AFB at Spokane in Washington State. From that early start as a personnel officer, her career included several "firsts" in many interesting and challenging assignments, culminating in her return to her home state. In February 2010, Mary Kight became the first female Adjutant General of California's National Guard and the first African American woman to hold such a post across the nation. She retired in the fall of 2011, after giving her country thirty-seven years of service. Her contribution to this book is accepted with pride.

ACKNOWLEDGEMENTS & INTRODUCTION

This book was inspired by an African American lady named Marie Brooks and is dedicated to her. We met in the summer of 2010 as I was preparing my lecture programs in California to promote and launch my book *Two Flights to Victory*. Her contributions and support were outstanding. The Tuskegee Airmen served in Jimmy Doolittle's 12th Air Force in North Africa in World War II and we discussed this extensively and the impact those men had on the transition from slavery to the desegregation of the United States Armed Forces by President Harry Truman in 1948. Those conversations led me to write a paper on the subject, which developed, on Marie's suggestion, into a lecture series of the same name as this book. It was presented at Black History Month events and she gave great support at those lectures. The synopsis of this book preceded the lectures, and then came the manuscript. Marie advised and made constructive suggestions throughout the creation of this work. I am truly grateful to the lady who "didn't do anything" (her words, not mine).

The core of this story is, as the title implies, the Tuskegee Airmen – the first all-black fighter unit of the US Army Air Forces formed in 1941, its trials and tribulations, those who helped to make it happen, as well as preceding and subsequent events in African American history. There is, therefore, much more to this story, going back to the days when up to 30,000 slaves of African birth or origin joined the two conflicting forces in the Revolutionary War. More than 5,000 joined Washington's armies, believing their freedom lay in an independent American nation, and around 20,000 joined the British forces of General Cornwallis, because they believed that King George would give them their freedom, forgetting that most of the slave traders still shipping their kinsmen to America's shores were British. Others joined the British because they were pressed to do so by owners loyal to the

David Styles in the back seat of an SNJ Navy trainer about to fly to photograph the B-25s that attended the 2003 Doolittle Raiders Reunion.

Crown. And yet amazingly, there were few all-black fighting units in either army – they fought with great valor alongside white comrades.

The next serious opportunity for slaves and former slaves to defend a cause was the American Civil War when again, many thousands – in the Union Army 179,000 (10 percent of the total fighting force) and 4,000 in the US Navy – volunteered to fight. Sixteen black Union soldiers were awarded the Medal of Honor. Far fewer served in the Confederate forces, about 13,000, though there were many more volunteers. They fought alongside white comrades and the Confederate Monument in Arlington National Cemetery marks that fact.

African Americans fought in the Spanish-American War in the 1890s and despite now being segregated by unit and by decorations for valor, five men won the Medal of Honor in that conflict. The Great War of 1914-1918 (World War I) saw 350,000 African Americans on the Western Front in 1917-1918. And there is the story of the first black aviator – Eugene Bullard, who had to go to France to achieve his ambition to fly, but today is commemorated by his own exhibit in the United States Air Force Museum.

World War II brought the famous and valiant Tuskegee Airmen into existence and they are still the core of this story, because it was their commitment and valor that brought the ultimate emancipation of the African American. They opened the doors to those many African Americans we recognize today as worthy of the honors they achieve, but who, without that record of 96 Distinguished Flying Crosses, 1,031 Air Medals, 60 Purple Hearts, a Silver Star, 14 Bronze Stars, 3 Distinguished Unit Citations, a Presidential Unit Citation and a Legion of Merit for their commander, would have found it so much more difficult to make their mark. A total of 2.5 million men registered for the draft in World War II and the first African American general in the US Army was appointed, Brigadier-General Benjamin O. Davis, whose son commanded the Tuskegee Airmen.

The story follows the desegregation of the US Armed Forces by Presidential Decree from Harry S. Truman, the Korean conflict and later, Vietnam. In Korea, the first black naval aviator to be shot down was Ensign Jesse Brown, and Tuskegee Airman Daniel "Chappie" James flew F-80s there as the first African American to command a USAF squadron. His old boss, Colonel Benjamin Davis, commanded the 51st Fighter Interceptor Wing. Colonel James went on to fly in Vietnam too, ultimately rising to the rank of four-star general, the first African American at that rank. Altogether some 600,000 African American men and women served in Korea and another 350,000 served through the Vietnam War.

Coming back to the core story of the Tuskegee Airmen, we see how these men changed the world of military aviation forever and today, how their sons and daughters – and the sons and daughters of other African Americans, are taking their rightful place on the frontiers of aviation, space exploration and leadership. Follow with pride, then, the great legacy these men have left and how African American men and women are today, 70 years on, living those dreams. In modern times, no greater accolade or tribute could have been paid to the Tuskegee Airmen survivors than the invitation they received from the first African American President of the United States, Barack Obama, to his inauguration. He said: *"I stand on these men's shoulders."* Four million fifty-seven thousand pairs of them since 1772.

I am grateful to many people during the time of this book's creation. Three men in particular gave great encouragement to my "Tuskegee" lecture program. They were Tod Ruhstaller, CEO of the Haggin Museum in Stockton, California, Joe Pruzzo, CEO of the Castle Air Museum at Atwater, California and Sergeant Major Dan Sebby, the Curator of the California State Military Museum in Sacramento, California's Capital City. It was this last institution that generously honored me with the appointment as its Aviation Historian.

These three people were also a significant part of the inspiration to embark on this new book so close on the heels of *Two Flights to Victory*. But that book also had a role to play, because it featured the Tuskegee Airmen, as members of Jimmy Doolittle's 12th Air Force in North Africa, then the 15th Air Force in Italy. This book is an outgrowth of that part of *Two Flights to Victory*.

Bob Fish is a Trustee of the USS "Hornet" Museum, located at Pier 3 on Alameda Point and whilst this story is not connected in any direct way with the "Hornet", again, the Doolittle connection was sufficient to attract his interest. Teasing out any slight clue for more information has been a valuable part of Bob's contribution to this production, which has enjoyed a remarkably quick gestation from idea to finished

ACKNOWLEDGEMENTS & INTRODUCTION, CONTINUED

work. Other contributions have come from United States Air Force-related websites. The value of their illustrations being in the public domain is inestimable, as has been the help from many un-named people connected with those websites and their resources. More fine detail came from Dr. Daniel Haulman and Mr. Craig Huntly – I am grateful to them both. Andre Swygert has been a keen researcher into Tuskegee Airmen affairs for over 20 years and his input to this text has been considerable, enthusiastic and invaluable. I am indebted to him.

Proofreading has been another important process throughout the creation of this book. Many people have read individual chapters, but I must especially thank my long-standing friend Mike Jacques and his wife, Sue, for their interest and observations. Carol French also worked her way through a substantial chunk of the manuscript and once more, Marie Brooks gave much time and energy to the manuscript and illustrations, offering advice and guidance on many of the potentially sensitive elements and on suitable images. My nephew Jonathan Styles and his wife Gill also followed progress with keen interest and offered many supportive comments. I am grateful especially to these named people and to all those unnamed people along the way who have answered queries, sometimes not knowing why, and helped to form what you now see here.

While we've had our moments during the editorial process, I have to acknowledge the tremendous amount of work done by my editors, Glyn and Jean Morris. They put in great effort to "get it right" and have helped very much to "smooth out" what you read here. Thanks Glyn and Jean – and I think we're still friends!

Designer Jodi Ellis has worked wonders with this book. Its attractive appearance is her handiwork, but she did much more. In taking the many corrections and revisions and running them into the text, she has done much to make the book what it is. Thank you, Jodi.

Finally, and I have offered this comment in previous works, I have tried to cater for all tastes and provide something for everyone, even those who derive pleasure from seeking out and highlighting mistakes. But seriously, anyone who does find an error or can add a further piece of fact, then please do address it to me, so that corrections can be embodied in any future edition of this work.

To everyone who has come into contact with this book along the way to its publication, I offer a warm "Thank you". That includes you, the reader of this Introduction now.

DGS, 2013, Stockton, California

The author wishes to acknowledge images sourced from: United States Air Force, United States Army, United States Navy, and NASA images in the Public Domain, as well as those from: Congresswoman Anna Eshoo, The Jimmy Doolittle Air and Space Museum, SMSgt Tim Day USAF, MSgt Scott T. Sturkoi USAF and Wikipedia images declared to be in the Public Domain. Other images came the author's own collection.

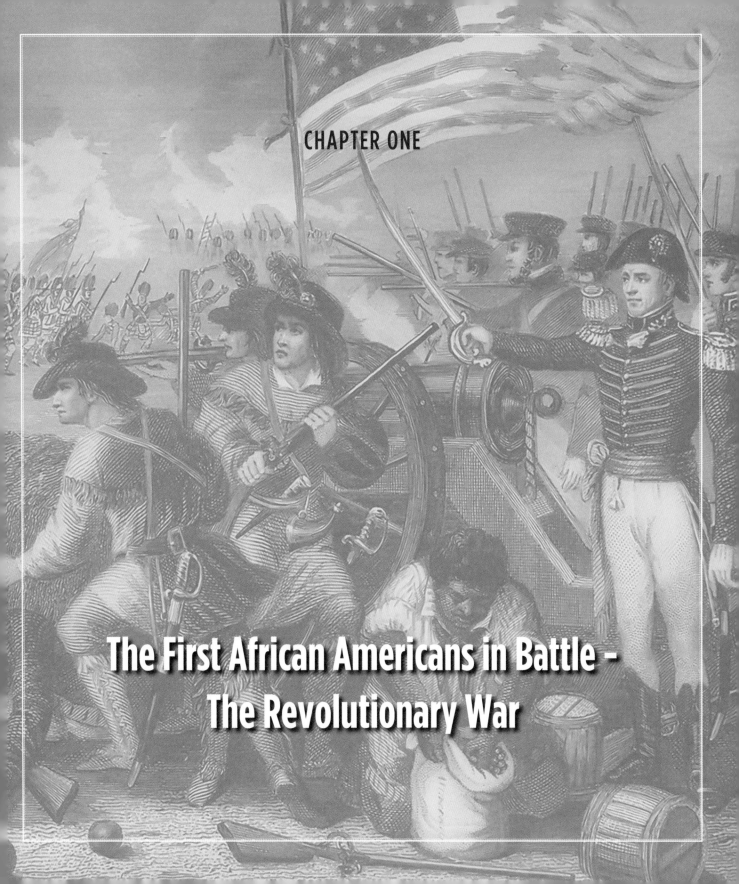

CHAPTER ONE

The First African Americans in Battle –
The Revolutionary War

African slavery has its roots in much earlier history than we address here. Among the first slave traders were the Arabs, who took African men and women into the interiors of Mesopotamia and the Arabian Peninsula – the men for hard-labor tasks and the women as housemaids, cooks, and for sexual gratification and the breeding of future generations of slaves to minimize trading costs.

A Roman slave market.

As the Roman Empire expanded into Northern Europe and the Middle East, almost 25 percent of the population was slaves and nearly half of them were of African origin –initially sold by Mesopotamian traders. Many of the tribal African men had powerful physiques and the Romans saw great sporting potential in them. In the outreaches of the Empire, fit young Africans were consigned to the amphitheaters as gladiators where they provided fine entertainment for the Roman generals and dignitaries, and soon there were black gladiators in the Coliseum of Rome.

Like the Mesopotamians, the Romans took to breeding slave children to provide future generations in preference to importing them with the risk of bringing to Rome disease and "imperfect specimens". Careful choices of studs and females gave the Roman Empire a slave stock that was the envy of the Mediterranean world.

Heirs to the Roman slave trade were the Spanish and the Portuguese who, in their explorations and colonization of South America, needed controllable and assured quality of labor. From the beginning, the use of African slaves provided the answer. One of the earliest recorded transactions in Brazil seems to have been in 1516. And soon, as the British colonists established a foothold in North America, they availed themselves of the opportunity of purchasing slaves. For example, as the Pilgrim Fathers settled in Virginia, the first African slaves, about 20 in number, were imported in 1619. Within a century, there were nearly half a million black slaves in America.

Slaves in Roman times were used for "entertainment" and put into the amphitheatres to fight wild animals.

Not all the early slaves in North America were fully owned by their masters, nor even were they all of African origin. Many Europeans had indentured themselves into virtual slavery for a given period of time to repay fares to the New World for their families, or to pay debts. There were also many Native Americans enslaved by early traders, but eventually a pattern established itself. Black slaves were easy to identify

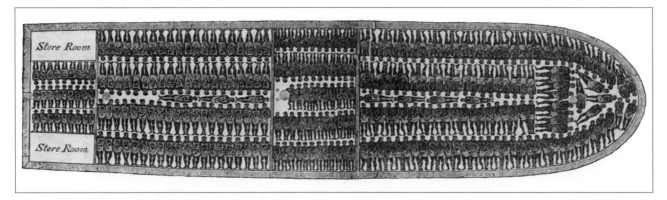

A slave ship "packing plan" from the 18th Century, showing how 278 slaves were transported across the Atlantic. Having bought them for somewhere between $150-$200 each, the "lucky" trader would realize around $800 per slave, yielding about $150,000 profit on one voyage.

Slaves being examined by a British trader.

Slaves being transported to ships.

by their color and were generally physically better "specimens" than their white counterparts, and they became the favored choice. Also the black slaves were easy to obtain as African tribal leaders of the time followed the pattern that went back centuries, selling as slaves captured prisoners of war and criminals.

When one considers the disgraceful conditions under which these human beings were taken, transported, and treated, it is extremely difficult to comprehend how they could possibly have become patriotic or loyal to any master by choice. But that did happen as second and third-generation slaves knew no other country. Additionally, as human beings they, like any other humans, developed friendships among themselves, which often became powerful loyalties – the more intense because associations with other groups were not available to them.

With growing unrest in the American Colonies of Great Britain, there was an increasing sense among slave groups of an opportunity to gain their freedom. That feeling was even fostered by some benevolent slave owners for there were many who released particularly loyal slaves where they had "earned" their freedom by some act of courage or special devotion and so there was a small, but growing, number of free African Americans in the country.

During the 1760s and into the 1770s, as the desire for American independence grew, there were public uprisings or paramilitary attacks on British military installations of which the Boston Riot and the Boston Tea Party were classic examples. And as that desire strengthened, so the boldness of the settlers came to the point where General George Washington raised an army to take on the British and seek independence. Militias were formed in the early 1770s and the Revolutionary War began in earnest in 1775, the Declaration of Independence coming on July 4, 1776. The war itself continued until 1783, when finally, the United States of America became a sovereign state and achieved recognition as such from Great Britain by the Treaty of Paris, signed on September 3, 1783.

Crispus Attucks, the man generally assumed to have been the first African American casualty of the Revolutionary War.

One incident, of many too numerous to detail in these pages, took place in Boston, Massachusetts. It arose from the dispatch by the British government of troops in 1768, to help the Colonial authorities enforce a series of Acts of Parliament known as the Townshend Acts, which created a means of imposing taxes on the colonies. This gave rise to formal resistance from the Massachusetts House of Representatives, and to a demonstration in 1770 that quickly expanded into what is now known as the Boston Riot. Two apprentices insulted a British officer and a soldier of his company, a Private White, struck an apprentice with the butt of his musket. In response citizens gathered round and harassed the soldier, and church bells began to toll. The bells were usually used as warnings, but now they became a signal for people to gather. As a crowd of 300-400 people surrounded the soldiers, they opened fire and among the several people killed was an African American sailor named Crispus Attucks, the first black casualty of the Revolutionary War. To African Americans, slave and free, he became a symbol of the struggle for freedom – firstly from the British, secondly from slavery.

As resistance expanded into war, some slave owners encouraged their slaves to join in the fray with the promise of freedom in the event of victory. It was a powerful incentive for male slaves to volunteer to fight, some for their country, the newly formed United States and others with the misguided hope of achieving freedom "from King George", believing that the British might be more benevolent towards them. Over 20,000 joined the British forces behind General Cornwallis because their British-born owners were loyal to King and Country. In contrast, only about 5,000 slaves chose to fight for the Union possibly because many Patriot slave owners did not encourage their slaves to enlist since they feared the slaves would band together and rebel to secure their freedom.

Consequently, the Battle of Lexington and Concord saw slaves fighting on both sides. The first shots of the Revolutionary War, were fired at Lexington, Massachusetts on April 18, 1775. The British General Thomas Gage sent 700 soldiers to destroy guns, ammunition and supplies the Patriots had stored in the town of Concord, just outside Boston and to arrest Samuel Adams and John Hancock, two prime leaders of the Patriot movement. The Patriots had secured excellent intelligence and, aware of the British plan, had moved all their

American Patriots facing British soldiers. This advance party of Patriots was a group of militia men known as Minutemen – the advance party awaiting Continental Army soldiers to take up the fight.

firearms from the warehouse, and another of their number, Paul Revere, had warned Adams and Hancock to escape.

The colonists had been expecting a fight with the British and they had organized a militia group, called the Minutemen, which included a number of slaves and free blacks. They were called Minutemen because they needed to be ready to fight on a minute's notice, a concept that went back to the 1650s when local militias were formed to protect communities from Indian raids. When the British soldiers reached Lexington, Captain Jonas Parker and 75 armed Minutemen were there to meet them. The Minutemen were greatly outnumbered. The British soldiers fired, killing eight of them and injuring ten others.

Soon Minutemen from nearby towns responded to messengers' warnings and the smoke from the burning supplies attracted local farmers and townspeople, and as the British soldiers headed back to Boston, they were attacked by a large force of patriots. By the time the soldiers reached Boston, 73 British men were dead and 174 more had been wounded, while 49 patriots were killed, and 39 others wounded. Throughout the day, black soldiers had fought with honor alongside their white compatriots.

The Battle of Bunker Hill was the next significant event in these early days of the Revolutionary War. Again, African and African-origin soldiers, both slaves and free men, fought for both sides. In the case of the Patriot soldiers, they thought they might gain their freedom and expand their civil rights in this new country. Many black men also served as guides, as messengers and even as spies in support of what they truly believed would be "the land of the free". Little did they realize that it would take almost 200 more years for true freedom to come to the African American. Nonetheless, in the belief at the time that this was their best option, many opted to join the Patriot cause and were seen fighting alongside white men.

At the same time, many others believed that the prospect of freedom might be better won by fighting with the British, and they fought alongside the Redcoats. The most significant reason for many slaves opting to fight for the Crown was because the British Parliament was already moving towards declaring slavery illegal throughout the Empire. An important legal test case took place in England in 1772, while the British colonies of America were still under Imperial rule. A British Customs officer from Boston, Massachusetts, Charles Stewart, owned a slave, James Somersett. Stewart took Somersett to England in 1769 and Somersett escaped in the summer of 1771. He was re-captured in November and imprisoned on a ship, the "Ann and Mary", bound for Jamaica. Before the ship set sail, three people claiming to be Somersett's godparents, John Marlow, Thomas Walkin and Elizabeth Cade (he had been baptized into the Anglican Church), made an application to the High Court for a writ of Habeas Corpus in respect of James Somersett, seeking to free him. It took three hearings to place the case before Lord Mansfield (an opponent of slavery), where a young lawyer, Francis Hargrave, in his first case, made a reputation for himself and secured Somersett's release and freedom.

In his summing up, Lord Mansfield said:

"The state of slavery is of such a nature, that it is incapable of now being introduced by Courts of Justice upon mere reasoning or inferences from any principles, natural or political; it must take its rise from positive law; the origin of it can in no country or age be traced back to any other source: immemorial usage preserves the memory of positive law long after all traces of the occasion; reason, authority, and time of its introduction are lost; and in a case so odious as the condition of slaves must be taken

strictly, the power claimed by this return was never in use here; no master was allowed here to take a slave by force to be sold abroad because he had deserted from his service, or for any other reason whatever; we cannot say the cause set forth by this return is allowed or approved of by the laws of this kingdom, therefore the man must be discharged".

As a consequence of this ruling, somewhere between 10,000 and 14,000 people held in bondage in Britain were set free. By 1833, the British government had declared slavery illegal throughout the Empire. Significantly, that was the year in which the great British abolitionist, William Wilberforce, died, but not before he had made his contribution to the abolition act and he had the pleasure of knowing of his success.

At the start of the Revolutionary War, it is said that the split of loyalties within the Colonial population was fairly even – one third committed to independence, one third committed to the Crown of England and one third neutral, not believing their lifestyles would change significantly either way. So those committed to independence would naturally bring pressure to bear on their slaves to support the independence cause, while those loyal to the King would persuade theirs to fight for Britain. The fact is that many of the slaves of

African Americans and new African migrant free men volunteered to fight in the Revolutionary War. The free would often volunteer to support the Patriots, while many slaves chose to fight for the British.

the "neutrals" would throw in their lot behind the British because they had been persuaded – even promised – freedom in return for a British victory. Hypothetical as it turned out, since neither side was put to absolute proof of its commitments, the British ultimately losing the fight. Such records as were kept suggest that approaching 100,000 slaves escaped, died or were killed during the Revolutionary War, something in the region of 20 percent of the total slave population of the time.

Meanwhile the British Governor of Virginia, Lord Dunmore, decided that he should expand the numbers in his army in order to preserve the authority of the Crown in that territory. In November 1775, he promised freedom to any slaves of "Patriots" or rebel masters if they would enlist in his newly formed regiment, to be called, strangely, the Ethiopian Regiment. What connection Ethiopia might have had with them would have been tenuous, but at least it was an African name and did seem to provide a recruitment incentive to some of those who enlisted.

Around 800 slaves left their masters, to become runaways liable to be shot on sight. They came from other places as well as Virginia. For example the free black community in Philadelphia almost certainly heard of Lord Dunmore's proclamation that slaves who fought would be set free in Virginia, so the number of 800 will have comprised quite a few from Pennsylvania, as well as several free men. The Ethiopian Regiment was trained in the basic skills of musketry and formation marching – at least to look like an orderly army. They were also given uniforms that had embroidered upon them the phrase: "Liberty to Slaves".

The Ethiopian's first engagement was at a place called Kemp's Landing in Virginia, where they scored an easy victory, over-running the Patriot troops encamped there. Confident of further victory and inspired by this first engagement, Lord Dunmore took his army, a combination of British regulars and the Ethiopian Regiment, on to Norfolk, engaging in the Battle of Great Bridge. Sadly for the Ethiopian, they were marching towards their enemy in formation and were an easy target. The Patriots brought down close to 100 men, less than half that number killed, but forced the British

Black soldier in the Ethiopian Regiment.

contingent to withdraw. Putting to sea at Norfolk, Dunmore withdrew his army and sailed north for New York. Smallpox struck as they sailed out of Virginia and only 300 or so soldiers of the Ethiopian reached New York, but there they were discharged and set free.

It seems that, when George Washington first took command of his Continental Army, he forbade the recruitment of black soldiers, even though many blacks had fought side-by-side with whites at Lexington & Concord and Bunker Hill. (Washington was a resident of the South and a slave owner himself, even though he assumed command of the Army in Massachusetts.) However, Washington did allow free blacks who had previously fought to re-enlist in 1775-76. But then, in the summer of 1776, the Continental Congress and all of the states of the intended Union, except Virginia, prohibited the recruitment of blacks whether free or slave. So Washington no longer had the power of decision in the matter of recruitment.

At the onset of winter of 1777-78, there were many black Virginians serving in every one of the state regiments. The Battle of Valley Forge was a particular example of where the Continental Army could not have functioned without them. Black soldiers froze, starved and died alongside their white comrades. By February 1778, the survivors were marching together through the snow, now practicing Baron von Steuben's quite unfamiliar military drills. Von Steuben was a German-born officer who had elected to serve with the Continental Army. When the Steuben-trained army proved its mettle at Monmouth in June, about 700 blacks fought side-by-side with whites. Eight weeks later, an army report listed 755 blacks in the Continental Army, including 138 in the Virginia Line. Von Steuben estimated some time later that this army was almost 50 percent black.

As the winter of 1777-78 advanced, the size of the Continental Army had dwindled significantly. Desertion (of white and black in similar numbers), injuries and disease had caused a drop of near 10,000, to just above 8,000 men. The Continental Congress had to do something drastic if it was to reinforce its numbers and be able to take on a rejuvenated British army, which had occupied Philadelphia. The solution came from the Rhode Island legislature, which set up a fund to purchase sufficient slaves to form a regiment consisting of both free blacks and slaves.

These men would be placed under the command of Colonel Christopher Greene and, when they had passed muster, they would be given their freedom. And for once, a regiment kept its word. The First Rhode Island Regiment fought with distinction for five years in the battles of Rhode Island, Point's Bridge, where it was especially commended, and Yorktown – and won their freedom, though their commander died in battle at Point's Bridge in 1781.

The State of Massachusetts also formed an all-black unit from

The First Rhode Island Regiment was commanded by Colonel Christopher Greene.

a mixture of slaves and free men. Beginning in early 1778 the state bought and emancipated slaves willing to become soldiers, and appointed the only black commissioned officer in the whole Continental Army to command it. His name was Samuel Middleton and his regiment became known as the Bucks of America. In October 1780, even Maryland accepted "any able-bodied slave between 16 and 40 years of age, who voluntarily enters into service... with the consent and agreement of his master." New York would begin to recruit slaves in March 1781. The tide was turning.

Then came the Battle and siege of Yorktown, a highly significant event for the First Rhode Island Regiment, for it was here that the surrender of General Lord Cornwallis was secured. The French had joined with the Patriots and provided a naval force to distract Britain's Royal Navy. They confronted the British at the Battle of the Chesapeake and British Admiral Sir Thomas Graves was defeated, allowing the French Navy to blockade New York and the neighboring coastline all the way down to Virginia, preventing any possibility of General Cornwallis escaping by sea. Cornwallis retreated into Virginia, where his forces commenced to construct a defensible deep-water port at Yorktown. General Washington's Patriot Army of over 11,000 men and the French 8,000-odd regulars under the command of Comte Rochambeau shadowed the British and were soon able to surround Cornwallis' army. On October 17th, Cornwallis asked for terms of surrender and after two days, the Battle of Yorktown became the decisive event of the Revolutionary War, for by 1783, the Treaty of Paris had been signed and Britain gave formal recognition to the United States of America.

The final act of compassion towards slaves participating in the Revolutionary War came from the Virginia House of Burgesses, which declared that all slaves who had fought in the Continental Army should be given their freedom in return for their loyalty to the Union. That declaration was issued on October 3, 1783 and so had the true force of law, in that the United States of America had now been formally recognized by the British government and King George. The Virginia House of Burgesses was the first legislature established anywhere within the British colonies of America. It first met on July 30, 1619, at a church in Jamestown, Virginia and its first ruling was the setting of prices for the sale of tobacco, a far cry from the journey through the War of Independence to the setting free of loyal slaves.

Now the United States could settle down to the peaceful construction of a nation. The Patriots still had a great deal to contend with in the route to great nationhood, not least dealing with the Native American tribes, upon whose lands the settlers were encroaching uninvited. As more immigrants came to the new country, problems arose with the westward migration of settlers, and the militias still had a job to do. They continued to recruit from the free black and slave communities, promising freedom to slaves in return for fixed periods of enlistment, five years being a common term.

But then, the political situation in the new United States began to change. Britain was at war with France, and in order to restrict the French finances, the British government instructed the United States to cease trading with them. Franco-American trade at that time was quite extensive and since the Americans saw the British dispute with the French to be nothing to do with the United States, the instruction was ignored. Great Britain's blockade of France during the Napoleonic Wars was a constant source of conflict because trading ships, French and American, were often prevented from sailing, stopped in the early stages of their voyage, or simply sunk. In addition, the British still continuously en-

gaged in impressments to force US citizens to serve in the Royal Navy, and they had also attacked the USS Chesapeake, which had nearly caused a war two year earlier. Disputes continued over the Northwest Territories and the border with Canada. War was thus inevitable – and with it, once more, the inclusion of black soldiers to fight for the Union. Amazingly, a large number of free or enslaved African Americans also volunteered to fight with the British.

The War of 1812, declared on June 12th, is one of the United States' forgotten wars. It lasted for more than two years, and ended in a stalemate, but it did achieve one significant fact and that was to confirm, once and for all, the independence and sovereignty of the United States of America. And it could have changed the face of political geography too if the US offensive against Canada had been successful. On the other hand, the British army was stopped when it attempted to capture Baltimore and New Orleans. In skirmishes at sea, there was a number of American naval victories in which American vessels proved superior to similarly sized British vessels.

At the time the United States declared war on Great Britain, the Navy was the only branch of the American Armed Forces allowing blacks to serve, although even they were officially barred from enlisting. The excuse made for the recruitment

HMS "Shannon" takes on the USS "Chesapeake" in Chesapeake Bay during the spring of 1813.

of slaves and former slaves was that they were "the best available in this time of need". And yet, the "Second War of American Independence" was primarily a naval war, so the greatest manpower needs fell upon the Navy. In March 1813 the Navy responded by officially reversing the policy of excluding African Americans from the fleet. Free blacks, and escaped slaves purporting to be free, reacted to that change of policy by joining the Navy in large numbers.

However, when the British fleet sent an expedition into Chesapeake Bay in the spring of 1813, they were stunned by the eagerness of slaves to desert their masters and join the Royal Navy. So many slaves recalled Lord Dunmore's proclamation in 1775 on his formation of the Ethiopian Regiment and the liberty won by those soldiers 38 years earlier that they were inspired to pursue the same path now promised to them. It has been estimated that 3-5,000 slaves from Maryland and Virginia fled to join the British. In April 1814, Vice Admiral Cochrane, of the Royal Navy, issued a proclamation welcoming aboard all slaves who wished to immigrate to Britain. They all had the choice of either serving a career with the British forces or being sent as free settlers to British possessions in North America and the West Indies.

As the war progressed, the African American component of the United States Navy represented up to 20 percent of the total naval manpower. Such records as exist tell that these men served with great courage and played a major role in the winning of naval battles. Captain Oliver Perry initially complained to Commodore Chauncey about the number of black sailors assigned to his command. Chauncey's response was that he had nearly 50 blacks on his own ship and many of them were among the best of his men, putting down Perry's complaint swiftly and decisively. The Battle of Lake Erie involved a naval force led by Perry and it defeated the British with blacks representing a quarter of the 400 man force aboard the ten vessel fleet. Their performance in that victory so impressed Perry that he later wrote to the Secretary of the Navy praising their fearlessness in the face of extreme danger.

In May 1814, British Admiral George Cockburn began to enlist and train runaway slaves for the marine unit on Tangier Island, in Chesapeake Bay, Virginia, a British base. The Marines saw their first action in late May during the successful British attack upon an American battery at Pungoteaque, on the peninsula that separates Chesapeake Bay from the Atlantic Ocean. The British commander of the expedition was highly impressed with the performance of the black Marines (not, incidentally, embodied into the Royal Marines, but described as the Corps of Colonial Marines) and continued to use them throughout the Chesapeake campaign, including the American defeat at Bladensburg, the burning of Washington, DC (the only time since the Revolutionary War that any foreign nation has ever occupied the American capital), and the British Armed Forces own defeat at Baltimore. The achievement of this Corps of Colonial Marines encouraged Cochrane and Cockburn to expand their use, but the war ended before they could put their ideas into action.

On land it was a similar story to the Americans' experiences at sea. For the United States, black soldiers played a key role in the last major land engagement of the war: the Battle of New Orleans. Louisiana had only achieved statehood some nine weeks before the United States declared war on Great Britain. With the sudden need for recruits, the state legislature authorized the recruitment of free black landholders into its militia. This re-formed the "Battalion of Free Men of Color", a body that had been disbanded in 1804. The unit's commanding officer was white, Colonel Michel Fortier, but Louisiana's governor, William Claiborne, decided to commission three black 2nd Lieutenants, the only African American commissioned officers in that state militia. It should be remembered that the honor of being the first African American commissioned officer in the United States was Samuel Middleton in the Continental Army back in 1778, leading the Bucks of America.

Having been soundly defeated in the Great Lakes and the Chesapeake campaign of 1814, the British switched their attention to the South. By the summer of 1814, when it became obvious to the Americans that Britain's next target would be New Orleans, General Andrew Jackson ordered the region to call up their militias into active service. Even with the New Orleans Battalion of Free Men of Color, Louisiana could

The Battle of New Orleans was the decisive event in the War of 1812, in which two battalions of the Free Men of Color made a major contribution to the defeat of the British in 1815. This was the confrontation which made the reputation of General Andrew Jackson.

not meet its quota of 1,000 men, so Governor Claiborne appealed for volunteers among the free black population of New Orleans, promising them the same pay, rations and bounty as for white volunteers. Many free blacks answered the call and raised the numbers of the Battalion of Free Men of Color from four companies to six, bringing the total number of men-at-arms to 353 men. On December 16, 1814, the battalion was absorbed into the United States Army under the command of Major Pierre Lacoste. The ranking black officer was Major Vincent Populus, the first African American to attain field grade rank in the United States Army's history.

On January 8, 1815 (only weeks after the peace treaty was signed between the United States and Great Britain) 8,000 veterans of the Napoleonic campaigns under the command of the British General Sir Edward Pakenham attacked New Orleans, fully expecting to win the battle against a mixed collection of men under the command of General Jackson. However, Pakenham encountered a massive surprise, because the two Battalions of Free Men of Color fought with great distinction, delivering to the British their worst defeat in many years, where they lost over 2,000 men in what could only be described as a frivolous encounter, especially as

American losses amounted to only 21 men. After the battle, General Jackson commended the performance of the two black battalions in a letter to Secretary of War James Monroe. Jackson noted that he believed General Pakenham, who fell in the battle, was brought down by a bullet of a Free Man of Color. When they were discharged, the black volunteers did receive the same pay and bounty as their white counterparts, but the promise of federal pensions and land grants of 160 acres each were never fulfilled. As the result of poor recruitment in peacetime, these black militia units ultimately faded away and were officially disbanded in 1834.

This period of African American commitment to military service in their quest for freedom could be expanded into a book of its own, but that is not the purpose here. The task is only to show how so many African Americans were willing to take up arms in what was essentially at that time the white man's struggle for freedom in the hope that some benefit of that freedom might reflect upon them. Sadly, it was to be almost 200 years before that was to be so – and without the valiant efforts of the Tuskegee Airmen – heirs in the first half of the Twentieth Century to their courage and determination, it may have taken much longer.

CHAPTER TWO

The Next Fight For Freedom – The American Civil War

In November 1860, Abraham Lincoln, a Republican, was elected President of the United States. He did not take office, as now, on January 20 in the following year, and it was March 4, 1861 before he occupied the White House. Leading up to his election and beyond, there had been moves by certain southern states to secede from the Union over the issue of slavery. Lincoln's political concern was less to do with the abolition of slavery than the integrity of the Union. His major goal was to keep the United States united as one nation, but it seemed he was fighting a losing battle. It is on record that Lincoln was not a supporter of slavery. In fact, he had made many speeches in opposition to the practice in his political career leading up to his presidency. Further, the United States of America had outlawed slavery, though putting that law into effect was another matter in many parts of the country. It is interesting to reflect that one of his senior army generals was Robert E. Lee and he too, opposed the

secession. But General Lee was a Virginian and he was not about to go to war with his own home state, and for that reason, Robert E. Lee withdrew to the Confederacy.

Seven states initially joined together – they were Alabama, Florida, Georgia, Louisiana, Mississippi, South Carolina and Texas. These states declared their secession from the United States on February 4, 1861, at the Montgomery Convention, in Montgomery, Alabama, just four weeks before President Lincoln assumed office. The Confederate States of America was formed and Jefferson Davis was elected as its first President. When, on April 12th, the Confederate Army attacked the United States Army outpost at Fort Sumter, there was little Lincoln could do but send troops to re-secure the fort. In that time, four more states, Arkansas, North Carolina, Tennessee and Virginia, seceded from the Union. Because many of the counties in the western districts of Virginia rejected the Confederacy, the United States government agreed to the formation of a new state – West Virginia, which was admitted immediately into the Union.

From the outset the Confederacy made a serious political misjudgment in believing that Abraham Lincoln had little concern for the plight of slaves and that the liberation of slaves was the first objective of the newly elected Republican government of the North. Certainly, the abolitionists had primarily come from the Republican Party, but in an extract from his inaugural address to Congress in March 1861, President Lincoln had this to say:

President (1860-1865) Abraham Lincoln.

"I do not consider it necessary at present for me to discuss those matters of administration about which there is no special anxiety or excitement.

"Apprehension seems to exist among the people of the Southern States that by the accession of a Republican administration their property and their peace and personal security are to be endangered. There has never been any reasonable cause for such apprehension. Indeed, the most ample evidence to the contrary has all the while existed and been open to their inspection. It is found in nearly all the published speeches of him who now addresses you. I do but quote from one of those speeches

THE TUSKEGEE AIRMEN AND BEYOND

when I declare that – "I have no purpose, directly or indirectly, to interfere with the institution of slavery in the States where it exists. I believe I have no lawful right to do so, and I have no inclination to do so"…

This misunderstanding of Lincoln's aims was the Confederacy's biggest error, closely followed in importance by the attack on Fort Sumter, for this act brought about the bloodiest war in America's history, with American killing and maiming American for minimal purpose.

It can be argued that the Confederacy was protecting its own best interests by seizing Fort Sumter, since it stood at the mouth of Charleston harbor. In December 1860, before the Confederacy was formed, and although the construction of Fort Sumter was not yet complete, its commander, Major Robert Anderson, proceeded to dismantle nearby Fort Moultrie and move its men and equipment to Fort Sumter. It was said that some form of agreement existed between the

State of South Carolina and the United States Government in Washington that all military properties would remain as they were until the issue of right of possession had been resolved – the argument being put by South Carolina that Fort Sumter belonged to that State. Major Anderson seemingly had no knowledge of such a political arrangement and was moving his men and equipment from Fort Moultrie to Fort Sumter for the purpose of self-protection.

Major Anderson was visited by representatives of the South Carolina Militia who requested his peaceful withdrawal from Fort Sumter and that he hand it over to the State of South Carolina. He was asked why he had transferred men and equipment from Fort Moultrie and he replied that he was concerned over the number of boats passing by the fort carrying soldiers of the South Carolina Militia and feared the possibility of attack from the north. His argument was not accepted, since it was stated that the patrol boats were seeking only to maintain law and order in and around the harbor, although no one had thought to forewarn Major Anderson.

An attempt was then made by the US government to reinforce the garrison by sending supplies in a large merchant steamer, "The Star of the West", but she was attacked by shots from the shore and retreated without unloading. Major Anderson did all he could with the limited resources he had to maintain his position but on April 11, 1861, when he refused to evacuate Fort Sumter, the guns of South Carolina opened fire and he was forced to surrender. The Civil War between the United States and the Confeder-

The image of the Confederate attack on Fort Sumter was published in *Harper's Weekly*.

Major Robert Anderson.

ate States had begun, heralding with it four years of bitter conflict and the worst war experience in North American history.

Rapid recruitment of soldiers was now vital to both sides. President Lincoln issued an edict to recruit 500,000 men, a tall order for an army starting with only around 16,000. It became essential to look at all aspects of recruitment, including black soldiers. Slaves and free blacks had been barred from enlisting in the United States Army since the War of 1812. But times were different now and there was a need for men from any source. At the height of the war, the ultimate size of the United States Army was 2.2 million, and of these, almost ten percent, or 179,000 were African American soldiers, recruited into black and mixed regiments.

The first action to bring black soldiers into the Union army was to confiscate slaves whose owners were in the Confed-

eracy, free them and enlist them into the US Army. Recruitment of free blacks was accelerated considerably when one famous free African American – Frederick Douglass – stood up to be counted – as did two of his sons. He gained great renown when he said:

"Once let the black man get upon his person the brass letter, US, let him get an eagle on his button, and a musket on his shoulder and bullets in his pocket, there is no power on earth that can deny that he has earned the right to citizenship."

As that profound statement echoed through the Spartan accommodations of slaves and only marginally better homes of free blacks, thousands of recruits flocked to join the United States Army in order, as they thought, to gain freedom, self-respect and citizenship on an equal footing with the white man – which was to take another century in coming – but the first true seeds of freedom were now being sown. A sense of patriotism for the nation was something most African Americans felt, but that smell of freedom was what motivated the great majority.

The Lincoln administration debated for some time the idea of recruiting black troops, for they were concerned that such a move might prompt more border states to secede. Proclamations were issued by General John C. Fremont in Missouri and General David Hunter in South Carolina to

Black and white soldiers of the Union and Confederate armies face each other in the 1861 Battle of Manassas, fighting side-by-side in their own battle lines.

Frederick Douglass.

lamation to his Cabinet. After the Union Army turned back General Lee's first invasion of the North at Antietam, Maryland, and the Emancipation Proclamation was subsequently announced, black recruitment was pursued in earnest. Volunteers from South Carolina, Tennessee, and Massachusetts filled the first authorized black regiments in the Union Army.

As the Army of the North was, by 1862, openly recruiting black soldiers to fight among its ranks, the Confederate Congress positively ruled that black volunteers should not be accepted into the army as a matter of policy. These actions had two effects on the Confederate Army – it demoralized the officers, who could only watch what was happening in the Union North and it demonized the Confederacy, for at every opportunity, the Union Army would make great capital from the large numbers of black soldiers in their battalions. By comparison, there were few enlisted in the south with only 13,000 engaged on the front line, although there were plenty of volunteers. However, the fighting units of the South were less well regulated from the top commands and many local militias found it expedient to take on black volunteers to fight alongside white soldiers. There was often a desperate need for numbers and any man, regardless of skin color, who would fight for his country was accepted. The dichotomy of this was that the African American volunteer abhorred and resented slavery as an insult to the human race, yet loved his country and was ready to fight for it. Nonetheless, those who did volunteer to fight for the South did so just as valiantly as their Northern adversaries.

The two Battles of Bull Run demonstrate how the African Americans fought and died for the South. One unit, the "Richmond Howitzers", was partially manned by black militiamen, and they saw action as early as 1861 in the first Battle of Bull Run, where they operated Battery Number Two. Add to that the two black infantry "regiments", one free and one slave, which also participated in the battle.

The Second Battle of Bull Run took place in August 1862 and once again, there were slave recruits fighting for the South. The total number of combatants on the battlefield in that two-day confrontation was 112,000, of which the Union Army fielded 62,000. Almost 20,000 men were killed or wounded,

emancipate slaves in their military regions and allow them to enlist, but their superiors would have none of it. However, by mid-1862, the rising numbers of former slaves (known as "contrabands") and the smaller number of white volunteers, created a situation that the government could no longer ignore. The Army was desperately in need of fighters and so the government had to reconsider and ultimately allow the recruitment of slaves into the army, with white officers and black non-commissioned officers.

On July 17, 1862, Congress passed the Second Confiscation and Militia Act, freeing slaves who had masters in the Confederate Army. Two days later, slavery was abolished in all the territories of the United States, and on July 22nd, President Lincoln presented the first draft of the Emancipation Proc-

Union cavalry charge in the first Battle of Bull Run.

and there were African American soldiers fighting and dying for both sides.

In July 1863, the bloodiest event of the Civil War was fought at Gettysburg in Pennsylvania, an awful, battle of three days duration. General George Meade led the Union Army of something under 94,000 men, with General Robert E. Lee heading up the Confederate Army of just under 72,000. The statistics of the battle are remarkably similar for both sides, with a few over 23,000 casualties and losses each, though far more Confederate soldiers died, some 4,700, than the Union's recorded total of 3,150. However, Union wounded were 2,000 higher than the Confederacy and there was about a 500-men difference in the numbers of captured and missing, the higher being on the Confederate side. There were black soldiers fighting for both sides, some in segregated regiments and

others alongside white comrades. Such was the emotion in the nation about Gettysburg that President Lincoln ordered that a military cemetery be constructed with a monument to those Union soldiers who died there. In November, he dedicated that monument and gave the historic Gettysburg Address – a short and simple declaration of the rights of men. Here it is:

"Four score and seven years ago our fathers brought forth on this continent a new nation, conceived in liberty, and dedicated to the proposition that all men are created equal.

"Now we are engaged in a great civil war, testing whether that nation, or any nation, so conceived and so dedicated, can long endure. We are met on a great battle-

field of that war. We have come to dedicate a portion of that field, as a final resting place for those who here gave their lives that that nation might live. It is altogether fitting and proper that we should do this.

"But, in a larger sense, we cannot dedicate, we cannot consecrate, we cannot hallow this ground. The brave men, living and dead, who struggled here, have consecrated it, far above our poor power to add or detract. The world will little note, nor long remember what we say here, but it can never forget what they did here. It is for us the living, rather, to be dedicated here to the unfinished work, which they who fought here have thus far so nobly advanced. It is rather for us to be here dedicated to the great task remaining before us – that from these honored dead we take increased devotion to that cause for which they gave the last full measure of devotion – that we here highly resolve that these dead shall not have died in vain – that this nation, under God, shall have a new birth of freedom – and that government of the people, by the people, for the people, shall not perish from the earth".

Just over a week after the Battle of Gettysburg, two more bloody battles were fought at Fort Wagner, on Morris Island – not too far from Fort Sumter – and adjacent to Charleston in South Carolina. The most famous fighting unit of those two battles was the 54th Massachusetts Volunteer Infantry, the volunteers being African Americans commanded by Colonel Robert Shaw. The most significant event of that battle was the first citation for the awarding of twenty-two Medals of Honor to African American soldiers in the Civil War – the

Sergeant William H. Carney was the first African American Medal of Honor recipient.

African American soldiers of the 54th Massachusetts Volunteers.

highest form of recognition of gallantry under fire that the United States can confer. The Medal of Honor was approved by Congress on July 12, 1862 as the "Highest Award for Valor" available. Specifically, it was awarded for "Conspicuous gallantry and intrepidity at the risk of his life above and beyond the call of duty while engaged in an action against any enemy of the United States; while engaged in military operations involving conflict with an opposing foreign force". The first recipient of the Medal of Honor was Sergeant William H. Carney of the 54th Massachusetts Volunteers. Sergeant Carney was nominated for the award just one year and one week after its institution.

Companion Medal of Honor awardee in the Civil War was Lieutenant Frank Welch, also of the 54th Massachusetts Volunteers and one of the very few black officers in that unit. This photograph shows him as a Major, commanding a battalion of the Connecticut National Guard.

which to draw. He concluded that the solution was to recruit from the slave population, and prepared a proposal to put to his fellow generals. His statement included this emotive passage:

> "Adequately to meet the causes which are now threatening ruin to our country, we propose, in addition to a modification of the President's plans, that we retain in service for the war all troops now in service, and that we immediately commence training a large reserve of the most courageous of our slaves, and further that we guarantee freedom within a reasonable time to every slave in the South who shall remain true to the Confederacy in this war. As between the loss of independence and the loss of slavery, we assume that every patriot will freely give up the latter – give up the negro slave rather than be a slave himself".

It was a controversial recommendation and one that was to be rejected by the generals who met with General Cleburne on January 2, 1864, among them Brigadier-General George S. Patton. The continuing desire to keep slaves subjected among some of his listeners inhibited Cleburne's promotion, for most had expected that he would be promoted Lieutenant-General and placed in command of the whole CSA Army. Instead, President Davis instructed that the document be kept confidential and no further action be taken in this direction.

Major-General Patrick Cleburne.

However, the situation for the Confederacy was truly dire when the Siege of Petersburg took place in June 1864 and resulted in a change of heart. Petersburg was an unusual city in Virginia in that around 50 percent of the population consisted of black people and around 35 percent of them were free, working in many trades in the town and mingling well

In the same way as the North was seeking to recruit soldiers from any available source, so by 1863 the Confederacy was looking at the same objectives and one especially interesting approach to this came from Major-General Patrick Cleburne, the senior Confederate officer of the time. He had contemplated the terrible rout of the Battle of Gettysburg and the later battles of the Civil War and was acutely aware that the Confederate army was being decimated. He knew he needed more fighting men and had no reserves upon

Black Confederate soldiers taking a rest during a lull in the fighting at the Battle of Petersburg in Virginia, in 1865.

A combination of black and white Union troops in the same battle.

with the white citizens. During the siege, African Americans continued working for the Confederacy, and in September 1864, General Robert E. Lee asked for an additional 2,000 blacks to be added to his labor force. Then in March 1865, with the serious loss of white manpower called for 40,000 slaves to become an armed force in the Confederacy.

The slaves-turned-soldiers were told that they would enjoy their freedom and undisturbed residences at their old homes in the Confederacy after the war. And the point was made without question that this would not be just toleration, but true and honorable freedom which, according to

the Petersburg Daily Express would be "...*won by the gallantry and devotion which grateful countrymen will never cease to remember and reward.*" We do not know how many men volunteered and in any event, the war ended before any major contribution could be made. However, there was one Confederate unit that was highly commended by its commander, the youthful, 24-year old, Colonel Shipp. This was the Jackson Battalion, which included two companies of African American soldiers. After combat at Petersburg, Colonel Shipp, reported to General Lee: "*My men acted with utmost promptness and goodwill... Allow me to state, Sir, that they behaved in an extraordinarily acceptable manner.*"

In March 1865, The Confederate Secretary of State, Judah P. Benjamin, gave a promise of freedom for all blacks who volunteered from the State of Virginia. Authority was granted by the State Legislature and on April 1, 1865, $100 bounties were offered to black soldiers. Benjamin exclaimed, "*Let us say to every Negro who wants to go into the ranks, go and fight, and you are free... Fight for your masters and you shall have your freedom.*" Confederate Officers were instructed to treat these soldiers with appropriate respect and protect them from "*injustice and oppression*".

Ultimately, a quota was set for 300,000 black soldiers for the Confederate States Colored Troops. President Jefferson Davis endorsed that quota and amazingly, 83 percent of Richmond's male slave population volunteered for duty. A special ball was held in Richmond to raise money to equip these men with uniforms and before Richmond fell, black Confederates in gray uniforms drilled in the streets.

However, before many of that 300,000 man army could be recruited, or even trained, the Civil War came to its end, with the surrender of the Confederate Army to the Union on April 18, 1865. A staggering 617,000 Americans had died, almost as many as in all of America's later wars combined worldwide. Tens of thousands more were maimed and injured. And the landscape of the beautiful South was ravaged and in parts is scarred to this day.

Most importantly of all, the hundreds of thousands of African Americans, Union and Confederate, who volunteered to serve did enjoy "freedom", but of an odd kind. They were free to work at places of their choice, which generally meant where they could get work. They were free to own their own homes, but in selected areas of cities and towns across America. Some prospered, often despite the system, not because of it. It was to be another hundred years and a great deal of civil bloodshed before they had a free democratic vote, the right to ride in public transport alongside white passengers and to buy goods in the same stores as anyone else. Freedom came, but a greater price had yet to be paid for liberty.

In Arlington, Virginia, stands the Arlington National Cemetery, a place to honor the military dead of many conflicts. It was originally created as a Confederate shrine – a place to bury the dead of the Confederate States Army and Militias, and it has the first military monument in the United States Capital to honor an African American soldier. The monument was designed by a Jewish architect, Moses Jacob Ezekiel, who was himself a Confederate soldier, and it was erected and dedicated in 1914. Ezekiel wanted to convey the mixed-race makeup of the Confederate Army and so an African American Confederate soldier is depicted marching in step with white Confederate comrades in arms, and a white soldier is represented giving his child to a black woman for protection. Moses Ezekiel is buried at the foot of that Monument. Arlington National Cemetery today is the final resting place for military Americans of all races.

By 1866, the Civil War was past, yet one of the most amazing stories from the US Army was about to unfold. This was when the first woman on record enlisted in the army, albeit as a man. Her name was Cathay Williams, but she was recorded on enlistment as William Cathey and she served in the Army for two years before it was discovered that she was female.

Cathay's story, as far as this book is concerned, began during the Civil War, when she and a number of other young girls were taken by the US Army from Jefferson, Missouri to Little Rock, Arkansas, to work as cooks and house servants for Army officers. Her father was an African American freeman, but her mother was a slave, belonging to William Johnson, a farmer who lived near Independence, Missouri, where she

The Confederate War Memorial at Arlington, Virginia, where black soldiers are depicted fighting alongside white soldiers.

was born. When she was a young girl, her master and family moved to Jefferson City, where he died. When the Civil war began and the United States soldiers came to Jefferson City they took Cathay and other slaves and former slaves to Little Rock.

Lieutenant-Colonel William Benton of the 13th Army Corps was the officer who instructed the removal and transportation of the group. He wanted Cathay to cook for the officers, but she had been a house girl, and had no experience of cooking. She learned to cook at Little Rock and was serving Army officers at the Battle of Pea Ridge in 1862, then moved on to Shreveport, Louisiana. She saw soldiers burn cotton to damage the Confederate States' economy and she was at Shreveport when the Confederate gunboats were destroyed on the Red River. After that, she spent some time in New Orleans, and Savannah, Georgia. When General Philip Sheridan raided the Shenandoah Valley and defeated the Confederate Army, she was working as cook and laundress to his staff. Ultimately, she finished up near her home, at Jefferson Barracks.

This wonderfully evocative picture is of Cathay Williams as Private William Cathey in the foreground, then shadowed in the background is Cathay as the woman she was.

It was perhaps this experience that led her, on November 15, 1866, to enlist in the Army as a male recruit. She gave her name as William Cathay, but because she was illiterate, she did not realize that her male name was written as "William Cathey". It is likely that she enlisted and took the chance of being discovered because as a civilian female cook, she would risk prolonged periods of unemployment and the pay would be half or less than the pay of a male cook in the Army. The fact that she was accepted speaks volumes about the quality of military medical examinations in those days. She certainly did not undress for that part of her enlistment and she equally would not have undressed completely in view of any of her comrades

There was a serious question about her health on enlistment, because she had not been in the Army long before she was sick. In fact she was sick with an unknown illness at the time she was assigned to Company A of the 38th Infantry along with 75 other black privates, at Jefferson Barracks. By April 1867, William Cathey and Company A had marched to Fort Riley, Kansas. On April 10th, she went to the post hospital complaining of "itch", the polite name for such afflictions as scabies, eczema, and lice, a typical hazard of the conditions of camp life. On April 30th, together with fifteen other privates, she was recorded as being ill in quarters. Because they were sick, all sixteen had their pay docked $10 a month for three months. She returned to duty on May 14th.

In June 1867, the company was located at Fort Harker in Kansas, and on July 20th, they arrived at Fort Union in New Mexico, after marching an amazing 536 miles. On September 7th, the company marched to Fort Cummings, also in New Mexico, arriving there on October 1st, and was stationed there for eight months. It does appear that William Cathey was capable of marching long distances without difficulty along with the men of her Company, and when they were not on the march, all the soldiers had to do garrison duty, drill and train, and scout for signs of hostile Native Americans. William Cathey did do her share of those duties, though there is no record that she ever engaged an enemy or saw any form of direct combat during her period of enlistment.

A cousin and a family friend, both members of Company A,

knew that Cathay had enlisted and they kept her secret for as long as they could. But when she reported sick in July 1868, she said, according to a report from the *St. Louis Daily Times*, of January 2, 1876:

> *"The post surgeon found out I was a woman and I got my discharge in October. The men all wanted to get rid of me after they found out I was a woman. Some of them acted real bad to me. After leaving the army I went to Pueblo, Colorado, where I made money by cooking and washing. I got married while there, but my husband was no account. He stole my watch and chain, a hundred dollars in money and my team of horses and wagon. I had him arrested and put in jail, and then I came here (St. Louis). I like this town. I know all the good people here, and I expect to get rich yet. I have not got my land warrant. I thought I would wait till the railroad came and then take my land near the depot. Grant owns all this land around here, and it won't cost me anything. I shall never live in the states again. You see I've got a good sewing machine and I got washing to do and clothes to make. I want to get along and not be a burden to my friends or relatives."*

Cathay Williams never became rich. Her health deteriorated and she attempted to claim a pension from the Army several years later, without success. Part of that may have been that she needed help in making her submission, due to her illiteracy, and part of it may be that it seems she was applying on questionable grounds. Most particularly, it may simply have been that those reviewing the claim decided unofficially that, because she was female, she was not eligible for a pension, so she did not receive one. Nor, like many others, did she receive her land grant. In those days, black soldiers were promised a land grant on completion of an enlistment, but again, it was not forthcoming, partly no doubt because she was a female and partly, because of that discovery, she did not complete her enlistment. The 1900 Census record does not list Cathay Williams as a resident of Trinidad, Colorado, where she had lived for some years and no trace of her exists beyond that time.

CHAPTER THREE

Six Medals of Honor - the Spanish-American War

The Spanish-American War took place in 1898, but has its roots in the quest for Cuban independence that occurred much earlier. The issue of colonies in the Americas goes back much further, into a philosophy called the Monroe Doctrine that was declared by President James Monroe in his seventh annual message to Congress on December 2, 1823. It said that the United States would neither accept nor tolerate continued European colonization of lands in the Americas, allowing only at that time the Spanish colony of Cuba to be exempt from the Doctrine, since Cuba was considered to be a province of Spain itself.

It has been suggested that the United States developed an interest in Cuba as the first step towards establishing an empire of its own. Traditionally, the US was regarded by most old-world colonial powers as an agricultural, isolationist nation with little interest in international affairs. But as America's industries developed, imports from the old colonial countries declined, the exporting of products began to be of interest to the United States, and it was anticipated by some that a Spanish Cuba could be an impediment to that growth. Consequently, US Presidents James Polk (1845-1849), Franklin Pierce (1853-1857) and Ulysses S. Grant (1869-1877) all made bids to buy Cuba from the Spanish Government.

Beginning in 1868 various native Cubans organized a series of insurgencies to gain independence from Spain. The Ten Years War took place from 1868-1878, and The Little War occupied 1879-1880. Fifteen years later, in 1895, a revolutionary from the first attempt at Cuban independence, Jose Marti, who had taken exile in Mexico and Guatemala, inspired another war of Cuban independence, by organizing a three-pronged attack on the island. One group would approach from Santo Domingo, a second from Costa Rica and the third from Florida, in the United States. Unfortunately, the US government discovered and blocked the attack from Florida, not wanting at this time to have a conflict in its own backyard. The revolution proved not to be the great show of force that Marti had planned. The potential of a quick victory through surprise was lost.

Each of the conflicts was put down brutally for it was important to Spain to quell the revolts and bring Cuba back into line, and as this latest conflict rumbled on, with guerrilla attacks on Spanish installations, General Valeriano Weyler y Nicolau was sent to Cuba. His harsh techniques had put down uprisings in several Spanish territories and

General Valeriano Weyler y Nicolau.

Cuban Cavalry 1898.

he was expected to succeed here. Weyler's opening strategy was to move villagers and town dwellers across the island to "re-concentration camps" and detain them there while the army set about its business of quelling the revolt.

On March 4,1897 William McKinley was inaugurated as the new President of the US. He was a severe critic of how the Spanish had handled the revolt and was quoted as saying that their reaction *"was not civilized warfare, it was extermination"*.

During the early 1890s the United States had experienced serious cash flow problems because the Cuban insurrection had interfered with trade, and tax legislation, known as the Democratic Tariff, had been passed in 1893 addressing a number of state revenue issues, but in particular, including the levying of income tax. It had proved extremely unpopular in business circles, had failed to yield sufficient revenue and had increased the public debt. After a challenge the tariff was declared unconstitutional by the Supreme Court. Immediately after his inauguration, McKinley sought an immediate revision of the tariff and revenue system of the country, with the result that the Dingley Tariff Bill was passed through both houses, and approved on July 24th.

Meanwhile, in Spain, a new prime minister, Praxedes Sagasta, entered discussions with the revolutionary group and an agreement was drawn up which allowed Cuba an autonomous government from January 1, 1898, though it would remain a colony of Spain. Cuba was regarded by the Spanish as an integral part of Spain and it is noteworthy that Havana's trading income was as high as that of Spain's biggest revenue-earning city, Barcelona. The loss of Cuba to independence would mean a significant decline in Spain's economic fortunes, and its retention as a province was therefore important.

As the situation in Cuba became worse, US popular opinion and commercial interests demanded that McKinley intervene on behalf of the native Cubans. Further, there was concern about the safety of Americans there and he responded by sending the USS "Maine" to the Havana harbor to evacuate if necessary, and the North Atlantic Squadron of the US

Cuban Cavalry.

Navy was ordered to anchor off Key West and standby in the Gulf of Mexico.

The situation erupted on the evening of February 15, 1898, when the USS "Maine" mysteriously sank in a massive explosion, with the loss of 266 lives. It was discovered that an external explosion had penetrated the ship's magazine and the magazine itself had exploded, taking the vessel with it. The backlash in the United States was immediate, making it certain that relations with Spain would deteriorate. In the Senate, Henry Teller of Colorado, put forward a proposition aimed at ensuring that the United States did not seek to annex Cuba as a US territory and establish permanent control over the island (there has, no doubt, been many a senator, Republican and Democrat, who might have wished the situation to be different down the years, not least John F. Kennedy in the 1960s Bay of Pigs Affair). The Teller Amendment demanded that Spain relinquish its claim to Cuba as sovereign territory and withdraw. It also sought to authorize the President to engage such force as was deemed necessary to secure Cuba's independence. That resolution was signed on April 20th and delivered to the Spanish government on the following day, with the result that Spain severed diplomatic relations with the United States. On the same day, the US Navy's North Atlantic Squadron blockaded Cuba from all maritime approaches. Such Spanish forces as were located on Cuba were now isolated and soon would confront the US Army. The war against Spain was more than just a war on Spanish forces in Cuba, and it became known as the Spanish-American War and lasted for less than six months.

One of the first units formed by Colonel Theodore Roosevelt (later President of the US) and Colonel Leonard Wood specifically to fight in this war was the First United States Volunteer Cavalry, which became famous as the "Rough Riders", perhaps appropriately when one considers the mix of recruits. The unit recruited men from the western frontier of the United States, who would be used to life in the saddle and could use firearms accurately on the move. Some Eastern States recruits were also accepted, where they could prove their fitness and skills in horsemanship. There were men from all walks of life – cowboys formed a large part and they were joined by such unlikely companions-in-arms as traders, professors and clergymen. It took six weeks to bring this cavalry regiment together and have them ready for shipment to Cuba, alongside the Regular Army units being prepared.

With a total of only 26,000 men and 2,000 officers, the army at the beginning of this war was severely limited. The great majority of experienced combat troops were located in garrisons throughout the west, so it was really no surprise that among the first units ordered to Cuba were the four black regiments, the 9th and 10th Cavalry and the 24th and 25th Colored Infantry Regiments. The basis of their selection for this duty was their recent experience on the Plains in the various Indian conflicts, but there was also the judgment of the War Department that blacks were immune to the diseases of the tropics and capable of more activity in high, humid temperatures. This erroneous thinking resulted in a concerted effort to recruit blacks for the formation of more "immune" troops. Whatever the motives for mobilizing black regulars, the soldiers themselves welcomed the opportunity to demonstrate their "soldierly qualities" and secure the respect they deserved for their race.

The four black regiments were sent to Chickamauga Park, Georgia, and Key West, Florida, during March and April 1898. Although excited to leave their outposts in the West, some

The USS "Maine".

The wreckage of the USS "Maine" in the Havana harbor after its sinking.

had regrets. In Salt Lake City the residents demonstrated enthusiasm and admiration for the 24th Infantry when they lined the streets of the city to bid farewell to the regiment. Only two years earlier, the whites of the city had vigorously protested the stationing of black troops at Fort Douglas. Yet, African American soldiers had won the hearts of the people

Men of the 9th and 10th Cavalry Regiments newly arrived in Cuba, without horses because of a foolish mistake in the shipping of these men, so they, and Colonel Teddy Roosevelt's "Rough Riders", all fought as infantrymen.

Sergeant Brent Woods, of the 9th Cavalry, was awarded the Medal of Honor in 1881 in New Mexico.

and for a period in their lives enjoyed an atmosphere that was not riven with racial prejudice.

Units were moved from Chickamauga to a staging area near Tampa and Lakeland, Florida, for six weeks during May and June 1898. They were joined there by the 1st Volunteer Cavalry – the Rough Riders. The atmosphere was distinctly different from that of Salt Lake City. Here, even their blue uniforms gave little or no protection from the anti-black prejudice of white soldiers and civilians alike. In the words of a Tampa newspaper, white citizens in the area refused "to make any distinction between the colored troops and the colored civilians and would tolerate no infractions of racial customs by the colored troops." Racial tension was nothing new for the southeastern United States, but the sudden arrival of African Americans unaccustomed to blatant discrimination created an explosive atmosphere. Inevitably, the soldiers were glad to leave and face whatever the battlefields would bring, expressing the hope that they would never have to return.

Chaos with the shipping arrangements meant that four companies of the Rough Riders never did embark and the 1st Volunteer Cavalry's horses were disembarked and not shipped at all. This meant that the soldiers had to fight as an

Lieutenant Benjamin O. Davis was an officer in the 9th Cavalry in Cuba. Seen here as a Captain, he became the first African American General in the US Army.

single file. The 1st United States Regular Cavalry followed a rough and irregular wagon road, running north and parallel with the Rough Riders. The two roads intersected about four and a half miles west. The third column, the 10th Cavalry, took a route approximately a mile further north through dense underbrush. It was intended that the three commands should move as nearly abreast as possible, but the difficulties the 10th Cavalry faced meant they were twenty to thirty minutes behind. One young officer in that column, of whom we shall read more later, was Lieutenant Benjamin O. Davis. He was to become the first African American general in the US Army.

The Rough Riders met the enemy's ambush 500 yards east of the junction of the two roads. The 1st Regulars, hearing the firing, hurried forward to join in and encountered a band of Spaniards to the north of where the Rough Riders were engaged. But, to the great credit of the Americans, neither column gave an inch. They held their ground until the men of the 10th Cavalry charged through the underbrush, delivered several volleys and advanced on the run. The Spanish broke ranks and fled, not making another stand against the Americans until San Juan Hill on July 1st. When the battle of La Quasina ended, there were 19 or 20 American men killed, only one of them black. This was the first major battle success for the African American soldiers. It would not be their last.

infantry regiment much to the annoyance of Colonels Wood and Roosevelt. Sailing from the west coast of Florida, the squadron of 32 ships carrying nearly 17,000 men landed at Santiago, in southeast Cuba, on June 22nd.

The initial battle was at La Quasina. First to engage was the 10th Cavalry, in reserve as the battle began, but who thrust forward into enemy fortified positions and secured a victory in company with the Rough Riders. On the morning of June 24th, three columns moved to the west. The 1st Volunteer Cavalry took a bridle path at the base of the mountain, where the underbrush was so thick the troops could only walk in

African American soldiers of the 10th Cavalry supporting Teddy Roosevelt's "Rough Riders" at the Battle of La Quasina.

Before the Battle of San Juan, four members of the 10th Cavalry demonstrated great acts of courage. On the evening of June 30, 1898, near a town called Tayabacoa, these four soldiers had a choice of ignoring six injured Cubans, not even their own comrades-in-arms, who were under fire from the Spanish. Death was a real prospect if they attempted a rescue. Private Dennis Bell, of Troop H, Privates Lee Fitz and George Wanton of Troop M and Private William Thompkins of Troop G, all volunteered to wade into the sea where the Cubans were hiding to evade enemy bullets, and pulled them to safety. Bell's commander, Lieutenant C.P. Johnson, called it "an almost foolhardy mission."

Private Dennis Bell.

For their heroism, all four Americans received the Medal of Honor almost a year later, on June 23, 1899. The citation for all four men read the same, that they: *"Voluntarily went ashore in the face of the enemy and aided in the rescue of their wounded comrades; this after several previous attempts at rescue had been frustrated"*. This was the only time in that war that four men were awarded the Medal of Honor for a single action in which all participated. They were the first Medal of Honor recipients in the Spanish-American War.

The following day, July 1st, saw the American force launch a two-pronged attack on the Spanish outpost at El Caney and on the entrenchments on San Juan Hill. The intention was that these positions would be secured prior to an all-out assault on Santiago in the south of the island. Troopers from the 25th Infantry were quick to secure El Caney after heavy fighting. At San Juan, it was a slightly different story. The Rough Riders were first into action, but as they advanced, they found themselves surrounded and at risk of being cut down. At this point, three regiments of black troops, the 24th Infantry, accompanied by the men of the 9th and 10th Cavalry, who were behind the Rough Riders, advanced. Hearing the commotion, they fired their way through the opposition to reach their stricken comrades. A New York reporter wrote of the 10th Cavalry, as he watched them advance: *"firing as they marched, their aim was splendid. Their coolness was superb and their courage aroused the admiration of their comrades"*. The last word on the Battle of San Juan Hill should go to an unknown white corporal who said: *"If it hadn't been for the black cavalry, the Rough Riders would have been exterminated."*

The next day another Medal of Honor was awarded. Advancing towards Santiago, Sergeant Major Edward L. Baker, of the 10th Cavalry, who had led part of the action on the previous day's fight on San Juan Hill, saw a wounded soldier lying in water. With no thought for his own safety, Baker left cover and attracted fire from the Spanish defenders. He

completed the rescue and saved the soldier's life. On July 3, 1902, he was presented with the Medal of Honor for: "Leaving cover and under fire, rescued a wounded comrade from drowning". That was the fifth Medal of Honor awarded to African Americans in just two days. There would be one more in this war, to a sailor aboard the USS "Iowa".

Sergeant Major Edward L. Baker.

The naval Battle of Santiago de Cuba resulted in a decisive victory for the United States and the total destruction of the Spanish fleet. Attempting to break out of Santiago harbor, Spanish Admiral Pascual Cervera's six ships were intercepted by American battleships and cruisers of the North Atlantic Squadron commanded by Rear Admiral William T. Sampson and the "Flying Squadron" commanded by Commodore William S. Schley. The total US force consisted of two armored cruisers, five battleships and two armored yachts. Admiral Cervera had at his disposal four armored cruisers and two torpedo boat destroyers. The battle began as Admiral Cervera opened fire on the USS "Brooklyn", Commodore Schley's flagship. Schley, in reply, advanced on the "Infanta Maria Teresa", joined by USS "Texas", USS "Iowa", USS "Indiana" and USS "Oregon". They made short work of Cervera's flagship and it ran aground in flames. The next Spanish cruiser out of action was the "Almirante Oguendo" which suffered a boiler explosion from a direct hit by USS "Iowa". The two torpedo destroyers were quickly disabled too, one sinking and the other running aground, once more in flames. The "Cristobal Colon" was the last of the Spanish ships and because "Brooklyn" was encountering engine problems, it was slowed down and could not catch the newer, faster, Spanish vessel. But USS "Oregon" had no problem in giving chase and catching up after an hour-long pursuit, forced "Cristobal Colon" to run itself aground in flames. In the end, the superior American firepower reduced Cervera's ships to burning wrecks, enabling the US land forces to lay the city to siege with no risk of fire from the now-decimated fleet.

After that battle the sixth Medal of Honor was awarded to an African American, Fireman First Class Robert Penn who, was aboard the USS "Iowa". The citation stated that he was: *"Performing his duty at the risk of serious scalding at the time of the blowing out of the manhole gasket on board the vessel, Penn halted the fire while standing on a board thrown across a coal bucket one foot above the boiling water which was still blowing from the boiler".*

The key objective of the American land forces on Cuba was to secure the city of Santiago de Cuba. Since the Battles of La Quasina, El Caney and San Juan Hill had been lost by the Spanish, there was little to do in defense other than to withdraw to Santiago. The

US and Cuban troops surrounded the city and on Monday July 4th, a .30 caliber Gatling Gun was moved up to Fort Canosa from Lieutenant John Parker's Gatling Detachment. In thirteen days, it fired 6-7,000 rounds into Santiago, doing significant damage.

Although on July 3rd, a relief column was able to break through to reinforce the Spanish General Toral's force, it was of no consequence, because on the following day, a cease-fire was arranged to evacuate some 20,000 civilians from the city. By July 8th, realizing that his situation was hopeless, Toral opened negotiations for surrender, making the condition that his troops could evacuate to another city. Needless to say, the US was having none of it, and General Shafter's force and the US Naval force under Admiral William Sampson, continued to bombard the city. While "surrender" was not used as a word in the capitulation document, the action could hardly be described as anything else. Major-General Nelson Miles, US Army Commander-in-Chief, went to Cuba on July 13th and entered discussions with Toral, accompanied by General Shafter, for the handing over of 23,500 troops and the concession to the US of Guantanamo City and San Luis. The final peace treaty was concluded by a protocol of peace signed in Paris on August 9th. That was almost the end of

The Spanish ship "Cristobal Colon", the fastest ship in the Spanish fleet.

The USS "Oregon," the only American ship fast enough to catch the "Cristobal Colon" which, rather than be blasted out of the sea with large loss of men, the captain decided to scuttle.

The armored cruiser USS "Charleston".

the Spanish-American War and was the true beginning of America's establishment of empire.

Since the United States was now formally at war with Spain, Cuba would not be the only location for confrontation between the two nations. The Asiatic Squadron of the United States Navy drove the Spanish Navy from the Philippines to secure that country as a territory under US protection. Guam also fell to the US to provide a further American foothold in the Pacific. Out of this Spanish-American War, the United States of America was about to emerge as a major international power from its earlier position as a self-sufficient nation of farmers. The conflict in Cuba, however, was still the major ingredient in this war and the United States had to prosecute its position vigorously if it was to be taken seriously, not only by Spain, but the whole of Europe, including Great Britain.

The final Treaty of Paris was concluded on December 10th, with the United States securing the Philippines as a protected territory, Guam and Puerto Rico as US territories and the independence of Cuba. In return, the United States paid Spain the sum of $20 million. This series of actions put the United States into a totally new world position, for now it had the facility to police the Pacific region as one nation had never before been able – if not even to take command of Pacific waters.

The last link in this chain of events is Hawaii, which was also secured as a sovereign US territory in 1898, but not this time by an act of war. Hawaii was an independent state before becoming a US territory by choice. The Kingdom of Hawaii had existed as an independent state between 1810 and 1893, until Hawaii's queen, Lili'uokalani, was ousted by a group of American and British businessmen. They established it as an independent republic, existing between 1894 and 1898. There were several attempts by the republic's administrators to persuade the United States to adopt the islands, but it took the Spanish-American War to persuade the US Government of the strategic value of Hawaii and in 1898, it was adopted as a US territory.

Hawaiian Queen Lili'uokalani.

CHAPTER FOUR

The War to End All Wars –
African Americans on the Western Front

The Great War – or World War I – began in August 1914 between Great Britain and Germany. It had its roots in disagreements and political ambition in Austro-Hungary, where there had been a desire for some time to take territory from the Serbians, but it needed an excuse to do so. That excuse was inadvertently provided by the assassination by a Serb of Austrian Archduke Franz Ferdinand and his wife in June 1914 in Sarajevo, because now Austro-Hungary was bent on "punishing" the Serbs for the assassination.

There were many treaties in place in Europe at that time. Serbia had a protection treaty with Russia, which undertook to come to Serbia's aid if it was attacked by an outside nation. Austro-Hungary had a deal with Germany to join it if it was attacked, as seemed likely if it struck at Serbia. Making the whole thing more unwieldy and complicated, the Franco-Russian Military Convention of 1892 guaranteed that if Russia was attacked or found itself at war, then France would

come to Russia's aid. The final piece of this convoluted jigsaw was Great Britain's guarantee to come to France's aid if it went to war. The house of cards began to collapse with Austro-Hungary's declaration of war on Serbia and its bombardment of Belgrade. France objected on behalf of Russia and Germany threw its weight behind Austro Hungary, ultimately bringing Britain into a reluctant confrontation with Germany. Neither of these countries wanted war with each other, since there was a strong bond of royal blood between Great Britain and Germany – Britain's Royal Household was closely linked to the House of Hanover, Germany's Royal Family.

Great Britain and the United States had already agreed their "special relationship", But even at that, President Woodrow Wilson had difficulty in thinking that the United States should back Britain in a war that was as much about European royal family disputes as anything else. He certainly wasn't

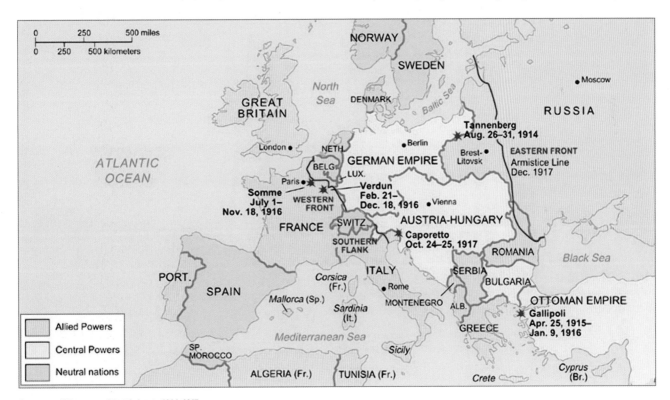

European Alliances and Battlefronts 1914-1917.

about to launch the United States into something that was none of its business. It stayed aloof and watched proceedings. However in 1915, the American public mood began to change, with the knowledge that German submarines were patrolling close to American waters and then came the first real shock.

In that year, the passenger liner "Lusitania" was sunk without a warning, killing over 120 Americans. One year later, German U-boats took the "Sussex" down and American citizens were outraged at these direct violations of their neutral rights at sea. At this point, a small percentage of Americans, including presidential hopeful Theodore Roosevelt, demanded "immediate warfare."

In 1916 President Wilson took a stronger stance toward the nation's foreign affairs policy by increasing the size of the US Armed Forces and issuing a warning to the Germans, basically telling them that if any more civilian passenger or freight vessels were sunk by German action, then the United States would sever diplomatic relations with Germany. This worked until the beginning of 1917, when notice was served on the United States to say that submarine attacks were to resume and that Germany was ending diplomatic relations with the US.

In an attempt to eliminate the threat of American involvement in a European war, Germany's foreign minister Alfred Zimmerman tried to provoke Mexico and Japan into attack-

RMS "Lusitania," the British luxury liner that was sunk by a German submarine on May 7, 1915. Out of 1,198 lost, 120 were Americans.

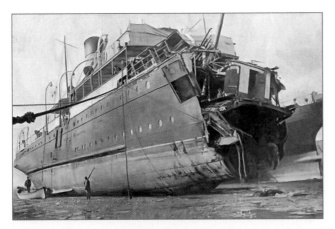

SS "Sussex" was a cross-channel ferry that was severely damaged by a German submarine in March 1916. While no American lives were lost, the action outraged the country and brought demands for war against Germany, in particular from Presidential hopeful Theodore Roosevelt.

three-day battle, the 28th Infantry captured Cantigny and then withstood five determined German counterattacks.

Here were born the "Black Lions of Cantigny", and here the prestige of the American fighting man was upheld before the world. The Black Lions also fought in the battles of Soissons, the Argonne and Sedan, and suffered more than 5,000 casualties in the war. Three Black Lions were awarded the Medal of Honor for their heroism and many more were awarded lesser medals for gallantry.

The Black Lion of Cantigny emblem.

ing the United States with the promise of German assistance when the European war had been won. A message containing that information was decoded by the British and sent to the US, further swaying Americans into action. Principally because of the resumption of submarine activity and the Zimmerman note, President Wilson asked Congress for permission to go to war, and on April 6, 1917, congress officially authorized the declaration.

The Great War, as it was known at the time (the term "World War I" was a 1940s manifestation) affected France perhaps more than any other country, for it was the principal battlefield. For four years, its towns and countryside were ravaged and millions of men died.

Following the US entry into World War I, the First Expeditionary Division, later designated the 1st Infantry Division, was constituted on May 24, 1917. A component of that division, the 28th Infantry Regiment, was assigned to it on June 8, 1917. On June 29th, at St. Nazaire, France, the men of Company K became the first American combat unit to set foot on European soil. The Regiment distinguished itself by conducting the first offensive operation by US troops in World War I at the town of Cantigny where, in a viciously fought

Eugene Bullard.

These Black Lions were not African Americans. They were given their badge, a black lion, the town's heraldic emblem, as a token of respect and gratitude by the citizens of Cantigny. But there was one Black Lion who was an African American – in fact he was the world's first black aviator. Eugene Jacques Bullard was born in Columbus, Georgia in 1894 to a former slave father from Haiti and Creek Indian mother. He left home when a teenager and stowed away on a ship which finally berthed in Scotland. His goal was to get to France, where his father had told him there was no prejudice against black people. While in England, he found he could defend himself quite well with his fists and so took up boxing, with some success.

He finally arrived in Paris in 1914 and when war began, Bullard decided to join the Foreign Legion and fought as an infantryman until the 1916 Battle of Verdun, where he was

Eugene Bullard beside his Les Ciqognes aircraft and with his pet monkey, Jimmy.

He was assigned to the famous Escadrille Lafayette. Shortly afterwards, when the United States entered the war, American airmen were trained in France to fly with the 94th and 95th Pursuit Squadrons – also initially forming part of the Escadrille Lafayette. Bullard as an American, wanted to fight for his country, so volunteered to join the US Army Air Service, but was refused because there were no black aviators in the US Army, and he remained in the service of the French.

Part of the Aeronautique Militaire was a squadron known as "Les Ciqognes" (The Storks) and there is one photograph of Eugene Bullard, showing him standing beside what is unquestionably his own aircraft and displaying his pet monkey "Jimmy". On the side of the fuselage is clearly part of the black portrayal of a stork and it was while he was flying with "Les Ciqognes" that he shot down two German aircraft. Of his experiences flying with "Les Ciqognes" Eugene Bullard generously said, *"I was treated with respect and friendship – even by those from America. Then I knew at last that there are good and bad white men just as there are good and bad black men."*

The first African American troops sent overseas in the Great War belonged to support units. Because the work that these units did was so vital to the war effort, commanders promised special privileges to soldiers in return for their long hours of hard work. As a result, they would often work for up to twenty-four hours at a stretch, unloading ships and transporting men and equipment to battlefield locations and to

seriously injured. Whilst convalescing in Lyons, where it had been pronounced he would probably never walk again, but did, he was offered an opportunity to join the French Flying Corps. An American friend of Bullard's bet him $2000 that he could not get into aviation and become a pilot. Eugene, perhaps inspired by the challenge, soon earned his wings from the aviation school in Tours on May 5, 1917, and just as promptly collected his reward. This made Eugene Bullard the first black fighter pilot in history.

Officer handgun training in France 1917.

railway depots. As the war continued and soldiers took to the battlefields, black labor units were given the tasks of digging trenches, removing unexploded shells from fields, clearing disabled equipment and barbed wire, and burying soldiers killed in action. Despite all the hard and essential work they provided, these African American uniformed laborers received the worst treatment of all black troops serving in World War I.

Two new combat divisions of African American soldiers were formed in late 1917, the first being the 92nd Division, assembled in October 1917, followed by the 93rd in December. Both were mainly white-officered, though by now, black junior officers were beginning to appear on rosters. Sadly, there was great personal animosity between the commander of the US Second Army, Lieutenant-General Robert Bullard (no relation to Eugene Bullard) and Brigadier-General Charles C. Ballou, the 92nd's commander. The sole basis of this hostility was racism. Bullard openly hated black soldiers and did his best to discredit them, using any means available to him, including sympathetic subordinate white officers. Regardless of what the 92nd Division did on the battlefield, it was almost impossible to counter the grossly biased comments and stories from prejudiced officers. The 92nd finally went into battle in August 1918.

Following some initial successes in Lorraine in mid-August, the 92nd was dispatched on September 20, 1918, to the Argonne Forest in preparation for the Meuse-Argonne offensive. The division reached the front lines just before the first assault. Its 368th Infantry Regiment was sent in to fill a gap between the American 77th Division and the French 37th Division. But there were serious problems, primarily due to their lack of training with the French, language difficulties, shortages of equipment, and unfamiliarity with the terrain. The regiment failed to complete its assignment and that failure tarnished the 92nd's combat record, and was used many times over the next thirty years to "demonstrate" the inadequacy of African American soldiers in combat.

After the disaster in the Argonne, the entire 92nd Division was sent to a quiet area of the front in the Marbache sector. Even there, however, their mission was dangerous. They were to harass the enemy with frequent patrols. The danger of the assignment was reflected in the 462 casualties sustained in just one month of patrolling. Although American commanders expressed dissatisfaction with the unit's performance, because they were bent on ensuring it had no credit for any of its actions, the French held a different opinion, and they decorated many members of the 365th Infantry and 350th Machine Gun Battalion for their consistent aggression and courage in the field.

By late 1918, when the German Army was in full retreat, the Allied Commander in Chief, Field Marshal Ferdinand Foch, wanted to force a decisive breakthrough and defeat. So the 92nd was ordered to take the heights east of Champney, France, on November 10, 1918. Although only lasting one day, the attack was fierce and bloody, costing the division over 500 casualties.

Brigadier-General Roy Hoffman, commander of the 93rd Infantry.

As the 92nd Division struggled to clear its reputation, the 93rd Division had a much more successful experience. Commanded by Brigadier-General Roy Hoffman, the 93rd Division was, unlike most other American infantry divisions, limited to four regiments, with many men among their numbers coming from National Guard units of New York, Illinois, Ohio, Maryland, Connecticut, Massachusetts, the District of Columbia, and Tennessee. Being made up of mostly draftees and National Guardsmen, the 93rd lacked cohesion initially. However, they soon gained an enviable reputation, partly because of their attachment to the French, but mostly due to the tenacity of the Divisional commander, General Hoffman and the determination of the soldiers under his and French command.

The 93rd's placement under French command came as the

result of a desperate appeal from the French to the United States for more fighting men. General John J. Pershing, commander of the American Expeditionary Force, gave them the four African American regiments of the 93rd Division because the French already had experience of black Senegalese soldiers in their army. The 93rd therefore quickly adjusted to their new assignment. Although experiencing some difficulties such as language and different equipment, the African American soldiers were welcomed and treated as equals.

Perhaps the most famous black regiment in that Great War was the "Fighting 369th". It remained on the front line for 191 days – longer than any other combat unit of the United States Army. It never lost a trench, it never retreated and not one of those men was taken prisoner by the enemy. The other regiments of the 93rd Division performed with courage and great credit too, the 370th being cited for courage on the Oise and Aisne rivers. The 371st and 372nd Infantry Regiments were also commended for bravery in the Argonne Forest. In addition to these regiments all receiving group awards of the Croix de Guerre from France, a further 34 officers and 89 enlisted men received individual awards of the Croix de Guerre. Not one received the highest award of their own country, the Medal of Honor – at least not at the time.

French Croix de Guerre.

The "Harlem Hellfighters" – men of the 92nd Infantry Division, proudly displaying their Croix de Guerre from a grateful French government on their return to the United States.

Soldiers of the 371st Infantry Regiment embarking for France.

There is one more tale of individual courage to be told here of the 93rd Infantry Division (Colored). It is the story of Corporal Freddie Stowers, the grandson of a slave, who was born in Sandy Springs, South Carolina. He was twenty-one years old, working as a farmhand and was married with a baby daughter when he was drafted into the US Army in 1917. After training, he was assigned to the 371st Infantry Regiment, under French command. Freddie was a young man committed to doing his best, demonstrated by the fact that inside a year, he had been promoted to the rank of corporal.

Freddie Stowers' story begins with him a squad leader in Company C of the 371st and they were given the task of leading the attack on a position known as "Hill 188" in the Champagne-Marne Sector. The success of the operation was due in no small part to the courage of Stowers, who died on the battlefield. Corporal Stowers' commanding officer submitted the recommendation for the award of the Medal of Honor immediately after the battle, with this citation that describes the action:

"Corporal Stowers, a native of Anderson County, South Carolina, distinguished himself by exceptional heroism on September 28, 1918, while serving as a squad leader in Company C, 371st Infantry Regiment, 93rd Infantry Division. His company was the lead company during the attack on Hill 188, Champagne Marne Sector, France. A few minutes after the attack began, the enemy ceased firing and began climbing up onto the parapets of the trenches, holding up their arms as if wishing to surrender. The enemy's actions caused the American forces to cease-fire and to come out into the open. As the company started forward and when within about 100 meters of the trench line, the enemy jumped back into their trenches and greeted Corporal Stowers' company with interlocking bands of machine gun fire and mortar fire causing well over fifty percent casualties. Faced with incredible enemy resistance, Corporal Stowers took charge, setting such a courageous example of personal bravery and leadership that he inspired his men to follow him in the attack. With extraordinary heroism and complete disregard of personal danger under devastating fire, he crawled forward leading his squad toward an enemy machine gun nest, which was causing heavy casualties to his company. After fierce fighting, the machine gun position was destroyed and the enemy soldiers were killed. Displaying great courage and intrepidity, Corporal Stowers continued to press the attack against a determined enemy. While crawling forward and urging his men to continue the attack on a second trench line, he

was gravely wounded by machine gun fire. Although, Corporal Stowers was mortally wounded, he pressed forward, urging on the members of his squad, until he died. Inspired by the heroism and display of bravery of Corporal Stowers, his company continued the attack against incredible odds, contributing to the capture of Hill 188 and causing heavy enemy casualties. Corporal Stowers' conspicuous gallantry, extraordinary heroism and supreme devotion to his men were well above and beyond the call of duty, follow the finest traditions of military service and reflect the utmost credit on him and the United States Army".

This montage depicts Corporal Freddie Stowers in uniform and across the front of the image, the Medal of Honor awarded 73 years after he died on the battlefield. His comrades in the attack on Hill 188 and his Croix de Guerre are also seen.

In the same timeframe, three other soldiers of the 371st Infantry were also recommended for the Medal of Honor, but the Army Decorations Board of the day commuted those awards to the Distinguished Service Cross, which ultimately those soldiers did receive. But the story is that Freddie Stowers' citation was lost in other paperwork. That may be supported by the fact that the other three did receive their awards, but it is still a possibility that this citation was "carefully put to one side". It was a Medals Review Board investigating recommendations for other would-be recipients that brought Corporal Stowers citation to light – more than seventy years later. The award was re-considered and approved and, some

seventy-three years after the battle for Hill 188, Freddie Stowers' sisters, Georgiana Palmer and Mary Bowens, were presented with their brother's Medal of Honor – the only one awarded to an African American soldier throughout the Great War of 1914-1918. In making the presentation, President George H. W. Bush said:

> *"Today, as we pay tribute to this great soldier, our thoughts continue to be with the men and women of all our wars who valiantly carried the banner of freedom into battle. They, too, know America would not be the land of the free, if it were not also the home of the brave."*

Corporal Freddie Stowers' Medal of Honor was presented by President George H.W. Bush in 1991 to his two surviving sisters.

The US Army was reckoned to be the most progressive of the Armed Forces in the issue of race discrimination. It had four regiments of African American soldiers in the United States – the 24th and 25th Infantry Regiments and the 9th and 10th Cavalry. They did not serve in France, but the regiments of the 92nd and 93rd Divisions did, as the only black soldiers on the battlefront in that war of 1914-1918. In this same period of time, the Navy and Coast Guard would only accept black volunteers (no draftees in either of those services) in menial, service supporting roles, like cook's mate or deckhand. The Marine Corps was excluded to black recruits. By contrast, at the end of World War I, there were cavalry, infantry, signal, medical, engineer, and artillery units, as well as men serving as chaplains, surveyors, truck drivers, chemists, and intelligence officers.

With the creation of African American units, there was a demand for African American officers. The War Department took the view that the soldiers would be more likely to follow men of their own race, so reducing the risk of any sort of uprising. Most leaders of the African American community agreed, and it was decided that the Army would create a segregated, but officially equal, officer training camp. In May 1917, Fort Des Moines opened its doors to black officer-trainees, with around 1,250 men attending at Des Moines, Iowa.

Around two hundred and fifty of the men going forward for officer training were already non-commissioned officers in the Army, while the other thousand were new recruits from civilian life. Of that number, only twelve percent scored "above average" in the tests set down by the Army, so the number who didn't make it from the beginning was quite high. The training was conducted by the West Point graduate officers of Fort Des Moines, with the support of a group of NCOs lifted from the four original black regiments. Sadly, the only staff members who took this training seriously were the African America NCOs and the recruits. Many of the officers selected to provide training were not especially interested, because they took the view that black soldiers were not up to standard and never would be.

The NCOs put their charges through foot drills, signaling, and physical fitness training. They also learned how to strip, reassemble and clean a rifle. They were taught military organization and close-quarter fighting, including the use of the bayonet. But the sloppy attitude of a number of the officers meant that the training was not up to normal military standard and the War Department concluded that the Des Moines training exercise had been poor and inadequate. What made matters worse was that nobody thought to bring someone from France to explain what the battlefields were like and how hard trench warfare really was.

Despite all the training problems, six hundred and thirty-nine newly commissioned officers left Fort Des Moines in October 1917. This was the only group to graduate from there, because the Army then closed it down. Commissions were appointed in the ranks of Captain, for senior NCOs who had come from the ranks of Sergeant Major or First Sergeant, 1st Lieutenant for other NCOs down to the rank of Staff Sergeant on entry and 2nd Lieutenant for the rest of the group. Their performance on the course was a key factor in the appointments, because some of those would become company commanders immediately. The whole class of Des Moines was assigned to the 92nd Division on graduation, to join infantry, artillery and engineer units. Future African American officer cadets would be trained as far afield as the Philippines, Hawaii and Panama, as well as training units within the continental United States. Altogether, the training programs yielded 1,353 black officers for war service. Some had been trained alongside white cadets, others were segregated – the Army had no formal policy at this time, but that would change in years to come.

Even though African Americans were moving up the ranks and into the Officer Corps of the Army, they still were not often receiving equal treatment or respect for their achievement. Black draftees were frequently treated with open hostility as they arrived at training camps. White enlisted men would simply refuse to salute black officers, forgetting that the principle of the salute is respect for the commission and its seniority, not the person wearing the uniform. Black officers were all too often barred from Officers' Clubs and even quarters. The War Department turned a blind eye, seeming to condone this appalling state of affairs – even to the extent that an order was issued to limit the number of black trainees in training camps to 25 percent of the total trainee numbers. That ruling was in response to complaints from white citizens in some southern states that there were too many black soldiers in local training camps. This dichotomy continued for some years – the contrast between the soldiers who had served in the west and been accepted as part of the community and appreciated for what they did, and the bitter segregation of others, usually in the southeast and even in the north of the United States.

As the conflict in Europe came to its end, it was time to count costs and the credits for the 92nd and 93rd Divisions. In a little over a year, the 92nd Division suffered 1,647 battle casualties and the 93rd Division endured 3,534. While American awards for bravery were sparse, partly because of the color of the soldiers' skins, they were officially justified because these units were under French field command. Demonstrating that black soldiers were decorated in a similar ratio to white soldiers, the French awarded the Croix de Guerre to the 369th Infantry Regiment as a Unit award, then made 171 individual awards for gallantry as well. That compared with many a French regiment and exceeded a number, simply because these Americans fought with such valor.

Seventy-one men of the 370th Infantry Regiment received the French Croix de Guerre for their action in the Oise-Aisne campaign, while 21 more were awarded the Distinguished Service Cross. The whole regiment of the 371st was again honored with a Unit award of the Croix de Guerre and 123 individuals were personally awarded the Croix de Guerre. Twenty-six officers and men received the Distinguished Service Cross from the United States and three officers were awarded the French Legion d'Honneur – this carried an automatic award of the Croix de Guerre with Palm as well. And then there was, 73 years later, Corporal Freddie Stowers' Medal of Honor – the only one awarded to a black soldier in the whole of the Great War of 1914-1918.

The fourth infantry regiment of the 93rd Brigade, the 372nd, demonstrated outstanding courage in the assault on Champagne and in the taking of Monthois. The resistance from the Germans was formidable and yet the 372nd engaged in hand-to-hand combat over a period of just under two weeks, enduring over 600 casualties in those two engagements alone. A Unit Croix de Guerre with Palm was awarded to the Regiment, and then 173 other gallantry awards were made by both the French and United States governments. Forty-three officers, 14 NCOs and 116 private soldiers were awarded a combination of the French Croix de Guerre and the US Distinguished Service Cross.

A fitting end to this Chapter is a reference to the Commanding General of the American Expeditionary Force in World War I, General of the Armies John J. Pershing. He, more than any other white officer, did much to ameliorate the appalling treatment of African Americans in the United States Army. Interestingly, and he took great pride in this, his service number was O-1 in the National Army of the United States. His nickname for most of his military life was "Black Jack". He

General John J. Pershing.

was the only officer to be promoted to the rank "General of the Armies" in his own lifetime, rather than "General of the Army" as others, such as Dwight D. Eisenhower and Henry H. Arnold, later were promoted.

Born in Laclede, Missouri in 1860, young John Pershing had two brothers and five sisters and went to school at Laclede High School, then to North Missouri Normal School, now Truman State University at Kirksville, Missouri. Returning to Laclede, he spent the years between 1879 and 1882 teaching African American children at the Prairie Mound School, because he recognized the appalling state of deprivation in that community and the lack of educational opportunity. That experience had a profound effect on the attitude of John Pershing for the rest of his life.

Not happy with the quality of education available to him locally, he sought entry into West Point Military Academy and was enrolled in the autumn of 1882. Graduating 30th in his Class of 1886, Pershing was assigned to the 6th Cavalry. In October 1892, he was promoted to 1st Lieutenant and given command of a company in the 10th Cavalry. The 10th Cavalry was a "colored" regiment of the regular Army and because of his compassionate treatment of his men, John J. Pershing was nicknamed, by fellow officers, as a derisive term, "Nigger Jack" (in those days any man remotely treating an African American with sympathy for anything would be described as a "nigger lover" – so it was with Pershing). In time, the label "softened" to "Black Jack", though the contemptuous intent remained. To his great credit, Pershing took pride in his nickname and continued to consider, as far as he could within the overall chain of command, the interests of African American soldiers.

While earlier a champion of the African American soldier, Pershing did not champion their full participation on the battlefield during World War I, understanding widespread racial attitudes among white Americans generally, plus President Woodrow Wilson's reactionary views on race. He also owed political debts to certain southern Democratic lawmakers. Even so, he exercised considerable discretion to soften the burden on African American soldiers in the field off the record. This is not an untypical situation of senior

General John J. "Black Jack" Pershing inspects his former regiment, the 10th Cavalry.

officers in the predicament of handling the progression of their future careers while addressing issues on the ground.

One point of great credit to General Pershing is that he always remembered his soldiers. He knew that the German fighting force his men had faced for over a year was superior in number and equipment to his own. So he ensured that his force was better trained, better able to "think on its feet" – and better respected. Whilst he allowed French field officers to command his two African American divisions, he insisted that final responsibility lay with American officers – so both the 92nd and the 93rd Divisions were ultimately commanded by American generals. He also monitored, as far as he was able, the awards of gallantry decorations to his officers and men to ensure as much fairness of distribution as he could. "Black Jack" Pershing was remembered with great affection by many thousands of African American veterans and much of the justification for that can be credited to those two years when he taught African American children between 1879 and 1882 and his time served with the 10th Cavalry. The name "Pershing" is to this day repeated in military circles with an expression of near reverence.

CHAPTER FIVE

African American Aviators – The Legend Begins

This Chapter tells of the many "firsts" in the world of African American aviators. And every single "first" was achieved against unremitting odds, especially the first of them all – Eugene Jacques Bullard. Without doubt, Bullard had some lucky breaks, but getting to where he did was almost like climbing Mount Everest unaided.

Eugene Bullard was born in Columbus, Georgia in October 1894. His parents, William Bullard and Josephine Thomas married and had ten children. William was born into slavery, his parents belonging to a man Wiley Bullard (hence the family name), a planter, in Stewart County Georgia. His father was born in Haiti and was sold into slavery when he was transported to the United States. William was nicknamed "Big Ox" for his physique and the way he worked. Gaining his freedom, he married Josephine, a Creek Indian, in 1882 and found a three-room house in which they could live and raise a family. Eugene was their seventh child.

William and Josephine were conscientious parents, for while William never had a formal education, his son Eugene later described him as "the most educated man I ever knew". He could read everything and anything that came into his hands. Poor as they were, William and Josephine made sure that Eugene, whom they perceived as a bright child, could read. He went to school at Columbus' 28th Street school between 1901 and 1906, leaving after fifth grade. William worked by this time for an up-and-coming cotton merchant, W.C. Bradley, who treated him well and probably helped to pay for his children's education because William was such a hard worker.

As he was growing up, young Eugene heard many stories from his father, who spoke French from his own father's Martinique origins, about how there was no segregation in France and how all men, black and white, yellow and pale brown, were treated equally with no racism. From his childhood, therefore, Eugene developed an ambition to see this "free" France. William Bullard constantly proclaimed that African Americans had just as much right to be proud of themselves as anyone else.

At the age of nine years, young Eugene witnessed an inci-

dent in his hometown in which his father came perilously close to being lynched, but luckily, he was able to break free from his captors and escape. Eugene never forgot that incident throughout his life and in 1906, decided, at the age of eleven, that it was time to leave home. So he ran away and tagged along with a family of English gypsies named Stanley. They told him that there was no such thing as segregation in England and encouraged him to pursue his dream. They looked after him and taught him how to care for horses, which they raced. Eugene learned to ride and even raced the Stanley horses on occasions, but by 1909, now fifteen, Eugene felt it was time to move on, and he left the Stanleys at Bronwood, Georgia and went to work for a family named Turner as a stable boy. The Turners treated Eugene well and encouraged him to ride, even entering him with one of their horses in the Terrell County Fair in 1911.

By 1912, the memory of his father's near lynching still haunted Eugene Bullard and he became more resolved to leave the racist society in which he lived. He was appreciative of the kindness Zachariah Turner and his family had shown him, but simply felt that he could not live with segregation for the rest of his life. As a result, he travelled north to Virginia and found his way to the seaport of Norfolk. His goal was to stow away on a ship that would take him to England. He found a German vessel, the "Marta Russ", which was to sail on March 4th for Aberdeen in Scotland. Eugene didn't know that Scotland wasn't England and worse, he had no idea how far Aberdeen was from the English border. But this ship would take him across the Atlantic which was his primary goal. His escape from the tyranny of racism was on the horizon, he thought. And whilst racism in Britain in those days was nothing to compare with Georgia, he was still to come across it occasionally.

Finding his way to Glasgow, Eugene worked for a gambling group as a lookout for a few months, because gambling was illegal, before moving to Liverpool in the northwest of England. He worked there as a longshoreman, on fish wagons and in an amusement park. He also took his chances as a prizefighter. A favorite haunt became Chris Baldwin's gymnasium in Liverpool, where he was coached and sparred with boxers. Discovering he had a talent for boxing, he was pitched against many opponents and ultimately found himself in the ring facing Billy Welsh for ten rounds. This started a brief boxing career that took him to France, the land of his father's dreams.

Returning to Liverpool, Eugene joined a vaudeville group that travelled across Europe, before finally returning to Paris. When the group was ready to move on, Eugene Bullard remained in Paris – but not for long. In August 1914, Britain declared war on Germany, and France was involved in the conflict, so Eugene decided to support his new country by joining the French Foreign Legion. He was assigned to the 170th Infantry Regiment in the Moroccan Division. In the Battle of Champagne, in September 1915, his company went into battle with five hundred men, and at the evening roll call, there were thirty-one left who answered their names. He was wounded twice in the Battle of Verdun in 1916. Awarded the Croix de Guerre, he was also declared unfit for infantry service. While convalescing in Lyons, he was offered an opportunity to join the French Flying Corps and by May 1917,

he had earned his wings from the flying school at Tours.

Joining the Escadrille Cicognes ("The Storks") Bullard went on to fly twenty missions in the company of such great aces as Charles Guynemer, France's top-scorer. Eugene's first mission was on September 8, 1917, flying a Nieuport that he called a real sweetheart, on a reconnaissance mission over the city of Metz, and from then on never missed a mission. Bullard claimed two "kills," but only one was confirmed, because the aircraft went down behind enemy lines. Nobody doubted he had shot it down, especially when his mechanics found seventy-eight bullet holes in his own plane. The second kill was in November 1917, when he shot down a German Pfalz after the pilot tried a maneuver called an Immelmann turn, which meant he flew nose up and then turned backwards to come in from behind. Bullard dropped into a cloudbank and came out below and to the right of the Pfalz, pulled in behind him and shot him down.

Many years later, in September 1949, when Eugene Bullard was living in New York and quietly earning his living virtually un-noticed by the world at large, he was badly beaten during a Peekskill Riot when walking through the grounds of Cortland Manor, in Westchester to attend a concert being given by the singer Paul Robeson, a contentious figure seen as a spokesman for the political left. These riots were anti-communist, anti-black and anti-Semitic but Bullard had no part in it and was trying to move out of its path when he was knocked to the ground and beaten by the angry white mob that included white members of state and local law enforcement. The beating was

Eugene Bullard, on the left, poses with a group from the Escadrille Lafayette.

A Pfalz DIII of the type that Eugene Bullard shot down, though this particular aircraft is one captured by the British.

The Tomb of the Unknown Soldier, which stands in the protection of the Arc de Triomphe in Paris. At the far end of the picture can be seen the crucible for the eternal flame. Eugene Bullard, as a French War hero, had the honor of sharing the re-kindling of the flame with two other French soldiers.

captured on film and despite this recorded evidence; no one was ever prosecuted for the assault. Graphic photos of Bullard being beaten by two policemen, a state trooper and a concert-goer were later published, but still no action was taken. It was an appalling demonstration of institutional racism at its worst.

The finale of Bullard's story comes in four parts – the first in 1954, when he was invited by the French government, in company with two French soldiers, to re-light the Eternal Flame on the tomb of the Unknown Soldier standing under the arch of the Arc de Triomphe. In 1959, the French Government honored him again by awarding him the Chevalier du Legion d'Honneur (Knight of the Legion of Honor). When visiting New York in 1960, President Charles de Gaulle publicly embraced Eugene Bullard as a true French hero. A year later, after his death, unrecognized as a war hero by the nation of his birth, his "grand finale" came in the form of an honor guard and color party sent from France, who draped his coffin with the Tricolor and laid him to rest, with full military honors, in the French Military Section of Flushing Cemetery in New York. It is said that he was buried wearing a French military uniform.

In all this time, the country of Eugene Bullard's birth paid little attention to him. He was a war hero in the truest sense, having laid his life on the line more than once. Much later, in 1971, when the United States was seeking to improve its reputation over the issue of race, it finally came to recognize Eugene Jacques Bullard by awarding him a posthumous commission in the rank of Lieutenant in the United States Air Force. How much better it would have been to have done that in his lifetime, thereby showing respect for a true living legend, as France had done for its adopted son.

Eugene Bullard's array of medals, all awarded by France.

Another famous early aviator was Elizabeth (Bessie) Coleman, born two years before Eugene Bullard, in Atlanta,

Bessie Coleman.

Bessie doing laundry.

Texas, the twelfth of thirteen children. Her family was desperately poor and of mixed race, her father, George, being a Native American and her mother, Susan, an African American. Early in her childhood, the family moved to Waxahachie, Texas, and Bessie grew up picking cotton and doing laundry with her mother to eke out a living. Life was horribly tough for the Coleman family. Bessie's father decided that he would move the family into Indian Territory in Oklahoma where he thought they would have better chances of a decent life. His wife was far from happy about spending her life on a reservation, so decided to stay in Texas.

Bessie and some of her sisters stayed with their mother. That was good for Bessie, because there was a traveling library that came through Waxahachie weekly and she was able to borrow books. Being bright and an avid student, she graduated from high school and then joined her father to study at the Colored Agricultural and Normal University (today known as Langston University) in Langston, Oklahoma. She could only afford to complete one semester there, and by 1915, to escape the drudgery of her present life, she decided to join two of her brothers who were living in Chicago. She studied at a beauty school and then went to work as a manicurist in a local barbershop. Her life was better already than it had ever been in Texas.

Bessie became interested in aviation and mentioned it to her brother, John. He had served in France in the Great War and had seen aircraft in action. He began to tease her and

say that in France, women flew aeroplanes, though in fact they didn't – yet. Brother John had also mentioned in a conversation that he had heard of a black pilot flying with a French squadron. Bessie did some searching and found out about this man who had won a Croix de Guerre, then gone on to fly with the famous "Storks". But his continuous teasing prompted Bessie to learn to fly. Remembering that Chicago was then "the" place for aviators, she traveled around to the flying schools but she was always turned away with the statement – "No, you're female and you're black."

Robert Abbott.

She left her job as a manicurist and went to work as the manager of a chili parlor, which was much better paid. Around this time, she also met a man, Robert Abbott, the publisher of the African American newspaper *The Chicago Defender* and he suggested to Bessie that she should move to France to achieve her ambition. After this, she enrolled in night classes to learn French, and in November 1920, she packed her bags and took off for France. Bessie Coleman was going to become a pilot. So confident was Robert Abbott that she would achieve her goal, he gave Bessie a sum of money that he and some friends had put together, to help her on her way.

She made her way to the flying school of René and Gaston Caudron. The Caudron brothers were renowned for their patriotism to France, in that they never patented any of their aviation designs, believing that the nation should benefit from their work. The G-3 was a reconnaissance and training biplane they built for the Aeronautique Militaire in the Great War and other companies manufactured the same aircraft in England and Italy without paying a license fee. Perhaps more famously though, they established a flight training school at their aerodrome at Le Crotoy, on the estuary of the River Somme in northern France.

The Caudron G-3.

René Caudron already knew that Mademoiselle Coleman would be coming, as Robert Abbott had warned him of her impending arrival. Going through some elementary tests, Bessie soon convinced her would-be tutor that she had the necessary attributes and considerable enthusiasm to be successful. She set about her lessons with diligence, both in ground school and in flight and it soon became apparent that her efforts to learn French before she left America had been worth every penny. She was thought the more of by the Caudron brothers because she had extended them that courtesy. As they saw it, it was a gesture of respect for France. She flew Nieuport Type 82s to gain her French National and FAI (Federation Aeronautique Internationale) International licenses. Out of sixty-two candidates on her course, Bessie was the only woman to complete the flight training program, to become the first woman to graduate from the Caudron School, the first African American woman to hold an aeronautical pilot's license of any kind – and most importantly of all, the first woman in the world to hold an international pilot's license.

Returning to the United States, no doubt with a contribution from Mr. Robert Abbott, who was all for her gaining publicity for black people and the African American cause, on the SS "Manchuria" in September 1921, Bessie was greeted by a whole corps of pressmen. It seemed that flying for entertainment was a lucrative business and the press had expected that Bessie would now do just that. But she quickly learned that stunt flying demanded certain flying skills she had not acquired so she returned to France, arriving in Le Havre on February 28, 1922, to train in a Caudron Nieuport, returning to New York in August that same year.

Once back in the United States, Bessie knew that in order to pursue her new flying career she had to have publicity to attract paying audiences. She created an exciting image of herself with a military style uniform and a presence that certainly belied her humble background. Her first appearance in an air show was on September 3, 1922 at Curtiss Field, near New York City. The show, sponsored by her friend Robert Abbott and *The Chicago Defender* billed Bessie as "the world's greatest woman flyer." More shows followed around the country including in Memphis and Chicago. On June 19, 1925, Bessie made her flying debut in Texas at a Houston auto racetrack, which had been re-named Houston Aerial Transport Field to mark the occasion.

In all the time between her 1922 flying debut in New York and her 1925 Texas debut, Bessie had nursed the ambition to establish a flying school for those from poor backgrounds, especially black people. However, in February 1923, Bessie suffered her first major flying accident while preparing for an exhibition in Los Angeles when her plane's engine stalled unexpectedly and she crashed. Knocked unconscious by the accident, Bessie suffered a broken leg, some cracked ribs, and a number of cuts to her face. Shaken quite badly, it took her more than a year to fully recover physically and mentally. She briefly toyed with the idea of a movie career to fund her proposed flying schools and she traveled to California to earn money to buy a plane of her own, crashed it after she had bought it and returned to Chicago to start afresh.

It was two more years before she was able to line up a series of lectures and exhibition flights in Texas. Once she was there, she defied racial and gender barriers, by insisting that everybody should pass through the same entrance gate. She appeared in San Antonio, Richmond, Waxahachie, Wharton, Dallas and several small towns and fields, performing barrel rolls and loops to excite the crowd. At Love Field in Dallas, she made a down payment on a Curtiss JN-4 "Jenny", fitted with a Curtiss OX-5 engine, from the Curtiss Southwestern Aeroplane and Motor Company.

Following another brief spell back in Chicago, Bessie went on a lecture tour delivering her message in black theaters in the states of Georgia and Florida. Shortly after arriving in

Bessie Coleman stands on one of the landing wheels of her Curtiss JN-4 "Jenny".

Florida, she opened a beauty salon in Orlando so as to generate more funds to start her first flying school. From time to time, she borrowed planes from others and did exhibition flying and later parachute jumping, as this was a new phenomenon in the aviation field. Parachutes were designed for safety, but they also made quite a spectacle to audiences who'd never seen them before – especially if the panels of the parachutes were all the colors of the rainbow. Always, as she did flying or parachute shows, she absolutely insisted that the entrance to the flying fields should not be segregated. Once inside the gates, the spectators were not further segregated.

Bessie made the last payment on her Curtiss Jenny in Dallas and arranged to have it flown to Jacksonville for her next engagement scheduled for May 1, 1926. On the day before, she was being flown by her mechanic and publicity agent, William Wills. She was not strapped into her seat in the back cockpit, because she was looking for suitable parachute landing sites. About ten minutes into the flight, the plane suddenly dropped into a steep nosedive, flipped over and catapulted Bessie to her death. Wills, who was still strapped into his seat, struggled to regain control of the aircraft, but died when he crashed in a nearby field and the aircraft burst into flames. After the accident, investigators discovered that Wills had lost control of the aircraft because a loose wrench had jammed the plane's controls.

There were five thousand mourners at the memorial service held for Bessie in Jacksonville on May 2, 1926, and among the personalities of the day who were there was Ida B. Wells, a prominent journalist and newspaper editor. Bessie's body was then transported by train from Orlando, after the formal funeral at Mount Zion Missionary Baptist Church, to Chicago. An estimated ten thousand people filed past her coffin at the Pilgrim Baptist Church in Chicago to pay their last respects before the burial. Thousands more were at the burial, when she was laid to her final resting place in Lincoln Cemetery.

It was only after her death that Bessie Coleman received the recognition that she deserved. Her dream of a flying school for African Americans came true when William J. Powell established the Bessie Coleman Aero Club in Los Angeles,

Bessie Coleman's grave at Lincoln Cemetery, in Chicago.

Cornelius Coffey was born in Newport, Arkansas, on September 6, 1903, a short time before the Wright brothers' first heavier-than-air flight. Young Cornelius took his first flight in an aeroplane when he was thirteen years old and promptly decided that aviation was his future. During 1925, he enrolled in a trade school on the South Side of Chicago to study motor vehicle mechanics along with his friend John Robinson who shared his burning ambition to fly.

Normal flying schools in Chicago, or elsewhere for that matter, would not accept them, but a black business man lent the two a vacant store front where they built a one-seat aeroplane powered by a motor cycle engine. They then set about teaching themselves to fly. These two young men were employed as auto mechanics by Emil Mack, the white owner of a Chevrolet dealership in Elmwood Park, Illinois, when they applied and were accepted at the Curtiss Wright School of Aviation in Chicago for an aviation mechanics training course. When they reported to the school to start classes, they were both refused admittance because they were black.

The school did try to reimburse the two for their tuition fees, but their employer, Mr. Mack, threatened to sue the school if the two young men were not accepted. The school backed down and allowed Cornelius and John to attend. Two years later they graduated at the top of their class. Building on that background, in the late 1930s, Cornelius Coffey established

California in 1929. After that, many more Bessie Coleman Aero Clubs sprang up all over the country. On Labor Day, 1931, these clubs sponsored the first all-African American Air Show, which attracted almost 15,000 spectators. That same year, a group of African American pilots established an annual flyover of Bessie's grave. Then, as a result of being affiliated, educated or inspired directly or indirectly, by the Bessie Coleman Aero Club, many famous African American flyers have continued to make Bessie Coleman's dream a reality. There have been many books about Bessie Coleman, aimed at inspiring young black women to reach out for their dreams. Bessie Coleman proved that people did not have to be shackled by their gender or the color of their skin to succeed and realize their dreams.

Cornelius Coffey.

Cornelius Coffey teaching at his engine school.

Harold Hurd.

the Coffey School of Aeronautics at Harlem Airport, located south of Chicago. From 1938 to 1945 more than 1,500 black students went through that school, including many who would later become Tuskegee Airmen. After World War II, Coffey served as an instructor at the Lewis School of Aeronautics in Lockport, and then at Dunbar Vocational High School in Chicago, training some of the first black mechanics to be hired by commercial airlines. He died in Chicago on March 2, 1994.

Cornelius Coffey was the first black person to hold both a pilot's and mechanic's license. He was a recipient of the "Charles Taylor Master Mechanic Award" from the Federal Aviation Administration and was the first black American to have had an aerial navigation intersection named after him by the FAA (the "Coffey Fix," a waypoint located on the VICTOR 7 airway over Lake Calumet, providing electronic course guidance to Chicago Midway Airport Runway 31 Left). Coffey also designed a carburetor heater that prevented icing and allowed aeroplanes to fly in all kinds of weather. Devices similar to his are still in use on piston-engine powered aircraft today.

Cornelius Coffey was the first African American to establish an aeronautical school in the United States. His school was also the only non-university affiliated aviation school to become part of the Civilian Pilot Training Program. His pioneering efforts led ultimately to the integration of African

American pilots into the American aviation industry.

Harold Hurd saw an African American man fly an aeroplane at an air show in 1929, and inspired by this, he became, three years later, one of the original class of all black graduates from Aeronautical University in Chicago where he secured his aeronautical mechanic's license in only six months. After graduation, he helped organize the Challenger Air Pilots Association and its 1937 successor organization, the National Airmen's Association of America, in efforts to expand black interest in flying. He underwrote his aviation interests by working at *The Chicago Defender* newspaper.

Cornelius Coffey was the man who taught Harold Hurd to fly at Chicago's Harlem Airport and in 1936 at the age of only twenty-four, Hurd gained his Private Pilot Certificate. During World War II, he taught mechanics and flying at Wilberforce University, the same university where Brigadier-General Benjamin O. Davis Senior was a professor. Hurd was drafted by the Army and eventually became a Sergeant Major. The Under-Secretary of the Navy Board instructed that Hurd should be transferred into the Army Air Corps, where he served with the Tuskegee Airmen. Harold Hurd was honorably discharged in 1946 and continued to fly until the 1970s. He was inducted into the Illinois Aviation Hall of Fame in 1991.

James Herman Banning was born in Oklahoma on November 5, 1899, to Riley and Cora Banning. Not much is known about his early life, but his parents moved to

James Herman Banning.

Ames, Iowa, in 1919, to enable their son to study electrical engineering at Iowa State College, but he only stayed there for one year. Young Herman had dreamed of aeroplanes and being able to fly from early boyhood, though in his early youth he did not see the possibility of it happening.

Leaving college and more interested in mechanical matters, he set up an auto repair shop on West Second Street, Ames in 1922, and later expanded his business into a bigger work-shop on Fourth Street. It was during this time that he went around the local flying schools trying to enroll in a flying course. But every one turned him down for the same reason – he was black. Finally, he found an ex-Army Air Service pilot, Raymond Fisher who ran a small flying school in Des Moines that undertook to teach him. Herman Banning became the first African American man to secure a pilot's license from the Department of Commerce in 1924 with License Number 1324. Whilst Eugene Bullard was the first African American to fly, he never flew in the United States and so was never licensed there, giving the accolade of "First Male African American Pilot License Holder" to J. Herman Banning.

Herman left Ames for Los Angeles in 1929 and linked his name to America's first woman African American pilot, Bessie Coleman, by accepting the job of Chief Pilot in William Powell's Bessie Coleman Aero Club. He taught flying and did some barnstorming in a White's Hummingbird biplane, to fund a scheme to be the first African American to fly across the Continental United States. He named his aircraft "Miss Ames", after the city in Iowa he had left behind.

FIRST TRANS-CONTINENTAL FLIGHT

Banning and Allen's flight across the continent as "The Flying Hoboes" was a magnificent effort, literally flying on a shoestring to cover 3,300 miles. However, theirs was the first from Los Angeles to New York, but not strictly the first flight across the continent. That honor falls to Lieutenant Jimmy Doolittle, who flew a DH-4 from Pablo Beach in Florida to Rockwell Field in California in September 1922.

Herman Banning aboard "Miss Ames", a White's Hummingbird.

Herman teamed up with a flight mechanic, Thomas Allen, also an African American who also worked at the Aero Club. The two spent hours dreaming and planning what was now to become their trip across the Continent. They bought a rather tired, six-year-old Alexander Eaglerock biplane for as much as they could afford. However, they had to do quite a lot of work on it to assure its airworthiness, including a total engine rebuild. They fitted new magnetos to the engine and since they couldn't find original inlet or exhaust valves, they modified a complete set from a Nash automobile. The engine ran better than before, so they felt they had done a good job.

The biggest problem was money to pay for fuel, oil and essentials, so they filled up as far as they could for the first leg and took off. They called themselves "The Flying Hoboes" and when they reached their first stop in Yuma, Arizona, a place Herman Banning had visited previously, they were greeted by an attendant who remembered him. The recollection was about a perfect three-point landing Herman had performed two years earlier before hitting a ridge in the concrete on the runway, bursting a tire and bending the wheel. The man said: *"Aren't you the pilot who landed here two years ago and blew a tire?"* Mildly surprised, Herman said he was and the reply then came, *"Well that's why we now have an up-to-date airport."* Banning's instant response was: *"That has to be worth a tank of gas."*, which the airport gladly gave to him.

It took them twenty-one days to cover the 3,300 miles from Los Angeles to Valley Stream Airport on Long Island. Only 42 hours were spent in the air, the rest of the time being taken with raising money to move on to the next stage. They hit on the idea of "selling" signature space to the people from the towns and cities they visited. Each person who contributed cash for fuel, oil, food and drink signed a wing of the aeroplane so as to follow it into posterity. It was a clever idea that worked and the pair received a hero's welcome in Harlem on arrival in New York.

A few months later, Herman Banning was due to fly a display at Camp Kearney in California. Bad weather delayed the event and then an aviation machinist's mate, Albert Burghardt, purporting to be a competent pilot, offered to fly Banning from Lindbergh Field in a Travelair two-seater. Banning had intended to take a young lady parachutist up with him and perform his display, but fate had something else in store. Burghardt, wanting to show off his prowess as a pilot, put the aircraft into a steep climb, stalled it and came plummeting down to earth, killing them both. Herman Banning had no chance to take control, because the front seat had no controls. This happened because Banning had tried to rent an aircraft himself and been refused, as the Chief Instructor of the school did not believe that Herman was a competent pilot, because he was black. He had to suffer the ignominy of being flown by a far less competent pilot, later thought not to be properly licensed, and plunge to his death for a foolish prank. A crowd of 2,000 people watched the awful spectacle. He was laid to rest at the Evergreen Cemetery in Los Angeles.

Another aviatrix, born in the same era as Bessie Coleman and Herman Banning, was Janet Harmon Bragg, born Jane Nettie Harmon on March 24, 1907 in Griffin, Georgia, to Samuel Harmon and Cordia Batts. Her mother was a Cherokee. She went to a boarding school in Fort Valley, Georgia and then studied nursing at Spelman Seminary. Once graduated, Janet went to work as a nurse at a mainly white hospital – blacks were treated in the basement. After two patients died

Janet Harmon strikes a relaxing pose.

due to lack of attention, she quit that job and moved north to Chicago. It was there, the home of America's aviation that she had the idea of learning to fly.

While she was working at Wilson Hospital in Chicago, she met and married Evans Waterford, but the marriage fell apart within two years and she moved on to work with practicing doctors. In 1933, she decided it was time to learn to fly and she enrolled at John Robinson and Cornelius Coffey's Aeronautical University. She was the only woman in a class of twenty-four black men. In 1934, having graduated from ground school, she bought the school's first aeroplane with $600 of her own money and progressed to gaining her private pilot's license.

When World War II was raging, Janet applied to join the Women's Air Service Pilots program. At an interview, she was plainly told that she could not join the service because she was black. It didn't matter that she could already fly and was therefore ahead of any other applicant. To gain her advanced license, she went to the Tuskegee Institute in Alabama and completed the Civilian Pilot Training Program there. She was denied a pilot's license in Alabama, because she was "colored", but she did gain her commercial pilot's license at Palwaukee Field in Illinois – the second African American woman to achieve that goal.

Janet's aviation career didn't "take off" as she had hoped, however, as between 1941 and 1951 she worked as a health inspector for an insurance company. In 1953 she married Sumner Bragg and together they managed nursing homes for the elderly in Chicago until their own retirement in 1972. Janet Bragg died in 1993 in Blue Island, Illinois. She had not fulfilled her aviation career as she had hoped, but she did keep flying and most importantly, left many more barriers of race and gender broken in her path.

During the mid-1930s in the period leading up to World War II, a group of dedicated individuals assembled in the Chicago area to form an organization that actively pursued the goal of participation for African Americans in the world of aviation and aeronautics. Led by Cornelius R. Coffey, his wife Willa B. Brown, and a man named Enoch P. Waters, the National Negro Airmen Association of America was formed with the specific purpose of furthering and stimulating interest in aviation among the African American community, and to bring about a better understanding in the field of aeronautics. Shortly thereafter, Claude Barnett, the director of the Association of Negro Press (ANP), with strong backing from Chauncey Spencer and Dale White, suggested that the word Negro be dropped from the organization and that it be re-titled, "The National Airmen Association of America". That proposal was adopted while maintaining the original objectives.

On August 16, 1939, an application for a Certificate of Incorporation was filed in Cook County with the Illinois Secretary of State, listing as Directors the following: Cornelius R. Coffey, Dale L. White, Harold Hurd, Willa B. Brown, Marie St. Clair, Charles Johnson, Chauncey E. Spencer, Grover C. Nash, Edward H. Johnson, Janet Waterford, George Williams, and Enoch P. Waters. Many of the charter members had originally come to Chicago to further their interest in aviation at the Coffey School of Aviation. Chauncey Spencer was encouraged to come to Chicago in 1934 by Oscar DePriest, a Congressional Representative, after being told by the Airport Operator in his hometown of Lynchburg, Virginia that, "they didn't teach coloreds to fly because they didn't have the intelligence."

A few months before the incorporation, the organization had undertaken an optimistic mission. Borrowing money and raising donations, two members were chosen to take a goodwill tour to stimulate interest in the "first national Negro air show to be held in Chicago". They would go to Washington, DC to talk to lawmakers about including African Americans in government-sponsored flight training and other aviation programs. Enoch P. Waters, Jr., a member of NAAA and city editor of *The Chicago Defender*, also suggest-

Willa B. Brown was the first African American woman to gain a commercial pilot's license and was the first woman officer in the Civil Air Patrol. She married Cornelius Coffey, her flight instructor.

ed the tour include a stop in Washington to urge Congressional representatives to push for inclusion of the Negro in the Army Air Corps.

A thousand dollars was donated by the Jones Brothers, Ed and George, of Chicago who controlled the "policy," a form of the numbers game, and also owned the Ben Franklin department store on 47th Street. With $500 that Chauncey Spencer had saved, the organization was able to rent a Lin-

A Lincoln-Paige PT biplane of the type used on the NAAA promotional flight.

Chauncey Spencer.

coln-Paige bi-plane from Art LaToure. Dale White, a pioneer flyer and the holder of an aircraft engine mechanic's certificate, and Chauncey Spencer who had met a few years earlier and had become close friends, were chosen to undertake this history-making mission. They left Chicago's Harlem Airport on May 9, 1939 but after three and a half hours were forced to land in a farmer's field near Sherwood, Ohio with a damaged crankshaft. Cornelius Coffey produced a replacement and they went on their way two and a half days later.

Refueling at Morgantown, West Virginia, they flew on to Pittsburgh without lights as night approached. They saw the beacon at Allegheny County Airport and followed a commercial aircraft in to land. The Civil Aeronautics Inspectors grounded the pair for flying too close and "endangering lives". Robert L. Vann, Publisher of the *Pittsburgh Courier*, came to the rescue and appeared on their behalf the next morning at a hearing where they were cleared. Mr. Vann then donated $500 to their cause and wrote several letters to influential representatives.

Edgar Brown, National Airmen's Association lobbyist, and the President of the Negro Federal Workers Employees Union met the pair in Washington. While there, they happened to meet Senator Harry S. Truman, the Democrat Senator from Missouri, to whom they gave an explanation of their mission. Truman seemed surprised when told that Negros were not accepted into the Army Air Corps and asked, *"Why aren't you in the Air Corps? Can't you get in?"* Edgar Brown explained that Negroes were not accepted.

"Have you tried?" asked Truman. The reply came: *"No sir, but others have tried and have been embarrassed. They have been turned away without regard for their training or ability. Only the color of their skin mattered."* Truman felt that they should try, but Dale White's response was that they felt they needed help to open the door to entry, because they were not able to break down the barriers themselves. Harry Truman's characteristic blunt manner led him to ask to see

Senator Harry Truman.

the aircraft. Later that afternoon he visited the airport and climbed up on the wing of the plane in order to look in the cockpit. He asked, "How much gas can this carry? How much did it cost to rent? Do you have insurance?" He was enthusiastic, and went on to say: *"If they've had the guts to fly this thing to Washington, I'll have the guts to back them."* Soon afterwards, Senator Truman helped steer legislation in the Senate to allow blacks to be trained along with whites under the Civilian Pilot Training Program.

Another key figure that White and Spencer met and talked with was Congressman Everett Dirksen, Republican for Illinois who later introduced the amendment to the Civil Aeronautics bill in the House of Representatives prohibiting discrimination in the administration of the benefits of the Act. Three years later a bill was passed to include African Americans in the Army Air Corps.

The Civilian Pilot Training Act was passed on June 27, 1939 and by August funds had been appropriated. After a few operational and bureaucratic procedures, the program went into operation at Tuskegee in late 1939. Two instructors from the Alabama Polytechnic Institute (Auburn University), Robert G. Pitts and Bloomfield M. Cornell, agreed to conduct the ground school portion of the training until the Tuskegee instructors were trained. They taught the four principal units of instruction, amounting to 60 of the 72 hours. The flight training initially was conducted by the Alabama Air Service, owned and operated by Joseph W. Allen out of the municipal airport in Montgomery, who stated that he had no reservations about teaching African Americans to fly.

On March 25, 1940 George A. Wiggs arrived in Tuskegee to administer the standard written examination required of all Civilian Pilot Training students. After administering and grading the exams, he revealed that the Tuskegee students had passed every subject. They had become the only southern school with a 100 percent pass rate, but had done so by a wide margin in comparison to Georgia Tech., Auburn, and North Carolina. Prior to that time in the seven southern states, no college had a record of a 100 percent pass on the first examination. The average score was 88 percent. One third of the students scored above 90 percent. The lowest

score was 78 percent and the highest scores were recorded by Charles R. Foxx, who averaged 97 percent, Alexander S. Anderson with 96 percent, and Elvatus C. Morris with 95 percent. The students almost matched the 100 percent pass rate on the flight evaluations and by the end of May 1940, when the flight phase of training was completed, all but one of the students had passed the flight examination set up by the Civil Aeronautics Administration inspectors and received their private pilot licenses.

Charles Foxx became one of the seven students in the southeastern region to compete for the Shell Intercollegiate Aviation Scholarship, and was one of only 49 students in the whole country to vie for the $1,500 scholarship. He had been selected not only for his near-perfect score on the written examination, but also because he was a superb pilot with superior flying skills. C. Alfred "Chief" Anderson recalled many years later that in his fifty years of flying he had "never seen a person as slick a pilot as Charlie Foxx. He was a natural born pilot." The National Airmen Association of America had done what no-one before them had achieved – they had broken the mold and set the scene for African Americans to take their rightful place in the annals of aviation and achieve equality of opportunity.

Dr. Lewis Jackson and Charles "Chief" Anderson pose together in the fuselage of a dismantled Waco UPF-7 training biplane. These would be used in the Civil Pilot Training Program later at Tuskegee, Alabama.

Dr. Lewis A. Jackson, had a passion for flying and a desire to change the world through his teaching. Even before graduation from Illinois Wesleyan University in 1939, he was teaching in local schools. His love for the classroom remained with him for the rest of his life, and his drive to excel in everything he did would eventually lead him to become President at Central State University. Dr. Jackson was captivated by aeroplanes as a child. His passion for innovation manifested itself at the age of 17, when he mounted a motorcycle engine on a monoplane, but unfortunately, a windstorm destroyed the invention before he could test fly it. By his twenties, he was barnstorming across Indiana and Ohio to earn money for college.

In 1939, Jackson earned his commercial license with instructor rating. Within a year he had joined forces with Cornelius Coffey to open Coffey and Jackson Flying School in Chicago. Later that year, Jackson completed advanced aerobatic training and moved to Tuskegee where he received additional aircraft training. He became director of training at the Army Air Forces 66th Flight Training Detachment, where, under his guidance, three groups of Tuskegee Airmen ranked first among the 22 schools in the Southeast Army Air Corps Training Command. After the war, Jackson moved to Ohio where he worked as an FAA Flight examiner for 13 years.

In 1974, Lewis Jackson fostered the Business Entrepreneur Program at Sinclair Community College in Sinclair, Ohio. His most creative venture was "An aeroplane in every garage." From his first test flight in 1956 until his death, he faithfully worked on designing a "roadable" aeroplane that could be

Dr. Lewis Jackson's "roadable" airplane.

stored at home and towed or driven to an airport. His 16-foot long, collapsible wing design attracted attention around the world.

The United States Army Air Corps, later Army Air Forces, first began to look at the question of training black aviators in the late 1930s. It was almost five years before a plan took shape but by 1941, the Tuskegee Airmen had been established, though they were not known by that name until much later. The Army plan was workable in a segregated Armed Forces environment and, as will be described later, the airmen distinguished themselves beyond anybody's wildest imagination. But neither the Navy nor the Marine Corps followed in the Army's footsteps and it was not until after World War II that the African American pioneers of Naval and Marine Corps aviation arrived.

The first African American to be trained by the Navy as an aviator was Ensign Jesse Leroy Brown. He was born in Hattiesburg, Mississippi, on October 13, 1926, enlisted in the Naval Reserve in 1946 and was appointed a Midshipman, USN, the following year. After attending pre-flight school and flight training, he was designated a Naval Aviator in October 1948. President Truman's edict banning segregation in the Armed Forces was now in full force. Midshipman Brown was then assigned to Fighter Squadron 32 (VF-32). He received his commission as Ensign in April 1949.

During the Korean War, Brown also became the first African American Naval Aviator to see combat when his squadron boarded the USS "Leyte" to fly F4U Corsair fighters in close support role. On December 4, 1950, while on a close air support mission near the Chosin Reservoir, Brown's plane was hit by enemy fire and crashed. His squadron comrades thought Brown was dead, until they saw him slide back his canopy and wave. His wingman, Lt.(jg) Thomas Hudner deliberately crash-landed his own Corsair in an attempt to save his friend, who was pinned in his aircraft. As daylight faded, with Hudner at his side, Jesse Brown died. He was awarded the Distinguished Flying Cross for his service in Korea and Lt. Hudner received the Medal of Honor for his actions that day. Jesse Brown had scored three "firsts" in US Naval aviation as an African American. He had completed Navy flight

Ensign Jesse Brown seated in an F4U-4 "Corsair".

Lt. (jg) Thomas Hudner at his Medal of Honor ceremony greeting Mrs. Daisy Brown, his best friend Jesse Brown's widow.

school, he was the first to go into combat for the Navy, and sadly, he was the first African American Naval aviator to die for his country.

Frank E. Petersen, Jr. was the first African American aviator serving in the United States Marine Corps. He was born on March 2, 1932 to Edith Sutterand Petersen and Frank E. Petersen, Sr. in Topeka, Kansas, where his father was a radio repairman. Frank Jr. grew up in South Topeka, attended Monroe Elementary School, and graduated from Topeka High School in 1949. Leaving Washburn College after just a year, he joined the US Navy in 1950 and entered the Naval Aviation Cadet Program a year later, graduating from flight training to be commissioned a 2nd Lieutenant in the Marine Corps (USMC).

2nd Lieutenant Frank Petersen climbs aboard his F4U-4 "Corsair" for another mission with VMF-212 from K-6 airfield at Pyong-Tek.

Petersen served in Korea with Marine Fighter Squadron 212 (VMF-212), flying Chance Vought F4U Corsairs on 64 combat missions out of K-6 Airfield in Pyong-Taek, reaching as far as the Yalu River. He was awarded the Distinguished Flying Cross and six Air Medals in that period. Converting to jets in the 1960s, his next combat experience was in Vietnam, where he flew Douglas Skyhawks (the A-4) with Attack Squadron 314 (VMA-314). He undertook a total of 314 combat missions in those two conflicts.

Rising through the officer ranks of the Corps, Frank Petersen scored another "first". On February 23, 1979 he was promoted to Brigadier-General becoming the first African American Marine Corps general. Then, in May 1983, he was promoted to Major-General and finally to Lieutenant-General on June 12, 1986. In July 1988, General Petersen stepped down as Commanding General, Marine Corps Combat Development Command at Quantico, Virginia and retired the next month.

The most recent significant African American aviator must surely be the USAF Thunderbirds Number Five – Major Tyrone D. Douglas. He is not the first African American to fly with the Thunderbirds, but he became the first African American solo leader in that team when he returned to it in 2009. After flying with the 20th Tactical Fighter Wing at Shaw AFB, Tyrone Douglas was assigned to the 36th Fighter Squadron in South Korea and then to Nellis AFB in Nevada as an Aggressor pilot. This squadron trains pilots deploying for combat operations on potential airborne and ground-based threats. Here, Major Douglas married Captain Trisha Harms, an Air Force Aerospace Physiologist, whom he had met at Shaw AFB. His first season with the Thunderbirds was in 2007, after leaving Nellis. He was accepted into the team immediately as a solo pilot, the 56th in team history and the first African American Solo. He completed a total of two years as a Thunderbird Solo, in his first season as the Opposing Solo and in his second, in 2009, as Lead Solo.

Tyrone Douglas was born in Missouri and attended Raytown High School there before going on to the University of Kansas to secure a degree in electrical engineering and computer science. He joined the Air Force in 1997 as an ROTC distinguished graduate and completed undergraduate pi-

lot training at Laughlin Air Force Base in Del Rio, Texas in 1998. He emerged as the distinguished graduate of class 98-12. Tyrone was then assigned to the 61st Fighter Squadron an F-16 Fighter Training Unit, where he earned top honors in Air-to-Ground Top Gun and Air-to-Air gunnery. He was deployed three times to Iraq and Afghanistan while he was assigned to his first operational unit.

Major Tyrone D. Douglas.

Major Douglas next became the Assistant Director Operations (ADO) of the 25th Flying Training Squadron. The primary mission is to produce new Air Force pilots who will go on to fly fighter or bomber aircraft. In 2009 Tyrone graduated from Touro University International earning his Master's Degree in Business Administration.

CHAPTER SIX

The Tuskegee Institute – Formation and Flight Training

Young Booker T. Washington.

The foundation of this Institute is the story of dreams coming true, thanks to the vision of one young man back in 1881. His name was Booker T. Washington and he was born a slave in 1856 on a small farm in the back country of Virginia. His father was a white planter and his mother a black slave. After the Civil War, his family moved to West Virginia to work in the salt furnaces and coal mines. From early boyhood, Booker was interested in learning and pursued what education he could with vigor, ultimately securing a secondary education at Hampton Institute. He toyed with the idea of pursuing further studies either in law or the ministry, but he was offered a teaching post at his old school, Hampton, which set the path of his career.

Already, Booker had a campaigning mind set and was dreaming of achievement for young blacks who, like him, had been born into slavery, but were now notionally free to make their way in life. He recognized his own privilege of gaining a secondary education, something usually reserved for young white men, and decided to put that to use for the benefit of young black men. He had one advantage from the beginning that was to serve him well in the future – an awareness of the white mentality of the time from his own white father.

Meanwhile, in 1880, Lewis Adams, a black political leader in Macon County, Alabama, agreed to support two Democratic Party candidates, both white, William Foster and Arthur Brooks in winning a local election. The arrangement was that they would, once elected, support the construction and establishment of a school for African Americans in the district. They were both elected and fulfilled their promise. Sometime later, Samuel Armstrong, principal of the highly successful Hampton Normal and Agricultural Institute in Virginia, was asked to recommend a white teacher to become principal of that school. However, he suggested that it would be a good idea to employ an African American and he recommended Booker T. Washington for the post.

In 1881, Washington left for Alabama and created the educational establishment to be called the Tuskegee Normal and Industrial Institute, modeled on his experiences of the Hampton Institute. What was so special about that? Not only the fact that he, a former slave, could go into the heart of the "black belt" of the south and establish such a school, but more significantly, he was only twenty-five years old when he did it.

The school was originally a shanty building owned by the local church and it was endowed with only $2,000 a year, just enough to pay the staff. The first class of twenty boys was to learn construction skills and Washington was only able to appoint one teacher initially.

Aware of the sensitivities of the establishment, Booker Washington made a conscious decision not to make his school a "trendsetter". He saw far more value in providing a place where young men could achieve solid work skills. He had already shown the value of his negotiating skills by persuading a group of white northern philanthropists to fund this project in the first place. Now, good teaching methods focused on the development of skills that would enable young people to take a place in society were more important than any sense of academic adventure. It would consolidate the school's reputation and help it ultimately become a part of that establishment.

Eventually, Mr. Washington was able to borrow money from the treasurer of his old school, the Hampton Agricultural Institute, to buy an abandoned plantation on the outskirts of Tuskegee, to build a brand new school. The school embraced practical subjects, which included farming, carpentry, brick making, shoemaking, printing and cabinetmaking. Booker Washington's astuteness already showed itself here clearly, for it enabled students to become involved in the building of that new school. Students worked long hours, rising at five in the morning and ending their day at nine-thirty at night.

By 1888 the school owned 540 acres of land and had over 400 students enrolled. Mr. Washington was able to attract good teachers, which

The original Tuskegee School buildings at the time of purchase in 1881.

The first fieldwork being carried out by women at Tuskegee in 1881. Soon the foundations of a real school would be built on this site.

Tuskegee students laying the foundations of one of the four Emery Halls of the Institute.

Students working in the Craft Workshop at Tuskegee.

plaint before being granted their political rights. From an early stage of his career, he took the view that confrontation would achieve far less than subversion. By raising the skill levels, the abilities and respect for his graduates, he believed that he would bring them to equality and liberty much more quickly. He knew well that he needed white support to ultimately achieve black suffrage.

In a short space of time, Booker Washington was to demonstrate a depth of political skill, combined with a perception that he was accommodating the white visions of the time of blacks in society, while working vigorously for the advancement of the African American cause across the whole spectrum of society. He did this by convincing white employers in the district, and his own governors, that the Tuskegee Institute would effectively educate and train young black men into skills that would keep them "down on the farm".

further enhanced the school's and his own reputation. Furthermore, his perceived conservative leadership helped to make it acceptable to the politically white-controlled Macon County. He proclaimed the belief that blacks should not campaign for the vote, since they needed to prove their loyalty to the United States by working hard without com- He was looking also by the middle 1890s to foster the support of new self-made white millionaires who were would-be philanthropists, such as the Rockefeller, Huntington and Carnegie families by promising them the traditional Protestant work ethic that they perceived so necessary to orderly society. They gave their support.

So what did he offer the black community that would convince them to support him and his Institute? In the post-reconstruction era of the South, he offered hope. Here was an opportunity for young men to escape the traditional vision of the black South. They could achieve self-sufficiency with an education that would equip them to become self-employed and grow at their own pace, they could own land by their efforts, and they could work in small businesses as partners. They could ultimately even win places in society

Booker Washington at the Atlanta Cotton States Exposition, delivering his Atlanta Compromise Address.

by going on from Tuskegee to become ministers or lawyers or teachers – all occupations that carried the beginnings of social influence and which hitherto had been virtually unavailable goals to African Americans. All this was part of Booker Washington's progressive philosophy to cultivate financial support from those who saw this as an institution of moderation. It worked, because he even persuaded the State of Alabama to give a small appropriation in support of the school's aims. He gained local white support and approval for his programs and most importantly, kept financial support coming in from his white northern supporters to such an extent that by 1900, the Tuskegee Institute was the best-supported black educational institution in the United States.

In September 1895, the Piedmont Center in Atlanta, Georgia, was the venue for the Cotton States Exposition, a grand showing of the innovations, creations and products of the South. Six states took part demonstrating, within the overall framework of the exhibition, the accomplishments of women and African Americans. It showcased the latest technology in many fields, including transportation, agricul-

ture, mining and manufacturing. Booker T. Washington, now prominent in local society, was a guest speaker on the opening day of that exposition.

Washington's delivery was known as the Atlanta Compromise Address. It focused on harmony in race relations, and he made it plain that blacks should concentrate on learning useful skills. He considered that black self-help and self-improvement would be far more useful tools in the advancement of the black population than violent resistance to segregation, disenfranchisement, and racial discrimination. That may have sounded at the time more like appeasement of the whites than advancement of blacks, but in principle, most people who listened to or read what he said had to agree that peaceful advancement of their cause would be far more productive in the longer term than violent confrontation.

Most important of all in this period of the development of the United States, when black soldiers were becoming accepted and respected in certain parts of the country, the "Indian Country" of the west in particular, Booker Washington's

Porter Hall, the first completed hall of the Tuskegee Institute.

the process of establishing acknowledgement of the contribution one group of black men made to the nation's success in war. Ultimately, this was the first major step forward in establishing equality between the races. It was the group that later became known as the Tuskegee Airmen.

Back to 1920, there was some recognition in government circles that black veterans of the Great War of 1914-1918 were being treated appallingly. The Treasury Department Hospitalization Committee found that it was almost impossible to secure proper treatment for African American soldiers in mixed hospitals for war veterans in the South. But the Treasury made available a fund to create a special hospital. Several locations were considered, but many were rejected by white communities who did not want a hospital for black veterans in their neighborhood. Tuskegee was finally chosen, partly because Robert Moton did all he could to bring it there and partly because Macon County was willing to accommodate it.

influence was having an effect and his views were listened to among leaders of white and black society. His wisdom and caution were respected by leaders of both sectors of society and he ultimately became the chief black advisor to two Presidents – Theodore Roosevelt (whose experiences of black American soldiers in the Spanish-American War had a profound effect on his views of race for the rest of his life) and William Howard Taft.

Booker Washington's pragmatic approach and constant efforts to improve the lives and standing of black people, quite apart from his continued development of the Tuskegee Institute, were his guarantee of a place in history right up to his death in 1915 at the modest age of 59. He had many critics who viewed his approach as one of keeping black people in a subordinate role to whites, but they did not see that his tactic of developing the skills and position of black people to a level equal to whites would essentially be a self-fulfilling prophecy. As the most profound mark of respect possible, he was interred in the grounds of the Institute he created. That Institute is today a National Monument.

Robert Moton was the second Principal of the Institute and during the 1920s and up to 1935, through some truly controversial times and issues, he also laid the foundation for what must be recognized as the most significant stepping stone in

Congress therefore authorized the Treasury to build a hospital solely for the care of more than 300,000 black veterans in the South. The hospital was built at a cost of $2,500,000 and consisted of 27 permanent buildings on a total of 464 acres of land alongside the Tuskegee Normal and Industrial Institute campus. Before it opened, however, there were many

The first VA hospital catering for sick and injured Colored War Veterans, this newly-built facility at Tuskegee was on the grounds of the Tuskegee Institute.

A group of "patients" being addressed during the Tuskegee Experiment.

American doctors to begin treating veterans in Tuskegee. He arrived there after graduating from Harvard and started his career as a young doctor working in psychiatry. Thirty-four years later, Dr. Tildon retired as the Tuskegee Hospital's Director.

In a celebration in 2008 to mark the eighty-fifth anniversary of the Tuskegee Veterans' Hospital, Central Alabama Veterans Health Care System Acting Director, Shirley Bealer, said:

"In 1923 young African American health care professionals were drawn to Tuskegee. They knew the nation would take stock in their ability and they knew they would not only be able to provide care for black veterans, but they would also serve as beacons for other young African Americans. Their commitment and professionalism would be scrutinized, measured and compared to the highest standards."

conflicts and Dr. Moton almost forfeited his position and reputation over it. The Macon County Fathers had expected this hospital to be operated by white doctors and nurses. Dr. Moton and many of his supporters had different ideas. Because black veterans could not get adequate treatment from existing mixed veteran hospitals, it was rightly expected that they would also be prejudiced here and so a campaign was launched to ensure that the hospital was staffed by African Americans. There was an open riot, which included even the Ku Klux Klan, and Dr. Moton had to appease all the different factions. Many people accused him of being an "Uncle Tom", but the ultimate settlement proved him right, for he achieved an agreement to staff the hospital with African American doctors and nurses.

The dedication ceremony of the Hospital for Sick and Injured Colored World War Veterans took place on February 12, 1923. Authority for the administration of the institution was passed from the US Treasury to the US Veterans Bureau (which became the Veterans Administration on July 21, 1930). Today, that hospital is known as the Tuskegee VA Hospital. Dr. Toussaint T. Tildon was one of the first six African

Sadly, the Tuskegee Hospital also had its dark side, with what became known as "The Tuskegee Experiment". This was a research program into the effects of untreated syphilis that involved almost four hundred African American men. The Public Health Service, working with the Tuskegee Institute, began a study in 1932 in which those men were enrolled. They were never told they had syphilis and were never treated for it. They were simply told they were being treated for "bad blood". It was a local term used at the time to describe a range of illnesses, one of which was syphilis.

In return for taking part in the study, these men were given free medical examinations and general medical care (except for syphilis), free meals and, ironically, free burial insurance. When all this began, there was no treatment for syphilis, so in some respects, the study program had some, minimal, legitimacy. But when the cure of penicillin became widely available in 1947, and when the experiments and study were continuing, the treatment was withheld from this group, because some nameless soul wanted to investigate how the disease spread and killed.

Finally, certain public health workers possessed of conscience could hold the story back no longer and it was leaked to the media. *The Washington Evening Post* ran a headline that read: "Syphilis Patients Died Untreated." By this time many men had died – and benefited from the free burial insurance. In 1973, the National Association for the Advancement of Colored People (NAACP) filed a "class-action" lawsuit and achieved a compensatory sum of $9 million. That meager sum was divided among the participants and distributed to survivors. This experiment will go down in history as one of the most blatant persecutions of men of one race "in the name of science" or for any other reason. It cannot be excused by the declaration that "some people react to certain diseases differently from others".

In 1997, President Bill Clinton made the best attempt he could to apologize, saying what the government had done was deeply, profoundly and morally wrong, to the survivors and to the victims' families, with these words:

> *"To the survivors, to the wives and family members, the children and the grandchildren, I say what you know: No power on Earth can give you back the lives lost, the pain suffered, the years of internal torment and anguish. What was done cannot be undone. But we can end the silence. We can stop turning our heads away. We can look at you in the eye and finally say, on behalf of the American people: what the United States government did was shameful. And I am sorry."*

Even that apology, profound as it was, couldn't do it all – the actions taken in the process of those experiments were indeed, shameful and a blight on the nation.

However in 1940, Tuskegee was about to become famous for a more uplifting reason. It was being considered as a site for use by the US Army Air Corps. A quite unusual question was placed in the hands of the commander of the Southeast Air Corps Training Center, Brigadier-General Walter R. Weaver, in November 1940 in a letter from the Office of the Chief of the Air Corps discussing the establishment of a pursuit squadron at Tuskegee, Alabama, crewed by "colored personnel". General Weaver had been aware for some time that a Negro training project was being considered and it was also widely thought that he would oppose a mixed race group for what were then obvious reasons. It was thought later that his motive for encouraging Dr. F. D. Patterson, President of Tuskegee Institute, to secure the location for colored flying activities, was to insure the segregation of the two races. If that was General Weaver's intention, then he was certainly successful.

Most of the detailed work for this experimental pursuit squadron was done in Washington, where it had already been decided that the entire establishment should be manned by colored personnel. It was considered then that only thirty-three pursuit pilots needed to be trained. But because of the Army's policy of segregation, nothing could begin until the enlisted mechanics and other ground trades needed were available and this would be twenty-two weeks after technical training had started, most probably at Chanute Field, Illinois. General Weaver was directed to submit a plan covering the setting-up of this flight training school at Tuskegee and to make recommendations about funds, personnel and internal organization. Finally, the Office of the Commander of the Air Corps letter pointed out (quite unnecessarily) that the whole concept should be on the basis that the new organization would provide a training standard in every way equivalent to that for white personnel.

In less than two weeks, the OCAC submitted to the Adjutant General a proposal. These plans were based almost word for word upon the recommendations sent in by the South East Air Corps Training Center. Their original estimate, that a total of 429 enlisted men and 47 officers would be needed, was upheld. Since it was virtually impossible to start elementary training immediately, it was proposed to enlist Civil Aeronautics Authority graduates from the secondary phase as flying cadets in the basic school as soon as they had been given military training. It had been established that there were already enough candidates for this to be practicable. The "icing on the cake" was that it had been recommended the Tuskegee site should be selected, because the only other available site, in the Chicago area, would not be suitable because of its climate.

In January 1941, a confidential telegram went to the SEACTC to advise that the Tuskegee project was approved and that funds would soon be secured. The decision was to be treated as classified "confidential" and news of this decision was not to be publicized in any direction. Soon afterwards, the Adjutant General was requested by OCAC to approve a plan to recruit 420

An early survey photograph of Tuskegee Army Airfield.

black soldiers, train them at Chanute Field, and send them to Tuskegee on October 1, 1941, when it was expected that basic flying training could begin. Advanced training was planned to commence on December 20th for an annual output of seventy-five pilots.

Major James A. Ellison, of the Southeast Air Corps Training Center, would be appointed the Project Officer for this program and in February 1941, he attended a conference in Washington to discuss the operation. He would ultimately be the first Commanding Officer of the Tuskegee flight school. It turned out that the original plan submitted by General Weaver would be modified in some aspects. And then, the War Department made it clear that it would have one of its own boards pass the project. It seemed that the original piece of land selected was not thought to be entirely suitable, so another one had to be selected to appease the engineers and some of Tuskegee's citizens. A new site was finally approved on April 30, 1941.

On February 7, 1941, SEACTC was formally advised that it was intended to organize a primary training civil establishment, contracted to Tuskegee on the same basis as similar flying schools. But, until this organization could function, it was anticipated that CAA secondary course graduates would go directly into basic military training. General Weaver was directed to initiate negotiations for the Tuskegee Institute and to make recommendations for the flow of students through the program. Mr. G. L. Washington, the director of aviation training at the institute, met General Weaver on February 15, and made it plain that from the Institute's point of view, he wanted a thoroughly safe and satisfactory airfield. His view was that the African American population deserved a successful experiment in flying training and that the success of black youth in the Air Corps depended heavily on the success of the Tuskegee project.

The man who was to become the focal center of this project in quite a short period of time was Charles Alfred Anderson.

Charles "Chief" Anderson with a student in a Waco UMF-7.

He was born in Bryn Mawr, Pennsylvania on February 9, 1907, the son of Janie and Iverson Anderson, and as a young boy was sent to live with his grandmother in Santon, Virginia, in the Shenandoah Valley. He later recalled that from the age of six years, he was captivated by flying. Since no flying instructor of his time would teach a black student, at the age of 22 he bought a used plane with his savings and some funds borrowed from friends and relatives, then began learning to fly without an instructor. He secured his private pilot's license in 1929 and went on to obtain a commercial pilot's license three years later, in 1932 – the first African American to earn a commercial license.

Charles Anderson had a close friend, Dr. Albert Forsythe, who was also "nuts about flying" and the two paired up to make a number of historic long-distance flights. They made the first round-trip trans-continental flight by black pilots, starting at Atlantic City, New Jersey and flying to Los Angeles, California. Amazingly, they had no navigation lights on their aeroplane, a Lambert Monocoupe Model D-145, no parachutes, no blind-flying instruments and no radio. Yet they found their way, using roadmaps to navigate.

This adventurous pair also made a long-distance flight to Canada and later flew an elaborate Pan American Goodwill Tour of the Caribbean in their Monocoupe, "The Spirit of Booker T. Washington." This island-hopping tour included the first flight of a land plane from Miami to the Bahamas and ultimately ended in Trinidad. These Anderson-Forsythe flights attracted worldwide attention and did a great deal to popularize aviation in the black community. The Tuskegee Institute snapped him up as its Chief Instructor in 1940. The legend of "Chief" Anderson was about to begin. His task was to develop a flight-training program for the Tuskegee school.

In Washington, Lieutenant-General Henry Arnold, Commanding General of the Army Air Corps authorized the elementary project, and his letter recommended the completion of a contract with the Tuskegee Institute. Then, the problem of finance raised its ugly head. It turned out to be unexpectedly complicated. Even though the Tuskegee Institute was successfully operating a flying school, certified by the CAA, and its President was willing to provide a separate dormitory, mess, hospital, classroom space and motor transportation, this project was expected to be expensive.

Dr. Patterson, President of the Institute, approached the Reconstruction Finance Corporation for funds and was refused on the grounds that the project might not continue over a long period of time. With the SEACTC's support, he turned to the Julius Rosenwald Fund in Chicago. In March 1941, a meeting of the board of that fund was held in Tuskegee with a surprise visitor, Mrs. Eleanor Roosevelt, in attendance. It was agreed in that meeting to lend the Tuskegee Institute the sum of $200,000, provided that the Tuskegee board put up $25,000 of its own money and agreed to amortize the entire amount as quickly as possible, though no specific time was

The Waco UMF-7. Several hundred Wacos were impressed into service with the Civilian Pilot Training Program.

The Lambert Monocoupe that once belonged to Charles Lindbergh and hung in St. Louis International Airport for some years. It is the same type and model that Anderson and Forsythe flew.

put on the amortization. As a result, construction quickly began and the project moved ahead.

After overcoming all the obstacles on the way to creating this new organization, and with some celebration, the elementary school at Tuskegee was opened on July 19, 1941, with an opening address from Major-General Weaver. The first commanding officer was Captain Noel F. Parrish who had previous experience of Negro students at the Glenview, Illinois, school where he had also been commanding officer. He remained at the Tuskegee elementary detachment until December 3, 1941.

The pre-flight school went into operation straight away, though it provided only military training in the first month. On August 21, 1941, Class SE-42-C-1, consisting of 12 cadets, including Captain Benjamin O. Davis, began its flying training. Captain Davis was the 20th Century's first African American graduate of West Point and was the first flight cadet trainee selected for this program. Only six of that original class finished the primary stage. The high attrition rate was credited by Captain Parrish to poor selection of cadets pre-enrolment. He pressed the need for future classes to be selected on the basis of potential ability not priority of application. He went so far as to suggest that the next course should come entirely from civil pilot training graduates. That did not happen and the elimination rate remained high. It was to be another year before more CAA graduates were drawn into the program. During this period, the four flying instructors and the one ground school instructor were white. But that was to change as soon as opportunity allowed and Charles "Chief" Anderson was to come on scene…

Major James A. Ellison, first Commanding Officer of the Tuskegee Flight School, was a man very sympathetic to the cause of the Tuskegee Airmen. Here, he reviews the first class of the Tuskegee program, included in which number was Captain Benjamin O. Davis. The aircraft in the background are Vultee BT-13s.

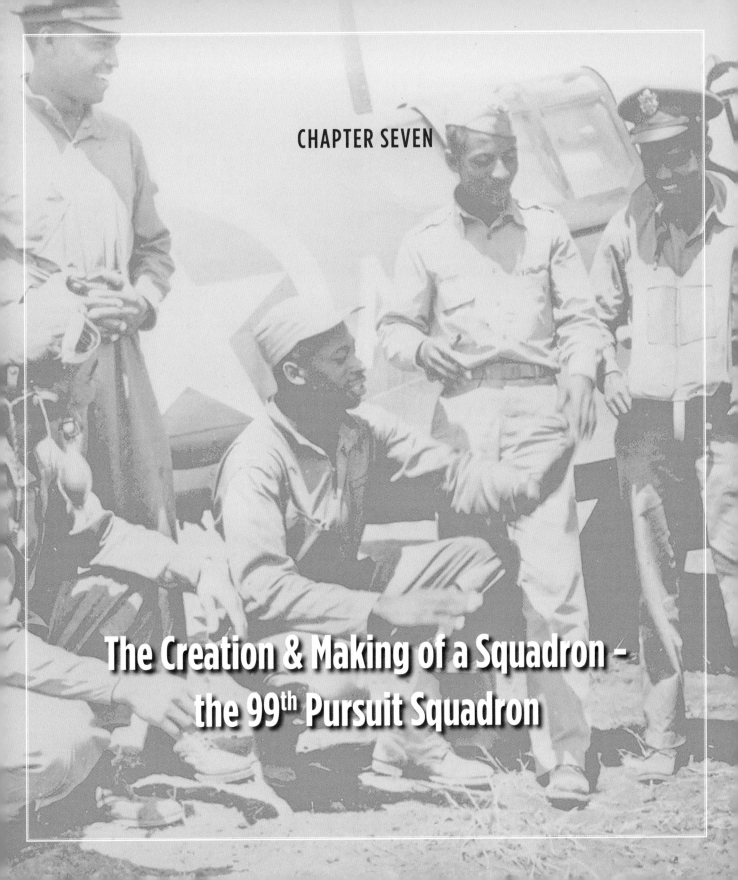

CHAPTER SEVEN

The Creation & Making of a Squadron – the 99th Pursuit Squadron

Imagine the excitement in the student crew room of the Tuskegee Institute when "Chief" Anderson announced that there was to be a pursuit squadron formed with all-black crews. It is possible to imagine the questions. "What's our squadron to be called?" – "What will we fly?" – "Who'll be the CO?" – "Where will we go into combat?" – "When will we go?" The one question that could be answered instantly was that they would be flying the aircraft they were already using in weapons and combat training – the Curtiss P-40 "Warhawk". Some were pleased, some were not – some took the view that at least they knew their aircraft and its quirks – others were hoping for something more advanced. But the P-40 it was to be – and some shabby examples at that.

The first person selected for the initial course of training for the new pursuit squadron was Captain Benjamin O. Davis. He was the son of the first African American General Staff Officer. His father was also accomplished in that he was commissioned into the 1st Volunteer Infantry in 1898, during the Spanish-American War, was mustered out of the Army in March 1899 and then enlisted as a private soldier, working his way through the ranks to Sergeant Major before he was commissioned again, having now served with the famous all-black 9th Cavalry. His re-commissioning was into the regular Army. Among his many assignments, he served with the 93rd Division in France and was one of the 179 Croix de Guerre winners. More significantly perhaps, he was assigned to Tuskegee Institute as Professor of Military Science and Tactics between 1920 and 1924. His promotion to Brigadier-General took place in October 1940. A hard act to follow for Benjamin Jr., but he finally outranked his father.

Benjamin Davis graduated from flight training, Course 42-C-I, in March 1942, along with four other black officers to form the core of what was to become the 99th Pursuit Squadron and he was appointed to command this new Tuskegee squadron. It was to be numbered "99" – the 99th Pursuit Squadron of the US Army Air Corps. As the Army Air Corps transformed into the United States Army Air Forces, so the designation of "Pursuit" squadrons changed to "Fighter" squadrons, though aircraft designations continued to be "P" for some years yet. The Navy, on the other hand, had used the designation "F"

Captain Benjamin O. Davis climbing aboard a North American AT-6, before moving on to the Curtiss P-40 "Warhawk".

for Fighter from the beginning of their aircraft type designations. The aircraft to be used by the 99th was the Curtiss P-40 "Warhawk", an obsolescent design by now, but nonetheless an aircraft that had proved itself in Royal Air Force service in the Western Desert of North Africa. And North Africa was where the 99th was going, to become a part of Brigadier-General James H. Doolittle's 12th Air Force.

But before all this happened, Tuskegee had to "produce the goods". Selection for enrollment into the Tuskegee Airmen was deliberately stiff so that its originators felt assured it would deter so many that numbers would fall far short of what was needed to form a viable fighting unit. They could then report to those on high that attempts to recruit suitably qualified numbers had failed and therefore so had President Roosevelt's idea of establishing an African American element to his fighting forces.

Not only did that philosophy fail, it seems to have worked against those who conceived it, the SEACTC training planners, for there were many young men who wanted to serve their country who were able to pass the elevated entry standards with ease and who, as a result, were probably better academically qualified than most of their white counterparts. The result was that there were many more college graduates than expected applying for places and joining the flying course. And when they arrived at Tuskegee, they were easily able to cope with the academic requirements of the course.

One of Tuskegee's civilian flight instructors, Linwood Williams, standing beside a Waco UMF-7 biplane trainer.

Pride and commitment are the two features that shine through in this picture. A group of the first graduating Tuskegee students who, by their appearance alone, are a great credit to the US Army. Soon their achievements would shine too and bring not only a significant contribution to the Allied victory in the North African and Mediterranean Campaigns, but more awards for courage in the air than any other Army Air Forces Fighter Group in those Theaters of Operations.

These men had pride in their achievements and in their country, but most of all, pride in their roots. They wanted to prove above all that African Americans could do anything that was asked of them every bit as well as any Caucasian American. And they set about doing it better – to prove a point. The ground crew technicians did the same. They were initially trained at Chanute Field at Rantoul, in Illinois until the Tuskegee facilities were upgraded. All these young men had two things to prove; that they could do the job as well as anybody else as individuals and that the color of their skin had no bearing on their ability to do the job. They were fighting for the Flag like anybody else.

It's interesting to reflect how that flight training took place. Certainly, a number of instructors were recruited into that task from civilian life, because they had been flight instructors before. But that accounts for only a few at the beginning. The Tuskegee Institute was a civilian organization and the early pilots were trained there under that civilian program, so that some could be further trained up to instructor standard, before becoming part of the Army Flight Training School at Tuskegee. But how did that happen, when there were no black military pilots up to that time. We know that the first four flight instructors on the civilian program were white, as well as the first ground school instructor. Those nameless white faces do occasionally appear in Tuskegee group photographs. But then came Charles "Chief" Anderson.

A great deal of work was done in the White House to support and encourage the establishment of the Tuskegee Institute as a feeder to the Army Air Corps for the foundation of what became known as the Tuskegee Airmen. The First Lady of the United States, Eleanor Roosevelt was much involved in securing the approval of the formation of the Tuskegee Army Flight School and in raising funding to ensure it could hap-

A group of students examining their next "steed", the Curtiss P-40.

pen. She visited the airfield in 1941, met many of the people who were to become influential in the creation and operation of the 99th Fighter Squadron and, flew with Charles "Chief" Anderson in a Piper Cub.

She was also influential in the decision to dispatch the 99th to North Africa into Jimmy Doolittle's command, where she thought the Tuskegee Airmen would best survive. That experience had its moments, especially when there was an attempt to dismantle the Tuskegee Airmen, but Lieutenant-Colonel Benjamin Davis' testimonial before the House Committee on Defense helped to deter that attempt – and Mrs. Roosevelt's behind-the-scenes influence at the White House sealed it. The Tuskegee Airmen lived to fight another day – and many more besides.

Selecting the aircraft type to be flown by the 99th Fighter Squadron was relatively easy – the Curtiss P-40 was available in some numbers, since it was being replaced in many front line squadrons by more up-to-date designs such as the P-47 Thunderbolt and the P-51 Mustang. While the P-40 was considered obsolescent, it was being put to extremely effective use by the Royal Air Force in several locations around the world. Three squadrons in North Africa, in the British 285 Wing – 112 Squadron Royal Air Force, 5 Squadron, South African Air Force and 27 Squadron Royal Australian Air Force – were already flying this aircraft type as the P-40K "Kittyhawk", with considerable success but all of theirs had been delivered new. And the earlier P-40B "Tomahawk" had been used by a few Army Cooperation (reconnaissance) squadrons in the Royal Air Force too, one notable among them being Number 208 Squadron. That squadron had been singled out by the Germans for mention in the failed Greek campaign, when they announced that "The vital communications link between forces in the field and British Headquarters – Num-

Mrs. Eleanor Roosevelt sitting in the back seat of a Piper Cub and looking very happy about the flight she is about to undertake with "Chief" Anderson. She had already met Anderson before and specifically asked for him to "take her up" during her visit to Tuskegee.

The P-40K and L were widely used by the Royal Air Force and Allied squadrons of 285 Wing in the Western Desert. This rare color shot of an Allison-engined 112 Sqn RAF P-40K shows it being "talked" out to takeoff position by a ground crewman sitting on the port wing.

ber 208 Squadron – has been destroyed". The escaping 208 Squadron crews had in fact set their aircraft on fire to stop the Germans getting them. An interesting aside here is that General Claire Lee Chennault "borrowed" the shark-mouth nose decoration of Number 112 Squadron RAF for his Flying Tigers in China and Burma. The Royal Air Force used more P-40s than any other air arm in World War II.

The 99th Fighter Squadron was formed as an entity in the United States under the supervision of Lieutenant-Colonel Davis, but the first commander of the 99th was Lieutenant George "Spanky" Roberts, whose promotion was accelerated to Major quite quickly. He took the squadron to North Africa, handing command to Colonel Davis upon his arrival at Fardjouna, just before the major bombing raid on Pantel-

The graduates of flight course SE–42–1 at Tuskegee. The eight men are: Nathaniel Hill, Marshall Cabiness, Herman Lawson, William T. Mattison, John Gibson, Elwood T. Driver, Price D. Rice and Andrew Turner.

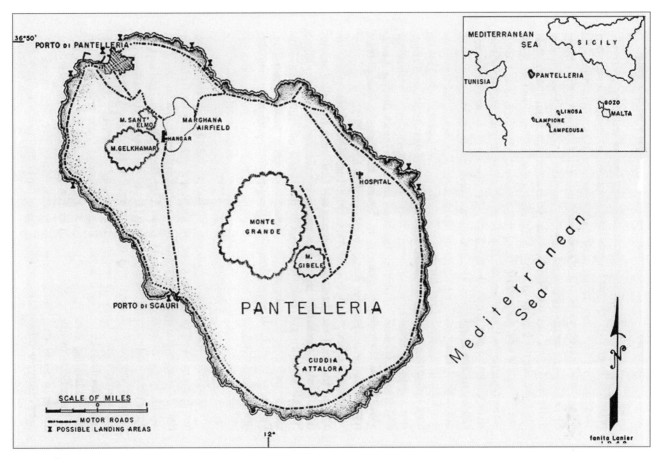

This map of Pantelleria shows the defensive installations. The major gun emplacements were jointly destroyed by the 17th and 320th Bombardment Groups from the air and the Royal Navy from the sea.

leria. Major Roberts, it appears, also led the earliest strafing runs on the island of Pantelleria before the squadron's first bomber escort mission.

The 99th's first missions were flown with a collection of "cast-off" P-40 Warhawks, which had not even been given a major service before being allocated to the 99th. They were aircraft which had been replaced by later types and which, as far as the squadrons from which they came were concerned, were likely to be scrapped and so there was no point in doing any major service work on them. A number probably were only fit for scrap. It is a tremendous testament, unsung,

to the ground crews of the 99th that they were able to improvise in the renovation of their aircraft to make them not just flyable, but reliably so. Since many of these mechanics had come from the world of auto-repair in the poorer black communities, they were already experts at "making do and mend", more widely known as "lashing-up". The camaraderie between aircrew and ground crew of the 99th became immensely strong and remained so throughout the War.

Arriving in North Africa in late April 1943, the first major mission allocated to the 99th was located at Oued Nja, near Fez in Morocco. They were there for seven weeks before being

THE TUSKEGEE AIRMEN AND BEYOND

assigned to the 33rd Fighter Group at Fardjouna, in Tunisia. Whilst there they were given the task of escorting the B-26 bombers of the 320th Bombardment Group, who were partners to the 17th Bomb Group, Jimmy Doolittle's old group in the Doolittle Raid on Japan the year before. The target was Pantelleria, a small island about sixty miles from Sicily, upon which was based a substantial enemy force and several squadrons of fighter and bomber aircraft. There were four islands – Pantelleria, Lampedusa, Linosa and Lampione – and all stood in the way of an Allied attack on Sicily, which was the next major target after the Allies had driven the German forces out of Tunisia. The job was to bomb Pantelleria into submission, because it was thought that this island, the biggest of the four, would cause the others to surrender. It certainly was not going to take just one day. Operation "Corkscrew" was planned to conclude with a landing on Pantelleria on June 11th.

A substantial Allied force was mounted to attack these four islands, with Britain playing a major naval role in the operation. The Royal Navy dispatched battle cruisers and destroyers from Gibraltar to bombard the islands on May 3rd, again on May 13th, and consistently into June. The destroyers HMS "Nubian" and "Tartar" took on the task of striking at the main gun emplacements on Pantelleria – there were 100 on the island in total and the volcanic rock took a massive shelling, as the guns were recessed into a combination of man-made and natural revetments. As May ran into June, the medium bombers of the 12th Air Force came into action as did the 99th Fighter Squadron. The arrangement was that the bombings from the air would prevent gun crews on the island from being fully effective, and the Royal Navy could shell with immunity.

The 99th would join the 33rd Fighter Group under its Commanding Officer, Colonel William Momyer. The first problem encountered by Lieutenant-Colonel Benjamin Davis was over the pre-flight briefing for their first mission. They had been in Fardjouna for a week and were left entirely to their own devices in finding their way around the airfield, locating fuel supplies and any kind of ground support. When it came to that vital pre-mission briefing, Lieutenant-Colonel

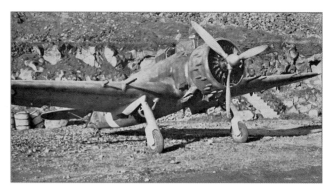

Air defense of Pantelleria consisted of many of these Italian Breda Br65 fighters, but as well as that, there were the much more formidable German Focke-Wulf Fw-190s, which the 99th Fighter Squadron faced over Pantelleria.

Davis was told quite bluntly by his Group Commander that neither he nor his crews would be allowed to attend the briefing, because they were "black".

Given little guidance from battle-experienced pilots, the 99th's first major combat mission was virtually doomed from the beginning. Yet Lieutenant-Colonel Davis called his own pre-mission briefing. He established the time of take-off for the bomb group and ensured that his pilots were in the air in readiness to provide escort cover.

What Davis and his crews did not know was what the enemy firepower might be, how alert the enemy fighter groups were, or in what formations they might be in the air. All this they had to discover as they flew. They soon did discover, because they were "jumped" by a German fighter group of FW-190 fighters – machines far superior to their worn-out and obsolescent P-40s. It was a miracle that the 99th did not lose a single aircraft in the skirmish, but succeeded in keeping the enemy off the bombers that were attacking the island. Events now were to turn ugly for the 99th Fighter Squadron and its commander when Colonel Momyer lodged a formal complaint that the 99th had failed in its task to escort the bombers, that the pilots of the squadron had panicked and run away from their charges, that they were incompetent and unable to fly their machines properly.

The B-26s of the 17th Bombardment Group (Jimmy Doolittle's old outfit from the Doolittle Raid) take off from North Africa.

B-26s of the 17th Bombardment Group on a bombing run.

A 17th BG B-26 "Earthquake McGoon" going home – mauled but still intact – and it flew all the way home.

Momyer's goal was to achieve the disbandment of the 99th Fighter Squadron and kill off the whole Tuskegee project. His report found its way to the House Defense Committee and the enquiry that ensued called for him and Lieutenant-Colonel Davis to give evidence. Colonel Momyer put the Pantelleria incident down to an argument that black pilots couldn't handle the complication of their mounts and that their ground crews couldn't keep the aircraft in the air, yet not one aircraft was lost. No consideration was given to the condition of the aircraft allotted to the 99th. In Momyer's view, all-black squadrons were a bad idea and the experiment should be abandoned. He reckoned without the tenacity of Lieutenant-Colonel Benjamin Davis, who was instructed to attend the inquiry as commander of the unit under investigation. Davis' evidence caused Momyer's recommendation to be overturned and established firmly the future of what would ultimately become the 332nd Fighter Group. And in the background, somebody had not reckoned for the views and influence of America's First Lady. In addition, the 99th Fighter Squadron was awarded a Distinguished Unit Citation for their actions over Pantelleria – a direct snub to Colonel Momyer.

Brigadier-General James H. Doolittle co-piloted a B-26 Marauder in that bombing raid over Pantelleria on June 10, just one day before the island surrendered to the Allies. He flew with one of his old 17th Bomb Group crews, former Doolittle Raider Major Jack Sims, commander of the 442nd Bombardment Squadron in the 320th Bombardment Group.

The 99th Squadron moved on from this attempt at disbandment and on June 11th, Pantelleria surrendered to the Allies, after being pounded by 6,131 tons of bombs from the air, together with countless shells from the sea. It was the first time in history that an enemy territory had surrendered without an attacking soldier setting foot on it. The Naval and aerial bombardment had beaten the occupants of the island into submission and opened the way for the invasion of Sicily.

The 99th now moved to Sicily, where it was to join up with the 79th Fighter Group, interestingly also flying P-40 Warhawks. It was then that Captain Charles B. Hall became the first African American pilot to shoot down an enemy aircraft, the

99th's first kill. On July 2, 1943, Buster Hall, escorting B-25s over Sicily brought down a Focke-Wulf Fw-190. Hall's victory brought important visitors to the 99th, including Major-General James H. Doolittle, Lieutenant-General Carl Spaatz and even the Supreme Allied Commander General Dwight D. Eisenhower. The Tuskegee Airmen were redeeming themselves after the nasty confrontation with Colonel Momyer. Shortly after this, Buster Hall shot down two more enemy aircraft and was awarded the Distinguished Flying Cross.

The 99th Squadron ground crews worked tirelessly to keep their P-40s in better shape than anybody else's. The aircrew's performance was a testament to the ground crew's dedication and resourcefulness.

As the Allies set up a beachhead on Sicily, on July 10th, the 99th flew patrols between Gela and Licata, where they would soon be based, to deter Luftwaffe aircraft from attacking the invasion and landing fleet. This was to be the last time the squadron would see enemy aircraft for quite a while, before late autumn of 1943, for they were now tasked with ground support. Despite the poor condition of their aircraft, the ground crews continued to work wonders with the P-40s and kept them flying up to six sorties a day against an average of four for their white squadron counterparts, who were flying newer and better condition machines.

With the reconstruction of Jimmy Doolittle's command, and his promotion to Major-General, the 12th Air Force was becoming less significant in the overall battle scheme. The Desert War had now shifted to Italy and the new 15th Air Force was formed. The 15th would absorb most of the flying units of the 12th, losing most of the Royal Air Force squadrons that had been attached to it, but picking up a couple of B-24 wings to make up numbers. The Consolidated B-24 was a four-engined bomber in the same league as the Boeing B-17, but could carry a heavier bomb load and had a slightly longer range. It was already making a name for itself in the Pacific, where long distances were being flown to and from targets and it was now being brought into the European Theatre of Operations. Now, the B-24 would take its place in history with the Ploesti Raids on Rumanian oil refineries and storage areas. Here, the US Army Air Forces suffered some of their most humiliating losses, as the oil installations were so heavily defended.

After the Senate Inquiry, the 99th Squadron, under the acting command of Major George Roberts, was re-assigned and absorbed smoothly into the 79th Fighter Group. The 99th pilots were pleasantly surprised to discover that their new Group Commander had none of the nasty traits of Colonel Momyer. Colonel Earl Bates took the view that he had just acquired a fighter squadron, equipped with competent fighter pilots, not a group of black men that were going to be a problem to him. It is significant to note that in none of the group war diaries was the color of skin mentioned. They were "men of names" and some of those men of names performed as formation leaders, regardless of skin color. Earl Bates was grateful to have a new squadron of men who were so dedicated to their task and proficient. There is even a story that the 85th Fighter Squadron, which had a reputation for the scantily-clad ladies it painted on its tails, presented the 99th with a spare pair of P-40s when two of its aircraft finally gave up the ghost.

A move to Madna, near Termoli in Italy, brought the squadron more intensive action for a while. In fact, on November 30th, the 99th flew nine missions in the one day – twice the average number of any other fighter squadron. But morale was dropping at this time – the notorious Italian winter mud, operating off "PSP" (pressed steel plate) runways and the

As the 99th swung into action over Anzio, so there were tales of hits and misses. The comradeship of the 99th Fighter Squadron was incomparable. The Tuskegee Airmen were already a brotherhood.

loss of one of their most popular members brought morale down still further. In mid-January, another member of the squadron, Willie Griffin, was shot down over enemy territory and he spent the rest of his war in a German prison camp. But then came a turning point, a move to Capodichino, near Naples. The landings at Anzio were imminent.

On January 22, 1944, the invasion at Anzio commenced and soon began to bog down. German aircraft appeared overhead and the 99th Fighter Squadron's morale was about to receive a boost. It was going back into action and air-to-air combat. Lieutenant Clarence Jamison found himself leading a formation of sixteen Warhawks into a formation of Focke-Wulf Fw-190s, which were dive-bombing shipping off the coastline. The Warhawks launched into a furious attack and, to the surprise of the Germans, shot down several of their number, despite the Fw-190 being at least seventy-five miles per hour faster than the P-40. This was a pure demonstration of superior skill with inferior aircraft.

The fight began with two of the 99th pilots, Jamison and Ashley, separating out the German flight leader and his wingman and giving chase. The Germans went low to escape, but Jamison opened fire on the leader and took chunks out of

B-26 Close-up.

his wing before the P-40's guns jammed and he could do no more damage. Ashley had better luck as he waded into his target and chased the German almost to Rome before finally getting him in his sights and opening fire with the desired result. The Fw-190 went down in flames.

Howard Baugh and Clarence Allen came in behind another fleeing Fw-190 and chased him down to the ground without even opening fire. Robert Diez saw another German on an almost parallel course, obviously unaware of his presence, and dropped in behind it, opening fire before the Fw-190 pilot could react and down he went. Ed Toppins picked up the tail of another Fw-190 and with a short burst, barely enough to do damage, he thought, took it out of the sky. Five so far and not a P-40 lost.

Leon Roberts found himself facing a more tenacious enemy – an Fw-190 pilot who decided to stay in the fray and, no doubt as far as he was concerned, take this inferior American out of the sky. He had a surprise coming. Roberts engaged in a real dogfight that lasted several minutes, but his patience ultimately paid off. The German was suddenly in front of him and Leon Roberts made no mistake, he opened fire and the German flipped over onto its back and went down. As this was happening, "Herky" Perry spotted enemy craft leveling out of a dive and ran down on to it. At a range of about 300 yards, Perry opened fire and raked the Fw-190. It fluttered momentarily, then dropped into the ground. Two more 99th pilots, Jack Rogers and Elwood "Woody" Driver intercepted an Fw-190 running for home and peppered it. However, they lost sight of their quarry in the smoke and so were only credited with a "probable" kill, though at 50 feet from the ground, it would certainly not have survived. But the rules of engagement were that the target had to be seen to go down to claim it as a "kill". The morning's count was eight with not a single 99th loss. But the afternoon was yet to come.

Lemuel Custis took a patrol in the early afternoon over Anzio. Not far inland, he and his patrol came across a mixed bunch of Fw-190s and Messerschmitt Bf-109s. The Germans saw the Americans coming and took up attack positions. One Fw-190 pilot thought he had an easy target as he approached Lieutenant Erwin Lawrence's P-40, but had a nasty shock as he was closing in for the kill. Out of the blue came Wilson Eagleson, who cut across the trajectory of the other two and as he turned through ninety degrees, opened fire on the German, taking him out of the sky instantly. Lawrence now found himself with another Fw-190 right in line in front of him and opened fire. He and Eagleson saw it go down, but not hit the ground, so it was another "probable".

The final two of that day were taken down by Lemuel Custis and Charles Bailey. Custis spotted an Fw-190 down low trying to hug the terrain to escape. In the process, he wasn't looking above him, because Custis closed in and opened fire for an easy "kill", watching the aircraft crash as he raked it with 50 caliber fire. The other Fw-190 downed that day was by Lieutenant Charles Bailey. He saw this Fw-190 also trying to escape the melee and with a deflecting shot at a shallow angle, he caused the aircraft to go out of control and the pilot to bail out. That was the last "kill" of the day, bringing the total to twelve. Two 99th pilots were shot down, though both parachuted out. The first was Allen Lane, who fell victim to four Fw-190s and the second was Sam Bruce who was later found dead on the ground. But this day, in the Battle of Anzio, was a particularly good day for the 99th Fighter Squadron of the 79th Fighter Group.

Colonel Bates, commander of the 79th Fighter Group was elated to learn of the successes of his new fighter squadron and made it plain to those in higher command that these men were worth their weight in gold. This was the first time the 99th Fighter Squadron had not just been given credit for what they had achieved – they were given the highest praise

possible. Morale noticeably rose, despite the loss of two of their planes in the air because at last , the "boys" of the 99th were truly appreciated. For their part, they appreciated the treatment they received from their comrades in arms in the 79th and the crew tent chat was like that of any other fighter group. But then came the icing on the cake. General

1st Lieutenant Charles Bailey downed an Fw-190 late in the afternoon of April 27, bringing the day's total "kills" for the 99th to twelve. Small wonder then, that the 79th Fighter Group was happy to have the 99th among its numbers.

Charles Bailey's P-40 all ready for its next sortie, armed up with antipersonnel bombs hooked on to the central rack under the fuselage.

Henry Arnold had the 99th Fighter Squadron awarded a Distinguished Unit Citation for their work at Anzio and Montecassino.

With all the past nastiness gone for the time being, the 99th Fighter Squadron was on a high. These young men were enjoying the kind of treatment that the 9th and 10th Cavalry had enjoyed in the West some 40-50 years before. But here it was different, for now, because the crews of the 99th – air and ground crew – were being treated as equals. Operational reports and the Group Operational Diary referred to individuals by name and many citations were put forward for the award of medals which carried no reference to the race of the intended recipient – only his name and his achievement. Small wonder then, that they should feel some sense of resistance and even animosity towards the prospect of being integrated into a segregated fighter group that was on its way to Italy and would soon absorb the 99th into its roster. It wasn't much consolation to these men who'd fought alongside white men and frequently been judged as better than their white peers by those white peers, that the group commander of the 332nd Fighter Group when it came would continue to be Colonel Benjamin O. Davis.

There were more incidents like those recounted above, in which time after time, the pilots of the 99th continued to prove that black pilots could perform every bit as well as their white counterparts, much more significantly, that they were able to take on far superior and more recent aircraft on equal terms and win. Time and again, these tired old workhorses, the Warhawks, kept going, thanks to the outstanding improvising skills of the ground crews and the flying skills of the pilots.

On February 5, 1944, a 99th patrol covering the Anzio beachhead, not expecting anything to happen, picked out almost a squadron of Fw-190s diving in from around 15,000 feet. They were heading for the beachhead where many allied soldiers were waiting and thus sitting targets for the Germans but they had not reckoned for the P-40s of the 99th. Turning into the German group, Elwood Driver followed an Fw-190 "down on the deck" and when he was just 300 yards behind it, opened fire. It ran for Rome in flames at 50 feet.

Clarence James and George McCrumby were being mobbed by a flight of six Fw-190s while Driver was dealing with his adversary and McCrumby's aircraft was hit. He lost control of the P-40 and decided he had to bail out. From 4,000 feet that should have been reasonably easy, except that his aircraft was in a dive and trying to escape was difficult. He climbed out of one side and the slipstream threw him back into his cockpit. Trying from the other side, he got out, but then discovered that his right foot was caught. He continued to struggle but fortunately at 1,000 feet the aircraft turned and released his foot at the same time. He pulled the ripcord on his parachute, after fumbling to find the handle, he reckoned the parachute opened at less than 800 feet. Even at that, he landed safely in a field and walked away.

A couple of days later, Leonard Jackson and Clinton Mills were patrolling and encountered a pair of Fw-190s, Once more, the sheer skill of the Americans shone through and the Luftwaffe lost two more of its finest. But now the Germans, having been bloodied savagely by all the fighter squadrons of the 79th Fighter Group, but especially the 99th because they were still flying more sorties per day than their contemporaries, decided they had to change tactics. It is a little surprising that the Luftwaffe pilots didn't tumble to this before, but they suddenly realized that the Fw-190 had at least 70mph speed advantage over the P-40. Instead of engaging, wherever they could, they would simply run away from the Warhawks.

March 19, 1944 was a momentous day for the 99th Fighter Squadron as they were tasked with knocking out the "Anzio Express", a rail-borne monster cannon that was throwing eleven-inch (283mm) diameter shells at the Allied Anzio landing force from a range of 55,000 yards. The barrel of this monster was over 70 feet long and the gun, on its massive frame and two 12-wheel rail bogies, weighed in at 218 tons. The vehicle needed to transport it overland was a 4-6-4 steam locomotive, but once the guns were in place a paired set of small diesel shunters were used to move the massive gun from inside its mountainside hiding hole. These were used partly because they could be instantly started and no time was lost when the gun was needed to be in position and also the exhaust was cleaner so no plumes of smoke would be seen from the air when the gun was being moved. Two of these guns were in use aimed at Anzio, named by the Germans as "Leopold" and "Robert", the former labeled by the Allies as "Anzio Annie" and the other "Anzio Express".

Eight 99th Squadron P-40s were dispatched to locate the "Express" and destroy it. They knew roughly where it was located, but the Germans had been quite skillful in picking mountainside caves that looked similar and they also were careful to ensure that, as far as possible, neither gun was exposed to view from the air. The pilots of the P-40s had to find the most likely tunnel openings and hope they had found the right one. The P-40 team located the right tunnel and almost "toss-bombed" the opening (a technique carefully developed fifty years later, but not formally known in those days) and effectively wrecking the exit, they went in and strafed the target as well. At the loss of no aircraft, though one P-40 was damaged by ground fire, the gun was perma-

nently silenced. After the war's end, both German guns were taken to the United States and one reassembled from the parts of the damaged two, where it is on view to this day at the US Army Aberdeen Proving Ground in Maryland.

In late June, the 99th was to leave the 79th Fighter Group and join the 324th Fighter Group at Cercola temporarily. The total tally of enemy aircraft downed by all the squadrons of the 79th was 49 – 15 by the 85th Fighter Squadron, two for the 86th, and 15 for the 87th. The 99th had proved its worth for it had downed 17 – the top-scoring squadron of the group. There were sad farewells from both sides as the 99th left, but it was soon to join a bigger fighter group, the 332nd – now an all-black assemblage of four squadrons. The Tuskegee Airmen had proved their point to all observers. Their courage and skill was no longer in doubt – and the consolidation of the 332nd Fighter Group would prove it beyond doubt in the coming months.

The sister gun to "Anzio Express", "Anzio Annie" or as the Germans named it: "Leopold".

CHAPTER EIGHT

Advancing the Battle –
The 332nd Fighter Group

The 332nd Fighter Group's journey into history began on December 22, 1943. A troop train bound for Fort Patrick Henry in Virginia was carrying just under 100 young men who were listed as fighter pilots. They were African American and they were the aircrew for three new fighter squadrons – the 100th, the 301st and the 302nd Squadrons. They had all been trained at Tuskegee and other locations and were now to come under the command of Colonel Benjamin O. Davis. On his first contact, he was disappointed. The cohesion that was present at the beginning of his own flight training, and which continued all the way through their training, was simply not present in this group, in his view. This was to be the 332nd Fighter Group, which would absorb the 99th Fighter Squadron into its ranks. He had some work to do.

The air and ground crew of the three squadrons were, as far as Benjamin Davis was concerned, a disorganized rabble. He had to instill some discipline and group cohesion before they could go into battle in Italy, or they would undermine the reputation of the 99th and then allow the predictions of such specters from the past as William Momyer to come true. He could not allow that to happen. The group embarked for Taranto, Italy from Virginia, a voyage of thirty-two days, and during this time, efforts were made to create a closer cohesion within the group, to form a team out of 100 men in four and a half weeks.

Next came another shock to morale. Rumors had been circulating, before they landed at Taranto, that the 100th Squadron would be equipped with the Lockheed P-38 "Lightning" or the Bell P-63 "Kingcobra", but when they arrived at Montecorvino, their home for the time being, they discovered the awful truth. The planes were old beat-up war-weary Bell P-39 "Airacobras", once again somebody's cast-offs.

The P-39 was a strange aircraft to begin with, because it was mid-engined, with the pilot sitting ahead of the power unit. The drive shaft from the engine to the propeller ran under the floor of the cockpit and an Oldsmobile-manufactured 37mm cannon fired through the propeller hub. The aircraft first flew in 1938 and was highly advanced for its time in a number of ways. For example, it had a tricycle undercarriage when most fighter aircraft were still equipped with a

tail wheel – "tail draggers". Its engine position was new so, as a result, was the shaft-driven propeller. The cannon firing through the hub of the propeller was reckoned to be the masterpiece of this aircraft – a machine designed around a weapons system for the first time, common in the 21st Century, but almost unique in 1938. The production models had self-sealing fuel tanks and substantial armor plating around the elevated seating position of the cockpit.

A 100th Squadron Bell P-39 "Airacobra" in Italy. This aircraft appears to have a different colored fin and rudder from the rest of the airframe, suggesting that this might have been one of the first "Red Tails". Note the darker rectangle containing the serial number.

Problems associated with this aircraft included the cannon, which had a low rate of fire and was prone to jamming. Whilst its rate of climb was intended to be stunning for the time, it was not, largely because the Allison V-12 engine didn't have the power for the weight of the aeroplane. North American Aviation encountered a similar problem with the earliest "Mustang" fighter and eventually switched to the Packard-built licensed Rolls-Royce Merlin. A similar fate had befallen the P-40, where its early Allison engines were supplanted by the Merlin in the P-40L, which the 99th Fighter Squadron was already flying. Many engineers and pilots said the P-39 lacked a reliable engine like the Merlin without a good supercharger system, so its intended rate of climb was far below expectation. All-in-all, not a good sign for the 100th Squadron.

The first task for the 100th Squadron was to understand the aircraft they were going to fly. Patrols again were the order of the day – covering an area from Cape Palermo to the

Ponziane Islands. Colonel Davis was quite distressed by this combination of a poor, clapped-out aeroplanes and a particularly hazardous task. As he observed, flying over the sea in an already battle-fatigued aircraft was a recipe for certain disaster, even before the enemy came on the scene. In mid-February, they were to discover just how bad the situation was with the P-39, when two pilots went up to intercept a German Junkers Ju-88 twin-engined reconnaissance bomber over Ponsa Point at the mouth of Naples Harbor. The P-39 pilots did some minor damage to the Ju-88, but its pilot then hauled back on the stick and out-climbed the pair of them. That was embarrassing and frustrating for the 100th Squadron pilots, because they had expected better of even these tired old war-horses – or were they mules?

Edward Gleed, commander of the 302nd Fighter Squadron and Robert Tresville, the 100th's CO decided they needed a bit of excitement. Without clearing it with Colonel Davis, they took sixteen P-39s up to the Anzio beachhead area in the hope of "meeting some Germans". Gleed encountered engine misfires and had to return to Capodichino. Coming back through the "flak corridor" between Rome and the beachhead was precarious enough, but with aircraft that were not the most reliable machines in the world, it was high risk, as one pilot, Walter Westmoreland, discovered as his aircraft was shot out from under him. This foolish venture incurred the wrath of Colonel Davis and Ed Gleed was relieved of his command.

A few more "antics" with the P-39 ensued before the whole

An unusual "late" shot of a Bell P-39, showing its firepower – central cannon, nose guns and wing-mounted 0.50 Calibers. The photograph is not exactly what it looks, however, because the aircraft is actually on the ground during a firing test and the photo has been tilted to make it look as though it is in the air.

332nd Group was consolidated into one location at Capodichino, alongside the squadron that would soon join their number, the 99th, with its now tired P-40s. News came soon after regrouping that the P-39s were to be replaced with the Republic P-47 "Thunderbolt". On April 25th, six P-47s arrived, cast-offs from the 325th Fighter Group. Each of the three 332nd squadrons received two initially, so they could discover what the P-47 had to offer over the P-39. At this time, the now-famous red tail color marking of the Tuskegee Airmen was confirmed.

As they waited for more P-47s, harbor patrols continued with the P-39. The odd air-to-ground firing took place too, though the pilots had discovered a need to treat their mount with a little respect when on ground-attack runs, as small bits of debris could bounce back up into the aircraft and do quite serious damage. The engine oil coolant radiators were quite vulnerable and if a piece of shrapnel were to penetrate one of the two radiators, it could cause the engine to seize in a couple of minutes with disastrous results. The pilots of the 332nd could not wait to get their hands on the P-47s.

In May, Lieutenant Woodrow Morgan was on a strafing mission in his P-47 when he was jumped by a German machine, shot down and captured – all because he was not alert to what was around him as he went in on his ground-firing run. On May 27, 1944, the 332nd was to depart from Capodichino and to leave 12th Air Force too. A new location, at Ramitelli, and a new Air Force awaited them. The group was now to be a part of the 15th Air Force and undertake a new role – the job for which it became the most famous, that of bomber escort. Now the 332nd Fighter Group squadrons would be flying deep into Germany, accompanying heavy bombing groups over the Alps on long-range escorts. The bombers would even go as far as Berlin, a 1,600 mile round trip. Gone were the Bell P-39s, replaced now entirely, albeit quite briefly, with the P-47.

The Republic P-47 Thunderbolt was a different kind of machine from anything the pilots of the 332nd Fighter Group had experienced before. To begin with, it was the heaviest single-engined fighter in the US Army Air Forces inventory. Powered by an 18-cylinder radial engine, the Pratt and Whit-

Colonel Benjamin Davis and his P-47.

ney Double Wasp of 2,000 horsepower, it had a propeller diameter the height of two tall men – twelve feet and two inches. Affectionately known as "the Jug", the Thunderbolt weighed in at eight tons when fully laden. Its two greatest assets were its capacity to take punishment under fire and its wide track landing gear, which made it relatively easy to land in almost any conditions. With an 800 mile operating radius and eight 50-caliber machine guns, the Thunderbolt made an excellent escort fighter.

Perhaps the most unfortunate early Thunderbolt incident for the 332nd was 2nd Lieutenant Lloyd Hathcock's experience. He was ferrying a P-47 from Foggia to Ramitelli just a couple

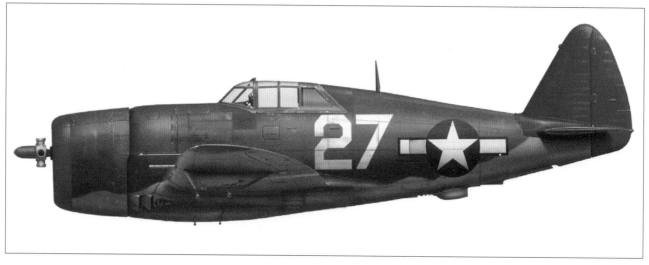

Lieutenant Lloyd Hathcock's P-47 as it was on the morning he took off from Ramitelli.

The aircraft as it was discovered by advancing Allied troops as they reached Rechlin almost a year later.

of days after the group's move there and he misjudged his returning direction. He flew 35 miles in the wrong direction, a most unfortunate error, as he landed at Rome-Littorio, where the Germans were still in control. Hathcock was dispatched to a Stalag Luft and his P-47 was sent to the Luftwaffe's test center at Rechlin in Germany, for evaluation against current German machinery.

With the early unfortunate loss of two Thunderbolts, Colo-nel Davis decided he had to "shake down" his group and get them into action. Within the first week of June, he had a formation of thirty-two P-47s airborne in the Ferrara-Bologna locality, conducting a fighter sweep. With little activity but occasional fire from the ground, all seemed well, until one pilot reported a loss of engine oil pressure. In a big engine like the R-2800 that powered these monsters, that was serious, so 2nd Lieutenant Carroll Langston, the pilot of the stricken machine, bailed out. His body was recovered some weeks later on a beach and his grave today is in his home state of Tennessee. Several other pilots reported similarly indicated pressure drops, but the gauges were found to be faulty. All the oil pressure gauges in the 332nd's P-47s were checked and the fault rectified. Sadly, if Carroll Langston had hung on and ignored the pressure gauge, he would have survived.

The day after that oil pressure gauge incident, the 332nd Fighter Group undertook its first official bomber escort mission. The task was to escort a group of B-17 "Flying Fortress-es" to targets in Pola, Italy. Thirty-two P-47s went aloft for that mission and it was here that Colonel Benjamin Davis "made his mark" as far as bomber escort duties were concerned. He had seen how other fighter groups did the job – escort the bombers in and then abandon them to find their own way home. As he said, many bombers are at their most vulnerable when they leave the target area, for enemy fighters are now looking for revenge and they're also looking for bomber crews who are a little less alert than they might have been approaching their targets. This is a natural state of affairs, when a bomber crew has been concentrating to its last ounce of energy to find and hit the target, the pressure is off momentarily and that's when they become less observant and vulnerable. Benjamin Davis' remedy for that was to ensure that his fighters escorted their bomber charges all the way to their targets and back home to base.

Colonel Davis' method was to have his escort fighters circling around the bombers at a safe distance to ensure they reached the targets, released their bombs and cleared the target area. Any aircraft that was damaged would have a fighter, or more usually two, to escort the crippled bomber to the nearest friendly airfield so that any injured crews could receive medical attention as quickly as possible and the aircraft was in danger for the shortest possible time. Davis would always ensure that somewhere between twelve and sixteen fighters were circling above the bombers under escort, so they could take action quickly in the event of enemy intrusion.

That first escort mission to Pola had gone well, but largely because there was no enemy air-to-air opposition. The next mission they flew, two days later, was not so uneventful. In fact, it was a classic demonstration of why bomber groups needed fighter escorts and what fighter escorts had to do to keep their bombers and themselves covered. On June 9th, 39 out of an intended 42 P-47s of the 301st and 302nd Squadrons left Ramitelli to accompany a large group of B-17s and B-24 "Liberators" from the 49th, the 55th, the 57th and the 304th Bombardment Groups to targets in Munich. This was their first Alpine crossing in an escort mission, so Colonel Davis needed to ensure as far as possible that his bomber groups stayed in tight formation and that his fighters gave top cover and missed nothing. It should be remembered that these aircraft were crossing the Italian Alps, keeping clear of the Swiss Alps because of Switzerland's neutrality, and so there was a possibility of enemy aircraft activity along the entire route.

As the massed group of aircraft approached Udine on their

way north, a flight of four Bf-109s jumped a group of B-24s in the formation and made a firing pass. As they came out of the pass, Lieutenant Wendell Pruitt locked in on one, rolling his P-47 into a dive to pursue it. He followed the 109 through a turn, hung on, firing as he went and sent it down in flames. As Pruitt was kept busy, another 301st Squadron pilot, "Red" Jackson, spotted half a dozen more Bf-109s above him. He climbed and closed in on one of them and opened fire on a "chance" shot, taking it out of the sky. As Jackson came away from that first interception, he discovered he'd lost his flight companions, so was now on his own. That was especially true in this situation, for suddenly he was confronted with a Bf-109 coming straight at him. He deliberately stalled his P-47 and avoided the head-on, but then the 109 was able to pick up his tail. Luckily for Red Jackson, a teammate gave chase and took the 109 out. With two pursuers on its tail, the German machine had no chance and plunged to the ground.

That day, there were five kills scored, two bombers lost, and one loss to the 332nd – Cornelius Rogers went down with his aircraft and a couple of others had picked up minor damage. After the mission, it was discovered that a group of officers from 15th Air Force was visiting Ramitelli along with a Republic Aviation representative. Their task was to give a briefing on "things that weren't in the book" about the P-47. Bearing in mind that these pilots had familiarized themselves with their new mounts "in the field", it was slightly late to point out the limitations of the airframe. As the major on the ground was telling the pilots they should never slow roll a Thunderbolt at a height of less than 1,000 feet because of its weight and the risk of not recovering, two pilots still airborne, Wendell Pruitt and Lee Archer were coming in fast and low, wingtip to wingtip. As they passed the assembled group on the ground, they lifted left and right into slow barrel rolls. It was said that the major on the ground almost fell off his pedestal and screamed at the two transgressors – *"You can't do that!"*, as if they could hear him, and as if they would have worried if they did hear. They were celebrating.

A couple of days later, in a run to Smedervo in Yugoslavia, the thirty P-47s airborne on that morning encountered little or no opposition. But in another run to Munich, thirty-two P-47s joined the bombers and, as they approached Udine, the Germans were in the air. Eleven Bf-109s joined the party that morning, but only four launched into any attack. One P-47 was slightly damaged in the confrontation, and all the bombers reached their targets and returned safely. It certainly seemed as though the Luftwaffe was losing heart, because on another bombing raid to Budapest, twenty-nine 332nd P-47s were airborne and as they approached the target area, some fifteen Bf-109s came up to meet them, accompanied by seven twin-engined German fighters, almost certainly Bf-110s. Amazingly, with twenty-two aggressors in the air to face the Thunderbolts, not a single one engaged with either bombers or fighters.

The last ten days of June saw some strange occurrences and some nasty mishaps. On June 23rd, Captain Robert Tresville led a wave of 41 Thunderbolts on a strafing run on the Airasco-Pinerolo landing ground in Northwest Italy. It didn't begin well, as one aircraft crashed on take-off, though the pilot was unhurt, and four more aborted shortly after take-off, leaving 36 to do the job. The P-47s were crossing the Tyrrhenian Sea in a light haze, which made the horizon so difficult to see that one aircraft went too low, hit the water hard and

exploded into flames, killing its pilot. Almost at the same time, another skimmed the water and pancaked – though the pilot escaped unhurt. Another pilot, trying to see if his companion was okay and could escape his aircraft, was not so lucky himself as he hit the water and went down with his machine. Three more aircraft touched the water, too, including Robert Tresville, who was said to have been looking at a map as he went in quite fast and was lost.

On June 25th, twenty P-47s went on a ground support and strafing mission in Yugoslavia in four flights. One of those flights was a four-ship and two of them had to abort the mission because one pilot's left jettisonable fuel tank would not release, so he and his wingman returned to Ramitelli. The two left were Wendell Pruitt and Gwynne Pierson and they continued on the mission, but lost the formation and never did find the target troop concentration. Strong winds had forced them off course and they found themselves flying up the Adriatic coast of Italy and over Trieste Harbor, where they could not believe their eyes. They had come across a ship they identified as an enemy destroyer at anchor. They flew in at the ship, broadside, side by side and opened fire together. In the commotion and with smoke now rising to

Lieutenant Gwynne Pierson's P-47, from which he shot the ship in Trieste Harbor. He and Wendell Pruitt were awarded DFCs for that action.

attract attention, three more P-47s joined in the fray and suddenly, Pierson struck the ship's magazine. It exploded in the harbor and almost took at least one Thunderbolt with it.

Leaving the ship to burn, the five P-47 pilots decided to have a "field day" and set about destroying a couple of radio/radar stations in the harbor area, a fleet of parked German trucks and then the wharf at Muggio. At that stage, as they flew low over Isola, a sailing boat opened fire on the aircraft; so they did no more than take it out too. Back at Ramitelli, Pierson's crew chief drew his attention to several jagged holes in the under-wing area of his P-47. They concluded it must have been from shrapnel sent up as the ship in Trieste Harbor blew up. For that mission, both Pruitt and Pierson were awarded the DFC.

The original caption to this photo suggested it was of 99th Fighter Squadron pilots at Pignataro checking a map rendezvous position before take-off. If that caption was correct, then very soon, they would become part of the 332nd Fighter Group, with Colonel Benjamin Davis in overall command. There is, however, some thought that it may have been posed at Tuskegee, but it's an interesting shot, whatever the location.

The Trieste mission was almost the Thunderbolt's swansong, for while a few "bubble-top" P-47s arrived to supplement and replace the most tired of the "Razorbacks" (aircraft with the cockpit canopy running back in line with the rear fuselage), there were the first signs of a new aircraft coming into the 332nd's inventory. The final P-47 mission was on June 30th, when 45 P-47s mounted an escort for five bomb groups going to Vienna. Two aircraft aborted before reaching their charges, so only 43 made the run. Fortunately, there were no incidents in either direction and the final Thunderbolt mission went out on a high.

The 99th Fighter Squadron was now briefly located at Pignataro, detaching frequently to Ciampo and Orbetelo and was still working with the 79th Fighter Group. This came to an end, for the 99th was to be integrated into the 332nd Fighter Group to make it a four-squadron group and moved to Ramitelli on July 3, 1944. Of course there were problems. Integrating a squadron that had been "race-less" for many months was difficult in itself, for many of the 99th pilots saw it as a retrograde step to return to segregation after they had proved so successfully how integration could and did work. Their experiences with the 33rd and 324th Fighter Groups had been one thing, but the demonstration of how an integrated Group could work caused many of them to ask why not widen the scope of this highly successful exercise and integrate the squadrons of the 332nd into other fighter groups? Sadly, part of the reason for that was that there were few group commanders like Colonel Earl R. Bates.

One of the problems with the four-squadron setup of the enlarged 332nd Fighter Group was that Tuskegee was not producing enough pilots to rotate the existing numbers, so crews of all four squadrons were now finding that they were serving longer tours of duty than their white counterparts. The upside to this was the re-equipment of the Group with the North American P-51 "Mustang". Even though, once again, the aircraft were somebody else's cast-offs, they were at least in better condition than some of the Thunderbolts had been in when they arrived at Ramitelli and another benefit was that the Mustang was a lighter aircraft, with a much better power to weight ratio and had longer range.

As usual, the transition from one aircraft type to the other was conducted "in the field" with pilots literally climbing out of one type and into the other, feeling their way around the cockpit to know where all the switches and levers were, then taking to the air, perhaps a little gingerly at first, but learning its quirks and faults as they went along. There was one occasion, when a pilot thought he had the Mustang under his control and flew aerobatics over the airfield, and ran down the runway inverted. At the end of the maneuver, he found he couldn't roll the aircraft over and went into the ground, wrecking the aircraft and killing himself. It was thought that his underbelly tank was full and the shift in center of gravity made it impossible to recover. Observers of that display learned from that.

The first Mustang escort mission was mounted on July 4, 1944 – a most appropriate day, some thought, though Colonel Davis had to hand over the leadership of the 40-ship escort group because his radio failed. On the following day, some fifty-two Mustangs escorted a bombing group, again without incident, though four aircraft were forced to land on Corsica because they were short of fuel. All the Mustangs now had the distinctive red tail of the Tuskegee Airmen, the intention being to let their own know that they were safe and to let the Germans know "attack at your peril". It did seem as though the latter taunt was working, for more escorts were taking place with little or no opposition, though on July 8th, that illusion came to an end as about 20 Germans took to the air to face up to the Red Tails.

While the 100th, 301st and 302nd Squadrons were undertaking escorts in early July, the 99th pilots were not finding it easy to convert to their new charges. Probably,

Arming up the guns of a P-51 for the next escort mission.

Colonel Benjamin O. Davis aboard his "new" P-51B Mustang.

they had been flying the P-40 for too long, bringing habits they had developed with the P-40 to the P-51 and discovering they did not work. The two aircraft types were not dissimilar in weight, but the Mustang was a more responsive aircraft and had more power. Some of the flying errors seemed inexplicable, but there was a question about their familiarity with the oxygen system – quite different from the P-40.

As this war progressed, "D-Day" had taken place on the Channel Coast of France and many German resources had been moved into the defense of Normandy. The Allies began to move inland, with the 332nd Fighter Group pressing further north in its pursuit of victory. On July 10th, 33 Mustangs went aloft to escort a 47th Bomb Group attack on the submarine pens at Toulon. That was an uneventful and successful mission, but a couple of days later, when the P-51s of the Red Tails were taking a formation of 49th Bomb Group B-24 Liberators to the railway marshaling yards in southern France, there was a strong resistance by 25 or so Fw-190s that came to meet them. One pilot, Joseph Elsberry, claimed four "Huns" that day and the mission was another success with every B-24 coming home.

Three days later, on July 13th, the bombers went for "targets at home", primarily the Pinzano railway bridge and the viaduct at Vinzone. Thirty-seven Red Tails joined the bombing group in an uneventful foray. A couple of days after that, the 99th Fighter Squadron was at last ready to try its hand at combat in their new steed, the P-51. This was expected to be a real trial, for the targets were the oil refineries at Ploesti. A total of 61 Mustangs accompanied the B-24s of the 55th Bombardment Wing, which had four Bomb Groups (each of three squadrons), the 460th, the 464th, the 465th and the 485th Bomb Groups – that represented 144 four-

Lieutenant Charles Bailey finally abandoned his old P-40 "Josephine" (named after his mother) for this new mount, a P-51B named "My Buddy" for his father.

engined bombers, delivering a total of 432 tons of bombs in a single drop. En route to the target, the air-to-air encounter was fairly light, with only eight Bf-109s to chase off as they were harrying three bombers that had fallen slightly out of formation.

Italy had formally changed sides in this war back in 1943 and Marshal Badoglio took initial control of the country after a vote of no confidence had been registered in Benito Mussolini. The next day, on July 25, 1943, King Victor Emmanuel had Mussolini removed from office and arrested. Marshal Badoglio was named Prime Minister and he then negotiated an armistice with the Allies, after which the Italians threw in their lot with Britain and the US. Despite all this, there were still Italians loyal to the Axis, who were flying aircraft still marked with the Fascist symbol, whereas the new Italian Regia Aeronautica sported red, white and green roundels, to make them easily identifiable to the Allies. On July 16th,

45 Mustangs flew a fighter sweep over Vienna and spotted a single Macchi MC-205 "Veltro" with Fascist markings, and thus loyal to Mussolini. Ultimately, four P-51s went after it and after a chase with some damage done to the Italian, it flew off and tried to follow the profile of a mountain, but ran into it after touching it with a wingtip, bursting into flames.

One incident worth recounting here, to demonstrate just how closely the Tuskegee Airmen stuck to Colonel Davis' rule of "never leave your bombers", because the bombers were "their own" and they did not want the repercussions that would come from leaving a bomber. This case involved a young 2nd Lieutenant named Maceo Harris. A B-24 Bomb Group had flown a successful raid on the Avignon railway marshaling yard in southern France. But one B-24 had strayed out of formation on departure from the target and was running into trouble.

The young Mustang pilot flew in to check out the B-24, spotting three possible adversaries closing in on the bomber from behind. Deciding they were P-51s, he rocked his wings to tell them that he had everything under control and they flew off. The upper gunner mistook Harris' P-51 for a Bf-109 and began firing at him. Realizing that this fighter was friendly, the gunner stopped and so Harris was able to close in and examine the damage. The B-24 had one engine feathered and another emitting smoke. They were about 40 miles from Corsica and when Harris discovered his companion couldn't radio to him, only receive, he gestured to the pilot to follow.

Maceo Harris could not make radio contact with Corsica either, so he resorted to "buzzing" the runway a couple of times to let people know he was there and then led the bomber in. It made a perfect three-point landing and rumbled to a halt as Harris landed too. Harris told the story that the bomber's crew was so delighted to not only have found a friendly fighter, but one that could get them down on the ground in safety that the pilot and his co-pilot hugged and kissed him, they were so pleased to have been rescued. That was what "sticking to your bomber" meant for so many of the 332nd Fighter Group.

Now, all four squadrons of the 332nd Fighter Group were fully engaged and several more escorts over Austria, Italy and Germany took place in the rest of July and early August. Many were uneventful and as many as 70 P-51s might be in the sky at one time. Quite often, a smaller number of enemy fighters would come up, but if they could not lure the Red Tails out of cover, they would abandon the fight. When the numbers in a fight were more equal, the Germans did stay and put up a fight, but rarely did they win. One day, with 66 Mustangs in the air, about 40 enemy aircraft came up to "have a go", but 11 of their number were quickly dispatched as the bombers went for Memmingen in Austria. There were many more incidents like this, dampened by the occasional loss of a Red Tail, but by and large, the Red Tails were successful to the point that many bomber crews had come to describe the 332nd Group as "The Red Angels". Few bomber crews knew at the time that their guardians

were African American, but it is surprising how many, even when they discovered that fact, did not change their view of this outstanding bomber escort group. And the "Never Lost a Bomber" soubriquet had already become the by-line for the Red Tails (though 27 were lost in total).

"Operation Dragoon" was to change the role of the 332nd Fighter Group for a while and sadly, the attrition rate for the group was to increase. From August 12th, the group was tasked with a ground attack "softening-up" role. The first of these tasks was to knock out a number of radar stations surrounding Marseilles Harbor. Each squadron was allocated its targets and the 99th went in to attack the Montpelier and Sete stations. It was a successful "hit", but 2nd Lieutenant Dick Macon was not so lucky. With his P-51 shot out from under him by ground fire, Macon crashed into a house and fractured a shoulder and four vertebrae in his neck and he was taken prisoner on the spot.

The 100th Squadron went for three targets close to Marseilles and Couronne and all three were destroyed without incident. The 301st attacked four targets in and around Toulon, but were not so lucky, in that they lost two aircraft and pilots – Lieutenants Joseph Gordon and his wingman both lost their lives to ground fire. The 302nd went for stations at Narbonne and Leucate and were successful in taking out their targets, along with a few secondary installations, but they were also less fortunate than the 99th or the 100th in losing two aircraft and their pilots, though the pilots were captured, not killed.

This kind of strafing activity continued for the rest of 1944, but was combined with high altitude bomber escort missions. In fact, at times, it was almost simply "high-low-high" day after day. There were also "highs" and "lows" in morale and incidents too. Some days, strafing runs or bomber escorts would go without a hitch, other days, pilots would be taken out of the skies, some surviving, some not.

A notable day in the history of the 332nd Fighter Group was September 10, 1944, when there was a General Staff Officer visit and an awards ceremony. This was Brigadier-General Benjamin O. Davis, Sr., who at that time was as-

Colonel Benjamin O. Davis, Jr. receives his Distinguished Flying Cross from his father, Brigadier-General Benjamin O. Davis, Sr.

signed to the Office of the Inspector-General of the US Army. General Davis was in the process of conducting an inspection tour between July and November 1944, examining units that contained African American soldiers, so it was opportune for him to visit the 332nd Fighter Group. In the same visit, he was assigned the task of presenting Distinguished Flying Crosses to, firstly, his son, Colonel Benjamin O. Davis, Jr., then to Captain Joseph Elsberry and 1st Lieutenants Jack Holsclaw and Clarence Lester. It seems there was a period in the history of the US Army, that Davis father and son were the only two senior African American officers in the entire army.

October 1944 was a month of heavy losses for the 332nd, with fifteen pilots lost. Apart from the obvious impact of such a loss, it caused other morale effects. The replacement rate of new African American pilots for lost crew members dwindled to nil and in-squadron pilots were flying 70 combat missions before rotating back to the US, while most other fighter group pilots were returning home after only 50. This compounded itself in two ways – not only were the pilots of the 332nd flying more missions per day than their Caucasian counterparts, they were flying more missions overall, with little or no sign of newly-trained pilots coming into the Group.

One bombing mission that merits mention was carried out by the 484th Bombardment Group's B-24s on October 20, 1944. The target was the Alfa Romeo factory in Milan which was probably the biggest single manufacturing unit in the Portello District of the city, so was quite easily identified from the air – even at 21,000 feet, the bomb drop altitude. It was an uneventful escort run for the Red Tails and so should have been a highly successful bomb run for the B-24s. But clearly, somebody did not accurately calculate the wind drift or the first aircraft let its bombs go too soon. The bomb fall plot photograph of the attack shows that less than 13 percent of the 261 bombs fell within the inner target circle of 400 yards. Most fell to the east and towards the south of the target. A primary school not far away took a direct hit and was destroyed, with most of its occupants. The Alfa Romeo factory only lost a couple of roofs and a few aero engines inside the factory. But here is the most ironic part of this particular bombing run – the Italians had switched sides a year before and were well and truly committed to the Allied cause. So why target this location at all?

A mixed bag of operations followed for the month of November. It began with the escort of a few bombing missions over Austria, then on November 3rd, Colonel Davis was to return to the US for a period and command of the Group passed on a temporary basis, once again, to Major "Spanky" Roberts. More escort duties followed, including the escorting of single reconnaissance aircraft over enemy territory with photo-reconnaissance aircraft, like the Lockheed F-5 (camera version of the famous P-38) the Lightning, B-24 Liberators and B-17s. Strafing railways, roads and river traffic over Hungary and Austria were interludes to more bomber escorts to oil refineries, factories and other targets. The winter weather was now beginning to hamper progress in any direction, so the 332nd, like many other groups, was slowing down.

Christmas Eve saw the return of Colonel Davis to command the Group and Christmas Day saw another bomber escort run with a group of B-26s with 42 Red Tails aloft covering. Forty-four P-51s were airborne for a bombing mission on the 26th and 52 the day after that. The bombing run on December 28th was a little unusual in that the bombers split into two groups to hit the oil refineries of Kolin and Pardubice in

Czechoslovakia, so the 50 P-51s split too, in order to cover all the bombers en route to and returning from the targets. A similar mission to Muhldorf and Landshut in Germany took place on the 29th and then the weather closed in. This gave Colonel Davis a chance to deliver a year-end address to the men under his command. He said:

> *"Unofficially, you are known to an untold number of bomber crews as those who can be depended upon and whose appearance means certain protection from enemy fighters. The bomber crews have told others of your accomplishments, and your good reputation has*

preceded you in many parts where you may think you are unknown".

A tough year ended for the 12th and 15th Air Forces and the 332nd Fighter Group too, with many pilots and aircraft lost in action, some heroically and some needlessly. But on the plus side, the Normandy Landings had been successful and the Allies were making headway across France and into Germany. As early as December 1944, there seemed to be an end in sight. But there was still a tough road in front of the 332nd Fighter Group – The Red Angels.

This bomb-fall plot photo is an aerial shot taken the day after the raid of October 20, 1944. It tells us the 484th Bombard ment Group dropped 261 bombs aimed at the Alfa Romeo factory in Portello, a district of Milan. But interestingly, the plot only identifies 171 bombs in this picture, so where are the other 90? Almost certainly in a trail south east of the prime target, following the wind direction. The inner circle is 800 yards across and the outer is 1600 yards across. By the former 12th Air Force Bomb Leader's standard (Lieutenant-Colonel Paul Tibbets), 209 of those bombs should have fallen inside the 800-yard circle to achieve 80% efficiency – as it was, this plot shows a bombing efficiency of 12.25%. Not a very good record for the 484th Bomb Group or the 49th Bombardment Wing. If this bomb drop had been 80% efficient, the Alfa Romeo factory would have disappeared from the face of the earth! As it was, a nearby primary school was hit, with the loss of sixty children.

CHAPTER NINE

World War II Ends – The Legend Grows

They were not to know it yet, but the dawn of 1945 would see the ultimate end for the 332nd Fighter Group – and indeed to all the participants – of this savage conflict that was World War II. A forced respite in combat activities was brought about by the weather in Ramitelli, but it was a time of movement for people. The 301st and 302nd Squadrons rotated out their squadron commanders as replacements arrived. And in those first days of the New Year, some 34 new pilots arrived at the 332nd Group Headquarters, easing the shortage of flyers and allowing a few to rotate back home.

January 3rd was the first day of the year when the weather eased enough to allow aircraft to take to the air again and a three-Mustang flight went up to accompany a camera-carrying Lockheed Lightning, the F-5, on a reconnaissance mission over Munich and Linz. However, the mission had to be aborted, because once they arrived over the target area, the weather turned again and the ground was obscured by a deep cloud cover. A second attempt was made later using a 60 Squadron South African Air Force Mosquito PRXVI – the

photo-reconnaissance version of the RAF's "wooden wonder". The Mosquito was built entirely of wood and turned out to be one of the most versatile twin-engined aircraft of World War II. They were built as light bombers, night fighters, ground-attack fighters and photo-reconnaissance – made famous by the motion picture "633 Squadron" with Cliff Robertson in the lead role. But even the Mosquito, on this day, did not come home with the "goods".

Five days later, the 47th Bomb Wing attempted to strike the Linz railway yards without the reconnaissance pictures they had asked for. Fifty-one Mustangs of the Red Tails went up to meet them, but when they reached the rendezvous point, there was not a B-24 to be seen. The bombers had discovered that there was once again heavy cloud over Linz and they abandoned the mission, but nobody had thought to tell the 332nd Fighter Group so that their Mustangs could stay on the ground. It was to be a further week before the weather lifted enough for another attempt. This attempt was was to be made by the 307th Bomb Wing, but they were not at the

Two of 60 Squadron SAAF's, Mosquito PRXVIs, part of the 3rd Photo Reconnaissance Group under Doolittle's command.

rendezvous point when the Mustangs went aloft, and the 47th was there (hopefully by co-incidence and not a week late) and the Red Tails took them as far as their remaining fuel would allow. This was one of those rare occurrences when the 332nd did not escort their charges all the way out and all the way home.

The weather continued to prevent bomber escorts, but there were reconnaissance flights to escort. On January 18th, an F-5 headed for Stuttgart for a photo mission and reached the target area with no problem, but the cloud cover over the city was dense and gave no opportunity for a photo run, so the F-5 and escorts returned home "with empty-camera". Then, on the same day, another escort, this time of six P-51s, accompanying an F-5 over Munich reached their target, the F-5 got its pictures and came home with the "goods". Another photo mission on the 18th came back with somewhat less success. This was a run to Prague but when they arrived, the weather had closed in to such an extent that the cloud base was up to 34,000 feet. The mission was aborted, but the F-5 pilot reported an engine misfiring and he disappeared into the clouds. Later the escorts picked up a radio message that the F-5 pilot was getting out.

Two days after that "trio of moments", on January 20th, four P-51s from the 99th picked up another F-5 en route to Prague. The run was uneventful into the target area, the F-5 pilot got his pictures and the quintet made for home. Flying low in the recovery trip, so as to avoid enemy radar, was a good idea and at any other time of year would have been no problem. But on this day, in probably the coldest winter of the War, these five aircraft ran into a snowstorm. They could not climb out of it because the cloud base was far too deep and they could not go any lower, so they simply had to try to hang on to each other and get back to Ramitelli. Inevitably, they split up and each pilot had to navigate his way home alone flying blind. Eventually, all four Mustangs got back, and it took the F-5 seven-and-half hours to make the journey.

The next bombing run of the month took place on January 21st, with 44 Mustangs airborne to meet a wave of bombers from the 5th Bombardment Wing leaving for Austria's oil refineries. The bomb leader radioed that they would be 30

minutes late at the rendezvous point so, as they often did, the Red Tails went on to the target area, with the intention of ensuring it was clear of defenders for the bombers to come

"After the Mission" – a group of pilots squat alongside a Mustang and chat about the day's work. From left to right: Lt. Dempsey W. Morgan, Jr.; Lt. Carroll S. Woods; Lt. Robert H. Nelson, Jr.; Capt. Andrew D. Turner; and Lt. Clarence P. Lester.

Captain Andrew Turner about to taxi out on a bomber escort with the 47th Bombardment Wing.

in and carry out their bombing run free of attackers. The only opposition that was seen on that day was four Me-262 jet fighters, which decided to keep their distance. The one Allied aircraft the German jet pilots were genuinely fearful of was the P-51, because its dive speed was faster than the Me-262 and on previous occasions, a number of 262's had been taken out of the sky in a diving attack from a P-51. This quartet was not about to risk it.

On February 1st, a mixed group of 300 bombers – B-17s and B-24s – from the 47th Bombardment Wing headed for the oil refineries at Moosbierbaum in Austria. Colonel Benjamin Davis led the fighter escort group, but when they reached the target area, the weather seemed to confuse the lead navigator and the whole bomb group went into a circling activity while the target position was resolved. Because of worsening weather, they failed to pick a precise spot for the target, so they abandoned the mission and flew on to Graz instead. By the time the bomber crews had re-allocated their target,

the escorts were low on fuel and so Colonel Davis called in another group from the 332nd to escort the bombers home, as his own group had to return to base.

Back to reconnaissance runs, four Red Tails flew an escort for an F-5 from the 19th Tactical Reconnaissance Squadron over Salzburg on February 5th, resulting in good photographs and free of enemy activity. A couple of days later, working from those photographs, the 19th's parent, the 47th Bombardment Wing flew a heavy bombing raid on Salzburg's main railway station and surrounding tracks with success, despite some intrusion from the weather. The weather en route to the rendezvous point for the escorts broke up the formation and left the fighters in scattered bunches across the sky. Luckily, there was no enemy aircraft action that day, and they had a safe run.

A dual bombing run on February 7th was set up to attack Moosbierbaum again. This time the 304th Bombardment

The fighters at Ramitelli were now being asked to cover ever longer distances in their escorts, so the jettisonable extra fuel tanks were an essential tool. Here TSgt. Charles K. Haynes, SSgt. James A. Sheppard, and MSgt. Frank Bradley fit a tank to a P-51.

Wing's B-24s would go in first, with a Red Tails escort of 33 P-51s, while the B-24s of the 47th Bombardment Wing would follow in a second wave with an escort of only 29 P-51s to cover them This second wave was not a quiet bombing run – there was anti-aircraft fire from below and a couple of Mustangs found themselves escorting a stricken B-24 to Ancona, where it could be repaired sufficiently well to get it home again.

A fighter sweep over Yugoslavia had been planned for the following day, to soften up the area around a drop zone for a transport aircraft to deliver supplies to a partisan group there. Once again, weather intervened and twelve Mustangs could not find one transport aircraft that was dropping the supplies and the mission was aborted. With improving weather, on February 8th, a further attempt was made. Visibility was excellent, so the Red Tails were able to ensure no enemy activity within sight. Once that had been achieved, a Royal Air Force Lysander of 148 Squadron came in, landed, delivered its contents and took off. 148 Squadron was one of the RAF's Special Duties squadrons that transported SOE (Special Operations Executive) personnel into partisan communities all across Europe.

More reconnaissance and bombing escorts took place over the next several days. While a small escort was provided to a 19th TR Squadron's F-5 in a photo run over Munich, Colonel Davis took 45 Mustangs up to escort the 49th Bombardment Wing's B-24s over Vienna, in a major assault on the central railway repair workshops and marshaling yard. There was virtually no opposition in the air in that attack, and all the bombers reached their targets and flew home. On the same day, a small escort group of twelve Red Tails took a smaller group of bombers into targets at Zagreb and Maribor in Yugoslavia and Graz in Austria. The year so far was progressing well as the weather was easing and it was interesting to note the inter-service cooperation that was taking place, for example with the Royal Air Force. The Red Tails' fame was spreading.

In the middle of February, a group of P-51s from the 99th Fighter Squadron was tasked with a ground strafing mission on a railway yard between Linz and Vienna, in Austria. It was

not a good day for 2nd Lieutenant Harold Brown, who was flying his 30th mission. It was to be his last of World War II.

Harold Brown had enlisted in his home town of Minneapolis and was assigned to the 99th Fighter Squadron in Italy after graduating from Class 44-E-SE. He was shot down twice – the first time he crash landed in friendly territory and returned to base at Ramitelli. The second time was during this ground strafing mission. He climbed out of his P-51 at about 1,000 feet over a wooded area. After landing, he was surrounded by an angry crowd of civilians who wanted to lynch him, but was rescued by a local policeman before being handed over to the German military authorities.

Harold Brown has said himself that in the PoW camp he was in (the "Oflag" of "Stalag XIII at Nuremberg-Langwasser), he was treated fairly by the Germans, officers and guards, and often asked how he could fight for a country that treated people of his skin color so badly. He replied that he still loved his country and believed it could change. At Nuremberg-Langwasser in the spring of 1945, there were only 45 American and 77 British officers held there, out of a total of almost 30,000 prisoners, more than half of them Russians). Brown was the only African American prisoner in the Oflag. He found little comradeship among his American compatriots, but the British were more friendly and accommodating.

Lieutenant Brown was a PoW for less than three months. He was handed over to General George Patton's advancing 3rd Army on May 3rd at Stalag VII-A in Moosburg, after being force-marched south from Nuremberg in company with almost 10,000 other Allied prisoners as the Russians advanced from the East. Having arrived at Moosburg on April 21st, Brown and his compatriots were there for only two weeks before being liberated.

February 14th saw Colonel Davis take 30 Mustangs airborne to escort the B-17s of the 5th Bombardment Wing. The 97th and 301st Bombardment Groups were part of 5th Bomb Wing at that time – these were two of the first USAAF groups in combat in World War II in Europe. The bomb wing was attacking the oil refineries of Lobau and Schwechat, near Vienna, and the Winterhafen oil storage depot. Event did not

"The Gruesome Twosome" were Lieutenant Lee Archer and Captain Wendell Pruitt. Archer was the only "Ace" of the 332nd Fighter Group. These two were formidable adversaries for any German fighter.

go quite as planned. First, a pair of Mustangs detached themselves to escort a small group of bombers that had been separated from the main formation. Then the whole escort became separated from their charges because of cloud. Fortunately, by the time they were able to re-group, the bombers were close to their targets and the run was a success. Just two aircraft, a B-17 and a B-24, became detached and were hosted by the Red Tails to a friendly landing ground and safety.

After another "split" escort mission on February 15th, in which 32 Mustangs escorted one half of the 49th Bombardment Wing, known as "Red Force" and another group escorted the 49th's "Blue Force", to Vienna's Penzinger Railway marshaling yards, a successful bombing run was made.

There were no German aircraft in the sky, but apparently a couple of P-38 Lightnings made a pass at some of the Red Tail escorts, before they realized that they were confronting friendly aircraft. As often happened, there were a few "lame" bombers escorted to safety by the Mustangs. On the next day, February 16th, there were more reconnaissance escort missions. This time, a de Havilland Mosquito (Canadian-built, as it happens) was escorted to gather images of Memmingen airfield. This Mosquito was almost certainly an aircraft from the 3rd Photo-Reconnaissance Group, a 12th Air Force unit which had a mixed bag of aircraft, including Lockheed F-4s and F-5s and half a dozen Mosquitoes, all based in Italy. Another 3rd Group photo-run was carried out the same day by an F-5 to Munich with a six-ship escort from the Red Tails. Again, reconnaissance runs started the day on February 17th, with a six-ship escort to a lone P-5 headed for Nuremberg. Then a four-Mustang escort accompanied another 3rd Photo-Reconnaissance Group Mosquito for a run over Munich. It has been said that the USAAF pilots didn't like the Mosquito, most probably because after flying a tricycle landing gear aircraft like the Lightning, a slightly "fatter" tail-wheeled aircraft was a bit more unwieldy. They certainly would not have liked the "steering wheel" control stick, the open wiring harness inside the aircraft, when most US aircraft had more paneling, but that apart, the Mosquito was a more stable reconnaissance platform with its larger wing area, by 35 square feet. Interestingly, the Mosquito was also faster than the Lightning, despite being a larger aircraft. One criticism of the Mosquito from US pilots was that it was a two-man crew machine, whereas the F-5 had only one – the pilot.

Shortly after these two photo missions were on their way, a 44 ship formation of Mustangs took off from Ramitelli,

heading for the Linz-Vienna railway line, looking for targets of their own. Trains were often a "productive" target, partly because most often they could not retaliate, and even when they could, the firepower from a train – even a freight train – was rarely powerful enough to defend it effectively, and there was the "bonus" that bombing a freight train meant cutting off quite a quantity of supplies and food, seriously affecting the German war machine. On this strafing run, two trains were taken out of operation and a couple of others damaged. Two locomotives were totally destroyed, while three more were damaged, as well as a number of trucks on railway wagons, several armored cars and buildings. Ground defense was poor, and no Mustangs were lost to ground fire.

February 19th was "just one of those days" when nothing went smoothly. It began with another 47th Bombardment Wing bomber escort. On the way to the target area, the Mustangs encountered a single RAF Spitfire, the pilot of which seemingly thought the P-51s were the enemy. He turned into

In February 1945, this P-51 of the 302nd Fighter Squadron, carrying standard drop tanks, took off for another escort mission.

The B-24s of the of the 451st Bomb Group, of the 49th Bomb Wing, launched an attack on the railway yards at Augsburg in late February 1945, under the watchful eyes of their red-tailed escorts.

the formation, aiming to make a run on them, but when he began his pass, three of the 48 Mustangs aloft turned into him, dropping their external tanks as they went. The Spitfire pilot clearly then thought better of his action, perhaps realized that these were not enemy aircraft after all, so made a hasty escape as to avoid embarrassment all round. It has been said by former RAF pilots that the P-51 did look a bit like a Bf-109 at a glance, especially if both aircraft were camouflaged. But these Mustangs were not olive drab finished – they were highly polished, the Red Tails' ground crews being extremely proud of their charges, so there should have been no case of mistaken identity here.

The last ten days of February were busy for the 332nd Fighter Group. They began with a reconnaissance escort of an F-5 heading for Nuremberg, but before they reached the target area, the Lightning suffered a misfire in one of its engines, so the five Mustangs and single F-5 aborted the mission and turned back, the Lightning putting in at San Severo. In the afternoon of the same day, 43 Mustangs went up to escort the 47th Bombardment Wing's Liberators on a bombing run to the Vipitento and Brenner railway yards, but when the Mustangs reached the rendezvous point, there were no B-24s in sight. Captain Turner, the Red Tails' formation leader, decided to send on 15 Mustangs to the target area and he circled the rendezvous area with the rest of the formation to await the Liberators. Some minutes later, the bombers arrived and the run was completed, but not without weather problems.

On February 21st, the 304th Bomb Wing was headed for the Vienna central rail marshaling yards, under the protection of 39 Mustangs. Apart from a single B-24 encountering mechanical problems, the run was without incident. The damaged machine was escorted by a pair of P-51s to Trieste and safety. Next came a bomber escort run to railway yards in southwest Germany, where the 5th Bombardment Wing was to be accompanied by 44 Mustangs, which had also been tasked with a ground strafing run on rail targets. But the weather closed in and the strafing run was aborted. More reconnaissance escorts followed on the 24th, with a 3rd PR Group Mosquito seeking pictures of Munich, then an F-5 following it in the next day, probably to fill gaps left by cloud cover. Out of those two reconnoiters came another strafing mission with 45 Mustangs covering movements in the areas of Munich, Linz, Ingoldstadt and Salzburg. Some aircraft provided top cover for others striking at rail targets. In all, they destroyed ten locomotives, damaged three others and wrecked several passenger coaches, oil tank wagons and 40 freight wagons. Then, one pilot spotted an airfield nearby, so they went for that and shot down three Heinkel He-111 bombers and a Bf-109 fighter. Ground fire brought one Mustang down and the pilot, Lieutenant George Iles, bailed out, but was captured by the Germans as he tried to escape to Switzerland. Lieutenant Alfred Gorham suffered a similar fate and was also captured.

It was a relief now for the 332nd to be given more reconnaissance escorts, since the number of pilots was dwindling, with no replacements coming from the US. After a Mosquito run to Munich once more, the 49th Bombardment Wing hit Augsburg railway yards, then the Red Tails took two more reconnaissance runs with F-5s to Prague. On that last day of February, Colonel Davis led a 34-ship escort to take the 5th Bomb Wing to targets in Verona. Difficulties arose as the pilot numbers were reduced to such a level that one of the four squadrons, the 302nd, had its remaining pilots switched to the other three, and by the first week in March, the 302nd was temporarily de-activated.

March opened with two pilots dying needlessly – the first was Flight Officer Thomas Hawkins, recently arrived in Italy, who crashed on take-off. Lieutenant Roland Moody lost his life even more tragically. He was in the pilots' tent at Ramitelli when a drop tank fell from an aircraft as it taxied by, hit one of the tent's poles, causing a spark, and the tent went up in flames. Roland Moody died from the burns he received in the incident.

The month's operations started quietly, with reconnaissance escorts to Prague and Stuttgart. In a bombing run to Vienna, which was diverted to Amstetten because of weather, the Red Tails came across a most unusual sight. They saw a formation of about a dozen Russian Ilyushin IL-2 "Stormovik" fighters flying near them and the bombing group. The Russians made no effort to intrude, but it was a clear sign of their progress across Eastern Europe, into Hungary, and that the Germans were now unable to prevent the air intrusion of the Russians. The German resistance in the air was now limited anyway, because fuel was desperately short and the Allies had virtually total control of the air. Ground resistance, on the other hand, was still fierce, as a strafing group of Red Tails discovered when they had been on a railway wrecking mission, finding little and so diverted to an airfield near Graz which was rather better protected than the attackers had anticipated. Lieutenants Robert Martin and Alfonso Simmons flew in low to attack and as they began their firing runs, were both brought down by flak. Simmons was killed, but as Martin was about to leave his aircraft, he radioed to base that he would "...walk in from here". Amazingly, he did just that and in mid-April was back at Ramitelli, none the worse for wear.

After a number of photo mission escorts, with Mosquitoes and F-5s over the next few days, the 5th Bombardment Wing was escorted to the railway marshaling yards at Bruck, and then the 47th Wing went for the Florisdorf oil refinery near Vienna. More railway yards were attacked by the 5th Bombardment Wing at Regensburg, then the Varazdin railway yards in Croatia in another 47th Wing raid. On March 14th, 23 Mustangs were dispatched to Hieflau, in southern Austria, where they attacked the Bruck-Leoben-Steyr railway and neighboring marshaling yard. They destroyed nine locomotives, 127 freight wagons, 37 flat cars and eight oil tanks. They also wrecked railway stations, including the one at Hieflau on the Rudolfsbahn railway.

More reconnaissance missions were interlaced with bomber escorts through the next ten days, as the pressure built up to destroy whatever was left of German resistance. Everybody sensed that this war could not last much longer. A transport escort took a C-47 Dakota over Yugoslavia to drop supplies

to the partisans, and then there were more photo sessions over Munich, Prague and Ruhland. A heavy bombing run to the oil refinery at Ruhland followed, with 43 Mustangs in escort. As the bombers and escorts turned for home, Lieutenant Lincoln Hudson ran into engine trouble and found it difficult to gain height to cross the Alps. He decided to go east towards the Russian lines, in the hope that he would find friendly territory. When this looked unlikely, he abandoned his Mustang over Tropau in Czechoslovakia, only to be mobbed and beaten by civilians. Ironically, it was the German army that rescued him and took him to Stalag Luft III.

The 15th Air Force was now about to launch its longest-range mission of the war – to Berlin. The round trip, on March 24th, would be 1,600 miles for 240 bombers in five bombardment groups, and just 59 Mustangs. As it happened, five Mustangs failed shortly after leaving the ground and aborted their mission. Of the remainder, 38 rendezvoused with the bombers and the other 16 went ahead towards the target area. Not long after the rendezvous, Colonel Davis had an engine problem with vibration at high manifold pressure, so he handed over

This B-24 of the 47th Bomb Wing flies home over the Alps after the longest bombing mission to a target from Italy, to Berlin. All but four bombers reached home from that mission.

THE TUSKEGEE AIRMEN AND BEYOND

the lead to Captain Armour McDaniel, the 301st Squadron's commander, though he did stay in the formation.

Close to Berlin, the Red Tails were scheduled to hand over their charges to the 31st Fighter Group, also flying P-51 Mustangs, but the 31st was late reaching the rendezvous point and the 332nd continued the run all the way to the target area, the Daimler-Benz tank manufacturing works. Just after mid-day, the fight began, with a couple of dozen Me-262 jet fighters confronting the Red Tails. Several dogfights ensued and the first Me-262 to go down was credited to Captain Roscoe Brown, who had spotted four heading north but as he turned towards them he saw spotted a lone 262 approaching him. He opened fire and both jet engines burst into flame, giving Roscoe Brown a definite "kill". A famous incident from this confrontation was when a 262 flew across the path of Lieutenant Earl R. Lane's P-51. Lane pitched in and as the Me-262 was peeling off, Lane came in at thirty degrees and from an amazing 2,000 feet range, fired and hit the jet, seeing pieces fly off it and the pilot, a German ace, Alfred Ambs, parachute out of his crippled machine. Lane saw the German jet go down and so his "kill" was official. It was an established fact that the German pilots were wary of being caught in a dive by a Mustang, because it had been established on several occasions that the P-51 was faster in a dive than the Me-262 and was rugged too.

Lieutenant Richard Harder was at 26,000 feet when he spotted three more Me-262s below, running in to attack the bombers. Harder was leading a flight of Mustangs and he had them turn inside the arc of the 262s and split them up. He then chased one of them and fired on it from a range of 2,000 feet, damaging it, but not taking it out of the sky. Flight Officer Joseph Chineworth fired on another Me-262 as he found himself in a similar position to Richard Harder earlier, but he could only claim a "probable". Almost immediately after that, Lieutenant Charles Brantly found himself cut across by another 262 and so he slammed open the Mus-

"Mission Accomplished" – the Red Tails make for home after the Berlin bomb run, with all but four bombers escorted there and safely back.

tang's throttle, taking the engine to the limit, and just hoped he could get close enough in the diving turn. As he closed in on the German, he opened fire and saw one engine burst into flames and the aircraft go down.

This run on Berlin had been the biggest task undertaken by the 332nd Fighter Group in the whole of the War and it had lost a number of pilots. Fortunately most of them were taken into captivity which, as it happened, would not last long now anyway, but sadly, the "never lost a bomber" myth was broken – four were lost on that day. The Mustang had proved beyond dispute its superiority in a dive to the Me-262 and had taken out four definite "kills" and up to five probables. And more interestingly, the Mustangs lost to enemy fire were lost to ground fire flak, not air-to-air. The German jets found the Red Tails invincible. It was a memorable day, for another Distinguished Unit Citation and the Presidential Unit Citation were awarded to the 332nd Fighter Group for its collective gallantry in an air battle that probably only lasted thirty minutes or so.

Buoyed by their success in the Berlin run, the 332nd scored probably its biggest haul of enemy aircraft "kills" of the whole war in the last days of March 1945. It was clear that this war was drawing to its close. Half of Germany had been shattered now by the Allies, yet the German fighter squadrons that still existed continued to put up what can only be described as a valiant fight. But it was a lost cause. The "Red Angels", as so many bomber crews were now describing them, were inspired by their latest Distinguished Unit Citation and pitched into battle with immense energy. In a strafing run, 332nd pilots brought down one Fw-190 and five Bf-109s. Within twenty minutes, during the same strafing run, another Fw-190 and three more Bf-109s were shot out of the sky. Three planes were lost in that strafing and, Ronald Reeves lost his life when he failed to recover from a tight turn at low level, but the other two pilots were taken into captivity.

Even so, that March 31st mission was a success, for the tally of two Fw-190s and eight Bf-109s was a significant achievement. Add to that, five locomotives destroyed, nine more seriously damaged and a "shopping list" of nine passenger

cars, 20 freight wagons, five oil tank wagons, five grain hoppers, a single road truck, a factory, a railway round-house, a railway station and a warehouse. It was an impressive score, but there was more yet to be done. Nobody yet knew that April would be the last complete month of the War in Europe, so the squadrons of the 332nd remained "tight" as the Allies advanced through Germany. The biggest battle of the War in Europe had taken place in the form of the Battle of the Bulge in the Ardennes, bordering Belgium and Luxembourg, where some 19,000 Americans lost their lives. This was George S. Patton's greatest battle and his greatest victory.

Even though the Germans were losing the battle on the ground, they were still putting up a spirited fight in the air. On April 1st, in a bombing run by the 47th Bombardment Wing, the 43 Mustangs in escort met some spirited opposition. Lieutenant Richard Harder spotted four Fw-190s below his flight of four and decided to go into the attack. They pulled more than they bargained for, for the four Fw-190s were decoys and there were twelve more Germans in the area waiting for just such an attack. Even at that, the Germans did not have it their way, as other Red Tails came to the rescue of Harder and his three companions. In the ensuing dogfight, three Fw-190s and seven Bf-109s went down to three Mustangs lost – two pilots lost and one captured.

The whole of April was taken up with a mixture of reconnaissance escort runs, fighter sweeps strafing enemy rail yards and strategic positions, as well as heavy bomber escorts to targets mostly now in Germany. The last enemy aircraft to be shot down by any of the 15th Air Force's fighter groups were credited to the 332nd Fighter Group. This incident on April 26, 1945 was for the escort of an F-5 on a reconnaissance run over Linz, Prague and Amstetting. It started with the Mustangs seeing a single aircraft below them, which they did not initially recognize. It turned out to be a 3rd Photo Reconnaissance Group Mosquito returning to its base. But as the three investigating Mustangs climbed back to their escort task they came across five Messerchmitt Bf-109s. Thinking they would be able to avoid confrontation, being probably as surprised to see the Americans as the Americans were to see them, the Bf-109s all waggled their wings in friendly gesture. Not inclined to believe the gesture, the Mustangs went into action. As two Bf-109s climbed, two Mustangs opened fire and both Germans went down. The other three Bf-109s dived for low cover, hoping that being "down among the weeds" would enable them to escape and run for home. They reckoned without the determination of the Red Tail pilots, who gave chase and brought all three down. This brought the total of enemy aircraft shot down by the 332nd Fighter Group in World War II to 111.

Just days from the end of the War in Europe, the 332nd Fighter Group left Ramitelli and moved to Cattolica. Their last operational mission had been a photo escort of an F-5 to Balzano, which was totally incident-free. Their next formal flying duty would be to take part in the 15th Air Force Review, on May 6th, flying over Caserta and Bari. After that, there was an expectation that they would relocate temporarily to the United States, prior to re-assignment to the Pacific, because that war was still raging fiercely. In fact, as the European War was coming to its close, the Battle of Okinawa had just begun and was to continue until June.

Many thousands of bomber crews flying from North Africa and Italy expressed their gratitude, respect and praise for the "Red Angels" – the Tuskegee Airmen who accompanied then to their targets and every time brought them home. Those same Red Angels destroyed 150 enemy aircraft on the ground in addition to tHe-111 in the air. Other fighter groups claimed higher scores, but they were in theatre longer than the 99th Fighter Squadron and the 332nd Fighter Group. The Red Angels took out 57 railway locomotives and over 600 pieces of railway rolling stock, as well as the "Anzio Express", the German K-5 giant cannon.

For their achievements in World War II, the 99th Fighter Squadron and the 332nd Fighter Group combined were awarded three Distinguished Unit Citations, the first from General Henry Arnold, Commanding General of the Army Air Forces, and a Presidential Unit Citation. Individually, there were 1,031 Air Medals, 96 Distinguished Flying Crosses, eight Purple Hearts, two Silver Stars, one Bronze Star and one Soldier's Medal awarded to these men. In addition, their Commander, Colonel Benjamin O. Davis, Jr., deservedly re-

"Somewhere in England", before embarking for France, the men of Dog Company, 761st Tank Battalion – "Patton's Panthers" prepare their equipment for action. Every weapon was cleaned and oiled, for each man knew that his own and his buddies' lives depended on it.

ceived the Legion of Merit, followed by two Oak Leaf Clusters to the same award.

There is a unit of the US Army that fought under the command of Lieutenant-General George S. Patton, Jr., which must be mentioned. This was the 761st Tank Battalion – "Patton's Panthers" – a group of African Americans who fought with equal valor on the ground as the Tuskegee Airmen did in the air. The 761st was formed in May 1943, under the command of Major Paul Bates. In October 1944, they went to war, crossing the English Channel to land on the Normandy beaches that had been the scene of such terrible slaughter and bloodshed on the days after June 6th – "D-Day". During the build-up period of the 761st, Major Bates was promoted to Lieutenant-Colonel and in the summer of 1944, General George Patton had asked for more tank units to reinforce his Third Army in readiness for the Battle of the Bulge. When the War Department replied to his request with the message that the only unit available was a Negro tank battalion, Patton replied "Who the **** asked about color? I asked for tankers!" And tankers he got – the 761st Tank Battalion.

Patton went to inspect the 761st shortly after their arrival in

THE TUSKEGEE AIRMEN AND BEYOND

France. When he arrived at St. Nicolas-de-Port, he instantly jumped on to the hood of an armored car, set his feet apart, and looked at the mass of black faces before him. His address to them was meant to inspire and encourage – and strike the fear of God into those who needed it. He said:

"Men, you are the first Negro tankers ever to fight in the American Army. I have nothing but the best in my Army. I don't care what color you are, so long as you go up there and kill those Kraut sonsofbitches. Everyone has their eyes on you and is expecting great things of you. Moreover, your race is looking forward to your success. Don't let them down and damn you, don't let me down. They say it's patriotic to die for your country. Well, let's

see how many [patriots] we can make out of those German sonsofbitches.

"There is one thing you men will be able to say when you go home. You may all thank God that 30 years from now, when you are sitting with your grandson on your knee and he asks: 'Grandfather, what did you do in World War II?', you won't have to say, 'I shoveled shit in Mississippi'".

The 761st fought with distinction. Eight enlisted men had been commissioned in the field. Three hundred and ninety-one were decorated for valor with seven Silver Stars (three of those posthumous awards), 56 Bronze Stars (Oak Leaf Clusters with three of them), a staggering 246 Purple Hearts

The 761st's most courageous fighter, Medal of Honor awardee Staff Sergeant Ruben Rivers.

Rivers in his tank, ready for the next phase, and for him his last, of the battle. Rivers quite consciously gave his life for the safety of his comrades. Yet his family had to wait fifty three years for his sacrifice to be recognized by his country.

CHAPTER NINE • 131

Lieutenant-General George S. Patton pins a Silver Star to the chest of Private Ernest A. Jenkins after securing Chateaudun in France.

Observer's Board about the "Negro Experiment". After all those men had done and achieved in battle, he failed them sadly. His replies to questions included answers that stated that black officers lacked initiative, and that their sense of responsibility was poor on average. The most cynical response was to the question: "Based on combat performance, what percent of colored officers do you regard as of field grade potential?" The response was "None!" There are many latter-day African American generals and admirals who have confounded that statement.

There are many incidents involving the 761st Tank Battalion that demonstrate their success, courage, initiative and commitment to fighting their war on three fronts all at the same time. They fought discrimination in their army, and discrimination in their nation and most significantly, when it mattered most, they fought their part of World War II with unflinching commitment, incredible initiative and immeasurable valor. Challenge the courage, if you dare, of the one man who could not take home his prize for valor – Staff Sergeant Ruben Rivers and his Medal of Honor.

Captain David Williams (a white officer who was assigned to the Negro Battalion because he shook hands with a black NCO.) was the commander of "C" Company of the 761st Tank Battalion. He told the story of Rivers' immense courage in the battle for Guebling in France. On two separate occasions, when already seriously wounded, Sergeant Rivers refused to be relieved and refused morphine to relieve the agony of his wounds. Instead, he told his commander that this was one order he would not obey and went back into battle.

The Company was faced with a German Tiger tank onslaught. The Tiger was Germany's biggest and most fearsome battle tank in World War II and Captain Williams radioed his tanks to pull back. Rivers response was that he saw them and would fight them. He took his tank, accompanied by the Sherman commanded by Sergeant Walter James, out of cover and directly into the face of the enemy. Captain Williams called for them to pull back again, but Rivers and James charged into the German line and bought enough time for the rest of the Company to re-group and escape fur-

and Oak Leaf Clusters on eight of them. One Medal of Honor was posthumously awarded to Sergeant Ruben Rivers 53 years after his death on the battlefield. To cap all of that, the 761st was awarded a Presidential Unit Citation, the highest award a unit can receive, from President Harry S. Truman. Yet another group of African Americans had made their mark on World War II and on the path to achieving equality for all races.

It is all the more appalling then to know the answers that Lieutenant-Colonel Hollis Hunt, the commander who replaced Lieutenant-Colonel Norman Bates when he was injured and hospitalized, gave when he was questioned by an

Tank Commander Harvey Woodard assessing the terrain before moving on.

ther damage. As they went forward, Rivers' tank was struck by an armor-piercing shell and brought to a halt. A second shell ripped off the turret and cut Rivers in half. Sergeant James was able to retreat and survived.

In 1997, President Bill Clinton finally presented the Medal of Honor to Ruben Rivers' sister, Grace Woodfork, in recognition of Captain Williams' citation, which read:

> *"For extraordinary heroism in action during 15-19 November 1944, toward Guebling, France. Though severely wounded in the leg, Sergeant Rivers refused medical treatment and evacuation, took command of another tank, and advanced with his company in Guebling the next day. Repeatedly refusing evacuation, Sergeant Rivers continued to direct his tank's fire at enemy positions through the morning of November 19, 1944. At dawn, Company A's tanks began to advance towards Bougaktroff, but were stopped by enemy fire. Sergeant Rivers, joined by another tank, opened fire on the enemy tanks, covering company A as they withdrew. While doing so, Sergeant River's tank was hit, killing him and wounding the crew. Staff Sergeant Rivers' fighting spirit and daring leadership were an inspiration to his unit and exemplify the highest traditions of military service".*

Another address from General George Smith Patton, Jr. says of these men all that needed to be said, as they ended their war in Steyr, Austria:

> *"In thinking of the heritage of glory you have achieved, do not be unmindful of the price you have paid. Throughout your victorious advances, your line of march is marked with the graves of your heroic dead, while the hospitals are crowded with your wounded".*

World War II, then, had ended with two "experiments" – the Tuskegee Airmen and the Patton Panthers – yielding success far beyond the expectations of the initiators of those "experiments". They had equaled, and frequently exceeded, the performance of any other battle groups in their proximity and left their mark in a profound way upon the annals of American military history. The Tuskegee Airmen, Patton's Panthers and many more had fought for the freedom and liberty of the world when they did not yet have freedom and liberty for themselves. The Legacy had begun…

CHAPTER TEN

Reflections and Myths
about the Tuskegee Airmen

There are many stories about the Tuskegee Airmen with varying levels of truth. Some of those tales are fundamentally untrue, while others need to be "taken with a pinch of salt". For example, there were stories abounding in the US Armed Forces at large, not just the Army, that African Americans were of low intelligence and low intellect, and were totally unsuited to any other military activity than those which were subservient, such as laborers, mess stewards, and infantrymen as long as they were kept separate, but even then, there were the views of some that they "lacked courage". Black men did menial tasks – that was the "logical way of things".

But when it was finally decided that an all-black air group should be formed, several of these myths were not just put aside, they were swept away. The first myth to put aside here is the story that Eleanor Roosevelt caused the Tuskegee Airmen to come into being. The decision was solely an Army recommendation, implemented by Brigadier-General (soon to be Major-General) Walter R. Weaver. It is, however, true to say that once the First Lady became aware of the coming existence of the Negro Flight Training Program, she took a positive interest, as a powerful campaigner in the Human Rights movement. And once she had visited Tuskegee Army Air Field, and flown with Charles "Chief" Anderson, she did become a vigorous campaigner on the Tuskegee Airmen's behalf, sometimes in public, more often behind closed presidential doors.

Walter Weaver was moved by the information that had been put before him and being, at the beginning of this "experiment", something of a "middle-of-the-roader", he needed evidence to persuade him of the courage, integrity and ability of black candidates for a flight training program. Most of the evidence was before him – he just had to look at it. Already, many African Americans had been awarded the Medal of Honor for their courage, one of the first being Sergeant William Carney in 1863, just one year after the institution of that decoration. Then, as recently as World War I, there was the record of 518 African American recipients of the Croix de Guerre from the French Government for their dauntless courage. Seventy-six black officers were awarded the Legion d'Honneur and this was enough to persuade General Weav-

er that African Americans did not lack courage. To quote a phrase from the recent motion picture "Red Tails" – "Courage Has No Color".

General Weaver's next concern was the academic ability of future black pilots and aircrew, bearing in mind that a bomber unit was being contemplated as well as a fighter squadron. Most white pilots were only high school graduates, but it was decided that the black pilots should only be selected from college graduates, to make sure that they were up to the level of intelligence and intellect that would be required from the pilot of a fighter plane. For those determined to see this whole experiment fail, they saw the requirement of a degree as an extra barrier to recruitment, which they believed would make it doubly difficult to recruit and help to kill the exercise before it began. They were in for a huge surprise.

When recruitment time came, in 1941, young black college graduates flooded into the Army's recruiting offices, to the great surprise of the officers involved in the flight training program experiment and to General Weaver, and his doubts were relieved. He knew that African Americans had courage, they had educational qualifications ahead of many of their white counterparts and their natural intelligence was beyond question too. General Walter Weaver was satisfied that the material he had available was "up to the job" so far. Now all they had to do was undergo the training program to prove they could learn to fly. They did not let the general down. There were failures, of course (but there was a similar attrition rate among white pilot trainees at the beginning).

The Civil Pilot Training Program began by using white instructors. In his eagerness to start the program, G. L. Washington, who was Director of Aviation at Tuskegee Institute, had recruited as early as 1939 a class group to undertake ground school. There were even three female applicants, and two, including Mildred Hemmons, completed the program as civilian pilots. Mildred Hemmons was the first female pilot to leave the Civil Pilot Training Program, earning her place in history on February 1, 1941, five months before the first Army cadet group entered Tuskegee, when she soloed with a Piper Cub. She was taught by none other than Charles "Chief" Anderson and her goal was to join the

WASPs (Women Air Service Pilots) to work as a ferry pilot for the US Armed Forces, but because of her race, she was rejected. At her interview, she was told she would not have been given an interview if her race had been known.

The story of Mildred Hemmons is fascinating, simply because she was the first "Tuskegee Airwoman" in her own right. She was not yet twenty years old when she successfully completed her flying training. And while she was at Tuskegee, she met a young man named Herbert Carter, a Tuskegee flying trainee and somehow, they managed to rendezvous in the air for their "dates". They used to fly to Lake Martin, about 25 miles from Tuskegee, on a Saturday. He would be doing a "check-flight" on a T-6 that had had maintenance work done on it and she would be flying a CPT Piper Cub. There is a stark difference in performance between the two aircraft, but the two would come together, he with flaps down and throttled back, she with throttle wide open so they could fly side by side for a few minutes, exchanging in sign language their expressions of affection for each other. They married in 1942, just after he won his pilot's wings, and were together for almost seventy years. When he went off to North Africa with the 99th Fighter Squadron, she remained at Tuskegee until they were reunited.

Much of Mildred Hemmons' story mirrors that of Bessie Coleman from some twenty years before, for Mildred was

Mildred Hemmons meets the First Lady, Mrs. Eleanor Roosevelt, at Tuskegee.

the first woman pilot to graduate in Alabama. Her instructor, Charles "Chief" Anderson rated her flying skills highly and, like her, was disappointed about her rejection by the WASP, for no other reason than that she was black. Even a whisper in the ear of First Lady Eleanor Roosevelt when she visited Tuskegee, was unable to reverse the WASP decision. Mrs. Roosevelt did try, but this time, she was unsuccessful because of the rule of segregation in the Armed Forces in that period.

In the early days of the Tuskegee flight program, G. L. Washington did not have long to organize his flight school instructors and there were no ground school instructors available near at hand, so he went searching outside his own locality. Visiting the Alabama Polytechnic Institute in Auburn, he persuaded Professors Robert G. Pitts and Bloomfield Cornell to deliver the four ground school course units for the same pay as the other Tuskegee Institute instructors received. As the flight-training program fell due to start, Mr. Washington had secured the services of Joseph Wren Allen, a white aviator who owned and operated a company called Alabama Air Services out of Montgomery. Initially, he had to transport his students to Montgomery and back, which made the days extremely long and proved not to be as successful as everyone would have liked. The flight classes were run in the afternoon, after a morning of ground school, and Joseph Allen took a group of ten at a time, in line with the CAA's requirements. He soon realized he needed more instructors and as travel arrangements were becoming more and more difficult, Washington had to find somewhere more local for the flight training part of the program.

Scouring the countryside, he came across a local site known as Kennedy Field, which was operated by three white aviators, Forrest Shelton, Stanley Kennedy and Joe Wilkerson. Initially, it was not CAA approved and needed to be so for government-approved flight training to take place there. Using the principle embodied into the Tuskegee Institute by Booker T. Washington so many years before, G. L. Washington employed his students to go to work on Kennedy Field to prepare it for flight training use. The students, under the supervision of Royal B. Dunham, supervisor of the Department of Mechanical Industries at Tuskegee, built a wooden hangar big enough to house three aircraft and including toilet facilities, a flight briefing shack and a fuel depot. By early 1940, the CAA had approved the field and it went into use.

July 1941 saw the first class of military aviation cadets come to Tuskegee and Moton Field, named after former Director of the Tuskegee Institute, Dr. Robert Russa Moton, was to be where flight training would begin. However, it didn't work out that way, because heavy summer rain in that year had prevented the construction work from being completed by August 23rd, when flight training was due to start. As a result, Kennedy Field continued to be used until early September, when aircraft were flown to Moton Field, then returned to Kennedy Field for overnight storage, because the hangar at Moton was not yet complete. Even after Moton Field had been formally completed, drainage problems there meant that Kennedy Field would continue to be used as a back-up field for some months yet.

By mid-1941, the team of flight instructors at Tuskegee consisted of four white instructors and three African Americans. The white instructors were: Joseph T. Camilleri, Dominic J. Guido, Frank Rosenberg and Forrest Shelton. The three black instructors were Charles (later nicknamed "Chief") Anderson, Lewis A. Jackson and George W. Allen. Linwood Williams later joined their number. This group of men were closely bonded as a team and set out to make the best aviators of their initial group of students that they could. This was Course SE-42-I, which included Captain Benjamin O. Davis in their number. In addition to these white instructors "Tuskegee Airmen", there were also two others essential to the success of this story. Major James A. Ellison and Captain, later Colonel Noel F. Parrish. These two men ran the operation on a day-to-day basis and were scrupulously fair in their dealings with their African American charges. There was no segregation in the flight school and the standards applied were what would apply anywhere else in the Army Air Corps. The quality of their "output" was soon to be demonstrated in North Africa.

Ground crews were also mixed and all were initially civilians. Austin H Humbles was an existing instructor in the aerome-

Army nurses arrive at Tuskegee to serve in the Base Hospital.

chanics training program at Tuskegee and was appointed Chief of Maintenance. Washington then went back to Alabama Polytechnic Institute to find more suitably qualified people and recruited Warren G. Darby as his chief instructor, as well as other white instructors. In his search for competent people to teach mechanics in ground school, Washington found one woman who shone above her peers, an African American and called Marjorie Cheetham, a licensed and certified aviation mechanic. Most of the early technician training was conducted at Selfridge Field in Illinois, but eventually it transferred to Tuskegee and Moton Field. This group of technicians was here to provide the essential maintenance and support for the Flight Training Program, as well as giving instruction in basic aviation mechanics as part of the course pilots undertook.

Thus, there were even Tuskegee Airwomen, as well as men. Apart from Mildred Hemmons Carter and Marjorie Cheetham, there was estimated to be some 41 women, serving mostly as nurses, but in other roles also.

Another love story that comes out of Tuskegee is that of Irma Cameron, who had the nickname "Pete" from childhood, and Charles "A-Train" Dryden. She was a nurse in the base hospital and he was a cadet on Course SE-42-C, the second pilot training course. On his graduation, they married. "Pete" Dryden was born and grew up in New York. She trained as a nurse in Harlem Hospital and volunteered to become a nurse at Tuskegee, believing that this could be her contribution to the war. She traveled by train with two friends, having no idea how her journey would affect her whole attitude to

Singer Lena Horne brought a "feminine touch" to the Tuskegee Airmen when she paid them a visit.

Captain Della Rainey was the Army Chief of Nursing at Tuskegee.

life. As the trio reached Washington, DC, they experienced the segregation of the South for the first time. There was no dining car in the "colored" section of the train and they were given strict and specific rules about when and where they could eat, behind a curtain, so as to ensure that the white passengers on the train did not have to acknowledge their existence. Irma Dryden said years later that she had never been exposed to anything so humiliating, but she drew great strength from that awful experience. She realized that from that moment she could overcome anything. She went on to spend a great deal of her time during her service at Tuskegee not only nursing physical wounds, but addressing stressful situations of the young men in her care too. Young pilot trainees who had problems with upcoming exams or flight tests would gain inner strength from her comforting words and Charles Dryden was one who passed through her care.

The first real trial of African American pilots came in the worst possible of circumstances. Lieutenant-Colonel Benjamin Davis took his 99th Fighter Squadron to North Africa to become part of the 33rd Fighter Group. Nobody had told him that his new Group Commander, Colonel William Momyer, had almost been repatriated to the United States as the result of a major error of judgment in which he had been strongly advised not to do what he did, in dispersing his fighters across parts of Tunisia, which were under German air superiority. Most of his aircraft were lost in his attempt to secure territory and Major-General James H. Doolittle was far from happy that he had to request new squadrons to re-equip the 33rd Fighter Group. In fact, if Momyer had taken Doolittle's and others' advice, he would not have had the 99th Fighter Squadron assigned to him.

The first attack carried out on Pantelleria by the 99th Fighter Squadron took place on June 2, 1943. It was a ground-attack mission in which they and other squadrons of the 33rd Fighter Group dive-bombed the German airfield on the island. And on at least one occasion, a 99th Fighter Squadron pilot, Clarence Jamison, flew as Momyer's own wingman and "covered his tail". So much for team spirit and loyalty. William Campbell was the other pilot participating in this first mission in which they flew as wingmen to element leaders of the 33rd Fighter Group, their parent unit. The second mission flown by the 99th was on the same day with the same unit and was flown by James Wiley and Charles Hall.

The debacle of Panetelleria was a serious undoing for Colonel Momyer, because he refused Lieutenant-Colonel Davis' request to join in the pre-flight briefing of the day before the first major bombing run, or even on the morning of the mission. The men of the 99th had already had to find their own accommodation and their own flight line space. Now they had to set up their own pre-mission briefing and find out what time the bombers were taking off. They were given no information about likely air defense of Pantelleria, so had to find out as they got near the target area. They could hardly have escorted the bombers all the way to their targets when they themselves were "jumped" by a German fighter group. But by keeping the Germans occupied the bombers were able to return unscathed.

The Tuskegee Army Nurses were not confined to hospital duties – they were trained as flight nurses too, and so perhaps should be included in the listing of "Tuskegee Airwomen". This group is comprised of Chief of Nursing Captain Della Rainey sitting in the back seat of the T-6, on the left is Nurse Abbie Voorhies (who married "Mac" Ross), next is Ruth Speight and on the right is Mencie Trotter. They are about to undergo flight orientation.

Ironically, it was the Pantelleria mission that earned the 99th its first Distinguished Unit Citation and equally ironically, it was after this that Colonel Momyer had the 99th doing "mopping-up" jobs instead of air-to-air combat. This was to build up his case for the removal of the 99th and its disbandment on the argument that "the experiment" had failed. He submitted his report to Major-General Edwin House, commander of 12th Air Support Command and he in turn passed it up to the North West Africa Tactical Air Force deputy commander, Major-General John J. Cannon, who by-passed his boss, Major-General James H. Doolittle and passed it "up the chain". That was a strategic mistake. The House Committee on Defense, as has been related elsewhere, took the evidence of Colonel Davis against the evidence of Colonel Momyer, with the result that the 99th was relocated and so was Colonel Momyer. The 99th came out best, as it was transferred to the 79th Fighter Group under the much more positive command of Colonel Earl R. Bates.

The issue of capability had now been thoroughly dispensed with. The Senate House Committee had sealed it and now the decision was being made to add three more squadrons to the "experiment" by establishing the 332nd Fighter Group, which would come under the well-earned command of Colonel Benjamin O. Davis. What had brought this about

THE TUSKEGEE AIRMEN AND BEYOND

was his steady guiding hand in command of the 99th Fighter Squadron and the extraction of absolute commitment to the winning of their part of the War and to the winning of their cause. That absolute dedication had brought them two Distinguished Unit Citations and several Air Medals.

Before leaving the "courage to do the job" and "fighting performance" issues, it is right to address an accusation that came from many different quarters. This was that, first the 99th and then the 332nd, had not produced a single fighter Ace and had, overall, shot down less than most of the other fighter groups in that Theater of Operations. There were seven fighter groups in the 15th Air Force. They were the 1st, the 14th, the 31st, the 52nd, 82nd, the 325th and the 332nd. The 31st was the highest-scoring of them all with 278 victories to its credit. The lowest scoring group was the 1st, followed by the 14th, with 72 and 85 victories respectively. In the middle sat the 332nd Fighter Group, with 94 (this does not include victories scored in North Africa by the 99th, which brings the tally to 138). It could hardly be said that the 332nd had a poor record of aerial victories, and much of the reason the figure is as low is that the 332nd stuck with its bombers on escorts, and had less opportunity to engage in dogfights. Fighter Aces have to engage with enemy aircraft consistently in order to become Aces. Getting bombers to their targets and safely home was more important to Colonel Davis and as a demonstration of that fact, we move naturally to the next "myth" of the Tuskegee Airmen.

It is recorded in many places that the Tuskegee Airmen "never lost a bomber". That would be a truly miraculous situation if it were true. But, it is not. It takes nothing away from the phenomenal achievements and reputation of the squadrons comprising the 332nd Fighter Group. They can say with pride that they were the most highly decorated group in the 12th or 15th Air Forces. And whilst they certainly did not "never lose a bomber", they lost far less than probably any other escort squadron, with just 27. The fact that between August 1944 and March 1945, they went seven months without losing a bomber is probably the single most significant factor in the propagation of that myth. However, Colonel Davis himself knew the statement was not true. The citation for his own Distinguished Flying Cross, contained in 15th Air Force General Order 2972 of August 31, 1944, says that on June 9, 1944, *"Colonel Davis so skillfully disposed his squadrons that in spite of the large number of enemy fighters, the bomber formation suffered only a few losses"*. Two, in fact, on that day.

The 332nd squadrons lost their bombers only on seven particular dates: June 9, June 13, July 12, July 18, July 20, and August 24, 1944 and March 24, 1945. The press of the day was reporting on the achievements of the "Red Angels" at this time and the "never lost a bomber" soubriquet suited their reporting objectives. *The Chicago Defender*, an African American newspaper, is one of those publications that perpetuated the myth. And amazingly, even on March 24, 1945, when the 332nd took down three Me-262 jet fighters in 15

The Italian Torpedo boat/minelayer "Giuseppe Misori" attacked in Trieste Harbor.

minutes over Berlin, only four bombers were lost. That is an impressive record and demonstrates just how close these fighter pilots stuck to their charges.

Another myth is that on June 25, 1944, Thunderbolts of the 332nd Fight Group sank a German destroyer in Trieste. The story is half right, in that they spotted a three-funnel ship in Trieste Harbor which looked like a destroyer. The "Giuseppe Missori" had originally been built as a destroyer, but before it went into service it was re-classified as a torpedo boat TA22, and then as a minelayer. It had been captured by the Germans from the Italian Navy in September 1943 and was moored in Trieste Harbor, flying the Kriegsmarine ensign, as Lieutenants Gwynne Pierson and Wendell Pruitt attacked. From gun-camera film, it was confirmed that Pierson's gunfire struck the ship's magazine to cause it to explode, and it was recorded as a "kill", but the ship did not sink. It was decommissioned in August 1944 but scrapped much later, in 1949, when the Italians were desperate for steel for their reviving industry.

How many Tuskegee Airmen were "Aces"? These men were not "Aces" in the accepted sense of five victories plus, but they were "Aces" to the crews of the aircraft they took to their targets and brought home. Not a single Fighter Ace came from the ranks of the Tuskegee Airmen in the two years they were in combat over North Africa and Italy. The closest any of them came was Lieutenant Lee Archer, who scored four victories and was variously credited with another half victory over Italy. An example of the esteem with which these men were held is the incident in which Lieutenant Maceo Harris brought a B-24 to safety in Corsica with no radio contact. The bomber pilot embraced Harris and thanked him with no thought of color or segregation in that gesture. The "Red Tails" were to become the "Red Angels" across so many of the Italian-based bomber groups for their outstanding commitment to "sticking with the bombers." Almost certainly the most famous of all the bomber escorts carried out by the 332nd, in company with other fighter groups, was the mission to escort 240 bombers on a long-range bombing run to Berlin. They covered 1,600 miles and lost only four bombers.

But there is another Tuskegee myth called "The Great Train

The standard 75-gallon drop tanks fitted to the P-51.

The larger 108 gallon paper tanks. These larger tanks fitted to the same mounting lugs as the standard tanks.

Tuskegee Liaison pilot Lieutenant Lloyd Taylor at Kennedy Field, close to Tuskegee and the original Tuskegee flying field, where most of the lightplane pilots were trained. The aircraft is a Piper L-4 Grasshopper.

Robbery." The story goes that, on March 23, 1945, when mechanics were preparing their P-51 Mustangs for an escort mission for bombers attacking Berlin, they realized that the standard "drop" tanks of 50- or 70-gallons capacity would not provide enough fuel for a full round trip of 1,600 miles. It is said that they heard about a shipment of larger fuel tanks on a train headed for another base. This unlikely story continues with the claim that a group of mechanics drove to where the train would pass and blocked its passage. They are then alleged to have removed the tanks they wanted, taken them back to Ramitelli and modified the aircraft to accept them. And it is claimed that they did all this before 6am on the 24th, which was the day of the escort. Good for a movie story line, but unfortunately, much less likely to be true than another story told by a line crew chief, an experienced aircraft maintenance technician, who recalled that he did not experience any difficulty in mounting larger fuel tanks to the wings of the P-51s he had in his charge. He also did not remember anybody needing to, or going to rob a train or warehouse to locate the larger fuel tanks. He offered the far more plausible suggestion that all aircraft parts and accessories normally came through the Army depot at Foggia, but this time, they did not. They had been delivered to a railhead at Chieuti and were collected by trucks from the 380th Service Group (and there is documentation to support that) for delivery to the 366th Air Service Squadron. That squadron's job was to provide service support to the 332nd Fighter Group, and its operational diary records that "a trailerload" of 110-gallon tanks was delivered to the 366th. Interestingly, those tanks were made of compressed paper, not aluminum alloy, so they were much lighter and, when jettisoned, did not give the Germans valuable scrap metal for their aircraft industry.

What of the myth of "150 Distinguished Flying Crosses and 744 Air Medals"? This particular myth is a "swings and roundabouts" story, in that there were less than 150 DFCs awarded to Tuskegee Airmen, but far more Air medals than the often-quoted 744. There was a staggering number of 1,031 Air Medals awarded to 265 men. That equates to almost four each for the two-year period in which the Tuskegee Airmen were involved. The individual award information appears in Appendix Five, but it is significant to note that a high number of pilots of the 332nd were awarded six and more Oak Leaf Clusters. And some people said these men had no courage.

The myth that all Tuskegee Airmen were fighter pilots has already been dispelled, but the story goes further. It is not true to say that the only Tuskegee Airmen in combat were fighter pilots, for 30 of their number were trained as liaison pilots to support the 92nd Infantry Division which was also in Europe from 1944. Liaison pilots flew small, unarmed light aircraft such as the Piper Grasshopper and Stinson Sentinel. Most of these aeroplanes were metal-framed and fabric-covered, and all were powered by small engines such as Lycomings of less than 175hp. The liaison pilots' job was to fly at low altitude, observe troop movements, and gather other important information about the enemy. They also did photo and "eyeball" reconnaissance, ferried spies into remote sites, shuttled people, including the injured, and delivered classified information to the front.

The 370th Infantry Regiment, of the 92nd Infantry Division, landed in Naples on July 30, 1944, to spearhead the arrival of the rest of the Division. They were preparing to be part of the IV Corps assault on Kesselring's Gothic Line across the Apennines in Northern Italy. The 92nd comprised this regiment plus the 366th and the 370th Infantry Battalions, as well as the 597th, 598th, 599th, and 600th Artillery Battalions. On September 1st, the three battalions of the 370th Regiment, along with elements of the 1st Armored Division, crossed the Arno River and advanced north for two to three miles. By the early hours of September 2nd,

The soldiers of the 370th Infantry Regiment pitching mortars at German positions to "soften up" the defensive line.

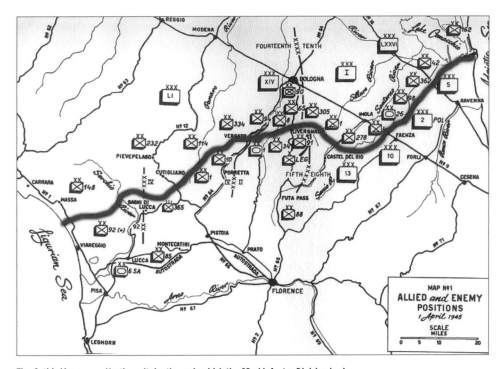

The Gothic Line across Northern Italy, through which the 92nd Infantry Division broke.

they had cleared minefields, worked on fords, and placed a treadway bridge across the Arno for the forthcoming armored infantry assault. The liaison pilots in this advance took greater risks with their lives than any other group of pilots. The aircraft were slow, barely reaching 100mph, and most cruised at between 65 and 70mph. The Piper Grasshopper had a Continental 65hp flat-four engine and two seats, one behind the other. Surprisingly few Grasshoppers were shot down, though quite a few suffered rifle-fire damage from the ground. It was a highly precarious occupation, especially as these pilots flew over the whole of the battle from just north of Naples up to the Gothic Line and beyond.

Continuing the advance, the 92nd broke through the Gothic Line at Giogio Pass on September 18th, moving forward to the Serchio Valley, where they consolidated the Allied position and ultimately securing Massa, Lama and La Spezia. The 92nd Division lost 2,848 men but reached all their objectives, capturing on the way an amazing 24,000 prisoners. They were awarded some 3,338 decorations between 12,000 men, and proved their value in one of the toughest battles of the Italian Campaign. The air observers in the aircraft of the 92nd Reconnaissance Squadron watched over their Division like mother hens, feeding back observation intelligence, photographing from the air, and occasionally picking up serious casualties. Like the 332nd Fighter Group,

A reconnaissance picture of the Giogio Pass.

they also earned a solid reputation for not abandoning their battalions.

With the end of World War II and the relocation of the 332nd Fighter Group to the United States, those heroes of the North African and Italian Campaigns who remained in the service of their country were about to receive a rude shock. There was a victory parade in New York City from which African American military personnel were excluded. Actions like this occurred throughout the whole country and Tuskegee Airmen found themselves shunned. In one incident a black soldier returning home from the war took the only vacant seat he saw on a bus and the driver ordered him to get off, because there were no seats for "coloreds". A large white soldier stood up and told the African American to sit down and proceeded to tell the driver that this man was just back from fighting for his country. He then said to all listeners, *"Anybody want to throw him off?"* There were no takers.

The 477th Bombardment Group was re-titled the 477th Composite Group after the war and became a combination of the Bombardment Group's B-25s and a number of newly issued (but not recently built) P-47 "Thunderbolt" fighters. The remaining members of the 332nd Fighter Group who decided to stay in the Service on their return to the US were drafted into this new Group. Their location was Freeman Field, in Indiana, having moved from Godman Field, near Fort Knox in Kentucky. The commander of the re-constituted 477th, as described elsewhere, was confirmed segregationist, Colonel Robert Selway.

After a period of unrest, Colonel Selway was relieved of his command and replaced by Colonel Benjamin O. Davis, who supervised the transfer of the unit from Freeman Field to Lockbourne Field in Ohio, where he faced an all-white civilian workforce that resented the influx of African Americans into the base. Many threatened some sort of action, including quitting their jobs, but Colonel Davis' skills of diplomacy, management and command enabled him to persuade them to rethink. He ultimately had one of the most contented civilian workforces on any base in the country.

In May 1947, the 477th was relieved of its B-25s and received more P-47s. Now re-numbered the 332nd Fighter Group again, it was soon to be allocated a group of Women's Army Corps soldiers (Tuskegee Women) as part of the support team. They were clerks, nurses, mechanics and parachute packers, and some were assigned to air traffic control. All were enthusiastic members of this somewhat diminished outfit, now virtually a squadron operating under the title of a group. While the women were mostly delighted to be at Lockbourne, the officers were becoming quite despondent because their group had shrunk as it became part of the newly formed United States Air Force and was retitled the 332nd Fighter Wing.

June 1948 was to see the Tuskegee Airmen's greatest battle campaign won in principle. This was the signing of President Harry Truman's Executive Order 9981, in which, segregation in the United States Armed Forces was to be outlawed. The process of implementation was slow, but African Americans in military uniform were now officially equal to anyone else. The mood in the 332nd was lifted to a new high, as progression opportunities appeared and some of those young men did see their careers advancing.

As the infant United States Air Force was getting to its feet, it began to organize ways of establishing and improving standards. One way of doing this was to hold competitions between groups and squadrons nationwide. The 332nd Fighter Wing's had a hands-down win of the "William Tell" Gunnery Competition in May 1949 at Las Vegas Air Force Base in Nevada (now Nellis Air Force Base). Three pilots — James Harvey, Harry Stewart and Alva Temple won the Team Prize in that event, the precursor of world-famous Exercise "Red Flag". Not only was it the first staging of this biggest annual gunnery exercise in the Air Force calendar, but an African American team also won it. How strange that the Air Force Almanac entered the word "unknown" against that inaugural win for 45 years, until a Tuskegee Airman, Colonel William Campbell, not only drew attention to the error, but also provided the complete data. Just a month after "William Tell", the 332nd Fighter Wing was disbanded. The 332nd Air Expeditionary Wing today is proud of its Tuskegee heritage in its operation as the premier combat wing in Iraq.

A 477th Bombardment Group B-25 being prepared for starting by a maintenance crew. The propellers of the B-25 needed to be rotated two or three full revolutions prior to starting so as to circulate oil in the engine.

When the 332nd Fighter Group was located at Lockbourne, Ohio, a group of Women's Army Corps African American soldiers were drafted into a wide variety of tasks – nurses, administrators, parachute packers, air traffic controllers and technicians.

CHAPTER ELEVEN

The Legacy Continues – Beyond the War and to Korea

With World War II ended and the 332nd Fighter Group re-assigned to the Pacific Theater of War, a decision had to be made at the Pentagon level concerning its future. Segregation still existed in the United States Armed Forces in mid-1945 and there would be some embarrassment in high quarters about this group of men who, regardless of skin color, were entitled to recognition. They were, after all, the most highly decorated group of men in the Mediterranean Theater of Operations in World War II and they had been held in the highest esteem by the many thousands of men they had escorted to and from targets – they were "The Red Angels".

You rest, using whatever you can find for comfort – like this Tuskegee Airman, using bombs as his cushions!

When these men returned to the United States, some had expected to be acknowledged for their service to their country, if not respected as the war heroes they were, just as men who had, like millions of others, served their country with dignity and honor. The city of New York was the first to officially snub them, when it organized a victory parade and, not only did not invite the Tuskegee Airmen, but it refused them participation. Suddenly, many men realized that in their homeland, nothing had changed, at least not for them. Like their predecessors, they learned that the battle at home against bigotry was greater than anything they had ever faced in war. However, change was on the horizon, a long way away, but there nonetheless.

Before that horizon was reached, the Tuskegee Airmen were subject to the gruesome, degrading racism many of them had already experienced in their early days of service, but thought they might have overcome by their efforts in the War. But there was no war now, and there was no obligation on anybody to be grateful for what they had done. The treatment meted out to these courageous men was on the instruction of the Commanding General, First Air Force, Major-General Frank Hunter. It perhaps comes as no surprise that Frank Hunter was born in Savannah, Georgia and carried with him all the traits of his birthright. In fairness to him, he was a fighter ace in World War I and an outstanding pilot, but an outstanding bigot too. He was the man who ordered that there would be no racial mixing under his command.

Contrast this with the ceremony at Cattolica in which Colonel Benjamin O. Davis was awarded the Silver Star for his outstanding leadership and courage on April 15, 1945, when he had led a strafing mission on German trains and railway installations. Davis was cheered by all the troops present, black and white. As soon as the ceremony was over, Colonel Davis and a group of 40 officers were boarded on to B-17s for return to the United States. They were to reconstruct the 477th Medium Bombardment Group into the 477th Composite Group (Colored), a collection of fighter and bomber aircraft ultimately located at Freeman Field in Indiana. The white commander of this group was Colonel Robert Selway, who took great pleasure in enforcing General Hunter's policy towards segregation.

Before the arrival of Colonel Davis and his entourage, Selway had instructed that the Officers' Club be split into two – Club Number One for black officers, "trainees" as they were called, and Club Number Two for white officers, or "instructors". The 477th officers were not impressed. On April 5, 1945, two young black officers entered Club Number Two and were immediately arrested by white military policemen. A third black officer, Roger Terry entered the Club and was treated the same way. The following day, in protest, 58 black officers entered the white Officers' Club and all were taken into custody. Four days after this debacle, Colonel Selway ordered all the officers of the 477th to sign a statement accepting his orders that the Officers' Clubs were to be segregated. It was not surprising that all 101 refused and were re-assigned to Godman Field, in Kentucky.

Selway had thought he had rid himself of the problem of black officers in his white Officers' Club, until he learned that every black officer at Freeman Field was planning to enter the club en masse. He closed the club and then had what he called the three "ringleaders" court-martialed. That did not work well for him either, for shortly after the court martial, Selway was relieved of his command and replaced by Colonel Benjamin O. Davis, Jr. on June 24th. A week later, on July 1st, Colonel Davis was appointed to command Godman Field itself, whereupon he appointed several of his old 332nd Fighter Group officers to senior positions at Godman.

Lieutenant Roger Terry.

Of the three officers court-martialed, only one, 2nd Lieutenant Roger "Bill" Terry, was convicted. This seems to have been an "example" conviction and, while it took fifty years, the US Government exonerated him, awarded a pardon and even reimbursed his $150 fine. Bill Terry went on to become National President of the Tuskegee Airmen Inc., a body he was actively involved in forming.

As the plan was to train the Tuskegee fighter and bomber crews for redeployment to the Pacific, the Mustangs that the 332nd Fighter Group had flown in Italy had now been replaced with Republic P-47N Thunderbolts, but before they could even reach the Pacific, leave alone become operational, the war in the Pacific was over. Japan had surrendered and so many of the pilots who had seen service in Italy were now returned to civilian life and the group shrank to just sixteen B-25s and twelve P-47s. Next came another relocation to Lockbourne Field, just outside Columbus, Ohio. Lockbourne Field became the only all-African American base in the country, and the men were far from welcome. The *Columbus Citizen* published an editorial that was simply insulting – saying that *"this is still a white man's country"* and questioning black men fighting for their country as so many had.

There was a group of white employees on the base at Lockbourne who were concerned about whether they would be allowed to keep their jobs. Colonel Davis called them into a meeting and assured them that all who wanted to remain employed would do so, as long as they performed their duties satisfactorily. Benjamin Davis complimented that group of employees as loyal stalwarts and reflected that they became staunch allies of the Tuskegee Airmen, acting as an excellent public relations link between the base and community at large. He then set about making his base *"the best in the Air Force"*. By April 1948, according to a report that said Lockbourne could be used as a model for all bases in the Air Force, it seemed he achieved his goal.

During May 1947, the B-25s of the 477th were withdrawn from Lockbourne and the remaining group reverted to the title of 332nd Fighter Group. A few months after that, it was re-titled the 332nd Fighter Wing and shrunk still further. Opportunities for advancement became more and more restricted, until President Harry S. Truman came to the rescue. He decreed in Executive Order 9981, issued on July 26, 1948, that all the Armed Forces of the United States would now be desegregated. His stated objective was that there would be

The Freeman Field Mutiny starts, when black officers are about to enter the Officers' club en masse.

The B-25s of the 477th Bombardment Group did a lot of flying training, but remained in the United States for the duration of the war. Finally, the unit was disbanded at Lockbourne and the 332nd Fighter Wing was established there.

sance exercise. One of their number, Harry Stewart, had an engine failure on the return trip from Shaw while flying at 20,000 feet. He dropped the aircraft to 10,000 feet, but realized that he was heading for mountains so, after flying 43 wartime missions Stewart decided the best part of valor was to bail out.

Ensuring first that the aircraft would not hit the community below, he trimmed the nose forward ready for his escape. Unfortunately, as he was set exit his aircraft, the slipstream grabbed him and threw him against the fin and broke his left leg in two places. As he floated down on the end of his parachute, with his left leg pouring with blood, he saw the

"equality and opportunity for all persons, without regard to race, color, religion or national origin". The greatest and major fight of the Tuskegee Airmen was now all-but over. They had achieved equal rights for African Americans throughout the Armed Forces.

Lieutenant Harry Stewart.

The 332nd Fighter Wing had no identifying "tag" to denote the color or identity of any of its manpower. It retained its connection to the Red Tails of wartime, by painting red the tops of the fin and rudders, as well as the rim of the engine cowling of their planes, and an individual identity letter was painted on each red fin top to mark it out from its neighboring squadrons. The group continued to train and on March 28, 1948, five P-47s were deployed to Shaw Air Force Base, near Sumter in South Carolina on a reconnais-

Lieutenant George Hardy at Lockbourne beside his P-47.

Thunderbolt crash into a hilltop and explode into flames. He must have lost consciousness, because the next thing he recalled was hearing a voice calling out, trying to locate him. A local man, Lafe Daniels took Stewart to his home, where his wife cleaned and patched his wounds before taking him to a clinic in Paintsville. When his leg had healed, Harry Stewart returned to active duty with the 332nd.

At the end of World War II, the Korean Peninsula was divided between the Western Allies and the Soviet Union, using the 38th Parallel North as the dividing line between the two territories. It had been agreed between the occupying powers that free elections would be held in 1948 to allow the people of Korea to select their own government. The peninsula had been occupied by the Japanese since 1910 but after the Japanese surrender, its former territories were being restored to individual entities. However, the Soviet Union had insisted on being involved in the post-war occupation of Korea as part of its strategy of securing territorial influence in the Far East. Their claim was based on the rather spurious concept that, being at war with the Japanese at the surrender, they were entitled to territorial influence – and territory. They had declared war on Japan on August 9th, the day of the second atom bombing there.

Tension was building over Korea, as the United Nations was pressing the Russians to agree to an election date. As time went on and 1949 came, the Soviet Union established a Communist government in Pyongyang. In some kind of retaliation, the United States urged the UN to recognize a government in Seoul for South Korea. This was seen by the Russians and the North Koreans as provocation and on June 25, 1950, North Korean troops crossed the 38th Parallel in force. The United States of America led a United Nations force to aid South Korea and repel the undeclared war from the North. United States troops began their counter-offensive on July 1st. The UN force drove the North Koreans back past the 38th Parallel and almost up to the Yalu River on the borders of the People's Republic of China. General Douglas MacArthur was the US and UN commander and it was what followed the drive to the Yalu River that ultimately lost him his job.

Fearing the risk of an invasion of the infant People's Republic of China, the Chinese leader, Mao Tse Tung, ordered his troops into Korea to support the Northern forces. The Chinese counter-attack pushed the United Nations forces back across the 38th Parallel and almost off the peninsula. It was at this point that General MacArthur proposed bombing the Chinese in Manchuria to drive them out of Korea. He sought permission from President Truman and when the President refused him, he took his suggestion to several congressmen and the press. As a result, President Truman relieved General MacArthur of his command immediately and replaced him with General Mark Clark. Throughout this war, the Soviet Union provided the weapons of war, including aircraft, and supplies and "advisers" to aid the North Korean and Chinese armies.

The 332nd Fighter Wing walked off with the Team Prize and this huge trophy at the first Nevada Gunnery Meet (now "Red Flag" at Nellis AFB), while Lt. Alva Temple took the Second Overall in the individual gunnery contest.

Whilst the key adversaries in the Korean Conflict were North Korea and the United Nations on behalf of South Korea, the key personalities were General Douglas MacArthur and Chairman Mao Tse Tung, leader of the People's Republic of China. Because MacArthur wanted to bomb China, he lost his command.

TOP SECRET

DECLASSIFIED
E.O. 11652 Sec. 3(E) and 5(D)
WHITE HOUSE PRESS RELEASE 4/11/51
By NARS Date 3.7.75

PROPOSED ORDER TO GENERAL MacARTHUR TO BE SIGNED BY THE PRESIDENT

I deeply regret that it becomes my duty as President and Commander in Chief of the United States military forces to replace you as Supreme Commander, Allied Powers; Commander in Chief, United Nations Command; Commander in Chief, Far East; and Commanding General, U. S. Army, Far East.

You will turn over your commands, effective at once, to Lt. Gen. Matthew B. Ridgway. You are authorized to have issued such orders as are necessary to complete desired travel to such place as you select.

My reasons for your replacement, which will be made public concurrently with the delivery to you of the foregoing order, will be communicated to you by Secretary Pace. and are contained in the next following message.

Harry Truman

This was the message from President Harry Truman to General Douglas MacArthur, relieving him of his UN and American Far Eastern commands. Lieutenant-General Matthew Ridgway took over temporary command, to be followed by General Mark Clark.

One young man worthy of mention here is Lieutenant George E. Hardy. At the age of nineteen, he had been assigned to the 99th Fighter Squadron in Italy and in the remaining month of the World War II flew 21 combat missions and before he was twenty, had been awarded two Air Medals. He was part of that group rotated back to the United States for re-training on the P-47N Thunderbolt prior to re-assignment to the Pacific in company with the 477th Bombardment Group. When the war with Japan came to an abrupt end in August 1945, these men and their machines were no longer needed, and George Hardy was released from the Service in November 1946.

As the war in Korea continued, Lieutenant Hardy returned to active duty, as a P-47 pilot with the 301st Fighter Squadron, 332nd Fighter Wing at Lockbourne in June 1948. That did not last long, however and in September that same year, he was assigned as a student to the Airborne Electronics Maintenance Officers School at Keesler AFB, Mississippi, graduating in August 1949. In September he was transferred to the 28th Bomb Squadron, 19th Bomb Group (B-29 aircraft), on Guam, as a Maintenance Officer.

Relocating from Guam, the 19th Bombardment Group operated from Okinawa, flying bombing missions over Korea. Captain Hardy, the youngest Tuskegee pilot, flew 45 combat missions over Korea as a member of that Group. From 1951 through 1962 he served in various Armament & Electronics Maintenance Squadrons in the Strategic Air Command and in Japan as Maintenance Officer and as a Squadron Commander. He received his Command Pilot Rating in 1959.

Lieutenant George Hardy, who joined the Tuskegee Airmen at the age of 19.

In June 1950, there were almost 100,000 African Americans

on active duty in the United States Armed Forces, equaling about 8 percent of the nation's total military manpower. In the Army, 9.7 percent of active duty service members were black, including 72,000 enlisted men and approximately 1,200 officers. In the Air Force, 4.4 percent of active duty personnel were black, including 21,000 enlisted men and 300 officers. About 6,000 African Americans, around three percent of the total personnel, served in the Navy and Marine Corps. By the end of the Korean War, more than 600,000 African Americans had served in the Armed Forces.

Just a month after the start of the war, the 24th US Infantry Division, still an all-black unit in the process of being desegregated, was facing the Chinese forces as they were repelling the UN forces from the Northern territory. In the defense of the UN position was Company M of the 24th. Amongst the Company was 23-year-old Private First Class William

H. Thompson at a machine gun post. He had been hit by Chinese fire, but stayed at his post to cover his comrades' escape, before trying to leave himself. He had been badly wounded and by the time he was hauled out of his machine gun post, he had lost a lot of blood. Two weeks after that incident, William Thompson died from his wounds, just days after his 23rd birthday. William Henry Thompson became the first recipient, and the first African American recipient, of the Medal of Honor in that war for his outstanding courage. His citation read:

"Pfc. Thompson distinguished himself by conspicuous gallantry and intrepidity above and beyond the call of duty in action against the enemy. While his platoon was reorganizing under cover of darkness, enemy forces in overwhelming strength launched a surprise attack on the unit. Pfc. Thompson set up his machine gun in the path of the onslaught and swept the enemy with withering fire, pinning them down momentarily, thus permitting the remainder of his platoon to withdraw to a more tenable position. Although hit repeatedly by grenade fragments and small-arms fire, he resisted all efforts of his comrades to induce him to withdraw, steadfastly remained at his machine gun and continued to deliver deadly, accurate fire until mortally wounded by an enemy grenade. Pfc. Thompson's dauntless courage and gallant self-sacrifice reflect the highest credit on himself and uphold the esteemed traditions of military service."

African American bomber crews of the 17th Bombardment Wing now flew B-26s in Korea, but the other B-26, the Douglas "Invader" (formerly A-26). Jimmy Doolittle's old Bomb Group now had African American pilots, bombardiers and gunners flying night intruder missions.

The air war over Korea had

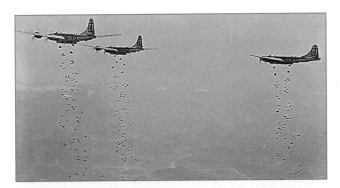

19th Bombardment Wing B-29s discharge their payloads of 20,000 pounds of bombs each on North Korean targets.

little to do with the North or South Koreans. It was more a battle of technology between the Soviet Union and the United States and a battle in the air between the United States (supported primarily by Australia, Great Britain and France), and the Chinese. Few Koreans were involved in the air war at all. The organization of the air action took a little time to pull together, because of the incompatibility of aircraft types and the complication of organizations. For example, the Australians had the British Gloster Meteor twinjet fighter in Korea, which quickly showed itself no match for the Russian-built MiG-15. But the Meteor made a good ground-attack aircraft because it was tough, so it was placed in action alongside the US Marine Corps' Corsairs, doing the same job. But there were British pilots attached to the Australian unit, Number 77 Squadron, and their participation had to be cleared with top brass.

The direct British contribution to the air war came from the Royal Navy, which had the aircraft carriers HMS "Triumph" and HMS "Unicorn" operating in Korean waters. The aircraft they carried were again far from air-to-air combat equipment. The Supermarine "Seafires" were used in ground attack work, while the Fairey "Fireflies" were used for anti-shipping activities. RAF pilots were supporting the Royal Australian Air Force as pilots with 77 Squadron and there was a small number of RAF pilots flying on secondment to the USAF, particularly in the squadrons of the 51st Fighter Interceptor Wing. As with the Royal Navy "Seafires", the US

Navy was fielding Chance Vought F4U "Corsairs" from, for example, the USS "Valley Forge" and the USS "Leyte".

Ensign Jesse Leroy Brown was mentioned in an earlier chapter, but since he was a participant in the Korean War and lost his life in that conflict, it is fitting to recall him again. Born in Hattiesburg, Mississippi, the son of a sharecropper, the ambition to fly and join the Navy as an aviator was about as possible as making a million dollars by the age of twenty. But somehow, young Leroy did it. He won scholarships and finally was able to enroll in Ohio State University, where only one percent of the students were African American. He worked hard on the assumption that nobody would ever give him a second chance and ultimately, he enlisted in the US Naval Reserve.

By pure chance, the man who became Jesse Brown's best friend in the Navy was graduating from the Naval Academy at Annapolis in Maryland as Jesse joined the Reserve. Both were bent on becoming flyers. That friend was Tom Hudner, who went on to flight school after serving a tour aboard the USS "Helena". Tom was the son of a wealthy Irish businessman in Boston, Massachusetts, so had none of the prejudices aimed at him that Jesse Brown experienced. For example,

HMS "Triumph" sails into Korean waters to provide British air to ground support for the UN forces and antishipping support for seaborne forces. "Triumph" was joined by "Unicorn" in the same role. Interestingly, both "Triumph" and "Unicorn" carried Afro-Caribbean crew members in mixed crews.

an ROTC instructor at Ohio State once told Jesse, *"No nigger will ever sit his ass in a Navy cockpit"*. But this courageous and determined young man was the only black American among the 600 cadets when at last he entered flight school in Pensacola, Florida, and he graduated.

Tom made Flight School a year later than Jesse. Both were assigned to the USS "Leyte" when the Korean conflict began and became instant friends. Living with Jesse Brown and flying with him from the flight deck of the "Leyte", Tom Hudner

Best friends Ensign Jesse Brown and Lieutenant (JG) Tom Hudner, playing backgammon in the ready room of USS "Leyte" before a mission.

discovered a great deal about Jesse's struggle to overcome racial prejudice and follow his dreams. The more he learned about this young African American, the more his admiration for him grew, especially as he discovered that Jesse was a father. Back home, awaiting his return was his wife, Daisy and his year-old daughter, Pamela. Jesse wrote to them almost daily, but he was never to see them again.

On December 4, 1950, US Marines and the US 7th Infantry Division up in eastern North Korea found themselves surrounded and cut off by the advancing Chinese in an area known as the Chosin Reservoir. Ensign Brown's section

was flying reconnaissance around that reservoir area looking for "targets of opportunity" to destroy. The Marines and soldiers fighting in the Chosin Reservoir were greatly outnumbered and their air superiority was the one advantage they had against the huge Chinese force. Corsairs from VF-32 swooped down low and fast and strafed every enemy position they could find in support of the soldiers and Marines on the ground. It was after one of these strafings that Ensign Brown called on his radio to say that his plane was losing oil pressure after a hit from an enemy gun.

The area around the Chosin Reservoir was mountainous and craggy, so Brown was in for a hard landing and his aircraft's condition made it worse. He crash-landed on the snowy slopes of a steep mountain at about 5,300 feet elevation. His plane broke apart on impact and his fellow Corsair pilots initially thought he had died in the crash. But, he opened the cockpit canopy and waved through the gap. Tom Hudner was delighted that his friend had survived the hard landing and he crash landed his own aircraft alongside Brown, in the hope that he could haul him out of the cockpit and get a rescue helicopter to pick them both up. It turned out not to be so simple.

Before the snows came, the Chinese didn't have it all their own way, as this picture shows. Pfc. Julius Van Den Stock from Company A of the 32nd Regimental Combat Team, 7th Infantry Division, rests in a Chinese bunker, armed with a Russian type Browning automatic rifle, along the slope of Hill 902 north of Ip-Tong.

Jesse Brown was seriously injured and trapped in his cockpit and Tom Hudner could not release him. He put out a fire in Brown's Corsair and called for a rescue helicopter from his own radio. The helicopter crew was unable to extract Brown and all Hudner could do was to keep his friend as comfortable and warm as he could. Jesse Brown died from his injuries and exposure, but in the company of his friend.

After the event, Tom Hudner concluded that he would almost certainly be court-martialed, or at least reprimanded, and his Naval career ended for crashing a perfectly sound Corsair in a failed attempt to save one man, a black man at that. However, Lieutenant Hudner's commander cited him for the nation's highest combat award, the Medal of Honor, and Ensign Jesse Brown was awarded the second highest honor for combat pilots, the Distinguished Flying Cross. Tom Hudner received his Medal of Honor on April 13, 1951 from President Harry Truman. Among the group of mostly white people who had congregated at the White House to witness the event was a lone young, African American woman, Daisy Brown. She stood next to Lieutenant Hudner as he was awarded his medal and he relayed the message that her husband Jesse Brown asked him to give her, that he loved her *(see photo on page 75)*.

In September 1949, Captain Daniel "Chappie" James, a Tuskegee airman who was a flying instructor during World War II at Tuskegee Army Airfield, was assigned to the Philippines as a flight leader for the 12th Fighter-Bomber Squadron in the 18th Fighter Wing, based at Clark Field. In late July, the 18th's group headquarters, together with two of its squadrons (the 12th and 67th Fighter Bomber Squadrons) deployed with Lockheed F-80 "Shooting Stars" to Taegu AB in South Korea.

Between July 28th and August 3rd, the 18th Group operated under the direct command on the 5th Air Force, but was then transferred to the 6002nd Fighter Wing. The F-80s were now exchanged for an aircraft certainly familiar to "Chappie" James – the P-51 (now F-51 under the Air Force's new type designations) "Mustang". The role was close air support, with such targets as tanks and armored vehicles, railway locomotives and trucks, artillery and anti-aircraft guns,

fuel and ammunition dumps, warehouses and factories, and troop concentrations – in fact, anything on the ground that belonged to the enemy.

During August, because of the massive advance of the counter-attack launched by the Chinese and insufficient aircraft parking at Taegu the 18th Fighter Wing was sent temporarily to Japan, but returned to Korea in September to support the UN counter-offensive. The front line was advancing rapidly and with it "Chappie" James and his squadron relocated, first to Pusan, then to Airstrip K-24 close to Pyongyang, the North Korean capital. In mid-November, Number 2 Squadron of the South African Air Force joined the 18th.

An early batch of F-80s located at Langley AFB in 1949. The aircraft in the foreground have their gun ports masked over, whilst some in the middle and background are not yet marked up in squadron colors, suggesting they are just entering service. The 18th Fighter Bomber Wing took its F-80s to Taegu in Korea.

Relocating in November 1950 to Chinhae, the 18th continued its ground support role until January 1951, when it earned for itself a Distinguished Unit Citation, having destroyed approximately 2,400 enemy vehicles and severely damaging five hundred or so more. From early 1951 until January 1953, the 18th moved from base to base in South Korea, such was the speed of change in the front line. It earned its second Distinguished Unit Citation for action

F-51 Mustangs of the 18th Fighter Bomber Wing arming up with rockets for another ground support mission from Taegu.

2nd, near the village of Chi-po-Ri, northeast of Seoul, his platoon faced heavy resistance in their attempt to take Hill 543. His platoon commander was wounded in the advance, so Cornelius took command of the unit and regrouped his men to lead a fresh assault against the hill. Wounded by a grenade, he refused medical attention, so as to continue to lead the charge. Sergeant Charlton died from his wounds, aged only twenty-one. For his actions during the battle, he was awarded the Medal of Honor.

Cornelius Charlton's Medal of Honor citation read:

between April 22 and July 8, 1951, when it flew 6,500 combat sorties while operating from rough earth and damaged runways to counter the enemy's 1951 spring offensive. Daniel "Chappie" James returned to the United States in July. His new assignment took him to Otis Air Force Base, Massachusetts, as an all-weather jet fighter pilot with the 58th Fighter-Interceptor Squadron.

Cornelius Charlton was another fighter. He was born in West Virginia to Van and Clara Charlton. In 1944, his family moved to the Bronx in New York City, and in 1946, Cornelius enlisted in the US Army. As an African American, Cornelius was entering a still-segregated army, but as a career soldier, he served with the US occupation troops in Germany after World War II and was transferred from there to Korea, assigned to an engineering group. He requested a transfer to an infantry unit and was subsequently placed in Company C of the 24th Infantry Regiment of the 25th Infantry Division.

In May, 1951, Charlton's unit pushed northwards and on June

Sgt. Charlton, a member of Company C, distinguished himself by conspicuous gallantry and intrepidity above and beyond the call of duty in action against the enemy. His platoon was attacking heavily defended hostile positions on commanding ground when the leader was wounded and evacuated. Sgt. Charlton assumed command, rallied the men, and spearheaded the assault against the hill. Personally eliminating two hostile positions and killing six of the enemy with his rifle fire and grenades, he continued up the slope until the unit suffered heavy casualties and became pinned down. Regrouping the men he led them

Sergeant Cornelius Charlton.

forward only to be again hurled back by a shower of grenades. Despite a severe chest wound, Sgt. Charlton refused medical attention and led a third daring charge, which carried to the crest of the ridge. Observing that the remaining emplacement that had retarded the advance was situated on the reverse slope, he charged it alone, was again hit by a grenade but raked the position with a devastating fire that eliminated it and routed the defenders. The wounds received during his daring exploits resulted in his death but his indomitable courage, superb leadership, and gallant self-sacrifice reflect the highest credit upon himself the infantry, and the military service.

In the last two weeks of this conflict, the US Air Force's 51st Fighter Interceptor Wing was protecting US airlifts of men and equipment from north of the 38th Parallel, because the Chinese were attacking any US or Allied aircraft on the north side of the border. On one morning late in July, a British pilot was flying with the 39th Fighter Interceptor Squadron and had a young USAF 2nd Lieutenant as his wingman. The British pilot, Flight Lieutenant John Granville-White, put his wingman in lead position to give him some experience and they were jumped by a pair of MiG-15s. The wingman couldn't shake the MiG off his tail, even when he went low, but Granville-White put his F-86 into a barrel roll to rise and get behind the MiG. He saw the aircraft in his gunsight when he was inverted and opened fire. The MiG went down in flames and its pilot ejected. Although Granville-White did not see the plane go down, he scored a confirmed and a probable "kill" that day.

For his courage and tenacity, Flight Lieutenant John Granville-White was awarded the United States Distinguished Flying Cross to add to his Air Medal. This was one of only fourteen US DFCs awarded to foreign pilots. An honor indeed – and the citation was signed off by the Commander of the 51st Fighter Interceptor Wing, Tuskegee Airmen Founder Member, Colonel Benjamin O. Davis.

Colonel Benjamin O. Davis, founding commander of the Tuskegee Airmen 99th Fighter Squadron and 332nd Fighter Group, leading a flight of F-86 Sabres over Korean skies in 1953.

CHAPTER TWELVE

New Tensions – Vietnam and African Americans

As the World began to think that peace might at last return and allow recovery from losses occasioned by the tragedy of war, the crucible of America's next conflict was bubbling. The place was a hitherto unknown location in what was still being described as French Indo-China, but is now called Vietnam. That unknown place was named Dien-Bien-Phu and the event that occurred in this obscure location was the French Foreign Legion's last stand against what was then known as the Viet Minh.

French paratroops dug in for the final fight for Dien Bien Phu. The battle lasted 55 days up to the French surrender.

The Battle of Dien Bien Phu was the climax of a series of political and military misjudgments made by the French after World War II. In the post-war re-distribution of territories, the French re-possessed Indo-China from the Japanese, as it had been a French territory since 1887. Like so many of the old Colonial powers, including Britain, France expected things to revert to how they were before the war. But they had reckoned without the rise of the People's Republic of China and the influence of Mao Tse Tung.

The background to Dien Bien Phu has its roots in an earlier confrontation with the Viet-Minh, at a place called Na San. The French principle was to created forward posts in a form called "the hedgehog concept". This was the establishment of a remote "air-land-base", where the forward post, a for-

tified encampment, would be supplied exclusively by air, since surface transportation was painfully slow and roads were often non-existent. At Na San, the French forces had it right, in that they had high ground, so the Viet Minh had to fight and travel uphill from any direction. The French had far superior firepower and, to aid the French victory at Na San, the Viet Minh commander, General Giap, simply used poor strategy.

The wisdom of the decision to follow the same strategy at Dien Bien Phu was questioned by several field officers, not least because the lie of the land was different, with Dien Bien Phu being surrounded by hills. This location was also farther away from French base camps and so would be more difficult to keep supplied. Being supplied by air meant that the senior staff officers would expect no problems, because who could take the aircraft out of the sky? This was the thinking of French Major-General René Cogny, who selected Dien Bien Phu as the next "hedgehog" garrison.

The objective of establishing the Dien Bien Phu garrison, deep in North West Indo-China was to cut off the supply route into and from Laos, and to defeat the Viet Minh, by drawing them into an open battle and destroying their capability to fight. The French had a rude awakening. First, the Viet Minh military leader, General Vo Nguyen Giap, unbe-

Desperately trying to hang on to Dien Bien Phu until air cover can relieve the pressure by air attacks on Viet Minh positions, the French paratroops put up a spirited fight.

After a fifty-five day battle, the French are simply outnumbered and out-gunned at Dien Bien Phu, so are forced to surrender There were black soldiers among this number.

time, though there was more American activity surrounding this battle than people realized at the time. There had even been discussion about organizing a bombing raid on Viet Minh positions, using sixty Boeing B-29 and possibly up to three nuclear weapons. Luckily, that did not happen, for the tinder box it would have lit would have set the scene for a major, even global, conflict, and Eisenhower knew it. But American air support was provided, in the form of twelve Fairchild C-119 transports and two squadrons of Douglas B-26 Invaders.

Subsequently, 37 American transport pilots flew 682 sorties over Dien Bien Phu in order to keep the French soldiers on the ground. Two American pilots were killed in the action. Ironic, perhaps that the French government waited so long, but in 2005, the seven surviving pilots of the original thirty-seven were awarded the Legion d'Honneur for their part in keeping the French going for as long as they could. They commented that dropping supplies at 2,000 feet presented risks of material dropping into the hands of the Viet Minh, but at 8,000 feet, it became a serious gamble that much would reach the intended recipients.

known to the French, had acquired heavy artillery and anti-aircraft guns, and the training to use them effectively. Even more devastating for the French was that, somehow, the Viet Minh had managed to position these weapons in strategi-cally strong sites above the French garrison in the highlands around Dien Bien Phu.

French intelligence was obviously lacking, because sud-denly, without realizing how it could have happened, the French were surrounded and quickly, the Viet Minh mounted an effective siege. They were able to bombard the French positions with ease and whilst vicious fighting took place on the ground, in which the Viet Minh troops were repeatedly thrown back, ultimately, the situation became progressively worse for the French. They had airdrops of supplies almost constantly, but the Viet Minh anti-aircraft guns were begin-ning to pick off the French transport aircraft. This meant that the aircraft had to drop supplies from higher altitudes, and they were losing more supplies to the enemy.

At this time, the United States, under the Mutual Defense As-sistance Act, provided the French with material assistance, including aircraft, pilots, weapons and mechanics. Presi-dent Eisenhower ruled out direct US involvement at that

The US government provided Fairchild C-119s in French markings, together with crews, to airlift paratroops and supplies to the beleaguered French at Dien Bien Phu.

As race riots took place in the United States, the Navy reviewed and modified its policy towards African American recruitment and accepted recruits into a wide range of specialist fields. On the left, a sailor is manning a .30 caliber machine gun on a utility boat cruising in the Rung Sat Special Zone. On the right, Commissaryman First Class Joshua Paige is holding "sick call" for children of Tam Toa village. This was a clear sign that the Navy was widening the scope of skills it made available to African American recruits.

Between 1952 and 1953, the Viet Minh took control of the key routes through Laos and as the artillery bombardments continued on Dien Bien Phu, the air drops to the French garrison were diminishing and ultimately, the Viet Minh over-ran the last bastion of French grip on the country. The result was that most of the garrison surrendered, though a few managed to escape and take the news of their defeat to Laos. This was the end of the French colony of Indo-China. The 1954 Geneva Accord established an agreement in which the French government agreed to withdraw all its troops as the two territories of what was now Vietnam were partitioned into Communist North and free Republican South. That lasted until 1959.

The Geneva Conference of 1954 began on May 8th, the day following the surrender of the Dien Bien Phu garrison. The North Vietnamese leader Ho Chi Minh represented the Democratic Republic of Vietnam, while the south of the country was administered by the French-supported State of Vietnam. The outcome of the agreement made in Geneva was that open democratic elections would take place across all of Vietnam, reuniting the country by the end of 1956. At that time, the French Armed Forces were withdrawn, but because no elections had taken place by the designated time, and because the United States had a stated policy of containing communism in the Far East. The South Vietnamese government, however, did not support the Geneva Accord

and accused the North of terrorizing people.

The Korean War influenced American thinking of the time and the indeterminate ending of that conflict in August 1953 left the US feeling vulnerable and wary. As the French withdrew, there was a vacuum in the view of the US government that simply had to be filled, so "advisers" were placed in Vietnam – less than a thousand to begin with, but by 1963, that number had increased enormously and by 1965, the United States was in open conflict with the North Vietnamese, with large numbers of US troops being located in Vietnam in a full-scale war.

As the United States involvement in Vietnam began in the 1950s with the provision of military advisers, so the conflict unfolded against the domestic scene of the civil rights movement. From the beginning, the use of African American troops brought charges of racism. And yet, this was the first military conflict in which the African American soldier was not segregated from other troops. Fully integrated regiments in the Army were now the norm, whereas Army regiments had still been segregated to the end of the Korean conflict. The Air Force, Navy and Marine Corps had all integrated much earlier.

Civil rights leaders and other critics, including the great champion of African American rights, Dr. Martin Luther King, Jr., described the Vietnam conflict as racist – it was *"a*

African American infantrymen rescuing a white soldier who clearly could not walk.

white man's war but a black man's fight," said Dr. King. He maintained that black youths represented a disproportionate share of early draftees and that African Americans faced a much greater chance of seeing combat. He was almost certainly right. But the other issue here was that recruitment of African American youths was stepped up significantly by the Armed Forces. More black youths were recruited and volunteered during this war than ever before.

"Project 100,000" was a program launched in 1966 by the Defense Secretary, Robert McNamara. It was part of President Johnson's "Great Society" and its intention was to improve opportunities for underprivileged youths from poverty-stricken urban areas by offering more lenient military entrance requirements. It did not do a lot of good, though over 350,000 men enlisted during the remainder of the Vietnam War, for which purpose it was deliberately created. It failed because, whilst it did improve recruitment figures, it did not fulfill its promise of giving training that would better prepare the recruits for a civilian career, nor did it give them enhanced progression in a military career. Forty-one percent of the recruits in this scheme were African American and large numbers of them drew combat assignments.

A disproportionate number of combat troops came from the African Americans community, though a high percentage of them had voluntarily enlisted. And even though they made up less than ten percent of the total number of American men under arms at that time, and about 13 percent of the total US population between 1961 and 1966, this group accounted for almost 20 percent of the combat-related deaths in Vietnam. In 1965 alone almost a quarter of the total number killed in action were African Americans. By 1968, increased recruitment meant that, whilst recruitment represented about 12 percent of total strengths of the Army and Marine Corps, it was African Americans who contributed half the number of front-line combat troops. So small wonder the activists were at work on the home front.

There were major riots in places like the Watts district of Los Angeles and in New York's Harlem, which did the reputation of the Armed Forces considerable harm. Then, the nationwide reaction to the 1968 assassination of Martin Luther King brought huge turmoil in the Armed Forces. Inter-racial discord was not generally an issue by this time among combat units because of the shared risk and responsibility. But in the rear areas and on domestic installations, the situation turned ugly. On the US Naval base at Cam Ranh Bay in Vietnam, it seems white sailors dressed in Ku Klux Klan-type outfits burned crosses and raised the Confederate flag. Af-

Not all race demonstrations were violent. For example, this peaceful march took place in Newark, New Jersey, in 1965.

The AC-119K Gunship was what Lieutenant-Colonel George Hardy flew in Vietnam. This picture is of a training aircraft at Lockbourne AFB – a place familiar to George Hardy from his time there in the 1940s, when he flew P-47 "Thunderbolts". He experienced race issues back in those days, when the Air Force was just being desegregated.

AC-119K Gunship.

Despite the unrest, there was a positive side to this too. There were men who had served their country in previous conflicts who were now ready to serve again and there were others who had not yet fought in combat who readily placed themselves in harm's way. Among these were George Hardy, the youngest Tuskegee Airman to fly in World War II and a veteran of the Korean conflict. In 1964, after earning a Master's Degree in Systems Engineering from the Air Force Institute of Technology, George was assigned to the Electronics Systems Division at Hanscom AFB, Massachusetts. Then, in August 1966 he was assigned as Chief of Engineering and Program Manager for Development and Installation for the 490L Overseas AUTOVON Communications System, the Department of Defense's first worldwide direct-dial telephone system. The initial sites in Europe, Panama and in the Pacific were successfully handed over in 1969.

rican American prisoners in the stockade at Long Binh in Vietnam, many jailed for violent crimes, rioted there. One white soldier died and several others were wounded during that event that ran for several weeks. The Marine Corps base at Camp Lejeune and the Army's Fort Benning were also among the important domestic military installations to witness serious racial problems.

In 1970 Major George Hardy was assigned to the 18th Special Operations Squadron in Vietnam as a pilot in AC-119K Gunships. He also served as the Operating Location Commander at Udorn Air Base in Thailand, as well as at Da Nang Air Base in Vietnam and flew 70 combat missions. He returned from Vietnam in April 1971 and retired in November 1971 with the rank of Lieutenant-Colonel. George Hardy's decorations include the Distinguished Flying Cross, the Air Medal with a staggering eleven Oak Leaf Clusters, and the Commendation Medal with one Oak Leaf Cluster.

A man well known to the world in his later years as a military commander was Colin Luther Powell, who was born in Harlem in 1937. His parents were Jamaican immigrants who had come to the United States to make a better life and who, as a consequence, stressed the importance of education and personal achievement to their son. Colin Powell grew up in the South Bronx, where he graduated from high school with no knowledge of what he might want to do in life. He entered the City College of New York to study geology and there, it seems, he discovered his calling on joining the Reserve Officers Training Corps (ROTC). He became commander of his unit's precision drill team and graduated in 1958 at the top of his ROTC class, with the rank of cadet colonel, the highest rank in the corps. He went on to transfer to the regular Army and was commissioned a 2nd Lieutenant.

Colin Powell became one of the 16,000 military advisors sent to South Vietnam by President Kennedy in 1962. In 1963, Lieutenant Powell was wounded by a punji-stick booby trap while patrolling the Vietnamese border with Laos. For that injury, he received the Purple Heart, and later in the same year he was awarded the Bronze Star. Captain Powell served a second tour of duty in Vietnam in 1968-69. During this second tour he was injured in a helicopter crash. Despite his own injuries, he managed to res-

Captain Colin Powell in Vietnam.

cue his comrades from the burning helicopter and was awarded the Air Medal and the Soldier's Medal. After Vietnam, Colin Powell returned to a post in Washington. You will read more of General Colin Powell later.

Another Tuskegee aviator who had already served his country in two major conflicts was Daniel "Chappie" James. An instructor in World War II, he managed to pull combat duty (in his case, because he wanted to) in Korea with the 12th Fighter Bomber Squadron and next he went to Vietnam. He was first appointed deputy com-

Colonel Daniel "Chappie" James in action again – a far cry from flying P-80 "Shooting Stars" in Korea. He stands in front of his F-4 "Phantom" in Vietnam.

Lieutenant Guion Bluford flew F4s with this unit, the 557th Tactical Fighter Squadron, in Vietnam.

mander for operations with the 8th Tactical Fighter Wing at Ubon Royal Thai Air Force Base, Thailand in December 1966. Then, he was promoted wing vice commander in June 1967. Colonel James flew 78 combat missions into North Vietnam, many in the Hanoi/Haiphong area, and led a flight into what was known as the Bolo Mig sweep, in which seven Chinese Mig 21s were destroyed, the highest total kill of any mission during the Vietnam War. His Wing Commander was Colonel Robin Olds, probably one of America's greatest fighter pilots and commanders. He frequently flew with "Chappie" James and two became close friends. As a flying duo in Vietnam, they carried the tag: "Blackman and Robin".

A man who was later to find a place in the United States Space Program, and who also flew in Vietnam was Colonel Guion Bluford. He graduated from Penn State University in 1964 as a distinguished Air Force ROTC graduate. Bluford attended pilot training at Williams Air Force Base, Arizona, and received his pilot wings in January 1966. He then went to F-4C combat crew training in Arizona and Florida and was assigned, as a

1st Lieutenant, to the 557th Tactical Fighter Squadron operating out of Cam Ranh Bay in Vietnam. He flew 144 combat missions, 65 of which were over North Vietnam.

Twenty African Americans were awarded the Medal of Honor for their courage in the field. The Medal of Honor list of African American recipients is as varied as any other part of the American community. Men from all walks of life – in a wide range of ranks – from all branches of the United States Armed Forces. Men who gave their lives for their country without thought of self or survival. Men of Courage – Men of Honor. Their acts of valor will now be described.

One of the first, in 1965, was Army Specialist Five Lawrence Joel, who was nominated for what President Johnson described as "a special kind of courage – the unarmed heroism of compassion and service to others". Lawrence Joel was a medical orderly who saved the lives of a number of US troops under fire, defying orders not to go through Viet Cong gunfire tending to soldiers' wounds, having been shot twice himself.

In October 1965, Private First Class Milton L. Olive III was serving with Company B, 2nd Battalion (Airborne), 503rd Infantry, 173rd Airborne Brigade. His platoon was moving through the jungle to find Viet Cong operating in the area. Although the platoon was subjected to a heavy volume of enemy gunfire and pinned down temporarily, it retaliated by assaulting the Viet Cong positions, causing the enemy to flee. As the platoon pursued the insurgents, Pfc. Olive and four other soldiers were moving through the jungle together when a grenade was thrown into their midst. Pfc. Olive saw the grenade, and saved the lives of his fellow soldiers at the sacrifice of his own by grabbing the grenade in his hand and falling on it to absorb the blast with his body. Through his bravery, unhesitating actions, and complete disregard for his safety, he prevented additional loss of life or injury to the members of his platoon.

Pfc. Milton Olive III.

On June 30, 1966, Sergeant Donald Russell Long of Troop C, 1st Squadron, 4th Cavalry, 1st Infantry Division, was taking part in a reconnaissance mission with Troops B and C of his squadron. They were moving along a road and were suddenly attacked by a Viet Cong regiment, supported by mortars, recoilless rifles and machine guns, from concealed positions beside the road. Sergeant Long abandoned the relative safety of his armored personnel carrier and braved a withering hail of enemy fire to carry wounded men to evacuation helicopters. As the platoon fought its way forward to resupply advanced elements, Sergeant Long repeatedly exposed himself to enemy fire at point blank range to provide the needed supplies. While assaulting the Viet Cong position, Sergeant Long inspired his comrades by fearlessly standing unprotected to repel the enemy with rifle fire and grenades as they attempted to mount his carrier. When the enemy threatened

Sergeant Donald Russell Long.

to overrun a disabled carrier nearby, Sergeant Long again disregarded his own safety to help the severely wounded crew to safety. As he was handing arms to the less seriously wounded and reorganizing them to press the attack, an enemy grenade was hurled onto the carrier deck. Immediately recognizing the imminent danger, he instinctively shouted a warning to the crew and pushed to safety one man who had not heard his warning over the roar of battle. Realizing that these actions would not fully protect the exposed crewmen from the deadly explosion, he threw himself over the grenade to absorb the blast and thereby saved the lives of eight of his comrades at the expense of his own life.

Private First Class James Anderson, Jr. was a Marine with the 2nd Platoon, Company F, 2nd Battalion, 3rd Marine Division. In February 1967 Company F was advancing in dense jungle northwest of Cam Lo in an effort to extract a heavily besieged reconnaissance patrol. Pfc. Anderson's platoon was the lead element and had advanced only about 200 meters when they were brought under extremely intense enemy small arms and automatic weapons fire. The platoon reacted swiftly, getting on line as best they could in the thick terrain, and began returning fire. Pfc. Anderson found himself tightly bunched together with the other members of the platoon only 20 meters from the enemy positions. As the fire fight continued several of the men were wounded by the deadly enemy as-

Pfc. James Anderson.

sault. Suddenly, an enemy grenade landed in the midst of the Marines and rolled alongside Pfc. Anderson's head. Unhesitatingly and with complete disregard for his personal safety, he reached out, grasped the grenade, pulled it to his chest and curled around it as it went off. Although several Marines received shrapnel, his body took the major force of the explosion. In this heroic act, Pfc. Anderson saved his comrades from serious injury and possible death. Pfc. Anderson was the first African American US Marine to be awarded the Medal of Honor.

Sergeant First Class Eugene Ashley, Jr. was a member of Company C, in the 5th Special Forces Group (Airborne), of the 1st Special Forces. On February 6 and 7, 1968, while serving with Detachment A-101, Company C., Sfc. Ashley was the senior Special Forces Advisor of a hastily organized assault

force whose mission was to rescue entrapped US Special Forces advisors at Camp Lang Vei. During the initial attack on the camp by North Vietnamese forces, Sfc. Ashley supported the camp with high explosive and illumination mortar rounds. When communications were lost with the main camp, he assumed the additional responsibility of directing air strikes and artillery support. Sfc. Ashley organized and

Sfc. Eugene Ashley.

equipped a small assault force composed of local friendly personnel. During the ensuing battle, Sfc. Ashley led a total of five vigorous assaults against the enemy, continuously exposing himself to a voluminous hail of enemy grenades, machine gun and automatic weapons fire. Throughout these assaults, he was plagued by numerous booby-trapped satchel charges in all bunkers on his avenue of approach. During his fifth and final assault, he adjusted air strikes nearly on top of his assault element, forcing the enemy to withdraw and resulting in friendly control of the summit of the hill. While exposing himself to intense enemy fire, he was seriously

wounded by machine gun fire but continued his mission without regard for his personal safety. After the fifth assault he lost consciousness and was carried from the summit by his comrades only to suffer a fatal wound when an enemy artillery round landed in the area. Sfc. Ashley displayed extraordinary heroism in risking his life in an attempt to save the lives of his entrapped comrades and commanding officer. His total disregard for his personal safety while exposed to enemy observation and automatic weapons fire was an inspiration to all men committed to the assault. The resolute valor with which he led five gallant charges placed critical diversionary pressure on the attacking enemy and his valiant efforts carved a channel in the overpowering enemy forces and weapons positions through which the survivors of Camp Lang Vei eventually escaped to freedom.

Private First Class Oscar P. Austin was serving with Company E, of the 2nd Battalion, 7th Marines, 1st Marine Division, (Rein), Fleet Marine Force when, on February 23, 1969, during the early morning hours Pfc. Austin's observation post was subjected to a fierce ground attack by a large North Vietnamese Army force supported by a heavy volume of hand grenades, satchel charges, and small arms fire. Observing that one of his wounded companions had fallen unconscious in a position dangerously exposed to the hostile fire, Pfc. Austin unhesitatingly left the relative security of his fox-hole and, with complete disregard for his own safety, raced across the fire-swept terrain to assist the marine to a covered location. As

he neared the casualty, he observed an enemy grenade land nearby and, reacting instantly, leaped between the injured marine and the lethal object, absorbing the effects of its detonation. As he ignored his painful injuries and turned to examine the wounded man, he saw a North Vietnamese Army soldier aiming a weapon at his unconscious companion. With full knowledge of the

Pfc. Oscar P. Austin.

probable consequences and thinking only to protect the marine, Pfc. Austin resolutely threw himself between the casualty and the hostile soldier, and, in doing, was mortally wounded.

The stories of all these men's deeds are taken directly from the citations for the Medal of Honor. In addition to those detailed here, which are given only as one example each for the year of the award between 1965 and 1969 and have no other preference of order. The remaining fourteen of the twenty recipients are given below, in the order of the date of the incident for which the award was made:

Platoon Sergeant Matthew Leonard, US Army
Company B, 1st Battalion, 16th Infantry, 1st Infantry Division. Near Suoi Da, February 28, 1967 – posthumous award.

1st Lieutenant Ruppert L. Sargeant, US Army
Company B, 4th Battalion, 9th Infantry, 25th Infantry Division. Hau Nghia Province, March 15, 1967 – posthumous award.

Sergeant Rodney Maxwell Davis, US Marine Corps
Company B, 1st Battalion, 5th Marines, 1st Marine Division. Quang Nam Province, September 6, 1967 – posthumous award.

Sergeant First Class Webster Anderson, US Army
Battery A, 2d Battalion, 320th Field Artillery, 101st Airborne Infantry Division (Airmobile). Tam Ky, Republic of Vietnam, October 15, 1967.

Captain Riley L. Pitts, US Army
Company C, 2d Battalion, 27th Infantry, 25th Infantry Division. Ap Dong, October 31, 1967 – posthumous award. Captain Pitts was the first African American commissioned officer to be awarded the Medal of Honor.

Specialist Fifth Class (then Pfc.) Clarence Eugene Sasser, US Army
Headquarters Company, 3d Battalion, 60th Infantry, 9th Infantry Division. Ding Tuong Province, January 10, 1968.

Specialist Fifth Class Dwight H. Johnson, US Army
Company B, 1st Battalion, 69th Armor, 4th Infantry Division. Near Dak To, Kontum Province, January 15, 1968.

Staff Sergeant Clifford Chester Sims, US Army
Company D, 2d Battalion (Airborne), 501st Infantry, 101st Airborne Division. Near Hue, February 21, 1968 – posthumous award.

Private First Class Ralph H. Johnson, US Marine Corps
Company A, 1st Reconnaissance Battalion, 1st Marine Division (Rein), Fleet Marine Force. Near the Quan Duc Valley, March 5, 1968 – posthumous award.

Lieutenant-Colonel Charles Calvin Rogers, US Army
1st Battalion, 5th Artillery, 1st Infantry Division. Fishhook, near Cambodian border, November 1, 1968. Lieutenant-Colonel Rogers was the highest ranking African American recipient of the Medal of Honor in the Vietnam War.

1st Lieutenant John E. Warren, US Army
Company C, 2d Battalion, (Mechanized), 22d Infantry, 25th Infantry Division. Tay Ninh Province, January 14, 1969 – posthumous award.

Private First Class Garfield M. Langhorn, US Army
Troop C, 7th Squadron (Airmobile), 17th Cavalry, 1st Aviation Brigade. Pleiku Province, January 15, 1969 – posthumous award.

Private First Class Robert H. Jenkins, US Marine Corps
3rd Reconnaissance Battalion, 3rd Marine Division (Rein), Fleet Marine Force. Fire Support Base Argonne, March 5, 1969 – posthumous award.

Sergeant First Class William Maud Bryant, US Army
Company A, 5th Special Forces Group, 1st Special Forces. Long Khanh Province, March 24, 1969 – posthumous award.

From this text, it will be appreciated that African Americans played a significant part in the war in Vietnam, for whilst the total number of those soldiers, sailors, airmen and Marines who served in Vietnam was almost double the number of African Americans fighting for the Union in the Civil War, the fact is that there were not almost 200,000 African Americans in Vietnam at any one time, whereas the 179,000 in the Union Army at its peak numbers were there until either they fell or the War ended.

The highest-ranking African American Officer in the Union Army in the Civil War was Lieutenant-Colonel William N. Reed. The highest-ranking African American officer to have served in the Vietnam War, was General Daniel "Chappie" James, who rose to be the first African American four-star general in the United States Air Force. General Roscoe

Brown was the first African American Army officer to reach four-star rank.

Also, the Medals of Honor awarded to African Americans in Vietnam were awarded over a slightly longer period of time than in the three years of the Civil War, yet still twenty awards were made for service in Vietnam, against twenty-two in the Civil War. The total number of Medals of Honor awarded in Vietnam was 242.

It is notable, too, that regardless of the risk of front-line duty, African Americans re-enlisted at a significantly higher rate in the Armed Forces. In 1964, they represented nine percent of all US military personnel; by

Lieutenant-Colonel Harold G. Moore in the battlefield.

1976 they represented greater than 15 percent of all personnel under arms. In that same period, the percentage of African American officers doubled, but they still accounted for less than four percent of the total.

The Vietnam War was America's least popular war. It was not a war of the participants' making, and in this war, men displayed some of the greatest courage ever witnessed. Of African Americans, this was certainly true and they deserved every word of accolade and praise given them. It took a hundred years for so many Medals of Honor to be awarded. Every one, and doubtless more, was earned.

Before leaving this Chapter, let us recall one of the bloodiest battles of the Vietnam War where a young Lieutenant-Colonel Harold G. Moore, is given the re-formed Seventh Cavalry, now an air cavalry unit using Bell Huey helicopters as its mounts instead of horses, to form a fighting unit to go to

Vietnam. He knew his destination was Vietnam, along with his four hundred soldiers. Moore was a remarkable man and his story is told in a book entitled, *We Were Soldiers Once – And Young.*

Colonel Moore reflected that President Lyndon Johnson, despite the many good things he was doing to acknowledge and establish the multi-racial, multi-cultural, society that was and is the United States of America, was determined not to declare the war in Vietnam a state of emergency because it would have cost money that he did not have. Harold Moore described this as "going to war on the cheap". But Lieutenant-Colonel Moore held similar views to his President, inasmuch as he was determined to integrate his fighting force into a single bonded unit where each man, regardless of race, color or creed, would fight as one. He did not recognize that some of his men had skin of yellow, light brown or black – they were soldiers and they were part of the Seventh Cavalry – and neither he nor his unit was going to suffer the ignominious fate that his military forebear, General George Custer, had suffered at the Battle of the Little Big Horn.

The Seventh Cavalry in the field during the Battle of Ia Drang. Lieutenant-Colonel Harold Moore vowed that every man who went into battle with him would return, regardless of race, creed or color – and they did.

Before leaving for Vietnam, Colonel Moore called his entire regiment together and delivered to them this inspiring address which, as it happened, was prophetic in much of its content:

> "Look around you. In the 7th Cavalry, we got a Captain from the Ukraine. Another from Puerto Rico. We got Japanese, Chinese, Blacks, Hispanics, Cherokee Indian, Jews and Gentiles – all American. Now here in the States some men in this unit may experience discrimination because of race or creed, but for you and me now, all that is gone. We're moving into the valley of the shadow of death, where you will watch the back of the man next to you, as he will watch yours, and you won't care what color he is or by what name he calls God. Let us understand the situation; we're going into battle against a tough and determined enemy. I can't promise you that I will bring you all home alive, but this I swear, before you and before Almighty God: when we go into battle, I will be the first one to set foot on the field, and I will be the last to step

> off. And I will leave no one behind. Dead or alive, we will all come home together. So help me God."

His prophecy was to come true. As the Seventh Cavalry went into battle with four hundred men to face a highly trained and skilled Vietnamese Army of 4-6,000 men, Harold Moore knew that not all of his men would come back alive. In theory, the Americans won that battle – in fact they certainly did not lose it. And after it, Colonel Moore was true to his word: every single man of the Seventh Cavalry returned to the United States – some physically unscathed, some mildly injured who would recover, some in wheelchairs and some in body bags. But he kept his promise – and the Vietnamese held off their fire when they realized what the Seventh Cavalry was doing, recovering its dead.

The point of the finale to this Chapter is that here was a man who was dedicated to his country, dedicated to his Service, but most particularly dedicated to his men, regardless of their origin. Perhaps the greatest hero of the Battle of Ia Drang was Harold Moore himself.

CHAPTER THIRTEEN

The First Tuskegee Generals - Barriers Fall

Back in 1942, there was one African American officer of Flag rank in the United States Armed Forces. That officer was Benjamin O. Davis, who made it to the rank of Brigadier-General against everybody's expectations of the time – including his own.

Benjamin Davis was born within reach of the nation's Capitol Building, in Washington, DC. There is some question over his date of birth, because his military record shows July 1, 1877, but his personal biographer, Marvin Fletcher, has researched birth records and come up with a date of July 1, 1880, suggesting that young Benjamin lied about his age, so as to enlist in the US Army without securing his parents' permission. Louis and Henrietta Davis were his parents and they placed him into M Street High School in Washington and while he studied there, he enrolled in the cadet program and when the Spanish-American War began, he joined the 1st Separate Battalion of the Washington, DC National Guard.

Lieutenant Benjamin O. Davis.

In July 1898, young Benjamin joined the 8th Volunteer Infantry Regiment as a 1st Lieutenant in Company G. He was located at Chickamauga in Georgia from July 1898 to March 1899, when the unit was disbanded. Having decided that the Army was a good career for him, Benjamin Davis then enlisted in the Regular Army and found himself assigned to Troop I in the 3rd Squadron of the 9th Cavalry, based at Fort Duschenes in Utah. His first duty was as the Troop Clerk, and in the spring of 1901, was assigned with his Troop to the Philippines. By the summer of that year, Davis had been promoted, probably because he had already served as an Officer in the National Guard, to the rank of Sergeant Major.

That August, Sergeant Major Davis was transferred to Troop F of the 10th Cavalry, where he was given the duties of a 2nd Lieutenant after passing the Officer's Qualification Test. There is an irony to that, in that Davis had already served in the Spanish-American War as a 1st Lieutenant. But he graciously accepted "the system" and returned to the United States with his troops to Fort Washakie in Wyoming. He remained there until September 1905, when he took up a new post, perhaps surprisingly, as a Professor of Military Science and Tactics at Wilberforce University in Ohio. He was in that post for just over four years, until mid-1909, when he returned to the Cavalry.

Here was an interesting assignment for Lieutenant Davis, for having only recently returned to Troop I of the 9th Cavalry, in April 1910 he was appointed military attaché to Liberia in West Africa. His task while there was to report on Liberia's military forces, returning to the US in November 1911. Once more, he found himself with Troop I of the 9th Cavalry from January 1912, located at Fort D.A. Russell in Wyoming. During 1913, the 9th Cavalry was assigned to Mexican Border Patrol and Davis was there until February 1915, at which point he returned to Wilberforce University to resume his old post of Professor of Military Science and Tactics.

Once again, on completion of his assignment to Wilberforce, Benjamin Davis returned to the 9th Cavalry in the Philippines. His appointment was as supply officer and commander of the 3rd Squadron. Later, he took command of the 1st Squadron of the 9th Cavalry and during that period of service, between 1917 and 1919, he achieved the temporary rank of Lieutenant-Colonel, though when he returned to the United States in March 1920, he reverted to the permanent rank of Captain, like so many officers who had returned from France in the Great War. So, in this respect, his reversion was not unusual. Even George S. Patton, Jr., a man who was to become the greatest battlefield commander in history, was reverted to the rank of Captain after World War I.

After another tour of duty with the 9th Cavalry, Captain Davis was to return to an academic life, but this time at the Tuskegee Institute.

Captain Davis' next move was back into the world of academia, but this time to a place that was to take on great significance for himself, for his son Benjamin Jr. and for the African American community as a whole. He was appointed Professor of Military Science and Tactics at the Tuskegee Institute, now a fully-fledged degree-granting university for African American students. He remained there for a full four years, before returning to a more regular military unit, the Second Battalion of the 372nd Regiment of the Ohio National Guard. Here, he served as an instructor until September 1929, when once more he returned to Wilberforce University in his former role as Professor of Military Science and Tactics. After a couple more years there, he took up the same role for a second time at the Tuskegee Institute, where he served this time for six years until August 1937. He then made his last move back to Wilberforce, before taking command of the 369th Regiment of the New York National Guard. In October 1940, Benjamin Davis, Sr. was promoted to the rank of Brigadier-General, the first African American officer to reach that rank in the US Army.

In January 1941, General Davis was made Commanding General of the 4th Brigade of the Second Cavalry Division, serving at Fort Riley, Kansas. That assignment lasted six months, as he was called to his birthplace, Washington, DC, to become an assistant in the Office of the Inspector General of the US Army. Whilst in that post, he also served on the Advisory Committee for Negro Troop Problems and between

1941 and 1944, he made inspection tours of African American soldiers throughout the Army. Between September and November 1942, then again between July and November 1944, he made inspection tours of African American units in Europe, including his son's command, the 332nd Fighter Group. It was at that time that he had the pleasure and honor of presenting his son with the Distinguished Flying Cross.

In November 1944, General Davis found himself assigned to work under the command of Lieutenant-General John C. H. Lee, the commander of the Communications Zone, European Theater of Operations. He worked with the General Inspectorate Section in that Theater of Operations from January 1945 until the end of the War in Europe in May. During this time, General Davis made a major contribution to the proposed policy of integration, which was ultimately enacted by President Truman in 1948.

In a conference at Cherbourg some time after D-Day, led by Lieutenant-General John Clifford Hodges Lee, Brigadier-General Benjamin O. Davis is seated second from the left. His role now was Special Assistant to the Commanding General, Communications Zone, European Theater of Operations in the Office of the Inspector-General.

General Davis' final assignment was as an assistant to the Secretary of the Army and in July 1947, he attended, as the United States' representative, the Centennial Celebrations of

Brigadier-General Benjamin O. Davis on an inspection tour in Europe.

Liberia. A year later, in July 1948, he retired in a ceremony presided over by President Harry S. Truman. He had given exactly fifty years of his life to his country. In his retirement, he was a member of the American Battle Monuments Commission up to 1961. On November 26, 1970, Benjamin Oliver Davis Sr., Brigadier-General US Army, died at Great Lakes Naval Hospital and was laid to rest at Arlington National Cemetery. He had the privilege of living long enough to see his son, Benjamin Oliver Davis Jr., rise above his own rank to reach Lieutenant-General.

The citation for Brigadier-General Benjamin O. Davis, Sr.'s Distinguished Service Medal could well be his epitaph:

"For exceptionally meritorious service to the Government in a duty of great responsibility from June 1941, to November 1944, as an Inspector of troop units in the field, and as special War Department consultant on matters pertaining to Negro troops. The initiative, intelligence and sympathetic understanding displayed by him in conducting countless investigations concerning individual soldiers, troop units, and components of the War Department brought about a fair and equitable

solution to many important problems which have since become the basis of far-reaching War Department policy. His wise advice and counsel have made a direct contribution to the maintenance of soldier morale and troop discipline and has been of material assistance to the War Department and to responsible commanders in the field of understanding personnel matters as they pertain to the individual soldier."

As the first African American officer to achieve General Officer rank, Benjamin O. Davis, Sr. had a great burden of responsibility and duty placed upon him, for he would be watched every step of the way through his career. He stood, and stands, as a proud example to all.

The early career growth of Benjamin O. Davis, Jr. has already been covered, and it is appropriate now to review his later career, advancing from the rank of Colonel to Brigadier-General, then, as his now-retired father watched the advance of his son's career, go beyond the achievements of his father.

Colonel Benjamin O. Davis, Jr. had commanded the 477th Composite Group and relocated it to Lockbourne in Ohio, where he and his men had encountered quite strong resistance from white workers to answer to black commanders, but his powers of persuasion and intense sense of fairness

Colonel Benjamin O. Davis, Jr., on the right of this picture, takes over command of the 477th Composite Group at Lockbourne AFB, before reverting it to the 332nd Fighter Wing and assuming command of Lockbourne AFB itself. His father, Brigadier-General Benjamin O. Davis, Sr., is on the left of the dais.

won his worker teams at Lockbourne over and established a thoroughly harmonious working atmosphere. It reached a point where Lockbourne became a valuable part of the community and the level of respect for Benjamin Davis rose to an unprecedented height. Nowhere else in the United States had such a level of cooperation and commitment from white workers under black supervision been achieved.

The influence of Benjamin Davis' performance and achievements in desegregating the working environment at Lockbourne had a profound effect on how affairs were handled during the separation of the Air Force from the Army in late 1947. The Deputy Chief of Staff for Personnel in the newly formed Air Force, Lieutenant-General Idwal H. Edwards, instructed that an extensive study into racial segregation be carried out. At this time, President Truman's mandate banning segregation in the Armed Forces was almost a year away, so Edwards' investigation was somewhat ahead of its time. He took into account the huge successes of the 99th Fighter Squadron and the 332nd Fighter Group, both during and post-World War II, and these factors weighed heavily in his recommendations to the Air Force Board.

General Edwards recommended unequivocally that racial integration should be the way ahead for the United States Air Force. His key argument was, of course, the performance of the Tuskegee Airmen in war and in peace – especially commending the conduct and command qualities of Colonel Benjamin O. Davis. As a direct consequence of Edwards' recommendations and reasons, the US Air Force was the first of the United States Armed Forces to implement racial integration in 1949, just months after the Truman mandate.

Benjamin Davis' next move was to the Air War College. Hitherto, no African American officer had been allowed to pursue that route, but promotion beyond the rank of Colonel was not available to any officer who had not attended that course, so for Benjamin Davis, it was vital. He succeeded in gaining entry and then faced the bigotry that prevailed in Montgomery, Alabama, the location of the Air War College. For example, he and his wife, Aggie, were barred from restaurants, hotels and even housing in certain districts. He bore the unpleasantness of his situation in order to graduate

and did so with distinction, with the result that his next assignment was to Headquarters USAF at the Pentagon.

The huge success he achieved in his post as Chief of the Air Defense Branch of Air Force Operations was noted by those above him. His supervision of white officers and enlisted men earned him great respect and, in the spring of 1953, a return to flying duties. He was appointed to command the 51st Fighter Interceptor Wing in Korea. The 51st was the premier fighter wing there and Davis' command of a mostly white group demonstrated that men in battle would give their loyalty to a black commander if he was scrupulously fair in his command and judgment. Some time after the Korean Armistice, clearly rewarding his Korean success, the Air Force appointed Colonel Davis as Director of Operations and Training in the Far East Air Forces. Just three months later, he matched his father's "first" by being promoted to the rank of Brigadier-General, the first African American to achieve that rank in the United States Air Force, as his father had been first in the Army.

Brigadier-General Davis was next assigned to become Vice-Commander of the 13th Air Force, as well as Commander of Air Task Force 13 (Provisional) at Taipei in Taiwan. His task was to create, from a clean sheet of paper, a defensive air force for General Chiang Kai Shek's Republic of China to deter the prospect of an attack from Chairman Mao Tse Tung's People's Republic of China, which had laid claim to Taiwan as an integral part of China. He achieved his goal inside two years and the testament to the success of his work lies in the fact that the Republic of China continues to exist to this day.

After a tour in Germany with the 12th Air Force, Davis was appointed Deputy Chief of Staff, Operations, for the US Air Forces in Europe. Promoted to Major-General, he

Lieutenant-General Benjamin O. Davis, Jr.

returned to the United States to become USAF Director of Manpower and Organization. During his four years in the Pentagon, he was promoted Lieutenant-General, the first three-star African American general. Upon that promotion, he was relocated to Korea to become United Nations Command Chief of Staff and of the US Forces in Korea.

Completing his second tour of duty in Korea, in August 1967, General Davis was given command of the 13th Air Force, covering the whole USAF activities in Asia, including Vietnam. His command responsibility carried a manpower complement of over 55,000 personnel.

He also had responsibility within that command for the Air of the Philippines. After just a year, he was recalled to the Pentagon to the become Deputy Commander in Chief of US Strike Command. In this command, General Davis made his personal business to understand the conditions under which the men and women under his authority lived and fought.

Retiring in 1970, Lieutenant-General Benjamin O. Davis, Jr., after 33 years' service on active duty, had left his Air Force a much better institution than the one he had joined. His contribution to the elimination of racial segregation in the US Air Force was so significant that his testament was the achievement of six percent of officers in the United States Air Force being African American. That does not yet represent a percentage equal to the percentage of African Americans in the total population of the United States, but it's almost halfway there, from a start of one – himself.

Another Tuskegee Airman

who distinguished himself by rising to General Officer rank was Colonel Daniel "Chappie" James. On his return from Vietnam, Colonel James was appointed Vice Commander of the 33rd Tactical Fighter Wing at Eglin Air Force Base, Florida in December 1967. While located there, he was nominated Florida's Outstanding American of the Year for 1969 by the Florida State Jaycees, and he received the Jaycee Distinguished Service Award. In August 1969, he took up probably the most sensitive post he had ever held. He was appointed to command the 7272nd Fighter Training Wing at Wheelus Air Base in the Libyan Arab Republic. This was just as Colonel Gaddafi's revolution created him President of Libya. Gaddafi wanted "the colonials" out of Wheelus Field, demanding that the air base be closed and its facilities turned over to the Libyan Arab Republic. This was a highly delicate situation for James to handle, requiring great restraint, tact, diplomacy, and determination. He possessed and displayed all of those qualities, and when he left Libya, he was rewarded with promotion to Brigadier-General.

On the left is Colonel Robin Olds and on the right is Daniel "Chappie" James. These two paired up to fly in Vietnam under the soubriquet "Blackman and Robin", to the amusement of all around them.

On his return to the United States in March 1970, General James was appointed Deputy Assistant Secretary of Defense for Public Affairs – a post which suited his talents well. In April 1973, he advanced as Principal Deputy Assistant Secretary of Defense for Public Affairs. He assumed duty as Vice Commander of the Military Airlift Command, with headquarters at Scott AFB, Illinois on September 1, 1974. In this period, General James was elevated in rank by two more stars. And now came the greatest African American achievement so far in history. Daniel "Chappie" James, Jr. was promoted to the rank of full General – the first African American four-star general. He was appointed Commander in Chief of the North American Air Defense (NORAD) Command. James was in poor health in the later years of his career and in 1977 he suffered a heart attack and decided that wisdom dictated his retirement. Just one month after his retirement, General Daniel James, Jr. had another major heart attack and died. He was laid to rest at Arlington National Military Cemetery.

General Daniel "Chappie" James, the first African American four-star general.

During his lifetime, General Daniel "Chappie" James became widely known as a public speaker and was popular in all circles. His key speeches covered Americanism and Patriotism and addressed the issues of the multi-racial society. Excerpts from some of his speeches were read into the Congressional Record and he was awarded the George Washington Freedom Foundation Medal in 1967. In 1970, he received the Arnold Air Society's Eugene M. Zuckert Award for outstanding contributions to Air Force Professionalism. The citation for that award read:

"A fighter pilot with a magnificent record, public speaker, and eloquent spokesman for the American Dream we so rarely achieve."

It is especially true to say that three men – Brigadier-General Benjamin O. Davis, Sr., Lieutenant-General Benjamin O. Davis, Jr. and General Daniel "Chappie" James, Jr. – probably did more than any other American to push open the door of opportunity for African Americans in military and wider society. True, their work and efforts were facilitated by a great American President – Harry S. Truman.

The man who did more in his time to break down racial prejudice in the United States than anyone up to his time. It was Truman as a Senator who met the deputation from the Negro Airmen's Association of America in the months leading up to World War II and took up their cause. He later signed the Executive Order 9981 in 1948, banning segregation in the United States Armed Forces, thus enforcing integration in the Navy, the Marine Corps, the Coast Guard, the Army and the Air Force.

One Tuskegee Airman who seems today to have disappeared into obscurity is Major-General Lucius Theus. Born in Madison County, Tennessee, in 1922, he graduated from Community High School in Blue Island, Illinois. In December 1941, during World War II, Theus entered the Army Air Corps as a private. After basic training, he attended the Army Administration School at Atlanta University and for the rest of the war, served as an administrative clerk, chief clerk, and first sergeant of pre-aviation cadet and basic training squadrons at Keesler Field, Mississippi.

Major-General Lucius Theus.

Entering Officer Candidate School after the War had ended, Lucius Theus graduated second in his class with a commission as 2nd Lieutenant in January 1946. After a one-year tour of duty as squadron adjutant at Tuskegee Army Air Field in Alabama, Lieutenant Theus was then transferred to Lockbourne Air Force Base, Ohio, as base statistical control officer under the command of Colonel Benjamin O. Davis, Jr., and became a Tuskegee Airman. In August 1949 he was assigned to Erding Air Depot in Germany as the analysis and presentation officer, and later he became commander of the Statistical Control Flight and Depot Statistical Control Officer.

Captain Theus was assigned in August 1952 to the Office of the Deputy Chief of Staff, Comptroller, Headquarters US Air Force in Washington, DC, where he was Chief of the Materiel Logistics Statistics Branch. In October 1957 Major Theus was transferred to Headquarters Central Air Materiel Forces Europe at Chateauroux Air Base in France, as statistical services staff officer. He was subsequently appointed technical statistical adviser to the comptroller, Headquarters Air Materiel Forces, Europe.

In January 1959 Lieutenant-Colonel Theus became Chief of Management Services Office in the Eastern Air Logistics Office in Athens, Greece. In February 1961 he was appointed Chief of Management Analysis, Headquarters Spokane Air Defense Sector, Larson Air Force Base, Washington, then in December 1962, Colonel Theus was assigned as base comptroller at Kingsley Field, Oregon. His next assignment was as base comptroller of Cam Ranh Bay Air Base in the Republic of Vietnam. For more than five months of this assignment, he also acted as deputy base commander of Cam Ranh Bay Air Base. In 1966 he graduated with distinction from the Air War College at Maxwell Air Force Base, Alabama.

In July 1967, Colonel Theus was attached to the Headquarters US Air Force, Office of the Comptroller of the Air Force, as a data automation staff officer, in the Directorate of Data Automation. He served initially as Chief, Technology and Standards Branch; then Chief, Plans, Policy and Technology Division; and later Chief, Program Management Division. During that assignment, Brigadier-General Theus also served as chairman of the Inter-Service Task Force on Education in Race Relations in the Office of the Secretary of Defense. The recommendations of the task force led to the establishment of the Defense Race Relations Institute and the Department of Defense-wide education program in race relations. In 1968 he attended the Department of Defense Computer Institute.

In July 1971 Brigadier-General Theus was assigned to the position of Director of Management Analysis, Office of the Comptroller of the Air Force. In June 1972 he was appointed Special Assistant for Social Actions, Directorate of Personnel Plans, Deputy Chief of Staff, Personnel, Headquarters US Air Force. On June 10, 1974, he was appointed Director of Accounting and Finance in the Office of the Comptroller of the Air Force, Headquarters US Air Force, and Commander of the Air Force Accounting and Finance Center, Denver, Colorado, rising to the rank of Major-General in the process.

General Theus spent much of his military career developing and implementing administrative systems to improve the life of the average airman and soldier. Programs such as direct deposit for military payrolls and better human relations are prime examples of his work. While assigned to the Pentagon, he chaired the inter-service task force whose recommendations led to a Department of Defense-wide race relations education and policy development and establishment of the forerunner to the Defense Equal Opportunity Management Institute. This Tennessee native with degrees from the University of Maryland and George Washington University was also the first African American to attend the Harvard Business School's Advanced Management Program. He has been named to both the Enlisted Men's Hall of Fame and the Michigan Aviation Hall of Fame.

Major-General Lucius Theus was only the third African American officer to reach General Officer Rank in the United States Air Force and was the first to rise from the rank of Private. He was not only the third African American General, but the third Tuskegee Airman to achieve that honor. He carried that banner with pride.

These first Tuskegee Generals were the trailblazers of liberty for African Americans. All had endured the hardships and rigors of segregation and bigotry. All had worked their way through those hardships and trials to achieve a better way of life and better social conditions for the tens of thousands of men who have followed them – in all ranks and all professions in the United States Armed Forces, not just the Air Force, though the Air Force was certainly their main focus.

All three of these generals – Davis, James and Theus, worked tirelessly in the communities where they served as well as in the Air Force establishments they served. They had a message and it was that any African American soldier or airman could serve their country and match the technical, management or administrative competence of any of their Caucasian counterparts if they were given the opportunity. After all, these three men achieved their goals against mountainous odds. Many more have followed them now, because they blazed the trail and cleared it of many obstructions on the way.

Gen. Lloyd W. "Fig" Newton was born in Ridgeland, South Carolina, where he graduated from Jasper High School. He graduated with a Bachelor of Science degree in aviation education from Tennessee State University in Nashville, where he was also commissioned as a distinguished graduate through the Reserve Officer Training Corps program in

1966. He underwent flight training at Williams Air Force Base and completed that course in June 1967, progressing to the F-4 "Phantom" course at George AFB in California. His first operational assignment began in April 1968 at Da Nang AFB in Vietnam, from where he flew 269 combat missions, 79 of those being over North Vietnam. A year later, he returned to the US for further training on the F-4D, after which he joined the 523rd Tactical Fighter Squadron at Clark AFB in the Philippines, where he was stationed for four years.

In November 1973, Newton was transferred to Luke AFB in Arizona as a flight instructor on the F-4D, where he served for a year. After that came the highlight of his career when he was selected to join the elite "Thunderbirds", the United States Air Force aerobatic display team. He was the first African American to join the team and flew as a slot pilot, as well as being the team narrator. He remained with the "Thunderbirds" until February 1978. Promoted to the rank of Major in January 1978, in the following month Major Newton became a student at the Armed Forces Staff College in Norfolk, Virginia, after which, in June 1978, he returned to the "Thunderbirds" as narrator and right wingman.

In December 1978, he left the "Thunderbirds" to become Congressional Liaison Officer to the US House of Represen-

Captain Lloyd "Fig" Newton.

tatives in Washington, DC. He remained in that post for just over three years, during which time, in October 1980, he was promoted Lieutenant-Colonel. At the end of that tour of duty, in February 1982, Lieutenant-Colonel Newton undertook conversion flight training to the F-16 and then, in June 1982, he was appointed Assistant Deputy Commander for Operations of the 8th Tactical Fighter Wing at Hill Air Force Base in Utah. In June 1983, he transferred to the same role with the 388th Tactical Fighter Wing, still at Hill AFB. By December 1983, he was promoted Colonel and left Hill in August 1984 to become a student at the Industrial College of the Armed Forces in Washington, DC.

Colonel Newton's next assignment was to be the Assistant Deputy Director for Operations and Training at Headquarters US Air Force in Washington, DC, where he took up his post in August 1985. He remained in that position until November 1986, when he was appointed Assistant Director of Special Projects, directorate of plans, still at Headquarters US Air Force. Leaving Washington in July 1988, Colonel Newton took command of the 71st Air Base Group, Vance Air Force Base, Oklahoma. Remaining at Vance, he then became Commander of the 71st Flying Training Wing there until May 1990, when he relocated to Randolph AFB in Texas to take command of the 12th Flying Training Wing.

In August 1991, Colonel Newton achieved his first star, being promoted Brigadier-General on August 3rd as he assumed command of the 833rd Air Division at Holloman Air Force Base in New Mexico. Leaving Holloman in June 1993, he took up the post of Director of Operations, J-3, in the United States Special Operations Command at MacDill Air Force Base in Florida in July of that year. One month later, he was promoted to Major-General, leaving MacDill in June 1995, after being promoted to Lieutenant-General, to become Assistant Vice Chief of Staff at Headquarters US Air Force. In June 1997, General Newton achieved the ultimate goal – he was promoted to four-star General and took up his final assignment. This was to be Commander of Headquarters Air Education and Training Command at Randolph Air Force Base in Texas. As General Officer Commanding, he was responsible for recruitment, training and education of Air Force

personnel. His command included Air Force Recruiting Service, two numbered air forces and the Air University. Air Education and Training Command consists of thirteen bases, more than 43,000 active duty members as well as 14,000 civilians. He retired from that post in March 2000.

General Lloyd W. Newton.

General Newton acquired the nickname "Fig" – a reference to the cookie by that name – *Fig Newton*. Throughout his career, he worked hard to dispel racism and to encourage young people from all walks of life with this statement:

> *"My point to youngsters is, they can grow to be anything and anybody their capabilities will allow them to be,"* he said. *"What's important to them is to continue to develop themselves to reach the summit they're trying to get to. The opportunities are out there. That doesn't mean it's going to be easy, doesn't mean someone won't try to stand in their way. They have to learn how to negotiate themselves around those problems."*

Lloyd Newton was not a Tuskegee General, but in spirit he was and his commitment to the neutralization of racism was as strong as any of the Tuskegee Airmen before him. In 2008 General Newton, now retired, endorsed Senator Barack Obama for election to President and appeared on stage at the Democratic National Convention at Invesco Field, in Denver, Colorado, with other former military leaders to lend support to Obama's campaign.

CHAPTER FOURTEEN

A Hesitant Peace and 21st Century Conflict

After the Vietnam War, the American people became skeptical of their Armed Forces and were distinctly unreceptive towards their war veterans. It is ironic to reflect that the attitudes displayed towards Vietnam Veterans brought about more suicides, it is said, than deaths in combat. The quality of government support for veterans was minimal and sometimes non-existent. It would seem that because this was the only war in United States history that America lost and for many years, was swept under the carpet. Nobody wanted to talk about defeat in Vietnam and so nobody wanted to support that war's veterans. Men from all sectors of the American community, mostly draftees – white, non-white, poor, badly educated and those who did not receive honorable discharges were deprived of medical benefits, and educational opportunities and benefits. As a result, so many of these 700,000 men found it difficult to secure work and keep jobs, to maintain normal family relationships (post-traumatic stress disorder was not recognized by the authorities) and many men ended up in jail.

Barely noticed in all the turmoil of this "hesitant peace" was the commissioning, in November 1979, of 2nd Lieutenant Marcella A. Hayes, who was the 55th woman out of a total of 48,000 officers to graduate from the Army Aviation School in Fort Rucker, Alabama. She was to become the first African American woman pilot in the modern US Armed Forces.

Lieutenant Marcella Hayes.

Against the background of Vietnam and the bad taste it carried for most Americans, the United States began its attempt to restore the integrity and trust of its Armed Forces. President Jimmy Carter was the Commander-in-Chief who

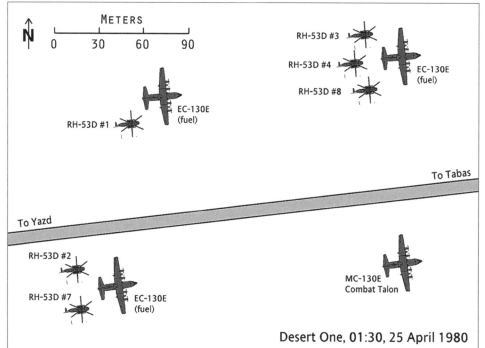

Desert One, 01:30, 25 April 1980

The original plan for aircraft distribution on the ground, the EC-130s being there to provide fuel to the helicopters, which were intended to keep their engines running the whole time they were on the ground, while the locations of the hostages were confirmed and they were recovered to the helicopters for movement to the waiting carrier "Nimitz" in the Gulf.

Iranian demonstrators scale the walls of the US Embassy in Teheran. The attack on the Embassy resulted in sixty six Embassy personnel being taken hostage, including twelve African Americans.

Not only were African Americans involved in this event as hostages, they were also among the intended rescuers too, but the whole program was to go wrong...

... as one helicopter began to move forward, flying low and slow, it was to collide with a C130 Hercules. Both were destroyed in the ensuing fire and eight men died.

The Iranians took great pleasure in parading some of their captives to show how superior they were to the mighty Americans. If the plan had gone without a hitch, it was almost certain that it would have been successful, even allowing for the lack of intelligence about the whereabouts of all the hostages.

authorized the first significant, albeit small in military scale, action to restore the nation's respect for its military men. The United States Embassy in Teheran was under siege in 1980 and fifty-three Americans were held hostage there. President Carter personally ordered their rescue by military means and a rescue plan, "Operation Eagle Claw" was put in place.

The operation proved to be a total fiasco, with two of the eight helicopters not reaching their destination, two more being disabled on location and another crashing into a C-130 Hercules in their attempt to leave. This was even more humiliating for the United States than Vietnam had been.

"Eagle Claw" was a failure because of a number of unpredicted issues. An aborted helicopter was carrying an inventory of helicopter spare parts to cater for any eventuality and another helicopter suffered damage to its hydraulic system and could not be repaired, reducing the number of available helicopters for the rescue to five. As a result of this, the commanders on the scene requested permission to abort the mission. President Carter reluctantly gave his approval.

Then, as the US force prepared to leave Iran, visibility was poor through a haze of dust and a helicopter crashed into a fuel-carrying C-130 Hercules as it was trying to move to a position where it could refuel and both went up in flames, destroying both aircraft and killing eight US servicemen. The remaining helicopters were abandoned in the interests of making a hasty withdrawal and the surviving personnel flew out by C130 to Masirah Island, off Oman, a former British base in the Middle East.

Because there was a growing sense of isolationism among the population of the United States, the next military action it became involved in started out from a difficult position. The neighboring Caribbean states asked the US to intervene in a violent power struggle that was taking place in Grenada in October 1983. Many people in the United States asked why their country should intervene in the affairs of such a small country as Grenada – what was it to do with the US?

But Operation "Urgent Fury" was mounted to put 1,000 US troops on to the island, including paratroops, Rangers and Marines to protect US citizens as well as to respond to the request. Quite apart from that, there was the expectation that the "People's Government" of Grenada were likely to allow Castro's Cuba to build an airfield with a 10,000 foot runway which would have been a strategic threat to the United States. Within days, they had secured the island, taking many military and civilian prisoners and gone some way to restoring the image of the United States Armed Forces in the process of restoring order in Grenada itself.

During this period of "hesitant peace", the North African state of Libya came into the world's headlines – first in 1981, when Colonel Moammar Ghadaffi, the President of Libya,

claimed that the Gulf of Sidra was Libyan sovereign territory, whereas the United States, which was conducting naval navigation exercises in the waters of the gulf, claimed it was international waters in accordance with normal conventions on territorial waters anywhere else in the world. Libya, however, sent two fighter jets to harass the US ships and two fighters were sent off the USS "Nimitz" to cover them. One Libyan aircraft fired a heat-seeking missile, which caused the US fighters to retaliate and shoot down both Libyan jets.

First on the ground in Grenada was the US 82nd Airborne, now a thoroughly integrated unit, with many African Americans on the ground and in command positions.

Artillery pieces, such as this Howitzer, were brought into use in Grenada in order to bring the uprising to a halt quickly. It lasted just days before order was restored.

Libya operated the Russian Sukhoi Su-22 fighter jet for quite some time as its main front line fighter, later supplemented by the MiG 25. But that would soon change as new aircraft became available to Libya.

With a variety of Russian aircraft in his inventory for many years, Colonel Ghaddafi finally yielded to the overtures of France and its President, Nicolas Sarkozy, and bought various marks of Mirage, the F1 being the most recent.

In March 1986, the Gulf of Sidra was again the focus of action between the US and Libya, when US ships were fired upon with Libyan missiles as they were once more conducting navigation exercises. The US responded with missiles, but there was no major damage to either side. However, a month later, US air and naval forces carried out bombing strikes on terrorist and military installations in Libya's capital, Tripoli, in retaliation for a terrorist bombing attack on a German disco which killed two American soldiers. The US government credited that attack to terrorists sponsored by

the Libyan government. Three years later, there was another incident about seventy miles north of Libya, when Libyan aircraft made threatening approaches to the USS "John F. Kennedy". Two F-14s took off from the "Kennedy" and shot down the Libyan aggressors.

In the meantime, the Arabian Gulf (Persian Gulf) was becoming the focus of attention for the world. A war between Iran and Iraq was raging, with neither side winning. During that period, for no obvious reason, in May 1987, the USS "Stark" was struck by two Exocet missiles fired from an Iraqi Mirage F-1, killing thirty-seven American sailors. This was the first military brush between Iraq and the United States. In another incident in the same period, in October 1987, Iran had attacked a US re-flagged Kuwaiti oil tanker with a Silkworm missile. The US retaliation was Operation Nimble Archer, in which the US attacked and disabled two Iranian oil platforms.

The guided missile frigate USS "Stark" suffered an unprovoked attack from an Iraqi Mirage that fired two French "Exocet" missiles at the ship, scoring a direct hit and killing thirty seven US sailors. The ship survived the incident, though was decommissioned in 1999 and ultimately scrapped in 2006.

When the Iraq-Iran War was near its end, in 1988, the United States adopted a policy of re-flagging Kuwaiti tankers, and increased its military presence in the Gulf region – ships in the Gulf and land forces in Eastern Saudi Arabia – so as to protect and escort those tankers out of the Gulf. President Reagan reported that US ships had been fired upon by both Iraqi and Iranian forces. The US escort action was the largest naval convoy operation that had taken place anywhere in the world since World War II. Finally, the cease-fire was signed between Iraq and Iran on August 20, 1988. The culmination of all this was the US Operation Praying Mantis, which was a mine-sweeping exercise after the Iranians had mined the Gulf and damaged, but not sunk, an American warship.

After the end of the Iran-Iraq War, the world began to think that peace was about to return to the Middle East. The United States reduced its presence in the Arabian Gulf and stability appeared to return to the region, but both the US and the British governments, maintained a vigilance in the region, not knowing what might come up next. This was the posturing of Saddam Hussein, Iraq's dictator, who consistently argued that Kuwait was rightfully Iraqi territory and yet it had been a stand-alone sheikhdom since the 18th Century, and when after World War I, the British and French governments, the two biggest influences in the region at the time, redistributed lands in the Middle East, Kuwait was re-established as an independent sheikhdom. The original state of Mesopotamia, lying between the Tigris and the Euphrates rivers was expanded beyond the shores of those rivers east and west to form the new Kingdom of Iraq. To its west was the Hashemite Kingdom of Jordan.

Oil was not yet a significant player in the politics of the Middle East and so all three countries were relatively poor and certainly had no military strength to protect themselves, so Great Britain entered treaties of protection for all three and over almost 40 years, through and after World War II, worked with those countries to build up their defensive strength, creating their air forces and donating military aircraft, mostly fighter planes, to all three. In 1958, a bloody and vicious revolution took place in Iraq, the Royal Family being massacred in its entirety as the first Republic of Iraq was established under General Kassem. King Hussein of Jordan appealed for British military protection against the threat of an Iraqi invasion. As the US protected Lebanon, so Britain protected Jordan from the potential aggression of the new tripartite United Arab Republics of Egypt, Syria and Iraq. For the time being, Britain underwrote the security of Jordan and guaranteed the independence of Kuwait.

In 1963, General Kassem declared that Kuwait was a sovereign territory of Iraq and mounted an invasion to take possession. Great Britain responded swiftly by placing a fighter squadron, Number 208 (its longest-serving Middle East squadron) on Kuwait's airfield. The squadron carried out a few ground attack strikes on Iraqi forces, which fled in response, and then maintained a presence for about six months. A young Saddam Hussein was in Kassem's administration at that time and in the fullness of time was to become Iraq's new dictator. In August 1990, Saddam decided to make a fresh claim on Kuwait and launched a large-scale surprise attack on the sheikhdom, seizing it and pillaging the tiny, now defenseless, state. The United Nations was called upon to intervene and ultimately, a coalition force consisting of US, British, French, Saudi Arabian, Egyptian, Syrian, Moroccan, Qatari, Omani, UAR, Danish, Belgian, Pakistani, Canadian, Australian and many more nations' troops formed to participate in Operation Desert Storm under the ultimate field command of US Army General Norman Schwartzkopf.

The attack on Iraq took place on 16th January 1991 with a major strike on Basra and in the open desert north of Kuwait. Within days, several thousand Iraqi soldiers had surrendered, ill-equipped for any kind of fight. Many simply didn't have adequate footwear. Many more had obsolete or dysfunctional weapons and a vast number simply lacked the will to fight. By the end of February, Kuwait had been liberated, with a significant and valuable contribution from the African American element of the US Armed Forces. A large contingent of the US component of the Coalition Force was US Reservists. Of the total US Force, approximately nine percent were African American, around 21,350 men and women.

In Desert Storm, African American women made a notable contribution to the success of the campaign. African American women served with distinction as officers, non-commissioned officers, and enlisted soldiers. Of the 35,000 females who went to Desert Storm, an estimated 40 percent of them were African Americans. According to Staff Sergeant Betty Brown of the Washington, DC, Army National Guard, all of these women endured the heat and the primitive conditions – no electricity, no running water, no bathrooms, and distinctly unpleasant sanitation conditions (for example ten-gallon trash cans used as toilets) alongside their male counterparts.

Army reserve Sergeant Pamela Davis stepped onto the sands of Saudi Arabia on Christmas Day 1990 with her unit, the 411th Engineer Brigade from Brooklyn, New York. A young African American woman officer, Lieutenant Phoebe Jeter, was commander of an all-male platoon in Desert Storm. She ordered thirteen Patriots to be fired (anti-missile missiles), destroying at least two Iraqi surface-to-air Scud missiles. Another African American female officer, Captain Cynthia Mosely, commanded Alpha Company of the 24th Support Battalion Forward, 24th Infantry Division (Mechanized). This was a 100-person unit that supplied everything from fuel to water to ammunition. Her unit re-supplied fuel for all the forward brigades because it was closest to the front lines. Desert Storm was the first military conflict in which women served in all combat activities. There was even the first African American female Navy pilot, Ensign Matice Wright, who was the Navy's first black female naval flight officer assigned to Fleet Air Reconnaissance Squadron 3 (VQ-3). Today, a civilian, Matice Wright is the Principal Director of Industrial Policy at the Department of Defense.

The United States Navy's first African American female helicopter pilot and first aviatrix in the Navy, Ensign Matice Wright.

Desert Storm was a total success for the Coalition Forces under the leadership of General Schwartzkopf and the African American contingent of the US Forces made its contribution to history in that action. Women in particular "upheld the honor of the Flag" when they were at last given the opportunity. This combat action was a major turning point in US military policy. It is somewhat amazing to realize that the first

Not quite such a happy picture, though a happy result. This is Army Specialist Shoshana Johnson after recovery from captivity as the first African American female prisoner-of-war. Held captive by the Iraqis for just over three weeks, she described her experience as "terrifying", though faith and thoughts of her family gave her strength.

black female pilot in the world, Bessie Coleman, preceded the first Navy's first African American female pilot by almost seventy years.

It is interesting to reflect on the make-up of the recruitment to and membership of the US Armed Forces shortly after Desert Storm. Black women in Fiscal Year 1993 represented 33 percent of Army female recruits, 22 percent of Navy female recruits, a remarkable 17 percent of Marine Corps female recruits and 18 percent of Air Force female recruits. One of the most amazing statistics is that 30.3 percent of females in the United States Armed Forces are African American women. Out of that number, some 33.6 percent serve in enlisted ranks, while 13.1 percent were commissioned and warrant officers. It should not be forgotten, that African American women undertook many dangerous roles as civilians for over a hundred years before, as nurses or intelligence gatherers for example, simply because they were not then allowed to enlist.

There was no major international conflict in the last decade of the 20th Century after what is now generally described as

Part of the protection process for Operation Provide Comfort was the provision of Coalition air cover by Operations Northern and Southern Watch, ensuring no-fly zones to Iraqi aircraft. Seen here are Sepecat "Jaguar" fighters from 54 Squadron of Britain's Royal Air Force.

"Gulf War One", and the world was essentially "at peace". In many parts of the world, however, that was far from the case. There were many minor "skirmishes" in that decade in which the United States was involved and in which many African American men and women of the US Armed Forces took part.

Between 1991 and 1996, the United States mounted Operation Provide Comfort, which involved delivering humanitarian relief and military protection for many Kurds who were fleeing their homes in northern Iraq. A small Allied ground force was based in Turkey to provide that protection if it was needed and supplies were airlifted and dropped into the Kurdish refugee areas. At the beginning of 1992, and extending for over ten years, to 2003, the UN approved the establishment of no-fly zones over Iraq. The United States, together with Great Britain, declared and enforced no fly zones over the majority of sovereign Iraqi airspace, prohibiting Iraqi flights in zones in southern Iraq and northern Iraq. Both the US and Great Britain conducted aerial reconnaissance and bombings in the central region and set up Operation North-

Two US soldiers checking a consignment of liquid containers, some empty, some full, as part of the aid for the Kurds in Northern Iraq. This picture displays not just the African American participation in this mission, it also shows how women are involved more and more in high risk operations.

ern Watch and Operation Southern Watch to protect those two areas of air space from Iraqi military incursion.

Also, in 1992, on August 3rd, the United States began a series of military exercises in Kuwait, after Iraq had refused to recognize the new border between Kuwait and Iraq set up by the United Nations. In addition, Iraq had also refused to cooperate with the United Nations inspection teams whose task it was to establish the whereabouts, if any, of weapons of mass destruction. This was the cause of much controversy later when a leader of those inspection teams confirmed at one time that he was convinced there were such weapons in Iraq, yet after the 2003 invasion, that same person said he believed there had never been weapons of mass destruction in Iraq – such mixed messages were a part of the intelligence that led to the 2003 invasion.

In Sierra Leone, West Africa, Operation Silver Anvil evacuated 438 people from that country after the overthrow of President Joseph Saidu Momo on April 29, 1992. That action was carried out by a US European Command Joint Special Operation Task Force, using C-141 aircraft from Air Mobility Command and C-130s from the US Air Force's Rhein-Main Air Force Base in Germany. The C-141s carried 136 people to Rhein-Main for onward flights to their homes, while the C-130s flew 302 more people to Dakar in Senegal.

Somalia was another country in Africa, the east this time, where there had been bitter fighting between factions wanting control of the country. Food had become a major currency in the region and was commonly stolen from relief agencies and traded for weapons. President George H. W. Bush, in one of his last acts as President of the United States responded to a UN appeal, which asked for assistance from member nations. President Bush proposed to the UN that United States combat troops could lead the intervention force. The UN accepted this offer and 25,000 US troops were deployed to Somalia. President Bush stated that this would not be an "open-ended commitment." The objective of Operation Restore Hope was to rapidly secure the trade routes in Somalia so that food could reach the people and the President stated that US troops would be home in time for Bill Clinton's inauguration in January 1993. In fact, they were not.

Upon his inauguration, President Clinton expressed a desire to scale down the US presence in Somalia and to let UN forces take over. In March 1993 the UN officially took over the operation, naming this mission UNOSOM II. The objective of this mission was to promote "nation building" within Somalia. One main target was to disarm the Somali insurgents. UNOSOM II stressed restoring law and order, improving the infrastructure, and assisting the people with setting up a representative government. Part of the US contribution to Operation Restore Hope was medical support and the 224th Medical Detachment of the 36th Medical Group provided a medical center.

Members of the 224th Medical Detachment pose outside their temporary medical center.

In Europe, there was civil unrest in Yugoslavia, which ultimately led to a bitter civil war, with tribal factions fighting for territory and, in some cases, renewed control of the whole country. In July 1992, Operation Provide Promise began. It was a humanitarian relief operation in the region of Bosnia and Herzogovina and ran for three and a half years, until January 1996. As this was taking place, on July 9, 1993, President Clinton reported the deployment of 350 US soldiers to the Republic of Macedonia to participate in the UN Protection Force to help maintain stability in that area of former Yugoslavia. Then, in 1994, the numbers in Macedonia were increased by a further 200 personnel. In 1995, NATO began its bombing of Bosnian Serbs in Operation Deliberate Force.

US UN Observers (right) discuss issues with a civilian Swiss UN policeman. African Americans played a key part in this operation.

LEFT: A massive USAF C-5 Galaxy from Travis AFB in California unloads a white-painted recovery truck at Skopje Airport.

Operation Deliberate Force came about because Bosnian Serb forces had advanced on the UN-declared Safe Area of Srebrenica. So on July 11, 1995, NATO aircraft attacked Bosnian targets in the Srebrenica area of Bosnia-Herzegovina identified by UN observers. Next, on July 25th, the North Atlantic Council authorized the deterrence of an attack on the Safe Area of Gorazde, and the use of NATO air power if this Safe Area was threatened or attacked. On August 1st, the Council took similar decisions aimed at deterring attacks on the Safe Areas of Sarajevo, Bihac and Tuzla. On August 4th, NATO aircraft conducted air strikes against Croatian Serb air defence radars near Udbina airfield and Knin in Croatia. As a result, NATO air forces were active in all these areas.

By April 1996, security in Liberia had deteriorated to such a level that it was felt US citizens were under threat, and President Clinton ordered the implementation of Operation Assured Response, to evacuate US citizens and certain third-country nationals who had taken refuge in the grounds of the US Embassy. A little over a month later, Operation Quick Re-sponse went into action to evacuate American citizens from Bangui, in the Central African Republic. The task was also to enhance the security of the US Embassy there while unrest continued. Men and women from the US Marine Corps element of the Liberian Operation Assured Response group provided that Embassy security, while at the same time evacuating 448 individuals, of whom approximately 200 were American. The Marines returned to Liberia on June 22nd.

A USAF F-16 lands at Aviano in Italy after an Operation Deliberate Force mission. Once again, African Americans took a significant role in these operations.

Further disturbances in Liberia in September 1998 caused a further military detachment of 30 personnel to increase the security of the US Embassy in Monrovia.

The Twentieth Century continued in this way, with actions in Haiti in 1994-1995 under Operation Uphold Democracy, where 20,000 US troops were deployed. In March 1997, Operation Silver Wake deployed men and machines to Tirana in Albania, to evacuate US government employees and a number of private citizens. During the same month, a standby force of US troops was deployed to Congo and Gabon, to provide enhanced security to US installations and to be prepared to evacuate US citizens from those two locations. No sooner was that operation complete than more military personnel were dispatched to Sierra Leone to prepare for and undertake the evacuation of US government employees and private US citizens.

Cambodia had not been a source of great US interest since the days of the Vietnam War, but on July 11, 1997, a US Task Force of around 550 men and women was deployed to Utapao Air Base in Thailand. The task was to ensure the security of American citizens in Cambodia during a period of conflict in that country. It was expected that US citizens might need to be evacuated from Cambodia and some were, but order was restored and so the US force withdrew.

Arabia and Africa returned to the focus of the US government in 1998. Operation Desert Fox saw United States and British air elements conduct a four-day bombing campaign over Iraq between December 16-19. It was put into effect because Iraq had failed to comply with United Nations resolutions and had interfered with UN inspection teams seeking to ensure there were no weapons of mass destruction either in store or being manufactured there. Once again, the leader of the inspection teams had expressed serious concerns about weapon materials being manufactured in Iraq. This bombing campaign had been planned and prepared as early as February 1998 and aroused extensive comment and criticism both at home in the United States and abroad. At first, Saudi Arabia, Bahrain and the UAE had all declared that they would not allow their air bases to be used in such a strike, though by December, they had relented and the

Short-range tactical strikes were carried out by 12 Squadron of Britain's Royal Air Force, operating out of Kuwait and Saudi Arabia.

Rockwell B-1B Lancers of the 28th Bomb Wing flew from Ellsworth AFB in South Dakota to Bahrain, from where they flew the heavy strategic bombing raids.

strikes took place. This campaign was a prelude to the invasion of Iraq took place in 2003 to remove Saddam Hussein from power.

Whilst Iraq was much in world focus, there were still issues in Africa that demanded US attention and President Clinton instructed the deployment of a military force to stand by to evacuate US citizens from Guinea-Bissau in June 1998. Operation Shepherd Venture placed the military detachment in Dakar, Senegal in readiness for the evacuation from the city of Bissau. In that same year, the US Embassies in Nairobi, Kenya and Daar es Salaam in Tanzania in August 1998 were attacked by al Qaeda terrorists. 258 people were killed and over 5,000 more injured in those two bomb attacks and the Clinton Administration reacted instantly with an aggressive response.

The United States launched cruise missiles on August 20, 1998, striking a terrorist training complex in Afghanistan

The devastated US Embassy in Dares-Salaam.

and destroying a pharmaceutical factory in Khartoum, the capital of Sudan, where it had been reported that nerve gas was being manufactured. Both targets were believed to have been financed by Osama bin Laden the founder of al Qaeda, the Islamist terrorist organization. Up to this time, the United States had been satisfied to comply with UN resolutions on sanctions, sometimes proposing them, or even requesting a UN resolution authorizing the

use of armed force, but in this case, it seemed clear that indifference both from the UN and some of the Muslim allies of the United States, particularly the Saudi Arabian view of a truck bombing that killed nineteen US service personnel, prompted the US to take a more aggressive line. It had to protect its embassies and published a warning to would-be aggressors of the likely consequences of such attacks.

Whatever peace existed at the turn of the 21st Century, within a year, it was shattered. September 11, 2001 was perhaps the most horrific day for the United States in modern history. Nineteen al Qaeda terrorists hi-jacked four airliners in the Continental United States. Two were flown into the twin towers of the World Trade Center in New York and the two buildings collapsed and over 2,700 people perished. Three hundred and forty-three New York firefighters and sixty New York Police officers lost their lives in their courageous attempts to rescue survivors from the two buildings. Among that number of firefighters were twelve African Americans.

A third airliner was crashed into the Pentagon building, killing 184 people and the fourth was intended to be flown into the Capitol Building or the White House. However, passengers on that aircraft had switched on cellphones to try to

This picture depicts ten of the African American New York Firefighters who lost their lives serving their city and their country. Sadly, none of the publicity pictures produced after the event featured them or their surviving comrades. They deserve recognition and will be remembered. Top from L to R: Leon W. Smith, Jr., Shawn E. Powell, Vernon Cherry, Andre Fletcher, Ronnie L. Henderson. Bottom from L to R: Gerard Jean Baptiste, Keithroy Maynard, William L. Henry, Jr., Karl Joseph, Tarel Coleman.

contact anyone they could and learned of the Twin Towers attack. As a result a number of the passengers took it upon themselves to try to overpower the terrorists in the hope that they might be able to rescue the aircraft. Unfortunately, their attempt failed and the aircraft crashed in a field near Shanksville, Pennsylvania. There were no survivors from any of the four aircraft.

Al Qaeda was clearly the first suspect for these horrifying events, the first such attacks on mainland United States. At first, Osama bin Laden denied responsibility, but eventually, in 2004, he proudly proclaimed that it was his organization that had carried out the strikes. The reasons given for the attacks were the United States' support of Israel, the fact that there were US forces in Saudi Arabia and the sanctions levied against Iraq. And yet, bin Laden was himself a Saudi, in fact a member of a highly respected Saudi family, who ultimately disowned him and his beliefs.

It is a sad fact that those twelve African American firefighters have been barely recognized down the years. It began with New York's Mayor Giuliani posing with a group of firefighters on the television program "Saturday Night Live", after the event. Every firefighter in the group behind the Mayor was white. And as so many people gave thanks across the City of New York for the survivors and remembered those who had perished, the African Americans were barely represented, except in their own communities. Those twelve firefighters were: Vernon Cherry, André Fletcher, Gerard Baptiste, Keith Glascoe, Karl Joseph, Tarel Coleman, William Henry, Ronnie Henderson, Vernon Richard, Leon Smith, Jr., Shawn Powell, and Keithroy Maynard.

One firefighter survivor who must be mentioned here is Firefighter Regina Wilson, one of only a few African American women firefighters anywhere. She was a member of the crew of Engine 219 and had just finished night shift. She was having breakfast with her crew members when the call came to go to the World Trade Center. Neither she nor her teammates had any idea what they were going into, but as they drove through the Brooklyn Battery Tunnel, it filled with smoke and dust. She and the other team members emerged from the tunnel and set about the rescue task that faced

them. They found bodies, parts of bodies, limbs and people in panic. They worked tirelessly and seven of Regina's crew gave their lives that day. It is a testament to the courage and fortitude of this young woman that she continues to serve in the Fire Department of New York, still a member of the crew of Engine 219.

A woman of courage and calling. New York Firefighter Regina Wilson poses in front of Engine 219 in September 2011, ten years after the most momentous event of her career.

This tragic set of events was the justification and basis of President George W. Bush's declaration of War on Terror. The first military move was to invade Afghanistan, where it was seen that the seat of control of al Qaeda was located. Osama bin Laden had been in Afghanistan for some years and knew the country well, and he eventually evaded capture for ten years. But the US campaign had to be also to dispel the Taliban rule of the country, for it was they who harbored and encouraged terrorist acts around the world. The United States also introduced the Patriot Act, which enabled law enforcement and security agencies to take much greater steps to minimize the opportunities for acts of terror to be committed. The Afghan War was distinctly unpopular with certain sectors of the US population, in fact, it was unpopular overall, because Americans do not like losing wars, and this did not look like a winner, as demonstrated by the Russians who had attempted to control the Taliban earlier with-

The downside of war. This nurse is closing the container in which the bodies of Americans who have died in Afghanistan will make their final journey home.

out success. As far as African Americans were concerned, it seemed to be much more of a white liberal conflict than one for them. Even so, many African Americans have fought there and many have died in their nation's cause.

On March 19, 2003, a coalition of forces from the United States, Great Britain, Australia and Poland, supported by smaller contingents from Peshmerga and Kurdistan, invaded Iraq, in what was seen by many, especially President George W. Bush, as a continuation of the original Gulf War of 1991. This invasion was variously called Operation Iraqi Freedom, the 2003 Gulf War or Gulf War 2. The alliance struck the Presidential Palace from the air on March 19th and this action was quickly followed by a ground offensive aiming for Baghdad. The Iraqi resistance was minimal and by April 9th, the city of Baghdad was secured by a joint American/British force.

General Tommy Franks commanded the US attack from Kuwait into Central Iraq and fought the Battle of Nasiriyah in Central Iraq on the way to Baghdad. The British Commander was Air Marshal Brian Burridge and his task force quickly secured Basra, and then joined the US force en route to Baghdad. Several other incursions took place against pockets of the Iraqi army including the capture and occupation

of Kirkuk on April 10th by the 173rd Airborne Division of the US Army, as well as the attack and capture of the town of Tikrit, Saddam Hussein's birthplace on April 15th. Saddam Hussein himself and the central leadership went into hiding as the coalition forces completed the occupation of the country. On May 1st, the end of combat operations was declared, so ending the invasion period and beginning of the military occupation.

Chief David Jones, a Navy Corpsman, holds a newborn baby his medical team delivered as the Battle for Nasiriyah was raging.

Some time after the capture of Tikrit, in December 2003, the US Army captured Saddam Hussein. After extensive interrogations by Staff Sergeant Eric Maddox of over three hundred people, on the day he was supposed to return to the US, he found himself interrogating Muhammad Ibrahim, Saddam's right-hand man. Eventually, Ibrahim took Maddox and a task force to the farm at Tikrit where Saddam was hiding. He did not want to "betray" his former master, but as he walked past a loop of rope sticking up from the ground he kicked it. The task force soldiers quickly realized that the rope was a handle to a trap door, which led to a deep hole in the ground where they found Saddam Hussein, now bearded and unkempt, as though he had been there for weeks or months. Saddam was returned to Baghdad, where he ultimately stood trial.

Women in combat. In the 2003 Iraq war, women were now right on the front line alongside the men and acquitting themselves well. Two young female combatants give comfort during a brief respite.

Former Chairman of the Joint Chiefs of Staff at the time of "Desert Storm", General Colin Powell was now Secretary of State in the Bush administration in 2003. Here, he displays a "dummy" vial of anthrax in his presentation in February 2003 to the UN Security Council on the issue of Iraq's possession of weapons of mass destruction.

US President George W. Bush and British Prime Minister Tony Blair both explained that the reason for the invasion of Iraq was to "disarm Iraq of weapons of mass destruction, to end the Saddam Hussein regime and his support for international terrorism, as well as to free the Iraqi people". There was a great deal of controversy over the invasion, with several of America's and Britain's traditional allies opposing it on the supposition that the war was illegal and expressing the view that the process of negotiation through the UN had not been exhausted. That particular contention will probably last a long time, but it should be noted that first, it was reported that the head of the UN inspection team, Hans Blick, had declared some time before the invasion that he believed there were weapons of mass destruction stockpiled in Iraq. The inspectors simply had not found them, because they had been obstructed by the Iraqis. Much later, after the war had taken place, Mr. Blick declared that he believed there had never been weapons of mass destruction in Iraq – yet he had been denied access to critical sites in Iraq, so how could he be certain?

Some time after the war, but still during the period of the Allied occupation of Iraq, the United States Central Intelligence Agency reported that no weapons of mass destruction had been found in Iraq. Many people since that time have said that there may not have been such weapons in Iraq now, but that did not mean they had never been there. In any event, the political leaders, especially Britain's Tony Blair, acknowledged that no weapons of mass destruction had been found in Iraq after the war and during the occupation, but made a strong, and valid, point that he was acting on the intelligence provided to him in the days before the decision to invade Iraq was taken. And on the basis of that intelligence, he considered there was a case to attack. Great Britain's Chief of the General Staff, General Sir Mike Jackson, reflected also on the question of whether this war was legal and satisfied himself that it was before ordering British forces into action.

During the occupation period, in May and June 2004, a young soldier of the British Army, 25-year-old Private Johnson Beharry, born in Grenada, in the West Indies, was serving with the 1st Battalion of the Princess of Wales' Royal Regiment. On May 1st, Beharry was driving a British Warrior tracked armored vehicle, which had been called to the assistance of a foot patrol caught in a series of ambushes. The Warrior was hit by several Iraqi-fired rocket-propelled grenades, damaging the vehicle and destroying its radio com-

Private Johnson Beharry in Iraq, readied for another patrol.

munication. The platoon commander, the vehicle's gunner and a number of others in the vehicle were injured. Because his periscope was damaged, Private Beharry was forced to open his hatch to steer his vehicle and so expose his face and head to Iraqi small arms fire. He drove the crippled Warrior through the ambush, with his own crew aboard and led five other Warriors to safety. He then pulled his wounded comrades from the vehicle as he was constantly exposed to further enemy fire. He was cited on this occasion for "Valour of the Highest Order".

Back on duty on June 11, 2004, Beharry was again driving the lead Warrior of his platoon through Al Amarah when his

vehicle was ambushed. A rocket-propelled grenade hit the Warrior six inches from Beharry's head, and he suffered serious injuries to his face and brain. Other rockets then hit the vehicle, incapacitating his commander and injuring several of the crew. Despite his life threatening injuries, Beharry retained control of the vehicle and drove it out of the ambush area before losing consciousness. He later required brain surgery for his head injuries. Queen Elizabeth II formally invested Private Beharry with the Victoria Cross, Britain's highest award for valor on April 27, 2005. The citation for Beharry's award read:

> *"Private Beharry carried out two individual acts of great heroism by which he saved the lives of his comrades. Both were in direct face of the enemy, under intense fire, at great personal risk to himself (one leading to him sustaining serious injuries). Beharry displayed repeated extreme gallantry and unquestioned valor, despite intense direct attacks, personal injury and damage to his vehicle in the face of relentless enemy action".*

This was the first award of the Victoria Cross in thirty years and the particular significance of it was that Private Beharry's commander had no thought of the fact that this young man was an African-Caribbean – he was a British soldier who had performed with outstanding valor. Interestingly too,

Private Beharry with General Sir Mike Jackson. Both were attending the same investiture.

General Sir Mike Jackson was made a Knight Grand Cross of the Order of the Bath at the same investiture in which Private Beharry received his VC and of Beharry, General Jackson said: *"I had never felt more proud of the British Army"* and following the investiture said that he was "overshadowed" by Beharry, *"and quite rightly so – it was an honor to stand alongside him"*. Praise indeed from one of Great Britain's greatest generals in modern times.

Of the US Forces in Iraq, since the beginning of the 2003 invasion and up to June 2011, some 4,469 American servicemen and women have died in combat or by terrorist action. Nine percent of that number, 402 persons were African American and more than half of them were under 25 years old. Frightening statistics, but still a fraction of the huge numbers of deaths in World Wars I and II.

The war in Afghanistan has raged for over a decade as this manuscript is being written and up to November 2011, 1,845 Americans have given their lives in Operation Enduring Freedom, as well as 389 Britons. Men and women have died in combat, from all races, creeds and colors. The task of this book is not to justify any particular viewpoint on the rights and wrongs of this or any other war in which African Americans have fought, but it is worth saying here that once

Navy Corpsman 2nd Class Lammont T. Hammond was awarded the Bronze Star Medal with combat distinguish device after exposing himself to enemy fire as he assisted wounded Marines in Afghanistan. At that time, he was assigned to the 1st Battalion, 5th Marine Regiment. He received his medal from Brigadier-General John Love while stationed at the US Naval Hospital in Naples, Italy.

"Operation Enduring Freedom" is a campaign aimed at just that single purpose – enduring freedom for Afghan people as well as for the world at large. Here, US soldiers engage with Afghan villagers, in the "hearts and minds" aspect of what is a very bloody war.

more, many people argued that this was not a war for African Americans. Whether it is or not, many African Americans have stepped up to the mark and volunteered for active duty, just as they have in all of America's wars past. For those who have lost their lives in the cause of freedom, all nations should be grateful.

CHAPTER FIFTEEN

From Helicopter through High Altitude – to Space

For some reason, people, especially men, do not expect to learn that a woman has flown a Lockheed U-2 spy plane. It comes as even more of a surprise to learn that not only has a woman achieved that distinction, an African American woman has done it. Merryl David Tengesdal first took to the air in a U-2 in March 2004 as a student pilot from Beale Air Force Base in California. Since then she has flown over Iraq, Afghanistan and Somalia, as well as many other undisclosed locations.

Merryl David was born in New York and grew up in the Bronx. From early childhood, she declared an undying enthusiasm for "Startrek" and watched every program she could access

Lieutenant-Colonel Merryl Tengesdal.

for several years. It was not surprising, then, that she decided she wanted to be an astronaut from early childhood. Born in 1974, she had made the decision as to where her future lay and everything she did in schools and leisure, ultimately led her to a career in aviation. Her first step on this road was to study at the University of New Haven, in Connecticut, where she earned a degree in Electrical Engineering.

Instead of joining the Reserve Officer Training Corps at university, she completed her degree and then enrolled in Officer Candidate School, to graduate and be commissioned as an Ensign in the US Navy. From there, she went to the Aviation Pre-Flight Training program at Naval Air Station Pensacola, in Florida, and then to Undergraduate Flight Training at NAS Corpus Christi in Texas.

David's first flight experience was in a Beech T-34 "Mentor". After completing fixed-wing training in September 1995, she applied for training in rotary-wing aircraft – helicopters – and was accepted. Ms. Tengesdal was on her way. Helicopter Flight

Lieutenant-Colonel Merryl Tengesdal poses in front of the aircraft she flies, the Lockheed U-2 – the first African American woman to achieve this distinction.

Training took place back at Pensacola and she graduated as a helicopter pilot in August 1996. A month later, she was promoted to Lieutenant (JG). Now located at NAS Mayport in Florida, she joined the SH-60B Fleet Replacement Squadron, emerging as an operational Sikorsky SH-60B "Seahawk" pilot in September 1997.

Over the next three years she undertook an operational tour of duty, with two long sea cruises and a number of short cruises and in September 1998, she was promoted to Lieutenant. Her tour of duty took her to the Middle

The SH-60B is a multi-mission helicopter originally built to an Army specification, but adapted for shipboard use. It is a combat capable machine and can be used in anti-submarine warfare, anti-surface action, medical evacuation and search and rescue roles.

The Air Force version of the T-6, named "Texan II" because of its number in the trainer numbering sequence and, of course, because of the illustrious predecessor. This aircraft is intended to train pilots up to pre-fast jet or pre-multi engine levels.

East, South America and the Caribbean. In 2000, she was selected for Instructor training and progressed to become a T-34C and T-6A instructor. Once she had completed the T-6A instructor program, she was assigned to the Joint Student Undergraduate Pilot Training School at Moody Air Force Base in Georgia. The T-6A is essentially the successor to the long-serving T-34, as a turbo-prop two-seat trainer, which can take students from ab-initio training all the way through to advanced level and has been in US Navy service since 2003.

When her Naval engagement was complete, Lieutenant Tengesdal transferred to the United States Air Force in the rank of Captain. In March 2004, her new and most exciting program of flight training began, for she had been successful in achieving selection to join Air Force Squadron One, the avenue to flying the incredible Lockheed U-2 spy plane, affectionately known as "the Dragon Lady". She was also promoted to the rank of Major. She became one of only five women to enter the U-2 program and one of only three African Americans, the first female. She completed her flying training in this exciting new leg of her career in April 2005.

Major Tengesdal's first assignment on completion of training was to remain at Beale Air Force Base, where she was deployed to fly missions over Afghanistan during Operation Olive Harvest and over Iraq, and the Horn of Africa to provide

intelligence in the process of combating terrorism and piracy in that region. During this time, she was also assigned to the duties of Chief of Flight Safety in the 9th Reconnaissance Wing and 9th Physiological Support Squadron Director of Operations. Major Tengesdal also became a U2 instructor pilot. By July 2007, she had become a U-2 and T38-A Instructor Pilot as well as 9 PSPTS Director of Operations at Beale up to November 2008. In November 2008, she was appointed Commander of Detachment 2/WR-ALC Plant 42 at Palmdale, California until December 2010. Her most recent assignment has great significance, in that, now as a Lieutenant-Colonel since February 2010, she was assigned to the 99th Squadron, taking up location in Korea. The 99th has great significance to all African American pilots, for it was the 99th Fighter Squadron that Major Benjamin O. Davis, Jr. took to North Af-

The Lockheed U-2 "Dragon Lady" high altitude reconnaissance aircraft.

rica and set the scene for the ultimate liberation of African Americans.

One can wonder if, when her parents gave her the name "Merryl", they might have anticipated where her future lay. Certainly, her name seems to have been almost prophetic, for in the French language, it translates to the word "Blackbird". However, rather than fly Lockheed's SR-71 "Blackbird", she was selected to fly the U-2 "Dragon Lady", at regular altitudes of up to 70,000 feet. In flying terms, the final frontier was the challenge of space. Merryl David Tengesdal has not reached that part of her personal goal, though she is young enough yet to achieve it during her Air Force career.

Robert Henry Lawrence, Jr. was born on October 2, 1935 and died on December 8, 1967. He was a Major in the United States Air Force and is said to have been the first African American astronaut. At the age of 16, he graduated in the top 10 percent from Englewood High School in Chicago and went on to graduate at the age of only 20 from Bradley University with a Bachelor's degree in Chemistry. At Bradley, he distinguished himself as Cadet Commander in the Air Force Reserve Officer Training Corps and was commissioned as a 2nd Lieutenant in the Air Force Reserve.

Major Robert H. Lawrence.

In June 1967, Major Lawrence successfully completed the Air Force Flight Test Pilot Training School at Edwards AFB, California. That same month he was selected by the USAF to become an astronaut in the Air Force's Manned Orbital Laboratory program, and technically becoming the first African American astronaut. However, he was killed on December 8, 1967 in the crash of a two-seat TF-104 "Starfighter" at Edwards AFB. He was flying backseat as instructor for a flight test trainee learning the steep-descent glide technique. The student pilot flared too late in his approach, and the air-

craft struck the ground so hard it collapsed the landing gear. The aircraft caught fire and while the student pilot ejected successfully, though severely injured, Major Lawrence was killed as he ejected while the aircraft was rolling on to one side. He died instantly and never had his chance at space flight.

The first African American who made it into space was Colonel Guion "Guy" Bluford. Guy Bluford, Jr. was born in Philadelphia, Pennsylvania in November 1942. His mother was a special education teacher and his father a mechanical engineer. The Blufords encouraged their sons to work hard and set high goals for themselves. Guy did just that.

Colonel Guy Bluford.

His Bachelor of Science degree in aerospace engineering came from Pennsylvania State University, where he enrolled in ROTC and learned to fly. Awarded his wings in 1966, he was assigned to the 557th Tactical Fighter Squadron at Cam Ranh Bay in Vietnam. Guy flew 144 combat missions, 65 of them over North Vietnam, and then spent five years as a flight instructor at Sheppard Air Force Base in Texas.

The crew of STS-8.

The Challenger patch for the STS-8 mission.

Returning to school, Guion Bluford achieved his Master of Science degree with a distinction in aerospace engineering from the Air Force Institute of Technology in 1974, then went on to a doctorate of philosophy in aerospace engineering with a minor in laser physics from the same institute in 1978. Also in 1978, he discovered that he had been selected as one of 35 astronaut candidates out of a field of over 10,000. He became an astronaut in August 1979. Bluford's first mission was STS-8 aboard the space shuttle Challenger 3, launched from Kennedy Space Center on Aug. 30, 1983. He thus became the first African American astronaut, flying 98 orbits of the earth.

Ronald Ervin McNair, PhD was born in Lake City, South Carolina on October 21, 1950 and died on January 28, 1986. He was a physicist and an astronaut. In 1971 he received his Bachelor of Science degree in engineering physics from North Carolina A&T State University in Greensboro, North Carolina. Dr. McNair received his PhD in Physics from Massachusetts Institute of Technology (MIT) under the supervi-

sion of Professor Michael Feld and became nationally recognized for his work in the field of laser physics.

In 1978 Dr. McNair was selected as one of only 35 successful candidates from a pool of 10,000 for the NASA astronaut program. He first flew on STS-41-B aboard Challenger in February 1984, as a mission specialist becoming only the

Dr. Ronald McNair and his crew from STS-51-L

The horrifying sight from the ground of STS-51-L as it exploded just 73 seconds after launch on January 28, 1986.

Dr. Ronald McNair working on a simulator.

The flight patch for the ill-fated STS-51-L crew.

The mission patch for STS-33 on left and STS-44 on the right.

second African American to fly in space, behind Colonel Guion Bluford. Following this mission, McNair was selected for STS-51-L, which was launched on 28th January 1986. He died during the launch of that mission, when Challenger disintegrated nine miles above the Atlantic Ocean only 73 seconds after lift-off.

Frederick Drew Gregory is a retired USAF Colonel and was born in Washington, DC on 7th January 1941. He is a former astronaut and also former NASA Deputy Administrator. He served briefly as NASA Acting Administrator in early 2005, covering the period between the departure of Sean O'Keefe and the arrival of Michael Griffin.

Colonel Gregory was the first African American to pilot a Space Shuttle.

Colonel Gregory was selected as an astronaut in January 1978 and after training was assigned as Astronaut Office representative at the Kennedy Space Center during the initial Orbiter checkout and was launch support officer for Missions STS-1 and STS-2. He was Flight Data File Manager and lead spacecraft communicator (CAPCOM). Next he was appointed Chief, Operational Safety at NASA Headquarters in Washington, DC, then Chief of Astronaut Training. He was a member of the Orbiter Configuration Control Board and the Space Shuttle Program Control Board. A veteran of three Shuttle missions he has logged approximately 456 hours in space. He was the pilot on STS-51B, which flew between April 29 and May 6, 1985 and then he was the space-

craft commander on STS-33, which flew during November 22-27, 1989. His final mission was aboard STS-44, again as spacecraft commander, between November 24 and December 1, 1991. Both of these missions carried Department of Defense payloads.

Colonel Gregory then served at NASA Headquarters as Associate Administrator for the Office of Safety and Mission Assurance between 1992 and 2001. He was Associate Administrator for the Office of Space Flight from 2001 to 2002 and on August 12, 2002, he was sworn in as NASA Deputy Administrator between February 20, 2005 and April 14, 2005. He vacated the position of Deputy Administrator on November 29, 2005.

Major-General Charles F. Bolden USMC was born in Columbia, South Carolina on August 19, 1946. He graduated from the United States Naval Academy with a Bachelor of Science degree in

STS-51B patch, Colonel Gregory's last mission.

Electrical Science and went on to achieve a Master of Science degree in Systems Management from the University of Southern California in 1977. Lieutenant Bolden gained flight training at Pensacola, Florida, at Meridian, Mississippi, and Kingsville, Texas before being becoming a naval aviator in May 1970. He flew more than 100 sorties into North and South Vietnam, Laos, and Cambodia, in the A-6A Intruder while assigned to VMA (AW)-533 at Nam Phong, Thailand between June 1972 and June 1973.

Major-General Charles F. Bolden.

Upon returning to the United States, Bolden began a two-year tour as a Marine Corps selection and recruiting officer in Los Angeles, California, followed by three years in various assignments at the Marine Corp Air Station in El Toro, California. In June 1979, he graduated from the US Naval Test Pilot School at Patuxent River, Maryland, and was assigned to the Naval Air Test Center's Systems Engineering and Strike Aircraft Test Directorates. While there, he served as an ordnance test pilot and flew numerous test projects in the A-6E, EA-6B, and A-7C/E aeroplanes. He logged more than 6,000 hours flying time, before being selected as an astronaut trainee in 1980.

Bolden graduated as an astronaut in August 1981. His technical assignments with NASA included: Astronaut Office Safety Officer; Technical Assistant to the Director of Flight Crew Operations; Special Assistant to the Director of the Johnson Space Center; Astronaut Office Liaison to the Safety, Reliability and Quality Assurance Directorates of the Marshall Space Flight Center and the Kennedy Space Center; Chief

Captain Bolden flew the A-6 "Intruder" in Vietnam from Nam Phong, known to Marines as "the rose garden".

of the Safety Division at JSC; Lead Astronaut for Vehicle Test and Checkout at the Kennedy Space Center; and Assistant Deputy Administrator, NASA Headquarters. A veteran of four space flights, he logged more than 680 hours in Space. Bolden served as pilot on STS-61C between 12th and 18th January 1986, then on STS-31, between April 24 and April 29, 1990.

He was the mission commander on STS-45 which flew from March 24 to April 2, 1992, then commanded STS-60 from February 3-11, 1994. General Bolden retired from the Marine Corps in the rank of Major-General. He was nominated in 2009 by President Barack Obama and confirmed by the US Senate, as the twelfth Administrator of the National Aeronautics and Space Administration, taking up the appointment in July of that year.

Dr. Bernard A. Harris was the first African American astronaut to take a walk in space. Harris first became interested

These are the four mission patches for the space journeys undertaken by Charles Bolden.

Dr. Bernard A. Harris, above, and below, his mission patches for STS-55 and STS-63.

in space when he watched the progress of Apollo 11 on television in 1969. He was born in San Antonio, Texas and graduated from the Sam Houston High School in 1974, to embark on a Bachelor of Science degree in Biology from the University of Houston. He went on to secure his MD from Texas Tech University School of Medicine in 1982. He completed his residency at the Mayo Clinic in 1985. Dr. Harris then completed a National Research Council Fellowship at the NASA Ame Research Center in 1987, and he went on to train as a Flight Surgeon at the Aerospace School of Medicine at Brooks Air Force Base in San Antonio in 1988.

On completion of his fellowship at Ame, Dr. Harris joined the Johnson Space Center as a clinical scientist and flight surgeon. Here, he carried out clinical investigations into space adaptation and developed a series of countermeasures to enable astronauts to overcome extended periods in space flight. He was selected by NASA in January 1990 and became an astronaut in July 1991, qualifying for as a mission specialist for future space flight crews. He served as the crew representative for Shuttle Software in the Astronaut Office Operations Development Branch. Dr. Harris was assigned as a mission specialist on

STS-55, Spacelab D-2, in August 1991. He flew aboard Columbia for ten days between April 26 and May 6, 1993. This was on the mission in which the Shuttle reached one year of accumulated flight time. Harris was part of the payload crew of Spacelab D-2, conducting a variety of research in physical and life sciences. During this flight, he logged over 239 hours and nearly 4.2 million miles in space.

Dr. Harris' second mission in space was as the Payload Commander on STS-63, from February 2-11, 1995. This was the first flight of the new joint Russian-American Space Program. In this mission, the first rendezvous with the Russian space station Mir took place and the Spartan 204 satellite was retrieved. It was also during this flight that Dr. Harris became the first African American to walk in space. At the same time, his fellow astronaut, Michael Foale became the first British-born astronaut to walk in space. Another detail of this space mission was that Eileen Collins became the first female Shuttle pilot. Dr. Bernard Harris logged 198 hours and 29 minutes in space, completing 129 orbits and covering over 2.9 million miles. He was the first African American man to go in space as one of NASA's research teams and was also involved in the construction of the Space Rover.

The first African American woman in space was a medical practitioner, Mae Carol Jemison. Dr. Jemison was born in Decatur, Alabama in October 1956. Her parents were Charlie Jemison and Dorothy Green. She was the youngest of three and her family moved to Chicago when she was three years old. Her father was a maintenance supervisor for a charity organization, and her mother worked most of her career as an elementary school teacher of English and Mathematics at the Beethoven School in Chicago.

It was in Chicago that an uncle introduced Mae to the

Dr. Mae Carol Jemison was the first woman ever in space.

Jemison at work in space.

Dr. Jemison has practiced medicine as a volunteer in a Cambodian refugee camp and with the Peace Corps in West Africa. It was while she was working as a general practitioner in Los Angeles, California that NASA selected her and 14 others to be trained as astronauts. Dr. Jemison became a NASA mission specialist in 1988. In September 1992, Mae Jemison was the first African American woman to go into space, aboard the Shuttle Endeavour. She was in the first class of astronauts selected after the Challenger accident in 1986 and she worked the launch of the first flight after the Challenger accident.

Dr. Jemison flew her only space mission from September 12-20, 1992 as a Mission Specialist on STS-47 and the first thing she saw from space was Chicago, her hometown. She was working on the middeck where there was no outside view, but as the Shuttle passed over Chicago, the commander called her to the flight deck. *"It was such a significant moment because since I was a little girl I had always assumed I would go into space,"* she said. STS-47 was a cooperative mission

STS47 patch.

between the United States and Japan that included 44 Japanese and United States life science and materials processing experiments. Dr. Jemison logged 190 hours, 30 minutes and 23 seconds in space.

world of science. At the age of only sixteen she enrolled at Stanford University and in 1977, and as a twenty-one year old, she graduated with degrees in chemical engineering and Afro-American studies. Her Doctor of Medicine degree came from Cornell University in 1981. Mae Jemison says she was inspired by Dr. Martin Luther King, but to her, King's dream was not a fantasy, as so many saw it, but a real call to action. *"Too often people think of him as something like Santa – smiley and inoffensive,"* she once said. *"But when I think of Martin Luther King, I think of attitude, audacity, and bravery."* She thought the civil rights movement was all about breaking down the barriers to human potential. *"The best way to make dreams come true is to wake up,"* she said. Dr. Mae Carol Jemison certainly woke up and followed her destiny.

Captain Winston Elliott Scott, a Naval officer, was selected by NASA in March 1992, and reported to the Johnson Space Center in August of that same year. He served as a mission specialist on STS-72 in 1996 and STS-87 in 1997, and logged a total of 24 days, 14 hours and 34 minutes in space, including three space walks, totaling 19 hours and 26 minutes.

Scott entered Naval Aviation Officer Candidate School after graduation from Florida State University in December 1972. He completed flight training in fixed-wing and rotary-wing aircraft and was designated a Naval Aviator in August 1974. He served a 4-year tour of duty with Helicopter Anti-Submarine Squadron Light, Thirty-Three (HSL-33) at Naval Air

Captain Winston E. Scott.

Station North Island in California, flying the SH-2F Light Airborne Multi-Purpose System (LAMPS) helicopter. In 1978 Scott was selected to attend the Naval Postgraduate School at Monterey, California, where he earned his Master of Science degree in aeronautical engineering with avionics.

On completing fixed-wing jet training in the TA-4J Skyhawk, Scott served a tour of duty with Fighter Squadron Eighty-Four (VF-84) at NAS Oceana, Virginia, flying the F-14 Tomcat. In June 1986 Scott was designated an Aerospace Engineering Duty Officer. He served as a production test pilot at the Naval Aviation Depot, NAS Jacksonville, Florida, flying two aircraft types, the F/A-18 Hornet and the A-7 Corsair. He was also assigned as Director of the Product Support (engineering) Department. He was next assigned as the Deputy Director of the Tactical Aircraft Systems Department at the Naval Air Development Center at Warminster in Pennsylvania. As a research and development project pilot, he flew the F-14, F/A-18 and A-7 Corsair II aircraft. Scott has accumulated more than 4,000 hours of flight time in 20 different military and civilian aircraft, and more than 200 shipboard landings.

The Kaman SH-2F "Seasprite" was Lieutenant Scott's first mount, before transferring to fixed wing aircraft.

Captain Scott's space experience began with STS-72 Endeavour, which was a nine-day flight on January 11 - 20, 1996. The crew retrieved the Space Flyer Unit satellite, which was launched from Japan ten months earlier. They also deployed and retrieved the OAST-Flyer satellite, and conducted two spacewalks to demonstrate and evaluate techniques to be used in the assembly of the International Space Station. The mission was accomplished in 142 orbits of the Earth, traveling 3.7 million miles and Captain Scott logged a total of 214 hours and 41 seconds in space, including his first Extra-Vehicular-Activity (spacewalk) of 6 hours and 53 minutes.

His second mission was aboard STS-87, from November 19 to December 5, 1997. This was the fourth US Micrograv-

The mission patches for Captain Scott's two space missions – STS-72 on the left and STS-87 right.

ity Payload flight, and focused on experiments designed to study how the weightless environment of space affects various physical processes, and also on observations of the sun's outer atmospheric layers. Captain Scott performed two spacewalks on this mission. The first, a 7 hour 43 minute walk featured the manual capture of a Spartan satellite, in addition to testing Extra-Vehicular-Activity tools and procedures for future Space Station assembly. The second spacewalk lasted 5 hours and involved space station assembly tests. Testing of the AERCam Sprint was conducted during this walk. The mission was accomplished in 252 Earth orbits, traveling 6.5 million miles in 376 hours and 34 minutes.

Robert Lee Curbeam, Jr. was born on March 5, 1962. He graduated from Woodlawn High School in Baltimore County, Maryland in 1980 and progressed to his Bachelor's degree in Aerospace Engineering from the US Naval Academy in 1984. He later achieved a Master's Degree in Aeronautical Engineering from the Naval Postgraduate School. Upon graduation from the US Naval Academy, Curbeam commenced Naval Flight Officer training in 1984. In 1986 he was assigned to Fighter Squadron 11 (VF-11) and was deployed to the Mediterranean and the Caribbean, as well as the Arctic and Indian

Lieutenant-Commander Robert Lee Curbeam, Jr.

Oceans aboard the USS "Forrestal". While serving with VF-11, he also attended the Naval Fighter Weapons School, the "Top Gun" academy. In 1989, Curbeam was named Fighter Wing One Radar Interceptor Officer of the Year and also was awarded the Best Developmental Thesis Award at the US Naval Test Pilots' School.

Lieutenant-Commander Curbeam's first space flight was aboard STS-85, between August 7 and 9, 1997. It was a twelve-day mission, during which the crew deployed and retrieved the CRISTA-SPAS payload and operated the Japanese Manipulator Flight Demonstration Robotic Arm. They also studied changes in the Earth's atmosphere and tested technology destined for use in the International Space Station. The mission took 189 Earth orbits, covering 4.7 million miles in 11 days, 20 hours and 27 minutes. Between this and his second flight, Curbeam served as a spacecraft communicator, responsible for relaying all voice communication between Mission Control and crews aboard the Space Shuttle and the International Space Station.

Commander Curbeam's second space flight was STS-98, which took off on February 7, and returned to Earth on February 20, 2001. This mission continued the work of building

and improving the International Space Station and delivered the US laboratory module Destiny. The Shuttle spent seven days attached to the Space Station while Destiny was secured. Curbeam logged more than 19 EVA hours during three space walks.

The crew also then relocated a docking port, as well as delivering supplies and equipment to the Expedition 1 crew already aboard the space Station. After this second flight, he also served as the CAPCOM Branch Chief. During the spring of 2002, he served as Deputy Associate Administrator for Safety and Mission Assurance, at NASA Headquarters in Washington, DC.

The F-14 "Tomcat" was one of the world's most potent fighting aircraft. A VF-11 F-14A on one of the steam catapults of USS "George Washington". Robert Curbeam was assigned to this squadron in 1986.

The mission patches for Robert Curbeam's first and second space missions – STS-85 and STS-98.

Captain Curbeam's third and final space mission was STS-116, which took off on December 9th and landed on December 22, 2006. This was another mission to the International Space Station and it involved installing a new truss segment

Robert Curbeam and Sweden's female astronaut, Christer Fugelsang space walk on STS-116.

and re-wiring of the Space Station's electrical system. This crew also returned ISS Flight Engineer Thomas Reiter to Earth after six months in space. Astronaut Sunita Williams remained on the space station. During the mission, Astronaut Curbeam was the EVA crew member for a record-breaking four space walks, three of which were conducted along with Swedish astronaut Christer Fuglesang, as well as another

STS-116 mission patch.

with Sunita Williams. Along with rewiring the station's electrical system, Curbeam and Fuglesang aided in the retraction of a sticking solar array on December 18, 2006. In performing this unexpected fourth EVA to aid in the retraction of the array, Captain Curbeam became the first person to perform four spacewalks on a single mission. One more African American first.

Michael P. Anderson was a United States Air Force Colonel and was one of the astronauts killed in the Space Shuttle Columbia disaster in February 2003, when the Shuttle disintegrated upon re-entry into the Earth's atmosphere. He was born in Plattsburgh, New York, but Spokane in Washington State was his chosen hometown. Selected by NASA in December 1994, Anderson arrived at the Johnson Space Center in March 1995. He completed a year of training and evaluation, and was qualified for flight crew assignment as a mission specialist. Colonel Anderson was first assigned technical duties in the Flight Support Branch of the Astronaut

Colonel Michael P. Anderson.

Office, and then was selected to fly on Mission STS-89 and later, STS-107, logging over 593 hours in space. The STS-107 Columbia mission took off on 16th January 2003 and made its re-entry on February 1st. The 16-day flight was a dedicated science and research mission. Working 24 hours a day, in two alternating shifts, the crew successfully conducted almost 80 experiments. The mission ended abruptly

The patches for STS-89 and the ill-fated STS-107.

The horrifying sight of STS-107 disintegrating on its re-entry to Earth's atmosphere just sixteen minutes from safety.

when Columbia and her crew perished 16 minutes before scheduled landing.

Robert Lee "Bobby" Satcher, Jr. was born on September 22, 1965 in Hampton, Virginia. He is a physician, and a chemical engineer with two Doctorates to his credit. He became the first orthopedic surgeon in space on Space Mission STS-129. He took part in two spacewalks during STS-129 and chalked up 12 hours and 19 minutes of EVA time.

Prior to being accepted into the astronaut program by NASA, Satcher was Assistant Professor at the Feinberg School of Medicine at Northwestern University, working in the Department of Orthopedic Surgery. Satcher held appointments as an Attending Physician in Orthopedic Surgery at the Chil-

Dr. Robert Lee Satcher notched up 259 hours in space on the STS-129 mission and made two space walks totalling 12 hours and 19 minutes.

dren's Memorial Hospital in Chicago, Illinois, specializing in Musculoskeletal Oncology. He also held an Adjunct Appointment in the Biomedical Engineering Department at Northwestern University School of Engineering. Selected by NASA in May 2004, Satcher completed Astronaut Candidate Training in February 2006 and went on to the STS-129 Mission as a mission specialist, spending more than 259 hours in space.

Stephanie D. Wilson was born on September 27, 1966 in Boston Massachusetts. She flew on her first space mission aboard the Space Shuttle Mission STS-121 and was only the second African American woman to go into space after Dr. Mae Jemison. Selected as an Astronaut Candidate in April 1996, Wilson completed two years of training and evaluation to qualify for flight assignment as a mission specialist. She was initially assigned technical duties in the Astronaut Office Space Station Operations Branch to work with Space Station payload displays and procedures. She then served in the Astronaut Office CAPCOM Branch, working in Mission Control as a prime communicator with on-orbit crews. Following her work in Mission Control,

Stephanie D. Wilson flew for thirteen days in STS-121, fifteen days in STS-120 and a further sixteen days aboard STS-131.

she was assigned to technical duties in the Astronaut Office Shuttle Operations Branch involving the Space Shuttle Main Engines, External Tank and Solid Rocket Boosters.

Ms. Wilson flew on three shuttle missions. On STS-121, she flew as a mission specialist from July 4 to July 17, 2006. It was a return-to-flight test mission and assembly flight for the International Space Station. During the 13-day flight the crew of Space Shuttle Discovery tested new equipment and procedures that increase the safety of space shuttles, repaired a rail car on the International Space Station and

STS121 patch.

duced never-before-seen, high-resolution images of the Shuttle during and after its launch. Ms. Wilson also supported the robotic arm operations for vehicle inspection, using the Multi-Purpose Logistics Module installation. She also embarked on EVAs and was responsible for the transfer of more than 28,000 pounds of supplies and equipment to the ISS. The crew performed maintenance on the space station and delivered a new member to the Expedition 13 crew. The mission was accomplished in 12 days, 20 hours, 37 minutes and 54 seconds.

Stephanie Wilson also flew on the STS-120 mission which operated between October 23 and November 7, 2007. It was another 6.25 million mile Space Shuttle mission to the International Space Station, delivering the Harmony module, and reconfiguring the P-6 truss in preparation for future assembly missions. STS-120 took up a new Expedition 16 crew member, Daniel Tani, and returned to Earth with Expedition 15 and 16 crew member Clayton Anderson. The crew carried out four space walks and used a previously untested repair method on the station's solar array. The mission was completed in 15 days, 2 hours and 23 minutes over 238 Earth orbits. In April 2010, Ms. Wilson also flew as a Mission Specialist on STS-131.

STS-120 (left) and STS-131 (right) patches.

Joan Elizabeth Higginbotham was born in Chicago on August 3, 1964. She graduated as an engineer from Southern Illinois University and began her career with the Kennedy Space Center in 1987 as a Payload Electrical Engineer in the Electrical and Telecommunications Systems Division. Inside six months, she was appointed lead for the Orbiter Experiments (OEX) on OV-102, the Space Shuttle Columbia. She later worked on the Shuttle payload bay reconfiguration for all Shuttle missions and conducted electrical compatibility tests for all payloads flown aboard the Shuttle.

Joan Higginbotham "dressed to go".

Ms. Higginbotham was tasked with several special assignments, including that of Executive Staff Assistant to the Director of Shuttle Operations and Management, where she led a team of engineers in performing critical analysis for the Space Shuttle flow in support of a simulation model tool. She also worked on an interactive display detailing the Space Shuttle processing procedures at Spaceport USA (the Kennedy Space Center's Visitor Center). Her next task was as backup orbiter project engineer for OV-104, Space Shuttle Atlantis, where she participated in the integration of the orbiter docking station (ODS) into the space shuttle used during Shuttle/Mir docking missions.

Two years later, she was promoted to lead orbiter project engineer for OV-102, the Space Shuttle Columbia. In this position, she held the technical lead government engineering position in the firing room where she supported and managed the integration of vehicle testing and troubleshooting. She actively participated in 53 space shuttle launches during her nine-year term at Kennedy Space Center.

Selected as an astronaut candidate by NASA in April 1996, Ms. Higginbotham was ultimately assigned technical duties in the Payloads & Habitability Branch, the Shuttle Avionics

Columbia, STS-116, landing.

from the School of Aerospace Medicine at Brooks Air Force Base in Texas in 1988. She then progressed to a residency in family practice at Ghent Family Practice at Eastern Virginia Medical School in 1992 and received certification as a senior aviation medical examiner from the Federal Aviation Administration in 1995. Yvonne Cagle was a member of the Astronaut Class of 1996. She is currently assigned to Johnson Space Center's Space and Life Sciences Directorate.

USAF Colonel Benjamin A. Drew was born in 1962 in Washington, DC. He has flown two space missions, the first being STS-118 to the International Space Station in August 2007, the second in early 2011 on STS-133, also to the International Space Station. On February 28, 2011, Drew became the 200th person to walk in space during STS-133's mission, in company with fellow astronaut Steve Bowen. STS-133 was

& Integration Laboratory (SAIL), the Kennedy Space Center (KSC) Operations (Ops) Support Branch, where she tested various modules of the International Space Station for operability, compatibility, and functionality prior to launch, the Astronaut Office CAPCOM (Capsule Communicator) Branch in the startup and support of numerous space station missions and space shuttle missions, the Robotics Branch, and Lead for the International Space Station Systems Crew Interfaces Section. Logging over 308 hours in space during the STS-116 mission, she operated the Space Station Remote Manipulator System. Joan Higginbotham was the third female in space after Mae Jemison and Stephanie Wilson.

Colonel Benjamin Drew.

Space Shuttle Discovery's last mission. While docked to the Space Station, Colonel Drew took part in two space walks.

Colonel Drew was selected to be an astronaut in NASA's Astronaut Group 18 in July 2000. Following his initial spaceflight, Drew spent almost a year at the Yuri Gagarin Cosmonaut Training Center in Star City, Russia. There, he oversaw NASA's training operations as Director of Operations. Benjamin Drew was the last African American to date to fly in a NASA space mission.

Colonel Yvonne Darlene Cagle was born in West Point, New York and received her Bachelor's degree in Biochemistry from San Francisco State University in 1981, then progressed to her Doctor of Medicine degree at the University of Washington in 1985. She did a transitional internship at Highland General Hospital in Oakland in California during 1985 and received a certificate in Aerospace Medicine

Colonel Dr Yvonne Cagle.

STS133 patch.

Leland D. Melvin was born on February 15th at Lynchburg, Virginia. Graduating from the Heritage High School in Lynchburg, he went on to a football scholarship at the University of Richmond, to gain a Bachelor's Degree in Chemistry. Then, in 1991 he gained his Master of Science degree in Materials Science Engineering, from the University of Virginia.

Leland Melvin "at work".

Melvin began working in the Nondestructive Evaluation Sciences Branch at NASA's Langley Research Center in 1989. His work included using optical fiber sensors to measure strain, temperature, and chemical damage in both composite and metallic structures. In 1994, he was selected to lead the Vehicle Health Monitoring team for the cooperative Lockheed-NASA X-33 Reusable Launch Vehicle program. In 1996, he co-designed and monitored construction of an optical Nondestructive-Evaluation facility capable of producing in-line fiber optic sensors.

Selected as an astronaut in June 1998, Leland Melvin was assigned, after training, to the Astronaut Office Space Station Operations Branch, and the Education Department at NASA Headquarters in Washington, DC. As co-manager of NASA's Educator Astronaut Program, Leland Melvin traveled across the country, discussing space exploration with teachers and students, and promoting science, technology, engineering and mathematics. He next served in the Robotics Branch of the Astronaut Office. Melvin flew two missions on the Space

STS-122 patch.

Shuttle Atlantis, as a mission specialist on STS-122, which flew between February 7-20, 2008, then as mission specialist 1 on STS-129 from November 16-27, 2009.

A final "face" in the African American space story is Kwatsi Alibaruho. His father, an economist, came from Uganda and his mother from Macon, Georgia. He grew up in Oakland, California and Atlanta, Georgia. Graduating from Massachusetts Institute of Technology with a Bachelor's degree in avionics, Kwatsi joined NASA's mission controller training program to become a Mission Control Flight Director, working mission control shifts at the Johnson Space Center in August 2005. He was the first African American Flight Director at the age of only 37. Leading a team of flight controllers, support personnel and engineering experts, a flight director has the overall responsibility to manage and carry out space shuttle flights and International Space Station expeditions. A flight director also leads and orchestrates planning and integration activities with flight controllers, payload customers, space station partners and others. The Class of 2005 consisted of Kwatsi, three women and five other males.

Kwatsi Alibaruho – the first African American Flight Director in NASA.

In late 2011, the "Space Odyssey" for manned space flight in the US Space Program is temporarily over. But in the future, there will doubtless be more men and women, including African American men and women, reaching out into space again in the interests and pursuit of science.

CHAPTER SIXTEEN

The Final Frontier –
African American Women Achievers

It is a worldwide social fact that women have always followed men to leadership in almost all career paths. In military circles, Great Britain was among the first nations to appoint women to its senior staff ranks, beginning in 1918 with the Women's Royal Air Force, when Violet Douglas-Pennant became the Commandant, although she was not accorded official General Staff (or "Flag") rank. She was succeeded by Dame Helen Gwynne-Vaughan, who also had no official military rank, but commanded women of Colonel rank below her. In and after World War II, the Commandants of the WRAF were of official General Staff rank and one of the most famous of their number was Air Commandant Jean Conan Doyle, daughter of Sir Arthur Conan Doyle, the 19th Century author of the famous Sherlock Holmes stories. But these women were not African American or Afro-Caribbean though they were the first female military commanders in modern times. Following are examples of some African American women who have achieved success.

Air Commandant Dame Jean Conan Doyle.

Willa Beatrice Brown was born on January 22, 1906 in Glasgow, Kentucky. She became the first African American woman to hold a commercial pilot's license in the United States and the first African American female officer in the Civil Air Patrol. As a young high school teacher in Gary, Indiana, and later a social worker in Chicago, Willa Brown decided that she was wasting her talents and that she wanted greater challenges in her life. Especially, Willa searched for something that was not normally available, especially to African American women. What better a challenge than flying?

Willa Brown began flight training with the renowned Cornelius R. Coffey, a certified flight instructor and expert aviation mechanic who had set up in business at Akers Airport, one of Chicago's racially segregated airports. Under Coffey's instruction, she gained her private pilot's license in 1937. Two years later, she and Coffey married and established the Coffey School of Aeronautics at Harlem Airport in Chicago, where they trained black pilots and aviation mechanics. Together with her husband and Enoch P. Waters, Brown helped form the National Airman's Association of America in 1939, whose main goal was to place black aviation cadets into the United States military. As the organization's national secretary and the President of the Chicago branch, Brown became an activist for racial equality.

Willa Brown.

She continually lobbied the United States government for the integration of black pilots into the segregated Army Air Corps and the federal Civilian Pilot Training Program (CPTP), which later helped persuade the United States Congress to vote to allow separate-but-equal participation of African Americans in civilian flight training programs. Her work was endorsed by the First Lady of the time, Mrs. Eleanor Roosevelt. The Coffey School of Aeronautics was selected by the US Army to provide black trainees for the Air Corps pilot training program at the Tuskegee Institute. Willa Brown eventually became the coordinator of war-training service for the Civil Aeronautics Authority and later was a member of the Federal Aviation Administration's Women's Advisory Board. She died from a stroke in Chicago in July 1992. Willa Brown was ultimately inducted into the Military Aviation Hall of Fame of the State of Illinois.

It was not until 1979 that an African American woman reached one-star rank as a Brigadier-General in the United States Armed Forces. She was Hazel Johnson who was appointed Chief of the US Army Nursing Corps. She became interested in nursing as she was growing up on a farm in Westchester, Pennsylvania, qualified as an operating room

Brigadier-General Hazel Johnson-Brown.

nurse at the Harlem School of Nursing in New York and then studied for her Bachelor's degree at Villanova University, joining the US Army Nursing Corps in 1955.

Lieutenant Johnson served in Japan at a US Army Evacuation Hospital, and in 1960 at Walter Reed Army Medical Center as a staff and operating room nurse. From 1963 to 1967, she was an operating room instructor and supervisor while on tour at three different hospitals, being appointed a Major in 1967. From 1969 to 1973, she helped develop new sterilizing methods for the Army's Field Hospital Systems as a staff member of the Army Medical Research and Development Command. In 1974, Johnson was promoted to Colonel and she became the director of the Walter Reed Army Institute of Nursing, an extension of the University of Maryland's nursing school.

Four years later Colonel Johnson was sent to South Korea where she was the chief of the department of nursing at the largest US Army hospital there. In May 1979, she returned to Washington DC and was promoted to the rank of Brigadier-General. A military ceremony was held in her honor at the Pentagon, where US Army Surgeon General Julius Richmond pinned on her uniform the Brigadier-General star and she was also sworn in as the sixteenth Chief of the Army Nurse Corps.

The awards and recognition throughout her military career include: the 1972 US Army Nurse of the Year, honorary doctorates from Villanova University, Morgan State University and the University of Maryland. The Army awarded her the Distinguished Service Medal, the Legion of Merit, the Meritorious Service Medal, and the Army Commendation Medal with Oak Leaf Cluster. Her military duties left little time to pursue other avenues of life, but two years before she retired from the Army, General Johnson married David Brown, and

so the 16th chief of the Army Nurse Corps became Brigadier-General Hazel W. Johnson-Brown. She retired from the US Army in 1984, and went on to pursue an academic career.

She has since served as an advisor to a number of surgeons general, and was a professor of nursing at Georgetown University in Washington, D.C., and finally at George Mason University in Virginia. At the latter, she was instrumental in founding the Center for Health Policy, designed to educate and involve nurses in health policy and policy design. Ms Johnson-Brown retired from teaching in 1997 when, she was appointed adjunct professor of nursing at Georgetown University. She has also served in a similar capacity at the University of Maryland.

Brigadier-General Clara Adams-Ender.

Following in the footsteps of Hazel Johnson-Brown was Clara Mae Leach, later Clara Mae L. Adams-Ender, who was born on July 11, 1939, in Willow Springs, North Carolina, the fourth of a family of ten children. She also rose through the Army Nurse Corps to the rank of Brigadier-General. Her parents were sharecroppers on a tobacco farm, and Clara Mae, along with the other nine children, spent much of her childhood in the fields. As a result she missed a lot of school. However, her parents, though lacking in formal education, understood that it was only through education that their children could break free from the toils of farm work. Clara Mae took the advice of her parents to heart and became an avid student. In order to make up for her missed time at school, she had classmates give her assignments to the local bus driver, who would drop them off in the evening. She also began reading with great enthusiasm. Her dedication paid off when she graduated second in her class from Fuquay Springs Consolidated High School at the age of 16.

Clara Mae wanted to study law, but her father thought that

nursing would be a more suitable career choice and in 1956 she enrolled in the nursing program at North Carolina Agricultural and Technical State University (A&T) in Greensboro. While at A&T, Clara received an army scholarship in return for her enlistment following graduation. During her junior and senior years, she held the rank of private in the North Carolina Army Reserve, and just before graduating in 1961 she was commissioned as a 2nd Lieutenant in the Army Nurse Corps.

In 1967, she became the first female in the Army to qualify for and be awarded the Expert Field Medical Badge and then received an MS from the University of Minnesota in 1969 and a Master of Military Arts and Sciences from the US Army Command and Staff College in Fort Leavenworth, Kansas in 1976. She was the first woman to earn this degree. In 1982, Clara Adams-Ender was the first African American Army Nurse Corps officer to graduate from the US Army War College.

Colonel Adams-Ender became a Brigadier-General in 1987 and was appointed Chief of the Army Nurse Corps at the same time. Following this post, she went on to serve as the Commanding General, US Army Fort Belvoir, Virginia and Deputy Commanding General, US Army Military District of Washington until she retired in August 1993. Clara Adams-Ender's prime motivation through a large part of her career was to improve standards of health care in the Army Nursing Corps and to widen the opportunities for young nurses entering the profession, whether military or civilian.

The first female US Air Force officer to be promoted to General Staff rank was Colonel Marcelite Jordan Harris. She became a Brigadier-General on May 1, 1991, and had a few other firsts to her credit, starting in the early part of her career when she was the first woman aircraft maintenance officer in the Air Force. She was one of the first two Air Officers commanding at the US Air Force Academy and then the first Deputy Commander for Maintenance.

Marcelite Jordan never envisaged a military career for herself. She had studied speech and drama at Spellman College, but after a number of unsuccessful auditions, she re-

Major-General Marcelite J. Harris.

alized how precarious her future was likely to be, and decided to look for a more stable profession that would satisfy her ambition. A year after graduation, she entered Officer Training with the USAF and started what became a highly successful career.

Lieutenant Jordan Harris was assigned to Travis Air Force Base in California in December 1965 as Assistant Director for Administration with the 60th Military Airlift Wing. Promoted to 1st Lieutenant on January 21, 1967, her next assignment was with the 71st Tactical Missile Squadron at Bitburg Air Base in Germany. Remaining at Bitburg, she transferred to the 36th Tactical Fighter Wing and was promoted Captain during 1969, returning to the United States in September 1970.

In September 1970, Captain Jordan Harris attended the Aircraft Maintenance Officer Course at Chanute Air Force Base in Illinois and began a tour of duty in the Far East, supporting the Vietnam campaign as Maintenance Supervisor for the 49th Tactical Fighter Squadron at Korat Royal Thai Air Force Base in Thailand. Returning to Travis AFB in June 1972, she became Job Control Officer, then Field Maintenance Supervisor for the 916th Air Refueling Squadron. She left Travis in September 1975 as a Major to move to Washington DC.

Until May 1978, Major Harris served as Personnel Staff Officer and White House Social Aide at Headquarters US Air Force. Then she was appointed Air Officer Commanding Cadet Squadron 39 at the US Air Force Academy at Colorado Springs, after which she spent the next two and a half years at McConnell Air Force Base in Kansas. Her first job there, from July 1980 to July 1981, was as Maintenance Control Officer with the 384th Air Refueling Wing. She was next promoted Lieutenant-Colonel in October 1981 as Commander of the 384th Avionics Maintenance Squadron at McConnell. In March 1982, Lieutenant-Colonel Harris was appointed

Commander of the 384th Avionics Maintenance Squadron, and then of the 384th Field Maintenance Squadron. On November 13, 1982, Lieutenant-Colonel Harris became Director of Maintenance at the Pacific Air Forces Logistic Support Center at Kadena Air Force Base in Japan. She remained in that post until March 1986, when she moved to the job of Deputy Commander for Maintenance at Keesler Air Force Base in Mississippi. As a full Colonel, in 1986 she was appointed Commander of the 3300th Technical Training Wing at Keesler, where she remained until September 1990. In 1990 she received a significant honor when she was nominated Woman of the Year by the National Organization of Tuskegee Airmen, a well-deserved award and a clear link in the thread of this book.

Between September 1990 and July 1993, Colonel Harris was Vice-Commander of the Oklahoma City Air Logistics Center at Tinker Air Force Base. Her next career move was her most significant, for her and for the Air Force when in May 1991, Colonel Harris was appointed its first female Brigadier-General. In July 1993, she took up the position of Director of Technical Training at Randolph AFB in Texas.

In September 1994, Brigadier-General Harris became the first female Director of Maintenance for the whole Air Force. She was located at Headquarters US Air Force in Washington and her final accolade came with promotion to Major-General on May 25, 1995. General Harris retired in 1997. Her post-Air Force career took her to Atlanta, Georgia, where General Harris is the Treasurer of the National Association for the Advancement of Colored People. She also serves as a director of the Peach Tree Hope Charter School and in 2010, President Obama appointed her to the Board of Visitors of the United States Air Force Academy, a job close to her heart as a former Air Officer Commanding of that institution. As her career advanced, Marcelite Harris worked tirelessly to improve opportunities for all women.

Brigadier-General Mary Kight was appointed the 45th Adjutant General for the California National Guard by Governor Arnold Schwarzenegger on February 2, 2010. In this position, she served as Director of the State of California's Military Department and led the largest, most heavily tasked National

Guard force in the United States, with an authorized strength of 18,000 Army and 4,900 Air members.

Upon enlisting into the active duty Air Force and receiving a commission in 1974, Mary Kight's career began as a Personnel Officer at Fairchild Air Force Base in Spokane, Washington State, followed by an assignment with the Department of the

Major-General Mary J. Kight.

Army. She ended her initial active duty career at Headquarters, Strategic Air Command, Offutt Air Force Base in Omaha, Nebraska. Wishing to continue in military service, she joined the Nebraska Air National Guard in 1981, performing duties as the Executive Officer, Group and Military Aide.

She returned to her home state of California in 1984, and joined the California Air National Guard at Fresno in California where she served as the Avionics Maintenance Officer and later the Field Maintenance Officer, Squadron, Consolidated Aircraft Maintenance, Tactical Air Command from 1984 to 1990, being promoted to Major in December 1987. Her next appointment was as Aircraft Maintenance Officer, Group, Air Combat Command until 1994. As a Lieutenant Colonel, she next served as the first Commander for the 144th Fighter Wing, Aircraft Generation Squadron, and later led the support group for the same unit while concurrently commanding the Detachment, 201st Mission Support Squadron for all members performing duty on Title 10 status in Fresno. In July 2001, Mary Kight was promoted to full Colonel, and in November 2004, General Kight accepted the position as the Assistant Adjutant General, Air, of the California National Guard.

In February 2006, she was selected to serve as the Assistant Adjutant General of the whole California National Guard, Joint Force Headquarters and a month later was promoted Brigadier-General. On February 10, 2010, she was appointed Adjutant General, the first female adjutant general of any

State National Guard and the first African American woman to occupy such a post. She was later promoted to Major-General and retired in the summer of 2011. In retirement, Mary Kight gives time to the California State Military Museum and is Vice-President of the George "Spanky" Roberts Chapter of the Tuskegee Airmen organization.

Major-General Irene Trowell-Harris was assigned as assistant to the director, Air National Guard, for human resources readiness in Washington, DC. She was responsible for assisting and advising the director on all human resource issues. In this capacity, she served as the chair of the Human Relations Quality Board, and advisor to the ANG Committee of Advisors. Her input had a major impact on force preparedness to meet the defense challenges of the future.

Major-General Irene Trowell-Harris.

Graduating in 1959 from the Columbia Hospital School of Nursing, 2nd Lieutenant Trowell-Harris was commissioned in the New York Air National Guard in April 1963. Assigned to an Aeromedical Evacuation Flight at Floyd Bennett Field in Brooklyn, New York, where she held the positions of chief nurse, nurse administrator, flight nurse instructor and flight nurse examiner between the years 1963 and 1973, rising to the rank of Captain. She was promoted to Major in September 1973 and assigned to the 137th Aeromedical Evacuation Flight before being re-assigned as a clinical nurse to the 105th USAF Clinic at Newburgh, New York in the same year. In March 1986, she was appointed commander, becoming the first nurse in Air National Guard history to command a medical clinic, and achieved the rank of Lieutenant-Colonel in 1980.

She subsequently served on active duty as ANG advisor to the chief, Air Force Nurse Corps in the rank of Colonel, and as ANG assistant to the director, medical readiness and nursing services, Office of the Surgeon General in Washington, DC, being promoted Brigadier-General in October 1993. In August 1998, General Trowell-Harris became the first female in history to have a Tuskegee Airmen, Inc. Chapter named in her honor, the Major-General Trowell-Harris Chapter in Newburgh, New York.

Lillian Elaine Fishburne was born on March 25, 1949 at Patuxent River in Maryland. She was raised in Rockville, Maryland and graduated from Lincoln University at Oxford, Pennsylvania in 1971 with a Bachelor of Arts degree in Sociology. She was commissioned an Ensign in the US Navy upon completion of Women Officers School at Newport, Rhode Island in February 1973. She was the first African American female to hold the rank of Rear Admiral (Lower Half) in the United States Navy. She was appointed by President Bill Clinton and formally promoted on February 1, 1998.

Ensign Fishburne's first duty assignment had been a Personnel and Legal Officer at the Naval Air Test Facility in Lakehurst, New Jersey. Between August 1974 and November 1977 she was assigned to Navy Recruiting District in Miami, Florida as an Officer Programs recruiter and later the Officer in Charge of the Naval Telecommunications Center, Great Lakes, Illinois until 1980. After two years as a student at the Naval Postgraduate School in Monterey, California, she reported to the Command, Control, Communications Directorate, Chief of Naval Operations (OP-940) where, she served as the Assistant Head, Joint Allied Command and Control Matters Branch until December 1984.

Rear Admiral Lillian Fishburne.

Lieutenant-Commander Fishburne's next assignment was as Executive Officer, Naval Communication Station, Yokosuka, Japan (the home of Japan's Naval Academy). In February 1987, she was assigned to the Command, Control, and

Communications Directorate, Chief of Naval Operations (OP-942) as a Special Projects Officer. After a tour with the Naval Computer and Telecommunications Station, Key West, Florida, Commander Fishburne studied at the Industrial College of the Armed Forces. Upon graduation in 1993, she was assigned to the Command, Control, Communications and Computer Systems Directorate, The Joint Staff, Washington, DC, where she was Chief of the Command and Control Systems Support Division (J6C).

In August 1995, now a Captain, Lillian Fishburne assumed command of Naval Computer and Telecommunications Area Master Station, Pacific at Wahiawa, Hawaii. In her final assignment, from February 1998, Rear-Admiral Fishburne served as the Director, Information Transfer Division for the Space, Information Warfare, Command and Control Directorate in the Office of Chief of Naval Operations in Washington, DC. She retired from naval service in 2001, having served her country for twenty-eight years.

Brigadier-General Stayce D. Harris is today the Mobilization Assistant to the Commander, 18th Air Force at Scott Air Force Base, Illinois. General Harris received a commission in the Air Force through the University of Southern California's Reserve Officer Training Corps program. She spent eight years on active duty and 18 years as a Reservist. She has commanded an airlift squadron, an air expeditionary group and an air-refueling wing. Graduating in 1981 with a Bachelor of Science degree in industrial and systems engineering from the University of Southern California, Los Angeles, Ms Harris was attracted to the Reserve Officer Training Corps during her studies, from which she was commissioned into the regular Air Force. Four years later, she graduated from the renowned Embry-Riddle Aeronautical University, with a Master of Aviation Management degree. From

Brigadier-General Stayce D. Harris.

November 1983 to October 1984 2nd Lieutenant Harris was a student in undergraduate pilot training at Williams Air Force Base in Arizona. In November 1984 she took the C-141B initial qualification course at Altus Air Force Base in Oklahoma, graduating in February 1985.

In March 1985, Lieutenant Harris became airlift operations officer and a C-141B aircraft commander. The next year, she was promoted to Captain and appointed squadron executive officer and Chief of Training, 14th Military Airlift Squadron at Norton Air Force Base in California until August 1990, after which she transferred to March Air Force Base in California as Air Operations Officer and a C-141B pilot with the 445th Airlift Wing. She was promoted Major on March 5, 1993, and from February 1995 to January 1997, Major Harris was Mobility Force Planner in the Office of the Deputy Chief of Staff for Plans and Operations at Headquarters US Air Force in Washington DC. Between January 1997 and January 2000, she was Individual Mobilization Augmentee to the Deputy Assistant Secretary of the Air Force. While in this post, she was promoted to Lieutenant-Colonel.

February 2000 saw Lieutenant-Colonel Harris appointed Reserve Deputy Commander to the 452nd Operations Group at March Air Reserve Base in California. After assignments with the 729th Airlift Squadron and the 507th Air Refueling Wing and promotion to Colonel, she became mobilization assistant to the Director of Strategic Plans, Requirements and Programs, Headquarters Air Mobility Command at Scott Air Force Base in Illinois. While in that position, Colonel Harris was promoted Brigadier-General and in July 2009, served at Bitburg, in Germany, before moving to her present job. In her civilian career, she is a first officer for a major airline flying routes to Asia and Europe.

Major-General Mary L. Saunders was Vice Director, Defense Logistics Agency, Fort Belvoir, Virginia. The agency provides a variety of logistics, acquisition and technical services to the Army, Navy, Air Force, Marine Corps and other federal agencies. These services include logistics information, materiel management, procurement, warehousing and distribution of spare parts, food, clothing, medical supplies and fuel, re-utilization of surplus military materiel, and document au-

Major-General Mary L. Saunders.

tomation and production. Approximately 23,300 civilian and military personnel perform this worldwide mission.

General Saunders was born in Nacogdoches, Texas, and grew up in Houston. She began her military career through the Officer Training School at Lackland Air Force Base, Texas. She was commissioned a 2nd Lieutenant and entered active duty in 1971. She has held various assignments in transportation and logistics plans, in the squadron, wing, numbered air force, headquarters and joint arenas. Prior to assuming her last position, from which she retired in 2001, General Saunders worked as Commander in the Defense Supply Center at Columbus, Ohio, and later, as the Director of Supply with the Office of the Deputy Chief of Staff for Installations and Logistics, Headquarters US Air Force, Washington, D.C.

The US Marine Corps was not without its female African American achievers either. Vernice Armour is one young woman deserving mention who did not become a General, for her goals and aspirations took her in a different direction, but in her time and with the right opportunities, it would be easy to imagine her making that step. She became the first female African American active duty combat pilot in the Corps.

Vernice was born in 1973 in Chicago, Illinois and grew up in Memphis, Tennessee, where she graduated from Overton High School, before going on to study at Middle Tennessee State University. While there, in 1993, she enlisted in the Army Reserve and then joined the University's ROTC. Not sure exactly where her future lay, she took time off from University to become a police officer in Nashville, Tennessee, where she was the first female African American in the motorcycle squad. Graduating from MTSU in 1997, Vernice joined the police force in Tempe, Tennessee as its first female African American police officer, but by October 1998, policing was not exciting enough for her, and she enlisted in the Officer Candidate School of the US Marine Corps. Commissioned as a 2nd Lieutenant in December 1998, Vernice was sent to flight school at Naval Air Station Corpus Christi in Texas, then on to Naval Air Station Pensacola, Florida. She graduated with her wings in July 2001, placing top of twelve candidates on her course, with a higher overall score than the previous two hundred graduates.

Lieutenant Armour was assigned to Marine Corps Depot at Camp Pendleton, near San Diego, California, where she was taught to fly the AH-1W Super Cobra attack helicopter and use its weapon systems. There she was named 2001 Camp Pendleton Female Athlete of the Year, twice winning the annual Strongest Warrior Competition. In addition to that, Vernice was a running back for the San Diego Sunfire women's football team.

Captain Vernice Armour USMC.

In March 2003, she flew with Helicopter Squadron HMLA-169 during the Second Gulf War in Iraq, so becoming America's first African American female combat pilot. She completed two combat tours in the Gulf and then was assigned to the Manpower and Reserve Affairs Equal Opportunity Branch as program liaison officer. Captain Vernice Armour demonstrated that she had what it took to reach the heights in the Marine Corps, but instead, she chose to leave the Corps and take up a career as a professional speaker and lecture on the topic of creating breakthroughs in life.

Gilda A. Jackson was born in Columbus, Ohio, and was educated at Bishop Hartley School. She enlisted in the US Marine Corps and achieved Sergeant rank before entering Ohio Dominican College to study for her Bachelor of Arts degree in Economics. She graduated in 1975. While at Ohio

Dominican, she enrolled in the Marine Corps Platoon Leader Course and gained her commission. A life-dedicated Marine, she declared: *"From the time I was old enough to vote and make adult decisions, I've been in the Marine Corps, so it's very special to me"*.

Colonel Gilda Jackson USMC.

September 1978 saw Captain Jackson assigned to Marine Aircraft Group 12 (MAG-12) in Iwakuni, Japan. Here, she served as the Group Aviation Supply Support Center Officer. A year later, she returned to the United States to the post of Group Fiscal Officer with Marine Air Group 16 in the 3rd Marine Air Wing at MCAS Tustin, California. She was next selected to attend the Amphibious Warfare School, in Quantico, Virginia, the legacy of perhaps the greatest Marine commander of all time and the architect of amphibious warfare, General Holland M. Smith. She graduated in June 1983 and her next assignment was to the Headquarters and Maintenance Squadron with MAG-13 at MCAS El Toro, California. Two years into that tour, now Major Gilda Jackson, she became Group Supply Officer to MAG-16, operating with Marine Helicopter Training Squadron 301.

In August 1987, Major Jackson attended the Marine Corps Command and Staff College, and then reported to the Navy Aviation Supply Office in Philadelphia, Pennsylvania, for duty as the F/A18 Weapons System Manager. She remained with ASO during Operations Desert Shield and Desert Storm and was promoted to Lieutenant-Colonel in August 1992. Lieutenant-Colonel Jackson was selected to attend Top Level School in 1996 and subsequently assigned to the Air War College at Maxwell Air Force Base, Montgomery, Alabama, and then to the 2nd Marine Aircraft Wing at MCAS Cherry Point, North Carolina where she held the post of Executive Officer until October 1, 1997, when Brigadier-General Clif-

ford L. Stanley pinned to her shoulders her "eagle" badges to elevate her to the rank of full Colonel. This made her the first African American full Colonel in the United States Marine Corps. Upon her promotion, Colonel Jackson was appointed Commanding Officer of the Cherry Point Naval Aviation Depot.

Gilda Jackson never forgot her roots and strove hard to eliminate racism wherever she went. She also took time to work with the Literary Council, giving support and working in programs for academically challenged children. In 2002, Colonel Jackson, now retired from the Marine Corps, was inducted into the Ohio Foundation of Independent Colleges Hall of Fame for her contribution to society and her efforts to ensure equality for all during her service. Here was a woman who, had the opportunity been there, would certainly have risen to Flag rank.

Even today, there is no female African American General in the US Marine Corps. But the time will come. That one star may have eluded Gilda Jackson, but she set a new benchmark and left just one step for the next African American Marine female career officer to reach for the stars. Today, women serve in 93 percent of all occupational fields, constitute 6.2 percent of Marine Corps strength, and are an integral part of the Corps.

Colonel Gilda A. Jackson retired from the Marine Corps with distinction. For her contribution to the defense of her nation, she was awarded two Defense Meritorious Service Medals, the Navy Commendation Medal, the Navy Achievement Medal and, the Marine Corps Good Conduct Medal from her enlisted days. Regardless of race, creed, color or gender, Gilda Jackson was and remains a role model to any aspiring young United States Marine embarking on a career with "The Few, The Proud".

Appendices

APPENDIX ONE
AFRICAN AMERICAN PILOTS REGISTERED IN 1939

Commercial Pilots

Name	State	Lic. No.	Expiration Date
Anderson, Charles A.	PA	7638	28 February 1939
Coffey, Cornelius R.	IL	36609	15 February 1939
Greene, John W., Jr.	MA	15897	30 April 1939
Renfro, Earl W.	IL	32546	15 May 1939

Name	State	Lic. No.	Expiration Date
Sully, Justo. R.	NY	34781	15 May 1939
Terry, Robert	NJ	29452	31 October 1939
Walker, Clinton T., Jr.	MI	35477	30 June 1939
Ware, Charles	NY	34381	30 April 1939
Wheeler, Rostell C.	MA	19196	30 June 1939
White, Dale L.	IL	34746	15 June 1939

Limited Commercial Pilots

Name	State	Lic. No.	Expiration Date
Allen, George W.	PA	32630	31 May 1939
Newkirk, Troy Webster	NY	34797	31 December 1939
Powell, William J.	CA	24335	15 March 1939

Private Pilots

Name	State	Lic. No.	Expiration Date
Aiken, William	CA	35071	15 July 1939
Brown, Willa Beatrice	IL	43814	30 June 1939
Cable, Theodore	IN	33738	30 November 1939
Chalmers, Willie. J.	NJ	34527	15 August 1938
Claytor, W.W. Schieffelin	DC	31533	15 December 1938
Cooper, Walter T.	NJ	49886	15 July 1939
Davis, Ralph H.	RI	45351	15 July 1939
Dillon, William H.	PA	33192	14 July 1939
Forsythe, Albert E.	NJ	27287	31 October 1937
Hutcherson, Fred, Jr.	IL	34679	31 May 1939
Jackson, Abram D.	PA	49866	31 May 1939
Mills, Thomas	NY	31780	15 May 1938
Nash, Grover C.	IL	30217	30 September 1939
Paris, William	IL	51064	15 August 1939
Payne, L. Verdell	NY	28358	31 July 1938
Rey, Ernst F.	NY	35216	31 July 1939
Robinson, John C.	IL	26042	31 July 1939

Solo or Amateur Pilots

Name	State	Lic. No.	Expiration Date
Cosby, Albert	IL	45027	30 April 1939
Darby, Dorothy	MI	38794	15 January 1940
Hankins, Roscoe, Jr.	DC	58107	11 November 1939
Hurd, Harold	IL	44998	30 April 1939
Johnson, Charles Richard	IL	43038	15 April 1939
Jones, Lola	IL	43703	15 April 1939
Ray, Herman	IL	45512	30 April 1939
Turner, Luther	NY	43940	15 April 1939
Walden, Coburn E.	MI	47366	15 May 1939
WA, Eddie	AR	47984	17 June 1939
Yates, Leonard L.	NY	43715	4 April 1939
Young, Perry H.	OH	43715	4 April 1939

Student Pilots

* Student licenses issued prior to November 1937 did not bear license numbers. NA = Not Available

Name	State	Lic. No.	Expiration Date
Adair, Frank B.	AR	54383	9 September 1939
Alleyne, Joseph S., Jr.	NY	33428	21 June 1939
Anderson, Grady Prince	SC	NA	4 August 1939
Ashe, Charles M.	DC	54573	29 September 1939
Avery, Delores	IL	NA	11 May 1937
Bemjamin, Zola A.	CA	NA	10 April 1938

Name	State	Lic. No.	Expiration Date	Name	State	Lic. No.	Expiration Date
Black, William, Jr.	NY	NA	28 October 1937	McDonald, Clarence J.W.	DC	48058	23 June 1939
Brooks, Jesse L.	NY	51134	18 July 1939	McFarland, William P.	IL	NA	2 May 1937
Brown, Aaron	MD	52476	19 August 1939	Mitchell, Frank Braddock	CA	NA	30 April 1938
Browning, Frank L.	IL	NA	7 June 1939	Moulden, William W.	CA	45437	4 May 1939
Bruce, Percy Lee	CA	55551	1 September 1939	Muldro, Joseph	IL	NA	11 April 1937
Caldwell, Walter M., Jr.	NY	51133	23 June 1939	O'Berry, Benny	FL	58434	16 November 1939
Chipps, Leon A.	NY	45531	30 April 1939	Paris, Leon D.	MD	NA	3 June 1939
Coleman, Gus	GA	NA	30 April 1939	Parks, Perry C., Jr.	CA	NA	10 April 1938
Cox, Alexander	IL	NA	16 June 1937	Payne, Verdell L.	NY	NA	3 June 1938
Davis, Albert Porter	KS	3902	4 June 1939	Perry, Lane G.	NY	54784	16 August 1939
Dickerson, Marie A.	CA	NA	17 March 1938	Porter, Ambers	IL	NA	22 March 1937
Edmonson, Charles Milton	CA	NA	29 April 1938	Procter, Charles Vincent	PA	52763	3 August 1939
Evans, Walter	NY	NA	April 15, 1939	Reed, Frank S., Jr.	IL	NA	15 June 1937
Fisher, Albert Hobert	CA	NA	21 October 1939	Reed, John D.	IL	46079	12 May 1939
Freeman, Arthur Willie	MI	57395	31 October 1939	Renfro, Anna Rosetta	IL	NA	2 May 1937
Gales, Richard Alfred	OH	NA	12 August 1938	Robinson, Robert Lee	CA	NA	27 April 1938
Gans, D. Louis H.	IL	NA	20 March 1937	Ross, Curtis	OH	NA	8 June 1939
Garrett, Leroy	IL	43305	6 April 1939	Ross, Harry M.	NY	NA	26 January 1937
Greene, Bene LaRue	CA	NA	27 April 1938	Ross, Timothy	OH	NA	8 June 1939
Grimmett, Theodore	IL	57404	1 November 1939	St. Clair, Marie Rowe	IL	NA	4 September 1939
Hampton, Clyde Barthaw	IL	NA	19 April 1939	Sansing, James	MS	NA	15 July, 1938
Hanson, Jesse McCoy	DC	NA	18 April 1939	Scott, David L.	MS	42257	17 April 1938
Harden, Rudy	WA	57282	29 October 1939	Sims, Willa Mae	CA	NA	17 April 1938
Hardy, Fred	IL	NA	1 August 1938	Smith, Archie	NY	53195	16 August 1939
Hawkins, Thomas	NY	NA	21 August 1939	Smith, Floyd Joseph	DC	48270	7 June 1939
Herndon, Edward L.	OH	41130	7 February 1939	Stanley, Milford	NJ	NA	25 December 1939
Howland, James H.	NY	NA	10 March 1939	Stephens, Everett Dewitt	DC	NA	16 November 1939
Jackson, Lola	NY	NA	8 October 1939	Stevens, Leslie T.	CA	NA	2 April 1938
Jefferson, Ann R.	CA	NA	27 April 1939	Strode, Bethel Julius	TX	NA	4 May 1939
Jefferson, Karl Garrett	CA	NA	3 April 1939	Thomas, Robert	NY	NA	3 April 1937
Jones, Albert S.	IL	NA	28 April 1937	Treadway, Timothy T.	NY	40081	7 January 1939
Julian, Hubert	NY	NA	28 April 1938	Walton, Bridget	CA	NA	8 May 938
Lilly, Joseph H.	VA	42770	1 April 1939	Waterford, Janet Harmon	IL	NA	17 June 1938
Love, Maxwell Lawrence	CA	NA	10 April 1938	Webster, George	IL	NA	2 May 1937
Lowe, William E.	IL	NA	1 August 1938	White, Harry C.	CA	NA	3 April 1938
Lundy, Russell G.	DC	48870	17 June 1939	Williams, Lee A.	CA	NA	18 May, 1938
Lytle, Laurence E.	NY	48206	17 May 1939	Williamson, James C.	NA	NA	27 April 1938

APPENDIX TWO
AFRICAN AMERICAN MEDAL OF HONOR RECIPIENTS

Name	Date/Place Of Action	Military Unit	Date of Award
Sgt. William Harvey Carney – Army	Jul 18, 1863 – Fort Wagner, SC	Company C, 54th Mass. Colored Infantry	NA
Contraband Robert Blake – Navy	Dec 25, 1863 – off Legareville, Stono River, John's Island, SC	US Steam GB Marblehead	Apr 16, 1864
Seaman Joachim Pease – Navy	Jun 19, 1864 – off Cherbourg, France	USS Kearsarge	Dec 31, 1864
Sgt. Decatur Dorsey – Army	Jul 30, 1864 – Petersburg, VA	Company B, 39th US Colored Infantry	Nov 8, 1865
Lnd. William H. Brown – Navy	Aug 5, 1864 – Fort Morgan & Mobile Bay, AL	USS Brooklyn	Dec 31, 1864
Lnd. Wilson Brown – Navy	Aug 5, 1864 – Fort Morgan & Mobile Bay, AL	USS Hartford	Dec 31, 1864
Lnd. John Lawson – Navy	Aug 5, 1864 – Mobile Bay, AL	USS Hartford	Dec 31, 1864
Engineer's Cook James Mifflin – Navy	Aug 5, 1864 – Mobile Bay, AL	USS Brooklyn	Dec 31, 1864
Pvt. William Henry Barnes – Army	Sep 29, 1864 – Chapin's Farm, VA	Company C, 38th US Colored Infantry	Apr 6, 1865
1st Sgt. Powhatan Beaty – Army	Sep 29, 1864 – Chapin's Farm, VA	Company G, 5th US Colored Infantry	Apr 6, 1865
1st Sgt. James H. Bronson – Army	Sep 29, 1864 – Chapin's Farm, VA	Company D, 5th US Colored Infantry	Apr 6, 1865
Sgt. Major Christian A. Fleetwood – Army	Sep 29, 1864 – Chapin's Farm, VA	4th US Colored Infantry	Apr 6, 1865
Pvt. James Gardiner aka: JD Gardner Army	Sep 29, 1864 – Chapin's Farm, VA	Company I, 36th US Colored Infantry	Apr 6, 1865
Sgt. James H. Harris – Army	Sep 29, 1864 – New Market Heights, VA	Company B, 38th US Colored Infantry	Feb 18, 1874
Sgt. Major Thomas R. Hawkins – Army	Sep 29, 1864 – Chapin's Farm, VA	6th US Colored Infantry	Feb 8, 1870
Sgt. Alfred B. Hilton – Army	Sep 29, 1864 – Chapin's Farm, VA	Company H, 4th US Colored Infantry	Apr 6, 1865
Sgt. Major Milton M. Holland – Army	Sep 29, 1864 – Chapin's Farm, VA	5th US Colored Infantry	Apr 6, 1865
1st Sgt. Alexander Kelly – Army	Sep 29, 1864 – Chapin's Farm, VA	Company F, 6th US Colored Infantry	Apr 6, 1865
1st Sgt. Robert A. Pinn – Army	Sep 29, 1864 – Chapin's Farm, VA	Company I, 5th US Colored Infantry	Apr 6, 1865
1st Sgt. Edward Ratcliff – Army	Sep 29, 1864 – Chapin's Farm, VA	Company C, 38th US Colored Troops	Apr 6, 1865
Pvt. Charles Veal aka: Veale – Army	Sep 29, 1864 – Chapin's Farm, VA	Company D, 4th US Colored Infantry	Apr 6, 1865
Corp. Miles James – Army	Sep 30, 1864 – Chapin's Farm, VA	Company B, 36th US Colored Infantry	Apr 6, 1865
Corp. Andrew J. Smith – Army	Nov 30, 1864 – Honey Hill, SC	55th Massachusetts Volunteer Infantry	Jan 16, 2001
Pvt. Bruce Anderson – Army	Jan 15, 1865 – Fort Fisher, NC	Company K, 142d NY Infantry	Dec 28, 1914
Lnd. Aaron Sanderson aka: Anderson – Navy	Mar 17, 1865 – Mattox Creek, VA	USS Wyandank	Jun 22, 1865
Sgt. Emanuel Stance – Army	May 20, 1870 – Kickapoo Springs, TX	Company F, 9th US Cavalry	Jun 28, 1870
Seaman John Johnson – Navy	Apr 12, 1872 – near Greytown, Nicaragua	USS Kansas	Jul 9, 1872
Seaman Joseph B. Noil – Navy	Dec 26, 1872 – Norfolk, VA	USS Powhatan	Dec 26, 1872
Pvt. Adam Paine aka: Adan Payne – Army	Sep 26 & 27, 1874 – Canyon Blanco tributary of the Red River, TX	Indian Scouts	Oct 13, 1875
Pvt. Pompey Factor – Army	Apr 25, 1875 – Pecos River, TX	Indian Scouts	May 28, 1875

Name	Date/Place Of Action	Military Unit	Date of Award
Trumpeter Isaac Payne – Army	Apr 25, 1875 – Pecos River, TX	Indian Scouts	May 28, 1875
Sgt. John Ward aka: John Warrior – Army	Apr 25, 1875 – Pecos River, TX	Indian Scouts, 24th US Infantry	May 28, 1875
Corp. Clinton Greaves – Army	Jan 24, 1877 – Florida Mountains, NM	Company C, 9th US Cavalry	Jun 26, 1879
Sgt. Thomas Boyne – Army	May 29 & Sep 27, 1879 – Cuchillo Negro River & Mimbres Mountains, NM	Company C, 9th US Cavalry	NA
Sgt. John Denny – Army	Sep 18, 1879 – Las Animas Canyon, NM	Company C, 9th US Cavalry	Nov 27, 1894
Sgt. Henry Johnson – Army	Oct 2 – 5, 1879 – Milk River, CO	Company D, 9th US Cavalry	Sep 22, 1890
Cooper William Johnson – Navy	Nov 14, 1879 – Navy Yard, Mare Island, CA	USS Adams	Oct 18, 1884
Sgt. George Jordan – Army	May 14, 1880 & Aug 12, 1881 – Fort Tularosa & Carrizo Canyon, NM	Company K, 9th US Cavalry	May 7, 1890
Seaman John Smith – Navy	Sep 19, 1880 – Rio de Janeiro, Brazil	USS Shenandoah	Sep 19, 1880
Sgt. Thomas Shaw – Army	Aug 12, 1881 – Carrizo Canyon, NM	Company K, 9th US Cavalry	Dec 7, 1890
Pvt. Augustus Walley – Army	Aug 16, 1881 – Cuchillo Negro Mountains, NM	Company I, 9th US Cavalry	Oct 1, 1890
1st Sgt. Moses Williams – Army	Aug 16, 1881 – Cuchillo Negro Mountains, NM	Company I, 9th US Cavalry	Nov 12, 1896
Sgt. Brent Woods – Army	Aug 19, 1881 – New Mexico	Company B, 9th US Cavalry	Jul 12, 1894
Ord. Seaman John Davis – Navy	Feb, 1881 – Toulon, France	USS Trenton	Oct 18, 1884
Ord. Seaman Robert A. Sweeney – Navy	FIRST AWARD – Oct 26, 1881 – Hampton Roads, VA	USS Kearsarge	Oct 18, 1884
Sgt. Benjamin Brown – Army	May 11, 1889 – Arizona	Company C, 24th US Infantry	Feb 19, 1890
Corp. Isaiah Mays – Army	May 11, 1889 – Cedar Springs, Arizona Territory	Company B, 24th US Infantry	Feb 19, 1890
Corp. William O. Wilson – Army	1890 – Sioux Campaign	Company I, 9th US Cavalry	Sep 17, 1891
Sgt. William McBryar – Army	Mar 7, 1890 – Arizona Territory	10th US Cavalry	May 15, 1890
Ship's Cook 1st Class Daniel Atkins – Navy	Feb 11, 1898 – Aboard Ship at Sea	USS Cushing	May 20, 1898
Pvt. Dennis Bell – Army	Jun 30, 1898 – Tayabacoa, Cuba	Troop H, 10th US Cavalry	Jun 23, 1899
Pvt. Fitz Lee – Army	Jun 30, 1898 – Tayabacoa, Cuba	Troop M, 10th US Cavalry	Jun 23, 1899
Pvt. William H. Thompkins – Army	Jun 30, 1898 – Tayabacoa, Cuba	Troop G, 10th US Cavalry	Jun 23, 1899
Pvt. George Henry Wanton – Army	Jun 30, 1898 – Tayabacoa, Cuba	Troop M, 10th US Cavalry	Jun 23, 1899
Sgt. Major Edward Lee Baker, Jr. – Army	Jul 1, 1898 – Santiago, Cuba	10th US Cavalry	Jul 3, 1902
Fireman First Class Robert Penn – Navy	Jul 20, 1898 – Santiago de Cuba, Cuba	USS Iowa	Dec 14, 1898
Seaman Alphonse Girandy – Navy	Mar 31, 1901 – Aboard Ship at Sea	USS Petrel	Mar 22, 1902
Corp. Freddie Stowers – Army	Sep 28, 1918 – Hill 188, Champagne Marne Sector, France	Company C, 371st Infantry Regiment, 93d Div.	Apr 24, 1991
Pvt. George Watson – Army	Mar 8, 1943 – Porloch Harbor, New Guinea	29th Quarter Master Regiment	Jan 13, 1997
Staff Sgt. Ruben Rivers – Army	Nov 15 – 19, 1944 – Guebling, France	Company A, 761st Tank Bn, 3d Army	Jan 13, 1997
Capt. Charles L. Thomas – Army	Dec 14, 1944 – Climbach, France	Company C, 614th Tank Destroyer Bn, 103d Div.	Jan 13, 1997
1st Lieutenant John R. Fox – Army	Dec 26, 1944 – Sommocolonia, Italy	366th Infantry 92d Infantry Division	Jan 13, 1997

Name	Date/Place Of Action	Military Unit	Date of Award
Staff Sgt. Edwd A. Carter, Jr. – Army	Mar 23, 1945 – Speyer, Germany	Company #1, 56th Armored Infantry, 12th Armored Division	Jan 13, 1997
1st Lieutenant Vernon J. Baker – Army	Apr 5 & 6, 1945 – Viareggio, Italy	Company C, 370th Infantry, 92d Infantry Div.	Jan 13, 1997
Pfc. Willy F. James, Jr. – Army	Apr 7, 1945 – Lippoldsberg, Germany	413th Infantry Regiment, 104th Division	Jan 13, 1997
Pfc. William Henry Thompson – Army	Aug 6, 1950 – Haman, Korea	Company M, 24th Infantry Regiment, 25th Infantry Division	Aug 6, 1950
Sgt. Cornelius H. Charlton – Army	Jun 2, 1951 – Chipo-ri, Korea	Company C, 24th Infantry Regiment, 25th Infantry Division	Mar 12, 1952
Pfc. Milton Lee Olive, III – Army	Oct 22, 1965 – Phu Cuong, Vietnam	Company B, 2d Battalion (Airborne), 503d Infantry, 173d Infantry Brigade	Apr 21, 1966
Specialist Sixth Class Lawrence Joel – Army	Nov 8, 1965 – Vietnam	HHQ, 503d Infantry, 1st Bn (Airborne), 503d Infantry, 173d Airborne Brigade	Mar 9, 1967
Sgt. Donald Russell Long – Army	Jun 30, 1966 – Vietnam	Troop C, 1st Squadron, 4th Cavalry, 1st Infantry Division	Feb 8, 1968
Pfc. James Anderson, Jr. – USMC	Feb 28, 1967 – Cam Lo, Vietnam	Company F, 2d Battalion, 3d Marines, 3d Marine Division (Rein) FMF	Aug 21, 1968
Sgt. 1st Class Matthew Leonard – Army	Feb 28, 1967 – Suoi Da, Vietnam	Company B, 1st Battalion, 16th Infantry, 1st Infantry Division	Dec 19, 1968
1st Lt. Ruppert Leon Sargent – Army	Mar 15, 1967 – Hau Nghia Province, Vietnam	Company B, 4th Battalion, 9th Infantry, 25th Infantry Division	Mar 10, 1969
Sgt. Rodney Maxwell Davis – USMC	Sep 6, 1967 – Quang Nam Province, Vietnam	Company B, 1st Battalion, 5th Marines, 1st Marine Division	Mar 26, 1969
Sgt. 1st Class Webster Anderson – Army	Oct 15, 1967 – Tam Ky, Vietnam	Battery A, 2d Bn, 320th Artillery, 101st Airborne Division (Airmobile)	Nov 24, 1969
Capt. Riley Leroy Pitts – Army	Oct 31, 1967 – Ap Dong, Vietnam	Company C, 2d Battalion, 27th Infantry, 25th Infantry Division	Dec 10, 1968

APPENDIX THREE
BADGES OF COURAGE – THE MEDALS AWARDED TO AFRICAN AMERICANS

This Appendix is not intended to be a compendium of medals and awards of the United States, but it is included to give insight into the decorations and medals awarded to the wide spectrum of people embraced by this book.

The Medal of Honor was approved as the United States highest award for valor by President Abraham Lincoln by Executive Order Number 82 on December 21, 1861. Since first approved, it has evolved through three designs to reach the modern-day versions awarded by the US Army, the US Navy and Marine Corps and the US Air Force. A fourth version was approved to be designed for the Coast Guard, but the only awardee received the Navy version of the Medal.

The first Medals of Honor awarded were all suspended medals, worn on the left breast at the head of any or all other medals awarded to the recipient. Originally, the Air Force did not have its own medal design, and before the Korean War, members of the Army Air Forces received the Army version.

First designed Army Medal of Honor.

The first recipients of the Medal of Honor were awarded their medals for acts of courage in the Civil War and the first African American to receive the Medal was Sergeant William Carney. This iteration of the medal remained in use until 1895, when the ribbon was changed from the "flag" type design, with a blue top panel and thirteen alternating red and white vertical stripes to a more simple three-color ribbon, still red, dark blue and white, but now two red edges of about one quarter of the total width of the ribbon, with a blue center vertical band, divided by a narrow white stripe. The metalwork of the medal remained exactly as in the original. This second type was used until 1904, when a more ornate design was introduced with a more open star and an enameled wreath behind the points of the star. The ribbon was now a pale blue moiré silk, with thirteen white stars placed centrally in two inverted chevrons of five and one chevron of three, all equally spaced. It was still a breast-worn medal.

The first design of Medal of Honor introduced by the United States Navy was less ornate than the Army version. It was designed and commissioned before the Army medal and while it used the same ribbon, the medal was different. The top clasp, by which the medal was pinned to the bearer's uniform, was a simple open rectangle. At the bottom of the ribbon was another open rectangular device, which had incorporated in it the bar from which the medal hung. From that plain bar was a single ring, linking to an anchor, which looped through the two rings suspending the inverted star

On the left is the first design of the Navy Medal of Honor, which was awarded unchanged until 1912. Next to it is the first revision of the Army design, awarded until 1903. In 1904, the version on the right was introduced and, apart from the ribbon and mounting pin, remains the same design to this day, except that now it is neckworn.

identical to the Army design. The first African American Navy Medal of Honor recipient was Seaman Robert Blake in 1864.

The third Army Medal of Honor had another change in its design, in that the image of the Roman Goddess of War, Minerva, repelling Discord, was replaced with a simple, helmeted head of Minerva. The words "United States of America" replaced the ring of 34 stars and the eagle that had once perched on cannon, saber in its talons, now perched on a bar bearing the word "VALOR" and the shafts of arrows. It became known as the "Gillespie" version, after Brigadier-General George Gillespie, who campaigned for the new design on two counts. His first reason was to make the ribbon more immediately distinguishable. His second was that the medal had been copied and to prevent that for the future, he personally took out a US Patent on the design and then transferred the patent to Secretary for War, William Taft, for retention by the government. Today, the Medal of Honor design is protected by law and, unlike the supreme award for valor of other countries, its sale is prohibited by any individual.

Shortly before World War I, in 1913, the Navy decided to adopt the same ribbon design as the Army, but retained the rectangular loops at the top and bottom of the ribbon and also retained the original Minerva-Discord obverse design. The reverse of the original Medals of Honor carried the inscription: "The Congress to:" with a space for the name of the recipient on an otherwise plain surface.

In 1919, the Navy took the unprecedented step of creating a second design of Medal of Honor, to be awarded to non-combatants. These would be people who had distinguished themselves with courage to the level where, had they been in combat, they would have received the Medal. It was designed by Tiffany and Company of New York and became known as the "Tiffany" Medal of Honor. It was in the shape of a Maltese Cross, not dissimilar from the British Victoria Cross, the highest award for courage awarded by the Monarch of Great Britain. The Tiffany Cross was suspended from the ribbon by a ring and was worn from a brooch-type pin, which carried the inscription "Valour" in English spelling. The inscription which had appeared on the reverse of the Medal was transferred to the reverse of the clasp.

A miniature version of the Navy Medal of Honor 1912-1942 (left) and the Tiffany Medal of Honor (right).

In modern times, there are three Medal of Honor designs, one each representing the United States Army, the United States Navy and since 1947, the United States Air Force. The Army and Navy Medals remain as they were before the ribbon was changed to a neck-worn type in 1923, while the Air Force version is similar in most aspects, in that it, too, is neck-worn, but the design is subtly different. It retains the inverted five-point star and features a similar green-enameled wreath to the Army design, except that the wreath ends at the upper two points of the star. The suspending device is a bar bearing the single word "VALOR", below which is a

Medals of Honor, left to right: Army (current), Navy/Marine Corps, and Air Force.

reproduction of the Air Force emblem and from that is suspended the inverted star by a ring. The star itself is different too, in that it retains the thirty-four stars that surround the central image, but the image of Minerva is replaced by one of the head of the Statue of Liberty.

There are nine different variations of a decoration that is held in the highest esteem worldwide. In terms of major powers, the Victoria Cross is the corresponding British and Commonwealth award, while the French (and Belgian) Croix de Guerre parallels the Medal of Honor in Continental Europe. Many Americans were awarded the Croix de Guerre (some by both France and Belgium in World War I) and among that number were almost 300 African Americans, whereas only one was awarded his own country's highest decoration, the Medal of Honor. That was Corporal Freddie Stowers.

Below are the three major corresponding European medals – the French Croix de Guerre, the British Victoria Cross and the Belgian Croix de Guerre. There have been black recipients of all three.

Badge of Military Merit.

which was the word "MERIT", and it was worn on the sleeve of the recipient. Only three were awarded during the Revolutionary War. A bill to Congress was launched in 1927 and by 1931, the medal was inaugurated on the bicentennial of the birth of George Washington, in recognition of the fact that it was he who had instituted the Badge of Merit. Douglas MacArthur instituted this revival of the Badge of Merit, which became known as the Purple Heart. It is awarded in all branches of the US Armed Forces to persons injured or killed in combat. In the order of wear, this medal takes precedence over meritorious service medals of any of the Armed Forces, but ranks behind the Bronze Star and medals ranking above it, such as the Distinguished Service Cross, the Navy Cross, the Distinguished Flying Cross and other higher awards. Ranking immediately below the Medal of Honor are the service Medals – the Distinguished Service Medal of the Army, the Navy, the Coast Guard, and the Air Force. Following them are the distinguished crosses – the Navy Cross, the Distinguished Service Cross, the Distinguished Flying Cross.

French Croix de Guerre.   British Victoria Cross.   Belgian Croix de Guerre.

Before the Medal of Honor was instituted, there was only one award for courage available for American soldiers or sailors. This was the Badge of Merit, awarded to those who had fought with outstanding courage in the Revolutionary War. It was not a medal as such, but an embroidered badge upon

The Legion of Merit ranks ahead of the Purple Heart, though the award is unique, in that its higher levels are neck-worn

Purple Heart.

and are only awarded to non-US citizens. The Officer and Legionnaire categories of the Legion of Merit can be awarded to US military personnel and one notable African American recipient of the Officer level of the Legion of Merit was the Tuskegee Airmen's first Squadron, then Group Commander Benjamin O. Davis, Jr., who incidentally, was also awarded the Purple Heart in Italy.

Key medals of distinction in the United States Armed Forces:

The four Distinguished Service Medals – from the left, the Navy Distinguished Service Medal, Army Distinguished Service Medal, Air Force Distinguished Service Medal and the Defense Distinguished Service Medal, instituted by President Richard M. Nixon in 1970 as the highest joint-service non-combat distinction awarded to military personnel. This last medal is primarily aimed at high ranking officers and is awarded to those serving in a joint-service role.

These four medals are the next step down from the Distinguished Service Medals. They are: the Navy Cross, the Distinguished Service Cross, the Distinguished Flying Cross and the Air Medal. The Air Medal was initiated as an Army Air Corps award, but has been awarded to members of all US Armed Forces where courage in the air has merited it. It is a unique cross-service award and examples of all have been awarded to Army, Navy, Marine Corps and Air Force personnel. Of particular merit is the number of Air Medals (1,031) and Distinguished Flying Crosses (96) awarded to members of the 99th Fighter Squadron and the 332nd Fighter Group in World War II – the Tuskegee Airmen.

From left to right: Silver Star, Bronze Star, Soldier's Medal and the Navy and Marine Corps Medal. The latter two, along with the Airman's Medal pictured on the next page, are awarded for life-endangering deeds not occurring in combat conditions.

The Certificate of Merit Medal, shown to the left of the Airman's Medal, is an obsolete award that was issued at the end of the 19th Century and early 20th Century, with broadly equivalent standing to the Soldier's, Navy and Marine Corps and Airmen's Medals. That medal was inaugurated to replace the Certificate of Merit, but was abandoned with the introduction of these other medals.

Congressional Space Medal of Honor.

One other unique decoration for valor, courage and heroism is the Congressional Space Medal of Honor. It is awarded to astronauts and is intended to recognize the great courage demonstrated by this unique group of people who, whilst not in "combat", are fighting the elements to achieve the nation's goals. Several have forfeited their lives in the pursuit of science. This medal is not seen as an equivalent to the Medal of Honor, but it is an award for valor and stands alone as recognition of achievements in space.

Medals for meritorious service are particularly relevant to this publication, because many African Americans have been recipients. The most significant of the "merit" awards is the Legion of Merit, one variation of which is the only other neck-worn decoration besides the Medal of Honor. The Legion of Merit is modeled on the lines of European orders of chivalry, such as Great Britain's Order of the British Empire. Like that Order, the Legion of Merit is awarded in four classes – Chief Commander, who wears only the 75mm breast badge: Commander, who wears the 57mm medallion about the neck, suspended on a ribbon of crimson and white: Officer, who wears the 49mm medallion suspended on a breast-worn ribbon with a 19mm gold effigy of the original badge in its center: and the Legionnaire, who wears the same 49mm medallion suspended from a plain ribbon, shown to the right.

The four degrees of the Legion of Merit: the breast badge of the Chief Commander and the neck-suspended Commander. To the right are the Officer and the Legionnaire, followed by the ribbons for each degree as worn in informal dress without the medals.

The Commander grade of the Legion of Merit is normally only awarded to non-US officers of Flag rank or to foreign dignitaries of equivalent status, whose service in support of the United States is seen to justify the award. One such example known to the author was the award of the Legion of Merit to a Royal Air Force Officer who was commander of the joint-service operations out of the Azores in World War II.

Ranking below the Legion of Merit is the Meritorious Service Medal, instituted in 1969 to be awarded to military personnel who had performed a continuous service in a duty of lesser responsibility or scope than would justify the award of the Legion of Merit. It can be awarded for service in a combat zone where the recipient is not engaged in combat at the time of the award.

The five variations of the Legion d'Honneur.

The Meritorious Service Medal

Also of interest are two significant French awards because they were presented in some number to African Americans in World War I. The first is the Legion d'Honneur, of which over one hundred were awarded in two classes to African American officers and soldiers. The Legion d'Honneur did not rank above the Croix de Guerre as an award for valor, but the French regard it as an equal in a different way. Every recipient of the Legion d'Honneur in battle automatically received the Croix de Guerre with Palm.

There are five classes of Legion d'Honneur. The highest is the Grande Croix, below which falls the Grande Officier, the Commandeur (the only neck-worn version of this decoration), the Officier and below that the Chevalier.

It is interesting to observe the similarities in appearance between the Legion d'Honneur and the Legion of Merit. The five-point "legs" of the "cross" are of similar shape and in both decorations, they are enameled white. The wreath in

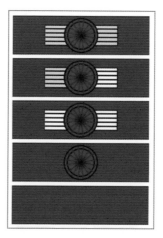

Legion d'Honneur ribbons, for wear without medals.

France's other top gallantry award, the Medaille Militaire.

the background and the circular center are also indicative that the person who designed the Legion of Merit was inspired by the Legion d'Honneur. However the thirteen stars in the center leave the observer in no doubt at all that it is an American award.

Service medals are awarded to all who served in a particular theater of war or in campaigns of action, some of which did not involve direct combat. They indicate a person's service record and commitment to his or her country.

Military medals have really only been a significant part of military history for a little over 200 years. Military campaign medals began to be awarded to British servicemen in the 19th Century, when such awards as the Military and Naval General Service Medals were authorized by Queen Victoria who reigned from 1837-1901. The earliest British campaign medal was authorized to mark Lord Howe's naval victory over the French in 1794. It was struck in gold and was awarded only to the officers who took part in that battle. It was later felt that medals for ordinary soldiers and sailors would be a morale boost and encourage people to either enlist or re-enlist. The awards were retrospective, since they bore an effigy of the Queen's head on the face (or obverse), yet commemorated battles like The Nile (1798), and Talavera (1809). This meant that they had to have been issued at least 40 years after the events for which they were awarded. Imagining the average lifespan of a soldier or sailor in those days,

it is clear that not too many medals were claimed or struck.

On the other hand, the earliest military award in the United States was the Badge of Merit, authorized by George Washington, which eventually evolved into the Purple Heart, awarded now for different reasons from those originally intended.

In the 21st Century, medals are a significant and integral part of military dress and custom. It is common today to see servicemen and women wearing several ribbons and medals of service quite early in their careers. There are also commemorative ribbons, which signify an award, but do not accompany medals. For example, the original Certificate of Merit ribbon told the observer that the bearer had received a Certificate of Merit, but the medal itself did not come into existence until 1905 and was discontinued in 1918.

The service medals relevant to African Americans who served the United States in its Armed Forces are displayed here in chronological order of the campaigns or events to which they relate, rather than the date of authorization, which may be much later. For example, the Civil War service medal was not authorized for issue until 1907 for the Army, over 40 years after the event. The Naval version of the same medal was authorized in 1908. Once again, the date of issue of this medal will mean that only a fraction of those entitled to receive it would have done so, because so many have predeceased its award.

From left to right: Civil War Medal 1861-1865, Indian Wars Medal 1869-1891, Spanish-American War Medal 1899, Philippines Campaign Medal 1899, World War I Victory Medal, WWI Army of Occupation Medal.

World War II Armed Forces Expeditionary Service Medal, World War II American Defense Service Medal, World War II European/African/Middle Eastern Campaign Medal, World War II Victory Medal, World War II Army of Occupation Medal and Prisoner of War Medal.

United States Korean Service Medal, UN Korea Medal, National Defense Service Medal (instituted by President Eisenhower in 1953), Southwest Asia Service Medal for the first Gulf War in 1991, the silver Kuwait Liberation Medal (issued by Kuwait to senior officers), and bronze Kuwait Liberation Medal 1991.

Saudi Arabian Kuwait Liberation Medal 1991, NATO Former Yugoslavia Medal, NATO Macedonia Medal (no clasp), US Armed Forces Expeditionary Medal (issued for Macedonia), UN Bosnia Medal, and NATO Kosovo Medal.

United Nations Kosovo Medal, UN Medal for Georgia 1993, UN Liberia Mission Medal 1993-97, UN Medal for Sierra Leone 1998 (all events to which the United States contributed and in which African-Americans took part), UN Macedonia Medal, and UN Cambodia Medal.

UN Medal for Croatia and Serbia (UNTAES Mission), Global War on Terror Expeditionary Medal (instituted after the events of September 11, 2001 in New York), Global War on Terror Service Medal, Afghanistan Campaign Medal, and Iraq Campaign Medal.

Commendation Medals, from left to right: Army, Navy and Marine Corps, Air Force and Joint Service.

APPENDIX FOUR
INFLUENTIAL PEOPLE

This Appendix addresses key people who influenced the inauguration of the Tuskegee Airmen and their subsequent success.

Harry S. Truman
US Senator 1935-1945
US Vice-President 1945
US President 1945-1953

Harry S. Truman was elected to the Senate, representing his home state of Missouri, in the 1934 elections. He was an early critic of powerful institutions like banks and what he saw as corporate greed. He had some voice for the "underdog", perhaps in part from his experience as a junior officer in World War I, when he was an artillery officer in the Missouri National Guard and was sent to France. While there, he served as battery commander of Battery D, 129th Field Artillery in the 60th Brigade of the 35th Infantry Division. This unit had a reputation for discipline problems, which manifested itself for Truman when, during a sudden attack by the Germans in the Vosges Mountains, the battery began to disperse. Truman ordered them back into position using the kind of profane language that would have been a credit to George Patton, and his men reassembled and followed him to safety. Under Captain Truman's command in France, the battery did not lose even one man. They provided support to Colonel George Patton's tank brigade during the Meuse-Argonne Offensive, a battle in which many African American soldiers fought. Truman's battery continued firing at German targets right up to the cease-fire on November 11th. It was here that he came across the 92nd and 93rd Infantry Divisions and admired their tenacity in a fight, which

was the start of Harry Truman's positive perspective on African Americans.

The year 1939 saw Dale White and Edgar Brown, leading figures in the National Airmen Association of America visit Congress by flying into Washington where they were met by Senator Harry S. Truman. He was an inquisitive man and wanted to know why they were denied admission when they declared the need for the Armed Forces to accept black pilots and ground crew. Their reply was simple – "Because we're black". Harry Truman took up their case and whilst it was 1941 before the decision was enacted, extensive research was conducted and African Americans joined the fighting forces in the air. In addition, Truman enlisted the help of Mrs. Eleanor Roosevelt in the quest for human rights and because of the outstanding military performance of the Tuskegee Airmen, President Harry Truman eventually invoked Executive Order 9981, which banned segregation in the United States Armed Forces 20 years before it was abolished in the nation at large. From a position of neutrality on the issue of race, Harry S. Truman became a true champion of the African American cause.

Congressman Everett M. Dirksen

Republican US Representative
1933-1949
Republican US Senator (IL)
1950-1969

Congressman Everett Dirksen was born in Pekin, Illinois, in 1896 to a German immigrant family. More than half of America has probably never heard of him, yet his influence in bringing civil rights legislation into being was significant. He took time out from his studies at the University of Minnesota Law School to serve his country in France in 1918-1919 and started his political career locally in 1927. By 1933, he was a Republican Congressman, with distinctly moderate views. He was another politician who met Dale White and Edgar Brown, representing the National Airmen Association of America, when they made their "flying visit" to Congress, because they were all from Illinois.

Congressman Dirksen was appalled to learn that these men, representing the interests of African Americans who wanted to fly for their country, were not acceptable to the Armed Forces just because of the color of their skin. He had seen men of the 92nd and 93rd Infantry Divisions in France and learned how many of them had been awarded the Croix de Guerre, individually as well as group awards to whole regiments. He reasoned that if such men could fight for their country with courage on the ground, why could they not do the same in the air? After that visit, Congressman Dirksen threw in his lot behind Senator Harry Truman and quietly campaigned for the admission of African Americans into the Army Air Corps.

Dirksen had a strange mix of views in his political career. He was an early supporter of Senator Joseph McCarthy in the 1950s, though later concluded that McCarthy had lost his sense of reason and distanced himself from that cause.

But most significantly, Everett Dirksen was the man who In 1964, as Southern Democratic Senators staged a blocking campaign that ran for fifty-four days to obstruct the passage of the Civil Rights Bill of 1964, introduced a substitute, slightly watered-down, bill that he and his supporters (who included Senators Mike Mansfield, Hubert Humphrey and Thomas Kirchel) hoped would attract enough Republican swing votes to end the stalemate. Their compromise bill was weaker than the official House version regarding government power to regulate the conduct of private business, but it was not so weak as to cause the House to reconsider the legislation. After 57 days, the substitute bill passed in the Senate and then the House-Senate conference committee agreed to adopt the Senate version of the bill, so bringing into being the Civil Rights Act to end segregation in society. At the end of his campaign, Everett Dirksen noted: *"Victor Hugo wrote in his diary substantially this sentiment, 'Stronger than all the armies is an idea whose time has come.' The time has come for equality of opportunity in sharing of government, in education, and in employment. It must not be stayed or denied."*

Mrs. Eleanor Roosevelt

First Lady 1934-1945
Human Rights Campaigner

Eleanor Roosevelt was born a Roosevelt as she was the fifth cousin of the man she married. In her early years, she joined the National Consumers League which had been created in 1898 by socially prominent women whose focus was to oppose the unregulated, dangerous and unhealthy working conditions known as "sweatshops". Eleanor Roosevelt's work consisted of visiting tenement apartments where workers both lived and worked, for example, turning out thousands of little artificial flowers to be used on hats and clothes and for which they were paid so little they remained in abject poverty. She made note of the workload, the physical toll on the workers, and the sanitary and safety conditions of the tenements. She also helped to create and disseminate publicity in the form of open letters to newspapers, press releases and other forms of media exposure about the Consumers League's "White Label" campaign. This was an endorsement given to manufacturers of products that were made under certain improved labor conditions, such as the elimination of unpaid overtime work, and hiring of workers only over the age of sixteen. After her marriage, and her husband, Franklin D. Roosevelt's, election to the Senate, she found herself working long hours as FDR's eyes and ears, especially in the area of human rights issues.

It was this human rights interest that brought Mrs. Roosevelt into contact with the Tuskegee Airmen. She had heard of the experimental project to set up a flying school for black student pilots and its incorporation into the Army Air Corps. With her campaigning perspective firmly in place, she visited Tuskegee in the spring of 1941 and while there, met Charles "Chief" Anderson, the chief flying instructor of the school. She asked Chief Anderson if black people could really fly aeroplanes and he invited her to fly with him around the field to see for herself. Their 40-minute flight together did much to advance the cause of black aviation, as she realized this man was a thoroughly competent aviator. After landing, she cheerfully announced, *Well, you can fly all right*. It has been suggested that the aircraft they flew in was a Waco biplane, but the picture taken of the two before flying clearly shows a Piper Cub high wing monoplane. Eleanor Roosevelt also used her influence as a trustee of the Julius Rosenwald Fund to secure a loan of $175,000 to purchase the land for Moton Field. She and Chief Anderson maintained a lifelong correspondence after that.

When Colonel Benjamin Davis was facing the possibility of his squadron being taken out from under him as Colonel William Momyer campaigned for the disbandment of the 99th Fighter Squadron, Mrs. Roosevelt took an interest from behind the scenes. She did not need to do too much, because Colonel Davis faced the Senate Committee on Defense robustly and held his ground as he explained how

his squadron had been refused attendance at the pre-flight briefing of their first mission and how he and his men had been left to find their own way around their airfield, how they had no information on the defenses of Pantelleria and how they had held off a German fighter group despite that, so allowing the bombers to reach their targets and return virtually unscathed. And then there was the bombshell, for Momyer, of the Distinguished Unit Citation awarded them by Lieutenant-General Henry Arnold. The result of that confrontation was the ultimate formation of the 332nd Fighter Group. Mrs. Roosevelt followed these developments closely and can always be described as an ally of the Tuskegee Airmen "in the right places".

General Henry H. Arnold
Commanding General, US Army Air Corps 1938-1941
Commanding General, US Army Air Forces 1941-1947
Commanding General, US Air Force 1947-1948
General of the Army 1945-1947
(5-star) General of the Air Force
(the only 5-star General of the Air Force in history)

Henry H. Arnold was appointed Chief of the Army Air Corps on September 29, 1938 and remained in that post through the reorganization of the Air Corps into the Army Air Forces in 1941. He was originally not sympathetic to the cause of recruiting black personnel into the Army Air Forces, not because he had any particular view on the subject, but because he was more personally concerned with the re-equipment of the Army Air Corps to fight the battles that he was confident would come, than the people who would fight it. However, there had been discussions in the corridors of Congress about the admission of black fliers into the Army and Senator Harry Truman had been asking questions. As a result, Major-General Arnold, who knew of the existence of the Tuskegee Institute's flying training program, sent a letter to Brigadier-General Weaver, commanding South East Air Training Command, asking for an investigation into the value of establishing all-black squadrons in the Army Air Corps. The prevailing view was that African Americans were simply not capable of matching the flying skills of white crews and that in any event, command would have to be given to white officers, simply because Army regulations did not provide for senior command positions to be occupied by black officers. General Weaver was a conscientious officer who, a little like General John J. Pershing, believed that blacks were capable of being trained and should be given a chance to prove themselves in the air.

General Arnold approved the basic plan put forward and had it presented to the Chiefs of Staff. The decision was made to base the training program at Tuskegee Institute, alongside the Civilian Pilot Training Program and while there was some local resistance, the program went ahead and Tuskegee Army Airfield was born. The first Project Officer was Major James A. Ellison, appointed in February 1941, who supervised the establishment of the military facility. It was several months before any activity took place, not least because there were extended discussions in Washington over funding and training numbers varied from seventy-five students a year to as low as fifteen. Finally, in July 1941, the elementary flying school was opened and the first flight course of twelve was inducted in August. Among that number was Benjamin O. Davis, Jr. who would lead the first fighter squadron, and ultimately was the first black General Staff Officer in the United States Air Force. He was the son of the first African American general in the US Army, General Benjamin O. Davis, Sr.

The 99th Fighter Squadron went into action in North Africa under the overall command of Brigadier-General Jimmy Doolittle and performed its first bomber escort for the 320th Bombardment Group over Pantelleria, a small volcanic island sixty miles off the Sicilian coast. Not the most successful mission in the history of that squadron, it was thwarted by the actions and obstructions of the Commander of the 33rd Fighter Group, Colonel William Momyer, who was strongly opposed to the idea of a black-crewed fighter squadron in

his group. There were problems which are addressed more fully elsewhere, but it is enough here to say that Colonel Earl Bates recommended a Distinguished Unit Commendation for the 99th which Arnold promptly endorsed. This was the first of three and was the defusing element in the Senate House Defense Committee Review of the 99th Fighter Squadron's future when Colonel Momyer was trying to get it disbanded.

Upon the expansion of the Army Air Corps in 1941, and its change of name to the Army Air Forces, Major-General Arnold was promoted to Lieutenant-General. Then, In March 1943, "Hap" Arnold's promotion to full General reflected his position in the membership of the Chiefs of Staff. Then, in December 1944, recognizing his achievements and huge contribution to the success of the Allies in World War II, General Arnold was promoted to five-star General of the Army, alongside General Marshall and later General Eisenhower. Henry Arnold's claims to distinction include winning the Air War in the Pacific, contributing to the winning of the Air War in Europe and being the only five-star general in two arms of the United States forces – the Army and the Air Force, for he was the founding Commanding General of the United States Air Force in 1947.

General Arnold died on January 15, 1950 and was buried in Arlington National Cemetery in Virginia, but his remains were later transferred to the grounds of the United States Air Force Academy, in Colorado Springs. For the USAF Academy Class of 2012 General Arnold was nominated Exemplar in recognition of his career-long achievements.

Lieutenant-General Idwal H. Edwards

Chief of Staff, European ETO 1943-1944
Chief of Staff Mediterranean ETO 1944-1945
Deputy Chief of Staff Personnel 1947-1950

Perhaps prophetically, Lieutenant-General Idwal H. Edwards was born in a town called Freedom, New York. At the outbreak of World War II, he was in command of Randolph Field, Texas. During the war he twice served as Assistant Chief of Staff for training on the War Department General Staff. In 1943, he was assigned as Chief of Staff of the European Theater of Operations under the command of Lieutenant-General Carl Spaatz, and then he became deputy commander of the US Air Force in the Mediterranean Theater during 1944 and 1945. This was where he first came into contact with the all-African American 332nd Fighter Group and its commander Colonel Benjamin Davis.

Major-General Edwards was appointed Commanding General of the US Air Forces in Europe from March 1946 to August 1947. He was then designated Deputy Chief of Staff, personnel, at Air Force headquarters in Washington, DC, in the rank of Lieutenant-General until March 1950, when he was named Deputy Chief of Staff, Operations. One of Idwal Edwards' key tasks was to investigate, through an intensive study, the impact and consequences of racial segregation in the Air Force. Available to him was his own limited experience of seeing the 332nd Fighter Group in action during World War II, but also was able to meet with Colonel Benjamin O. Davis, once again commander of the 332nd Fighter Wing and of Lockbourne Air Force Base.

Benjamin Davis' achievements in desegregating Lockbourne had a profound effect on how affairs were handled during the separation of the Air Force itself from the Army in late 1947 and the attitudes to segregation. General Edwards was able to use the evidence of the smooth transition from segregated to integrated operation of Lockbourne as an example of how it could (and perhaps should) be done and these factors were a distinct influence on his recommendations to the Air Force Board. He appointed his deputy, Brigadier-General Richard Nugent to head the investigative team that produced the material for his report and recommendations.

General Edwards made the unequivocal recommendation that racial integration was the way ahead for the United States Air Force. His key argument was, of course, the performance of the Tuskegee Airmen in war and in peace – especially commending the command qualities of Colonel Benjamin O. Davis. It followed, therefore, that Edwards' recommendations were that the US Air Force should be the first of the United States Armed Forces to implement racial integration – and it did, just months after President Truman's Executive Order 9981.

APPENDIX FIVE
JAMES H. DOOLITTLE – FOUNDING GENERAL 12TH AND 15TH AIR FORCE

Brigadier-General James H. Doolittle was the founder of the 12th United States Army Air Forces in North Africa during World War II. It was his job to build a bombing force to help Major-General George Patton and British General Bernard Montgomery push the Germans out of North Africa. Not only did he need bomber crews with a high level of expertise, he required fighter cover that would stick with the bombers and give them confidence and reassurance to enable them to do a better job.

As a gunnery instructor in the 1920s, Doolittle had learned how valuable air-to-air firepower was and made it very plain that bomber escorts should not abandon their bombers when they saw the chance of a fight. That was playing into the enemy's hands for the Germans had developed a tactic of luring away the escorting fighters which allowed more German fighters to attack the now unprotected bombers.

This explains why the better bomber escort squadrons shot down fewer enemy aircraft than defensive groups.

Doolittle's own aviation career was magical to many young men who sought to join the Army Air Corps. They would almost certainly never be able to emulate his flying career, but they saw him as a role model. The bomber crews of the 477th Bombardment Group could relate to Doolittle as the bombardment leader of the Doolittle Raid on Japan because they were expecting to fly into combat with the same model of aircraft, the North American B-25 "Mitchell". The soon-to-be fighter pilots could envisage themselves as the same type of daredevil they understood Jimmy Doolittle had been in his racing days.

The reason this forty-something General was so inspirational to these young pilots, whatever their race or color, was that

A US Army Air Service DH-4 – unusual in that has a two-bladed propeller, where most had four blades. It looks fairly new into service with the shiny under-surfaces to the wings and has not yet been fitted with underwing mountings for bombs and other "stores".

Jimmy Doolittle stands on one of the pontoons of his Curtiss R3-C racing biplane prior to the 1925 Schneider Trophy Race, which he not only won, but secured a new seaplane speed record in the process. This was the United States' second Schneider Trophy win.

The Curtiss P-1C in flight. The "C" model was "cleaner" than its earlier variants.

Lieutenant Jimmy Doolittle beside his aircraft before the first test flight. The experiment was completely successful and finally dispelled the fear for pilots of flying in poor weather or at night.

he had been the world's greatest aviator before the war began and in the years when they were growing up. He had made the first transcontinental flight across America in 1922, with a flight time of 21 hours and 19 minutes.

Then, in 1925, Lieutenant Doolittle flew a Curtiss R3-C Navy biplane to victory in the Schneider Trophy Race, an international race for floatplanes established in 1912. Doolittle's expert flying and hairpin turns gave the United States its second win in that event, with an average speed of 232.6 miles per hour. After the Schneider Trophy Race, Doolittle demonstrated his prowess as a fighter pilot by taking a Curtiss P-1 "Hawk" to Chile on a successful visit to promote the aircraft to that country's infant air arm. His next achievement was in 1928, when Lieutenant Doolittle became the first man to fly an outside loop – that is, flying with the pilot on the outside, not as was customary, on the inside of the loop. Again, he flew a Curtiss Hawk.

He had been planning to leave the Army when he was approached by Harry F. Guggenheim, the son of a multi-millionaire businessman and philanthropist, Daniel Guggenheim. Guggenheim Senior had set up a $2.5-million fund for the promotion of developments in aviation and Harry wanted Doolittle to participate in a series of experiments flying in fog. This is how Doolittle became the first man to "fly blind", using instruments to guide him rather than visual contact with the world outside his cockpit.

After the blind flying trial, Jimmy Doolittle resigned his commission in the Regular Army in 1931, and transferred to the Reserve in the rank of Major. He took the job as manager of Shell's Aviation Fuels Division, and resumed racing, flying in the Bendix Trans-continental Trophy Race from Los Angeles to Cleveland. Doolittle won the race and then went on to set a new coast-to-coast record by flying to New York. A year later, he won the Thompson Trophy Race in the Gee-Bee RC-1.

By the time the Japanese attack on Pearl Harbor took place, James H. Doolittle had returned to active duty and was a Lieutenant-Colonel, working as a staff officer to General Henry H. Arnold, commander of the Army Air Corps. In this position, Doolittle achieved his greatest personal aviation

The USS "Hornet" CV-8, the carrier which took the Doolittle Raiders on their journey.

B-25s lashed to the deck of the carrier en route.

President Roosevelt pins the Medal of Honor to Brigadier-General Doolittle's chest after the highly successful raid. Generals Arnold and Marshall, with Mrs. Doolittle between them, look on.

Madame Soong Mei Li (wife of General Chiang Kai Shek) presents the Order of Yung Hui to Jimmy Doolittle and Major John Hilger.

success, leading what became known as the Doolittle Raid on Japan. He took sixteen B-25 bombers from the aircraft carrier USS "Hornet" to bomb five cities in Japan in retaliation for Pearl Harbor which caused the Japanese to pull back approximately five per cent of its forces from the Pacific Islands. It also set Jimmy Doolittle on the path to se-

nior command, with his promotion by President Roosevelt to Brigadier-General and the award of the Medal of Honor. Shortly after that, he left to form and command the 12th Air Force in North Africa.

Barely had General Doolittle established himself in North Africa than he was to discover one of his crack fighter groups, the 33rd, had lost most of its aircraft due to the foolhardy action of its commander, Colonel William Momyer who had spread his squadrons out over remote airfields in Tunisia, thinking he could break the German control of the air. He had been advised against taking this action, but went ahead anyway, with disastrous consequences, and his group had to be withdrawn to re-form.

Doolittle made it plain to Momyer that he did not approve of what had happened and it can only be presumed that Momyer escaped a court-martial because of his previous success in introducing the Curtiss P-40 into Britain's Royal Air Force service in the Western Desert and his personal skill as a fighter pilot. But he was now faced with being told that, instead of having the pick of the Army Air Forces' elite, the first three fighter squadrons to arrive in North Africa would be allocated to him. Colonel Momyer did not bargain for what was to come, for among these squadrons was the 99th Fighter Squadron, the first African American unit in the Army Air Forces. Colonel Momyer came from Savannah, Georgia, where segregation was almost a religion in those days.

So well did the 99th Squadron perform that it quickly won a Distinguished Unit Citation from Lieutenant-General Henry Arnold, and it was also later expanded after the debacle of Colonel Momyer's attempt to disband it, to become the 332nd Fighter Group, a four-squadron unit that went on to become the most highly decorated fighter group in the North African and Mediterranean Theaters of Operation.

In March 1943, Doolittle became Commanding General of the North African Strategic Air Forces and was promoted to Lieutenant-General. Moving from North Africa with the Allied advance, Doolittle was given the job of establishing and commanding the 15th Air Force in the Mediterranean Theater and into that air force was placed the 332nd Fighter Group. The Consolidated B-24 Liberator was the most common bomber in the 15th and made its name in the raids on the Ploesti oilfields. Many of those raids were escorted by fighters from the 332nd Fighter Group under withering fire from German ground and air defenses.

In England, Lieutenant-General James H. Doolittle as commander of 8th Air Force, just before he took the 'Mighty Eighth' to the Pacific.

The Air Force Association certificate presented to its first President, Jimmy Doolittle.

Between January 1945 and the end of the war in September of that year, General Doolittle commanded the 8th Air Force in Europe and the Pacific. On May 10, 1946 he reverted to inactive reserve status and returned to Shell Oil as a vice president and later a director. Doolittle retired from the Air Force Reserve in February 1959 and in 1985 was promoted to General of the Air Force by President Ronald Reagan. General Doolittle died in California on September 27, 1993 and was buried in Arlington National Cemetery, with his high school sweetheart, Josephine Daniels Doolittle.

APPENDIX SIX
THE TUSKEGEE AIRMEN - ROSTER AND CLASS LIST

Thanks in no small part to the efforts of Mr. Andre Swygert, a long-standing student of Tuskegee matters, it has become possible to list below the class details of every pilot who passed through the Tuskegee Flight Training Program. This initial list details the fighter and bomber pilots. The second list details pilots trained for Service Pilot Duties.

Following these two lists is a third roster of pilots, who were trained for liaison flying duties with the 92nd Infantry Division, bringing the total to 994 men. While this third group of pilots did not fly combat duties, they were every bit as much at risk of being shot down, from the ground or from the air. Their work was much closer to the ground and at lower speeds and the value of their contribution to the success of the Italian Campaign is confirmed by the fact that it was the 371st Infantry Regiment, a unit of the 92nd Division, that broke through the Gothic Line first. These men can therefore claim their entitlement to be listed as Tuskegee Airmen just as much as any others.

NAME	CLASS	GRAD DATE	RANK	HOMETOWN
Adams, Paul	43-D-SE	29-Apr-43	2nd Lt.	Greenville, SC
Adams, John H., Jr.	45-B-SE	15-Apr-45	2nd Lt.	Kansas City, KS
Adkins, Winston A.	44-B-TE	08-Feb-44	2nd Lt.	Chicago, IL
Adkins, Rutherford H.	44-I-I-SE	16-Oct-44	2nd Lt.	Alexandria, VA
Alexander, Robert R.	43-F-SE	30-Jun-43	2nd Lt.	Harrisburg, PA
Alexander, Harvey R.	44-D-TE	15-Apr-44	2nd Lt.	Georgetown, IL
Alexander, Halbert L.	44-I-SE	20-Nov-44	2nd Lt.	Georgetown, IL
Alexander, Walter G.	45-D-SE	27-Jun-45	2nd Lt.	Orange, NJ
Allen, Clarence W.	43-C-SE	25-Mar-43	2nd Lt.	Mobile, AL
Allen, Walter H.	44-J-TE	28-Dec-44	F/O	Kansas City, KS
Allen, Carl V.	46-C-SE	28-Jun-46	2nd Lt.	Bronx, NY
Allison, James M.	46-C-TE	28-Jun-46	2nd Lt.	Chicago, IL
Alsbrook, William N.	43-I-SE	01-Oct-43	2nd Lt.	Kansas City, KS
Alston, William R.	44-I-SE	20-Nov-44	2nd Lt.	Huntington, WV
Anders, Emet R.	44-H-SE	08-Sep-44	2nd Lt.	Carbondale, IL
Anderson, Robert D.	44-D-TE	15-Apr-44	2nd Lt.	Indianapolis, IN
Anderson, Paul T.	44-I-I-TE	16-Oct-44	1st Lt.	Woodbine, NY
Anderson, Rayfield A.	44-K-TE	01-Feb-45	2nd Lt.	Indianapolis, IN
Archer, Lee A., Jr.	43-G-SE	28-Jul-43	2nd Lt.	New York, NY
Armistead, Richard S. A.	44-F-SE	27-Jun-44	F/O	Philadelphia, PA
Armstrong, William P.	44-H-SE	08-Sep-44	F/O	Providence, RI
Ashby, Robert	45-H-TE	20-Nov-45	2nd Lt.	Jersey City, NJ
Ashley, Willie	42-F-SE	03-Jul-42	2nd Lt.	Sumter, SC
Askins, Montro	44-K-SE	01-Feb-45	2nd Lt.	Baltimore, MD
Audant, Ludovic F.	44-B-SE	08-Feb-44	UNK	Port au Prince, Haiti
Bailey, Charles P.	43-D-SE	29-Apr-43	2nd Lt.	Punta Gorda, FL

NAME	CLASS	GRAD DATE	RANK	HOMETOWN
Bailey, Harry L.	43-G-SE	28-Jul-43	2nd Lt.	Chicago, IL
Bailey, Terry C.	45-C-SE	23-May-45	F/O	Richmond, VA
Bailey, William H.	45-E-SE	04-Aug-45	2nd Lt.	Pittsburgh, PA
Baldwin, Henry, Jr.	45-H-TE	20-Nov-45	F/O	Philadelphia, PA
Ballard, Alton F.	43-H-SE	30-Aug-43	2nd Lt.	Pasadena, CA
Barksdale, James M.	46-A-SE	23-Mar-46	F/O	Detroit, MI
Barland, Herbert C.	44-H-SE	08-Sep-44	2nd Lt.	Chicago, IL
Barnes, Gentry E.	44-D-SE	15-Apr-44	2nd Lt.	Lawrenceville, IL
Barnett, Herman A.	45-E-SE	04-Aug-45	F/O	Lockhart, TX
Bartley, William R.	43-G-SE	28-Jul-43	2nd Lt.	Jacksonville, FL
Bates, George A.	46-A-TE	23-Mar-46	F/O	Chicago, IL
Baugh, Howard L.	42-J-SE	10-Nov-42	2nd Lt.	Petersburg, VA
Bee, Clarence, Jr.	45-B-SE	15-Apr-45	2nd Lt.	Kansas City, MO
Bell, Rual W.	44-D-SE	15-Apr-44	F/O	Portland, OR
Bell, Richard H.	44-E-SE	23-May-44	2nd Lt.	Chicago, IL
Bell, John J.	44-I-SE	20-Nov-44	F/O	Jersey City, NJ
Bell, Lloyd W.	44-K-SE	01-Feb-45	2nd Lt.	Pulaski, IL
Bell, George E.	46-C-SE	28-Jun-46	2nd Lt.	Altoona, PA
Bennett, Joseph B.	45-I-SE	29-Jan-46	2nd Lt.	Halesite, NY
Bibb, William V.	45-H-TE	20-Nov-45	2nd Lt.	Ottumwa, IA
Bickham, Luzine B.	45-A-SE	11-Mar-45	F/O	Tuskegee Inst., AL
Biffle, Richard L. Jr.	44-K-SE	01-Feb-45	F/O	Denver, CO
Bilbo, Reuben B.	45-D-SE	27-Jun-45	F/O	Fresno, CA
Bing, George L.	44-G-SE	04-Aug-44	2nd Lt.	Brolyn, NY
Black, Samuel A.	43-K-TE	05-Dec-43	2nd Lt.	Plainfield, NJ
Blackwell, Hubron R.	43-H-SE	30-Aug-43	2nd Lt.	Baltimore, MD

NAME	CLASS	GRAD DATE	RANK	HOMETOWN
Blaylock, Joseph	45-D-SE	27-Jun-45	2nd Lt.	Albany, GA
Blue, Elliott H.	44-A-TE	07-Jan-44	2nd Lt.	Hampton, VA
Bohannon, Horace A.	44-J-SE	28-Dec-44	F/O	Atlanta, GA
Bohler, Henry C. L.	44-J-SE	28-Dec-44	F/O	Augusta, GA
Bolden, Edgar L.	43-K-SE	05-Dec-43	2nd Lt.	Arlington, VA
Bolden, George C.	45-F-TE	08-Sep-45	2nd Lt.	Pittsburgh, PA
Bolling, George R.	42-F-SE	03-Jul-42	2nd Lt.	Hampton, VA
Bonam, Leonelle A.	44-E-SE	23-May-44	2nd Lt.	Pascagoula, MS
Bonseigneur, Paul J. Jr.	44-H-TE	08-Sep-44	2nd Lt.	Chicago, IL
Bowman, Leroy	43-C-SE	25-Mar-43	2nd Lt.	Sumter, SC
Bowman, James E.	44-K-SE	01-Feb-45	F/O	Des Moines, IA
Bradford, Clarence H.	43-K-SE	05-Dec-43	2nd Lt.	St. Louis, MO
Brantley, Charles V.	43-K-SE	05-Dec-43	2nd Lt.	St. Louis, MO
Brashears, Virgil	44-D-TE	15-Apr-44	2nd Lt.	Kansas City, MO
Braswell, Thomas P.	44-B-SE	08-Feb-44	2nd Lt.	Buford, GA
Bratcher, Everett A.	43-H-SE	30-Aug-43	2nd Lt.	Poplar Bluff, MO
Brazil, Harold E.	43-K-TE	05-Dec-43	2nd Lt.	Joplin, MO
Brewin, Irvin O.	44-I-SE	20-Nov-44	2nd Lt.	Chicago, IL
Briggs, John F.	43-E-SE	28-May-43	2nd Lt.	St. Louis, MO
Briggs, Eugene A.	46-A-SE	23-Mar-46	F/O	Boston, MA
Bright, Alexander M.	43-F-SE	30-Jun-43	2nd Lt.	Chicago, IL
Broadnax, Samuel L.	45-A-SE	11-Mar-45	F/O	Oroville, CA
Broadwater, William E.	45-E-TE	04-Aug-45	F/O	Bryn Mawr, PA
Brooks, Sidney P.	42-D-SE	29-Apr-42	2nd Lt.	Cleveland, OH
Brooks, Milton R.	43-E-SE	28-May-43	2nd Lt.	Glassport, PA
Brooks, Tilford U.	45-B-SE	15-Apr-45	F/O	East St. Louis, IL
Brothers, James E.	43-D-SE	29-Apr-43	2nd Lt.	Chicago, IL
Brothers, James E.	44-G-TE	04-Aug-44	F/O	Philadelphia, PA
Browder, Cecil L.	43-I-SE	01-Oct-43	2nd Lt.	Wilmington, NC
Brower, Fred L. Jr.	44-C-SE	12-Mar-44	2nd Lt.	Charlotte, NC
Brown, James B.	43-J-SE	03-Nov-43	2nd Lt.	Los Angeles, CA
Brown, Roger B.	43-J-SE	03-Nov-43	2nd Lt.	Glencoe, IL
Brown, Roscoe C. Jr.	44-C-SE	12-Mar-44	2nd Lt.	New York, NY
Brown, Walter R. Jr.	44-C-SE	12-Mar-44	2nd Lt.	Hampton, VA
Brown, Harold Haywood	44-E-SE	23-May-44	2nd Lt.	Minneapolis, MN
Brown, Harold Howard	44-G-TE	04-Aug-44	2nd Lt.	Weleetka , OK
Brown, Augustus G.	44-H-TE	08-Sep-44	2nd Lt.	Houma, LA
Brown, Robert S.	44-H-TE	08-Sep-44	2nd Lt.	Minneapolis, MN
Brown, James W.	44-I-I-TE	16-Oct-44	2nd Lt.	Detroit, MI
Brown, Lawrence A.	44-K-SE	01-Feb-45	F/O	Jamaica, NY
Brown, George A. Jr.	45-E-TE	04-Aug-45	2nd Lt.	Baltimore, MD

NAME	CLASS	GRAD DATE	RANK	HOMETOWN
Brown, Reuben H. Jr.	45-F-SE	08-Sep-45	2nd Lt.	Kansas City, MO
Browne, Gene C.	43-I-SE	01-Oct-43	2nd Lt.	New York, NY
Bruce, Samuel M.	42-H-SE	06-Sep-42	2nd Lt.	Seattle, WA
Bruce, Reginald A.	44-G-SE	04-Aug-44	F/O	Indianapolis, IN
Bryant, Leroy, Jr.	44-J-SE	28-Dec-44	F/O	Houston, TX
Bryant, Grady E.	45-D-SE	27-Jun-45	2nd Lt.	Los Angeles, CA
Bryant, Joseph C. Jr.	45-E-TE	04-Aug-45	F/O	Dowagiac, MI
Bryson, James O.	45-D-SE	27-Jun-45	F/O	Columbus, GA
Burch, John A. III	45-A-SE	11-Mar-45	2nd Lt.	Indianapolis, IN
Burns, Isham A. Jr.	44-J-SE	28-Dec-44	2nd Lt.	Los Angeles, CA
Burns, Charles A.	46-B-TE	14-May-46	UNK	Unknown
Bussey, Charles M.	43-E-SE	28-May-43	2nd Lt.	Los Angeles, CA
Butler, Jewel B.	46-A-SE	23-Mar-46	2nd Lt.	Denison, TX
Bynum, Rolin A.	44-A-TE	07-Jan-44	2nd Lt.	Montclair, NJ
Byrd, Willie L. Jr.	43-K-TE	05-Dec-43	2nd Lt.	Fayetteville, NC
Cabiness, Marshall S.	42-I-SE	09-Oct-42	2nd Lt.	Gastonia, NC
Cabule, Ernest M. Jr.	45-A-SE	11-Mar-45	2nd Lt.	Detroit, MI
Caesar, Richard C.	42-H-SE	06-Sep-42	2nd Lt.	Lake Village, AR
Cain, William L.	44-I-I-TE	16-Oct-44	F/O	London, OH
Calhoun, James A.	44-C-SE	12-Mar-44	2nd Lt.	Bridgeport, CT
Calloway, Julius W.	44-I-SE	20-Nov-44	F/O	Louisville, KY
Campbell, Herman R. Jr.	43-J-SE	03-Nov-43	2nd Lt.	New York, NY
Campbell, Lindsay L.	44-J-SE	28-Dec-44	F/O	Washington, DC
Campbell, McWheeler	44-J-SE	28-Dec-44	2nd Lt.	Cambria, VA
Campbell, Vincent O.	45-A-SE	11-Mar-45	2nd Lt.	Corona, NY
Carey, Carl E.	44-H-SE	08-Sep-44	2nd Lt.	St. Louis, MO
Carpenter, Russell W.	44-I-SE	20-Nov-44	2nd Lt.	Plainfield, NJ
Carroll, Alfred Q. Jr.	43-J-SE	03-Nov-43	2nd Lt.	Washington, DC
Carroll, Lawrence W.	45-H-TE	20-Nov-45	2nd Lt.	Chicago, IL
Carter, Herbert E.	42-F-SE	03-Jul-42	2nd Lt.	Amory, MS
Carter, James Y	43-D-SE	29-Apr-43	2nd Lt.	Winst-Salem, NC
Carter, Lloyd A.N.	44-K-SE	01-Feb-45	2nd Lt.	York, PA
Carter, Clarence J.	45-D-SE	27-Jun-45	F/O	Chicago, IL
Carter, Floyd J.	46-A-TE	23-Mar-46	F/O	Norfolk, VA
Carter, William G.	46-C-SE	28-Jun-46	2nd Lt.	Pittsburgh, PA
Casey, Clifton G.	45-B-SE	15-Apr-45	F/O	Birmingham, AL
Cassagnol, Raymond	43-G-SE	28-Jul-43	UNK	UNK, Haiti
Chambers, Charles W.	46-A-SE	23-Mar-46	2nd Lt.	Camden, NJ
Chandler, Robert C.	44-B-SE	08-Feb-44	2nd Lt.	Allegan, MI
Charlton, Terry J.	42-J-SE	10-Nov-42	2nd Lt.	Beaumont, TX
Chavis, John H.	44-D-SE	15-Apr-44	2nd Lt.	Raleigh, NC

NAME	CLASS	GRAD DATE	RANK	HOMETOWN
Cheatham, Eugene C.	43-K-TE	05-Dec-43	2nd Lt.	Philadelphia, PA
Cheek, Quinten V.	45-F-TE	08-Sep-45	2nd Lt.	Weldon, NC
Cheek, Conrad H.	46-C-SE	28-Jun-46	2nd Lt.	Weldon, NC
Chichester, James R.	44-I-I-TE	16-Oct-44	2nd Lt.	Santa Monica, CA
Chin, Jack	46-C-SE	28-Jun-46	2nd Lt.	Chicago, IL
Chineworth, Joseph E.	44-E-SE	23-May-44	F/O	Memphis, TN
Choisy, George B.	45-E-TE	04-Aug-45	2nd Lt.	Jamaica, NY
Cisco, Arnold W.	43-D-SE	29-Apr-43	2nd Lt.	Alton, IL
Cisco, George E.	44-E-SE	23-May-44	2nd Lt.	Alton, IL
Clark, Herbert V.	42-F-SE	03-Jul-42	2nd Lt.	Pine Bluff, AR
Clayton, Melvin A.	45-A-TE	11-Mar-45	2nd Lt.	Salem, NJ
Claytor, Ralph V.	45-C-SE	23-May-45	2nd Lt.	Roanoke, VA
Cleaver, Lowell H.	44-K-SE	01-Feb-45	2nd Lt.	Prairie View, TX
Clifton, Emile G. Jr.	44-B-SE	08-Feb-44	2nd Lt.	San Francisco, CA
Cobbs, Wilson N.	45-D-SE	27-Jun-45	2nd Lt.	Gordonsville, VA
Coggs, Granville C.	45-G-TE	16-Oct-45	2nd Lt.	Little Rock, AR
Colbert, William A. Jr.	44-K-SE	01-Feb-45	F/O	Cumberland, MD
Cole, Robert A.	44-J-SE	28-Dec-44	F/O	Northfield, VT
Coleman, William C. Jr.	44-D-TE	15-Apr-44	2nd Lt.	Detroit, MI
Coleman, James	44-H-SE	08-Sep-44	2nd Lt.	Detroit, MI
Coleman, William J.	45-A-SE	11-Mar-45	2nd Lt.	Columbus, GA
Collins, Gamaliel M.	44-I-I-TE	16-Oct-44	F/O	Los Angeles, CA
Collins, Russell L.	45-E-SE	04-Aug-45	F/O	Davenport, IA
Connell, Victor L.	45-D-SE	27-Jun-45	2nd Lt.	Nutley, NJ
Cook, Martin L.	44-D-TE	15-Apr-44	F/O	Purcellville, VA
Cooper, Charles W.	44-H-SE	08-Sep-44	F/O	Washington, DC
Cooper, Edward M.	45-F-TE	08-Sep-45	2nd Lt.	Sharon, LA
Corbin, Matthew J.	45-D-SE	27-Jun-45	F/O	Pittsburgh, PA
Cousins, Augustus	44-D-TE	15-Apr-44	2nd Lt.	Toledo, OH
Cousins, William M.	44-H-SE	08-Sep-44	2nd Lt.	Philadelphia, PA
Cowan, Edwin T.	44-J-TE	28-Dec-44	F/O	Cleveland, OH
Cox, Hannibal M. Jr.	44-D-SE	15-Apr-44	2nd Lt.	Chicago, IL
Craig, Lewis W.	44-D-SE	15-Apr-44	2nd Lt.	Asheville, NC
Craig, Charles E.	44-K-SE	01-Feb-45	F/O	Detroit, MI
Criss, Leroy	45-B-TE	15-Apr-45	F/O	Los Angeles, CA
Crockett, Woodrow W.	43-C-SE	25-Mar-43	2nd Lt.	Little Rock, AR
Cross, William, Jr.	43-I-SE	01-Oct-43	F/O	Cleveland, OH
Crumbsy, Grover	44-K-TE	01-Feb-45	F/O	Pensacola, FL
Cummings, Herndon M.	45-A-TE	11-Mar-45	2nd Lt.	Montrose, GA
Curry, John C.	45-E-TE	04-Aug-45	2nd Lt.	Indianapolis, IN
Curry, Waiter P.	45-F-SE	08-Sep-45	F/O	Washington, DC
Curtis, Samuel L.	43-G-SE	28-Jul-43	2nd Lt.	Yeadon, PA
Curtis, William J. Jr.	45-A-TE	11-Mar-45	F/O	Pittsburgh, PA
Curtis, John W.	45-B-SE	15-Apr-45	2nd Lt.	Detroit, MI
Custis, Lemuel R.	42-C-SE	06-Mar-42	2nd Lt.	Hartford, CT
Dabney, Roscoe J. Jr.	45-F-TE	08-Sep-45	2nd Lt.	Lakewood, NJ
Daniels, John	43-G-SE	28-Jul-43	2nd Lt.	Chicago, IL
Daniels, Harry J.	43-H-SE	30-Aug-43	2nd Lt.	Indianapolis, IN
Daniels, Robert H. Jr.	43-K-SE	05-Dec-43	2nd Lt.	Corona, NY
Daniels, Virgil A.	44-A-TE	07-Jan-44	F/O	Jacksonville, FL
Daniels, Thomas J. III	44-I-I-SE	16-Oct-44	F/O	Wetumpka, AL
Darnell, Charles E.	44-C-TE	12-Mar-44	2nd Lt.	Dayton, OH
Dart, Clarence W.	43-J-SE	03-Nov-43	2nd Lt.	Elmira, NY
Davenport, Harry J. Jr.	44-E-SE	23-May-44	2nd Lt.	Beaumont, TX
Davis, Benjamin O. Jr.	42-C-SE	06-Mar-42	Capt.	Tuskegee, AL
Davis, Richard	42-G-SE	05-Aug-42	2nd Lt.	Ft. Valley, GA
Davis, Alfonza W.	43-C-SE	25-Mar-43	2nd Lt.	Omaha, NE
Davis, John W.	44-E-SE	23-May-44	2nd Lt.	Kansas City, KS
Davis, Claude C.	44-G-TE	04-Aug-44	1st Lt.	Pittsburgh, PA
Davis, Donald F.	45-F-SE	08-Sep-45	F/O	Detroit, MI
Davis, Sylvester S.	45-F-SE	08-Sep-45	2nd Lt.	Cleveland, OH
Davis, Clifford W.	45-F-TE	08-Sep-45	F/O	Chicago, IL
Dean, Vincent C.	44-C-SE	12-Mar-44	2nd Lt.	Corona, NY
DeBow, Charles H.	42-C-SE	06-Mar-42	2nd Lt.	Indianapolis, IN
Deiz, Robert W.	42-H-SE	06-Sep-42	2nd Lt.	Portland, OR
Derricotte, Eugene A.	46-B-TE	14-May-46	UNK	Unknown
Desvignes, Russell F.	45-B-TE	15-Apr-45	F/O	New Orleans, LA
Dickerson, Charles W.	43-J-SE	03-Nov-43	2nd Lt.	New Rochelle, NY
Dickerson, Tamenund J.	44-I-SE	20-Nov-44	F/O	Detroit, MI
Dickerson, Page L.	45-G-SE	16-Oct-45	F/O	St. Louis, MO
Dickson, Lawrence E.	43-C-SE	25-Mar-43	2nd Lt.	Bronx, NY
Dickson, Othel	43-K-SE	05-Dec-43	2nd Lt.	San Francisco, CA
Dickson, DeWitt	44-J-SE	28-Dec-44	F/O	New York, NY
Diggs, Charles W.	44-B-TE	08-Feb-44	2nd Lt.	Roxbury, MA
Dillard, James M. Jr.	45-I-TE	29-Jan-46	2nd Lt.	East Beckley, WV
Dillon, Oliver M.	45-I-TE	29-Jan-46	2nd Lt.	McComb, MS
Dixon, Edward T.	44-G-SE	04-Aug-44	2nd Lt.	Hartford, CT
Doram, Edward D.	44-I-I-SE	16-Oct-44	2nd Lt.	Cincinnati, OH
Dorkins, Charles J.	45-A-TE	11-Mar-45	2nd Lt.	Baltimore, MD
Doswell, Andrew H.	43-H-SE	30-Aug-43	2nd Lt.	Cleveland, OH
Doswell, Edgar A. Jr.	45-A-SE	11-Mar-45	F/O	Lynchburg, VA
Dowling, Cornelius D.	44-I-I-SE	16-Oct-44	2nd Lt.	New Rochelle, NY

NAME	CLASS	GRAD DATE	RANK	HOMETOWN
Downs, Walter M.	43-B-SE	16-Feb-43	2nd Lt.	New Orleans, LA
Driver, Elwood T.	42-I-SE	09-Oct-42	2nd Lt.	Trenton, NJ
Driver, Clarence N.	44-A-SE	07-Jan-44	F/O	Los Angeles, CA
Drummond, Charles H.	44-I-I-TE	16-Oct-44	2nd Lt.	Roxbury, MA
Drummond, Edward P.	46-C-SE	28-Jun-46	2nd Lt.	Philadelphia, PA
Dryden, Charles W.	42-D-SE	29-Apr-42	2nd Lt.	Bronx, NY
Dudley, Richard G.	45-B-SE	15-Apr-45	2nd Lt.	Norristown, PA
Duke, Charles H.	44-A-SE	07-Jan-44	2nd Lt.	Portland, OR
Duncan, Roger B.	45-E-SE	04-Aug-45	2nd Lt.	St. Louis, MO
Dunlap, Alwayne M.	43-C-SE	25-Mar-43	2nd Lt.	Washington, DC
Dunne, Charles A.	43-H-SE	30-Aug-43	2nd Lt.	Atlantic City, NJ
Eagleson, Wilson V.	43-D-SE	29-Apr-43	2nd Lt.	Bloomington, IL
Echols, Julius P.	45-G-TE	16-Oct-45	F/O	Chicago, IL
Edwards, Jerome T.	42-J-SE	10-Nov-42	2nd Lt.	Steubenville, OH
Edwards, William H.	44-G-SE	04-Aug-44	F/O	Birmingham, AL
Edwards, John E.	44-G-SE	04-Aug-44	2nd Lt.	Steubenville, OH
Edwards, James E. Jr.	44-J-TE	28-Dec-44	F/O	Wenatchee, WA
Elfalan, Jose R.	45-H-TE	20-Nov-45	2nd Lt.	Prospect, KY
Ellington, Spurgeon N.	43-E-SE	28-May-43	2nd Lt.	Winst-Salem, NC
Ellis, William B.	43-G-SE	28-Jul-43	2nd Lt.	Washington, DC
Ellis, Carl F.	44-F-SE	27-Jun-44	2nd Lt.	Chicago, IL
Ellis, Everett M.	45-I-TE	29-Jan-46	2nd Lt.	Baltimore, MD
Elsberry, Joseph D.	42-H-SE	06-Sep-42	2nd Lt.	Langston, OK
Esters, Maurice V.	43-E-SE	28-May-43	2nd Lt.	Webster City, IA
Ewing, James	44-F-TE	27-Jun-44	F/O	Helena, AR
Exum, Herven P.	44-I-I-TE	16-Oct-44	F/O	Wilson, NJ
Farley, William H.	44-B-TE	08-Feb-44	2nd Lt.	Savannah, GA
Faulkner, William J.	43-D-SE	29-Apr-43	2nd Lt.	Nashville, TN
Fears, Henry T.	44-I-TE	20-Nov-44	F/O	Muncie, IN
Finley, Clarence C.	45-A-SE	11-Mar-45	2nd Lt.	Chicago, IL
Finley, Otis	45-F-TE	08-Sep-45	2nd Lt.	St. Louis, MO
Fischer, James H.	44-G-SE	04-Aug-44	F/O	Stoughton, MA
Flake, Thomas M.	44-J-TE	28-Dec-44	F/O	Detroit, MI
Fleming, Rutledge H. Jr.	45-A-TE	11-Mar-45	F/O	Nashville, TN
Fletcher, Henry F.	43-J-SE	03-Nov-43	2nd Lt.	San Antonio, TX
Ford, Harry E. Jr.	45-E-TE	04-Aug-45	F/O	Detroit, MI
Foreman, Walter T.	43-D-SE	29-Apr-43	2nd Lt.	Washington, DC
Foreman, Samuel	44-E-SE	23-May-44	F/O	Tulsa, OK
Francis, William V.	45-D-SE	27-Jun-45	F/O	Philadelphia, PA
Franklin, George E.	44-H-SE	08-Sep-44	2nd Lt.	Joliet, IL
Franklin, Earl N.	45-C-SE	23-May-45	2nd Lt.	Joliet, IL
Freeman, Eldridge E.	45-B-TE	15-Apr-45	F/O	Chicago, IL
Friend, Robert	43-K-SE	05-Dec-43	2nd Lt.	New York, NY
Fulbright, Stewart B. Jr.	43-K-TE	05-Dec-43	2nd Lt.	Springfield, MO
Fuller, Willie H.	42-G-SE	05-Aug-42	2nd Lt.	Tarboro, NC
Fuller, William A. Jr.	45-E-SE	04-Aug-45	F/O	Detroit, MI
Funderburg, Frederick D.	43-K-SE	05-Dec-43	2nd Lt.	Monticello, GA
Gaines, Thurston L. Jr.	44-G-SE	04-Aug-44	F/O	Freeport, NY
Gaiter, Roger Bertram	44-B-SE	08-Feb-44	2nd Lt.	Seaside Hgts., NJ
Gallwey, James H.	46-A-SE	23-Mar-46	2nd Lt.	Oswego, NY
Gamble, Howard C.	43-K-SE	05-Dec-43	2nd Lt.	Charleston, WV
Gant, Morris E.	44-H-SE	08-Sep-44	F/O	Chicago, IL
Garrett, Alfred E. Jr.	45-G-SE	16-Oct-45	F/O	Fort Worth, TX
Garrison, Robert E. Jr.	44-G-SE	04-Aug-44	2nd Lt.	Columbus, OH
Gash, Joseph E.	45-A-SE	11-Mar-45	2nd Lt.	Denver, CO
Gaskins, Aaron C.	45-E-SE	04-Aug-45	2nd Lt.	Hartford, CT
Gay, Thomas L.	44-B-SE	08-Feb-44	2nd Lt.	Detroit, MI
Gibson, John A.	42-I-SE	09-Oct-42	2nd Lt.	Chicago, IL
Giles, Ivie V.	45-D-SE	27-Jun-45	F/O	Kansas City, KS
Gilliam, William L.	45-B-SE	15-Apr-45	F/O	New York, NY
Givings, Clemenceau M.	43-E-SE	28-May-43	2nd Lt.	Richmond, VA
Gladden, Thomas	44-I-SE	20-Nov-44	2nd Lt.	Washington, DC
Glass, Robert M.	44-I-I-SE	16-Oct-44	F/O	Pittsburgh, PA
Gleed, Edward C.	42-K-SE	13-Dec-42	2nd Lt.	Lawrence, KS
Glenn, Joshua	44-K-SE	01-Feb-45	F/O	Newark, NJ
Goins, Nathaniel W.	45-H-TE	20-Nov-45	1st Lt.	St. Paul, MN
Golden, Newman C.	44-G-SE	04-Aug-44	F/O	Cincinnati, OH
Goldsby, Charles S.	45-A-TE	11-Mar-45	F/O	Detroit, MI
Gomer, Joseph P.	43-E-SE	28-May-43	2nd Lt.	Iowa Falls, IA
Goodall, Ollie O. Jr.	44-K-TE	01-Feb-45	F/O	Detroit, MI
Goodenough, Purnell J.	43-I-SE	01-Oct-43	2nd Lt.	Birmingham, AL
Goodwin, Luther A.	44-H-TE	08-Sep-44	1st Lt.	Bakersfield, CA
Gordon, William M.	43-C-SE	25-Mar-43	2nd Lt.	Mobile, AL
Gordon, Elmer	43-C-SE	25-Mar-43	2nd Lt.	Portsmouth, VA
Gordon, Joseph E.	44-B-SE	08-Feb-44	2nd Lt.	Brolyn, NY
Gorham, Alfred M.	44-B-SE	08-Feb-44	2nd Lt.	Waukesha, WI
Gould, Cornelius Po, Jr.	44-B-SE	08-Feb-44	F/O	Pittsburgh, PA
Govan, Claude B.	43-B-SE	16-Feb-43	2nd Lt.	Newark, NJ
Gray, George E.	43-E-SE	28-May-43	2nd Lt.	Hemphill, WV
Gray, Leo R.	44-G-SE	04-Aug-44	2nd Lt.	Roxbury, MA
Gray, Elliott H.	45-F-SE	08-Sep-45	2nd Lt.	Tuskegee Inst., AL
Green, William W.	43-G-SE	28-Jul-43	2nd Lt.	Staunton, VA

NAME	CLASS	GRAD DATE	RANK	HOMETOWN
Green, Smith W.	43-H-SE	30-Aug-43	2nd Lt.	Los Angeles, CA
Green, Paul L.	44-G-SE	04-Aug-44	2nd Lt.	Xenia, OH
Green, James L.	44-I-TE	16-Oct-44	F/O	Philadelphia, PA
Greenlee, George B. Jr.	43-G-SE	28-Jul-43	2nd Lt.	Pittsburgh, PA
Greenwell, Jacob W.	46-A-SE	23-Mar-46	2nd Lt.	Fort Worth, TX
Greer, James W.	44-J-SE	28-Dec-44	F/O	Detroit, MI
Griffin, William E.	43-B-SE	16-Feb-43	2nd Lt.	Birmingham, AL
Griffin, Jerrold D.	45-E-TE	04-Aug-45	2nd Lt.	Philadelphia, PA
Griffin, Frank	45-I-SE	29-Jan-46	F/O	Asbury Park, NJ
Groves, Weldon K.	43-F-SE	30-Jun-43	2nd Lt.	Edwardsville, KS
Guilbaud, Eberle J.	44-D-TE	15-Apr-44	UNK	Port au Prince, Haiti
Guyton, Eugene L.	44-J-SE	28-Dec-44	F/O	Cleveland, OH
Haley, George J.	43-I-SE	01-Oct-43	2nd Lt.	Bath, NY
Hall, Charles B.	42-F-SE	03-Jul-42	2nd Lt.	Brazil, IN
Hall, Milton T.	42-K-5E	13-Dec-42	2nd Lt.	Owensboro, KY
Hall, Richard W.	43-G-SE	28-Jul-43	2nd Lt.	Albany, GA
Hall, James L. Jr.	44-C-SE	12-Mar-44	2nd Lt.	Washington, DC
Hall, Leonard C. Jr.	45-D-SE	27-Jun-45	2nd Lt.	Philadelphia, PA
Hamilton, John L.	43-E-SE	28-May-43	2nd Lt.	Greenwood, MS
Hancock, Victor L.	45-F-TE	08-Sep-45	F/O	St. Louis, MO
Harden, Argonne F.	45-A-TE	11-Mar-45	2nd Lt.	Philadelphia, PA
Harder, Richard S.	44-B-SE	08-Feb-44	2nd Lt.	Brolyn, NY
Hardy, George E.	44-H-SE	08-Sep-44	2nd Lt.	Philadelphia, PA
Hardy, Bennett G.	45-F-SE	08-Sep-45	2nd Lt.	Kokomo, IN
Hardy, Ferdinand A.	46-B-TE	14-May-46	UNK	Unknown
Harmon, Arthur C.	45-G-TE	16-Oct-45	2nd Lt.	Los Angeles, CA
Harper, Samuel W.	44-A-TE	07-Jan-44	2nd Lt.	Oliver Springs, TN
Harris, Cassius A.	42-G-SE	05-Aug-42	2nd Lt.	Philadelphia, PA
Harris, Richard H.	43-F-SE	30-Jun-43	2nd Lt.	Montgomery, AL
Harris, Herbert S.	43-F-SE	30-Jun-43	2nd Lt.	Philadelphia, PA
Harris, Maceo A. Jr.	43-I-SE	01-Oct-43	2nd Lt.	Boston, MA
Harris, Stanley L.	43-K-SE	05-Dec-43	2nd Lt.	St. Paul, MN
Harris, Louis K.	44-E-SE	23-May-44	2nd Lt.	St. Louis, MO
Harris, Edward	44-G-SE	04-Aug-44	F/O	Pittsburgh, PA
Harris, Bernard	44-I-TE	20-Nov-44	2nd Lt.	Detroit, MI
Harris, James E.	44-J-SE	28-Dec-44	2nd Lt.	Xenia, OH
Harris, Archie H. Jr.	44-K-TE	01-Feb-45	2nd Lt.	Ocean City, NJ
Harris, John S.	45-E-TE	04-Aug-45	2nd Lt.	Richmond, KY
Harris, Thomas D. Jr.	45-F-SE	08-Sep-45	2nd Lt.	Brolyn, NY
Harris, Alfonso L.	45-G-SE	16-Oct-45	F/O	Dallas, TX
Harrison, John L. Jr.	43-K-TE	05-Dec-43	2nd Lt.	Omaha, NE
Harrison, James E.	45-D-SE	27-Jun-45	2nd Lt.	Texarkana, TX
Harrison, Lonnie	45-G-TE	16-Oct-45	F/O	Huston, LA
Harrison, Alvin E. Jr.	45-H-TE	20-Nov-45	F/O	Chicago, IL
Harvey, James H. Jr.	44-I-SE	16-Oct-44	2nd Lt.	Mountain Top, PA
Hathcock, Lloyd S.	43-K-SE	05-Dec-43	2nd Lt.	Dayton, OH
Hawkins, Kenneth R.	44-A-TE	07-Jan-44	2nd Lt.	S Bernardino, CA
Hawkins, Thomas L.	44-E-SE	23-May-44	F/O	Glen Rock, NJ
Hawkins, Donald A.	44-I-TE	20-Nov-44	F/O	S Bernardino, CA
Hayes, Reginald W.	44-C-TE	12-Mar-44	2nd Lt.	Holicong, PA
Hayes, Lee A.	45-I-TE	29-Jan-46	F/O	East Hampton, NY
Hays, Milton S.	44-D-SE	15-Apr-44	2nd Lt.	Los Angeles, CA
Hays, George K.	44-E-SE	23-May-44	2nd Lt.	Los Angeles, CA
Haywood, Vernon V.	43-D-SE	29-Apr-43	2nd Lt.	Raleigh, NC
Heath, Percy L. Jr.	44-K-SE	01-Feb-45	2nd Lt.	Philadelphia, PA
Helm, George W.	45-C-SE	23-May-45	2nd Lt.	Reidsville, NC
Henderson, Eugene R.	44-I-TE	20-Nov-44	2nd Lt.	Jacksonville, FL
Henry, Milton R.	43-F-SE	30-Jun-43	2nd Lt.	Philadelphia, PA
Henry, Warren E.	44-H-TE	08-Sep-44	2nd Lt.	Plainfield, NJ
Henry, William T.	44-K-SE	01-Feb-45	F/O	New York, NY
Henson, James W.	45-B-SE	15-Apr-45	2nd Lt.	Baltimore, MD
Herrington, Aaron	44-E-SE	23-May-44	2nd Lt.	Raleigh, NC
Herron, Walter	44-J-TE	28-Dec-44	1st Lt.	Memphis, TN
Hervey, Henry P. Jr.	43-K-TE	05-Dec-43	2nd Lt.	Chicago, IL
Heywood, Herbert H.	44-C-SE	12-Mar-44	2nd Lt.	St. Croix, Virgin Isles
Hicks, Frederick P.	44-B-TE	08-Feb-44	2nd Lt.	San Francisco, CA
Hicks, Arthur N.	45-C-SE	23-May-45	2nd Lt.	Dayton, OH
Higginbotham, Mitchell	44-K-TE	01-Feb-45	2nd Lt.	Sewickley, PA
Highbaugh, Richard B.	43-K-TE	05-Dec-43	2nd Lt.	Indianapolis, IN
Highbaugh, Earl B.	44-E-SE	23-May-44	2nd Lt.	Indianapolis, IN
Hill, Nathaniel M.	42-I-SE	09-Oct-42	2nd Lt.	Washington, DC
Hill, William E.	43-H-SE	30-Aug-43	2nd Lt.	Narragansett, RI
Hill, William L.	43-K-SE	05-Dec-43	F/O	Huntington, WV
Hill, Charles D.	44-B-TE	08-Feb-44	2nd Lt.	Washington, DC
Hill, Louis G. Jr.	44-B-TE	08-Feb-44	1st Lt.	Indianapolis, IN
Hill, Charles A. Jr.	44-F-SE	27-Jun-44	2nd Lt.	Detroit, MI
Hillary, Harold A.	43-K-TE	05-Dec-43	2nd Lt.	New York, NY
Hockaday, Wendell W.	44-E-SE	23-May-44	2nd Lt.	Norfolk, VA
Hodges, Jerry T. Jr.	45-F-TE	08-Sep-45	2nd Lt.	Heth, AR
Holbert, Bertrand J.	45-A-SE	11-Mar-45	2nd Lt.	Dallas, TX
Holland, Henry T.	45-E-SE	04-Aug-45	2nd Lt.	Baltimore, MD
Holloman, William H. III	44-H-SE	08-Sep-44	2nd Lt.	St. Louis, MO

NAME	CLASS	GRAD DATE	RANK	HOMETOWN
Holloway, Lorenzo W.	45-G-SE	16-Oct-45	2nd Lt.	Detroit, MI
Holman, William D.	45-C-SE	23-May-45	F/O	Suffolk, VA
Holsclaw, Jack D.	43-G-SE	28-Jul-43	2nd Lt.	Spokane, WA
Hopson, Vernon	44-I-SE	20-Nov-44	F/O	San Antonio, TX
Houston, Heber C.	43-D-SE	29-Apr-43	2nd Lt.	Detroit, MI
Hubbard, Lyman L.	45-H-SE	20-Nov-45	F/O	Springfield, IL
Hudson, Perry E. Jr.	43-J-SE	03-Nov-43	2nd Lt.	Atlanta, GA
Hudson, Elbert	44-C-SE	12-Mar-44	2nd Lt.	Los Angeles, CA
Hudson, Lincoln T.	44-F-SE	27-Jun-44	2nd Lt.	Chicago, IL
Hughes, Samuel R. Jr.	45-B-SE	15-Apr-45	F/O	Los Angeles, CA
Hughes, Andrew James	46-B-TE	14-May-46	UNK	Unknown
Hunter, Willie S.	43-F-SE	30-Jun-43	2nd Lt.	Albany, GA
Hunter, Charles H.	44-A-TE	07-Jan-44	2nd Lt.	Washington, DC
Hunter, Henry A.	44-I-I-SE	16-Oct-44	2nd Lt.	Williamsport, PA
Hunter, Samuel	44-J-TE	28-Dec-44	2nd Lt.	Col Springs., CO
Hunter, Marcellus L.	45-G-TE	16-Oct-45	2nd Lt.	Washington, DC
Hurd, James A.	44-H-TE	08-Sep-44	1st Lt.	Leavenworth, KS
Hurd, Sylvester H. Jr.	45-H-SE	20-Nov-45	F/O	Chicago, IL
Hurt, Wesley D.	45-E-SE	04-Aug-45	2nd Lt.	Philadelphia, PA
Hutchins, Freddie E.	43-D-SE	29-Apr-43	2nd Lt.	Donaldsonville, GA
Hutton, Oscar D.	43-J-SE	03-Nov-43	2nd Lt.	Chicago, IL
Hymes, William H.	44-K-SE	01-Feb-45	2nd Lt.	Lincoln Univ., PA
Iles, George J.	44-E-SE	23-May-44	2nd Lt.	Quincy, IL
Irving, Wellington	43-K-SE	05-Dec-43	2nd Lt.	Belzoni, MS
Jackson, Melvin T.	42-J-SE	10-Nov-42	2nd Lt.	Warrenton, VA
Jackson, Leonard M.	43-D-SE	29-Apr-43	2nd Lt.	Fort Worth, TX
Jackson, Charles S. Jr.	44-A-SE	07-Jan-44	2nd Lt.	Chicago, IL
Jackson, Charles L.	44-D-SE	15-Apr-44	F/O	Circleville, OH
Jackson, William T.	44-F-TE	27-Jun-44	F/O	Chicago, IL
Jackson, Frank A. Jr.	44-I-I-SE	16-Oct-44	F/O	Youngstown, OH
Jackson, Julien D. Jr.	45-G-SE	16-Oct-45	F/O	Norfolk, VA
Jackson, Donald E.	45-H-TE	20-Nov-45	F/O	Kansas City, KS
Jamerson, Charles F.	43-C-SE	25-Mar-43	2nd Lt.	Pasadena, CA
James, Daniel, Jr.	43-G-SE	28-Jul-43	2nd Lt.	Pensacola, FL
James, Voris S.	44-J-TE	28-Dec-44	2nd Lt.	San Antonio, TX
Jamison, Clarence C.	42-D-SE	29-Apr-42	2nd Lt.	Cleveland, OH
Jamison, Donald S.	45-F-TE	08-Sep-45	F/O	Wilmington, DE
Jefferson, Lawrence B.	43-H-SE	30-Aug-43	2nd Lt.	Grand Rapids, MI
Jefferson, Samuel	43-H-SE	30-Aug-43	2nd Lt.	Galveston, TX
Jefferson, Alexander	44-A-SE	07-Jan-44	2nd Lt.	Detroit, MI
Jefferson, Thomas W.	44-E-SE	23-May-44	F/O	Chicago, IL

NAME	CLASS	GRAD DATE	RANK	HOMETOWN
Jenkins, Stephen S. Jr.	44-H-SE	08-Sep-44	2nd Lt.	Columbus, OH
Jenkins, Silas M.	44-I-I-TE	16-Oct-44	2nd Lt.	Lansing, MI
Jenkins, Joseph E.	44-I-I-TE	16-Oct-44	2nd Lt.	Ardmore, PA
Jenkins, Garfield L.	44-I-SE	20-Nov-44	2nd Lt.	Chicago, IL
Jenkins, Edward M.	45-A-SE	11-Mar-45	2nd Lt.	Nutley, NJ
Johnson, Langdon E.	43-E-SE	28-May-43	2nd Lt.	Rand, WV
Johnson, Wilbert H.	43-F-SE	30-Jun-43	2nd Lt.	Los Angeles, CA
Johnson, Charles B.	43-I-SE	01-Oct-43	2nd Lt.	Philadelphia, PA
Johnson, Carl E.	43-I-SE	01-Oct-43	2nd Lt.	Charlottesville, VA
Johnson, Rupert C.	44-F-SE	27-Jun-44	2nd Lt.	Los Angeles, CA
Johnson, Conrad A. Jr.	44-G-SE	04-Aug-44	2nd Lt.	New York, NY
Johnson, Robert M.	44-H-SE	08-Sep-44	F/O	Pittsburgh, PA
Johnson, Alvin	44-I-SE	20-Nov-44	2nd Lt.	Chicago, IL
Johnson, Andrew, Jr.	44-I-SE	20-Nov-44	2nd Lt.	Greensboro, NC
Johnson, Louis W.	44-I-SE	20-Nov-44	2nd Lt.	San Antonio, TX
Johnson, Charlie A.	44-I-TE	20-Nov-44	F/O	Marshall, TX
Johnson, Theopolis W.	45-B-TE	15-Apr-45	2nd Lt.	Carbon Hill, AL
Johnson, Earl C.	45-C-SE	23-May-45	F/O	Baltimore, MD
Johnson, Clarence	45-D-SE	27-Jun-45	2nd Lt.	Newark, NJ
Johnston, William A. Jr.	45-D-SE	27-Jun-45	F/O	Sewickley, PA
Jones, Hubert L.	43-H-SE	30-Aug-43	2nd Lt.	Institute, WV
Jones, Edgar L.	43-I-SE	01-Oct-43	2nd Lt.	New York, NY
Jones, Major E.	44-D-SE	15-Apr-44	2nd Lt.	Cleveland, OH
Jones, Beecher A.	44-K-SE	01-Feb-45	F/O	Chillicothe, OH
Jones, Robert, Jr.	45-A-SE	11-Mar-45	F/O	Jamestown, NY
Jones, Frank D.	45-C-SE	23-May-45	F/O	Hyattsville, MD
Jones, William M.	45-G-SE	16-Oct-45	2nd Lt.	Columbus, OH
Jordan, Lowell H.	45-B-TE	15-Apr-45	2nd Lt.	Fort Huachuca, AZ
Keel, Daniel	45-G-TE	16-Oct-45	F/O	Boston, MA
Keith, Laurel E.	44-F-TE	27-Jun-44	2nd Lt.	Cassopolis, MI
Kelley, Thomas A.	45-D-SE	27-Jun-45	F/O	Pasadena, CA
Kelly, Earl	45-F-SE	08-Sep-45	2nd Lt.	Los Angeles, CA
Kennedy, Elmore M.	43-K-TE	05-Dec-43	1st Lt.	Philadelphia, PA
Kennedy, James V. Jr.	45-A-TE	11-Mar-45	2nd Lt.	Chicago, IL
Kenney, Oscar A.	43-F-SE	30-Jun-43	2nd Lt.	Tuskegee Inst., AL
Kimbrough, Benny R.	44-G-SE	04-Aug-44	2nd Lt.	Cincinnati, OH
King, Earl E.	42-G-SE	05-Aug-42	2nd Lt.	Bessemer, AL
King, Haldane	43-J-SE	03-Nov-43	2nd Lt.	Jamaica, NY
King, Celestus	44-D-TE	15-Apr-44	2nd Lt.	Los Angeles, CA
Kirkpatrick, Felix J.	43-E-SE	28-May-43	2nd Lt.	Chicago, IL
Kirksey, Leeroy	44-J-SE	28-Dec-44	F/O	St. Louis, MO

NAME	CLASS	GRAD DATE	RANK	HOMETOWN
Knight, William H.	45-B-SE	15-Apr-45	F/O	Topeka, KS
Knight, Calvin M.	45-D-SE	27-Jun-45	F/O	Norfolk, VA
Knight, Frederick D. Jr.	45-H-TE	20-Nov-45	2nd Lt.	Columbus, OH
Knighten, James B.	42-E-SE	20-May-42	2nd Lt.	Tulsa, OK
Knox, George L.	42-E-SE	20-May-42	2nd Lt.	Indianapolis, IN
Kydd, George H. III	44-D-TE	15-Apr-44	2nd Lt.	Charleston, WV
Lacy, Hezekiah	43-F-SE	30-Jun-43	2nd Lt.	River Rouge, MI
Laird, Edward	43-J-SE	03-Nov-43	2nd Lt.	Brighton, AL
Lanauze, Harry E.	46-A-SE	23-Mar-46	2nd Lt.	Washington, DC
Lancaster, Theodore W.	44-I-I-SE	16-Oct-44	2nd Lt.	Rochester, NY
Lane, Allen G.	42-F-SE	03-Jul-42	2nd Lt.	Demopolis, AL
Lane, Earl R.	44-D-SE	15-Apr-44	2nd Lt.	Wickliffe, OH
Lane, Charles A. Jr.	44-H-SE	08-Sep-44	F/O	St. Louis, MO
Langston, Carroll N. Jr.	43-I-SE	01-Oct-43	2nd Lt.	Chicago, IL
Lanham, Jimmy	44-E-SE	23-May-44	2nd Lt.	Philadelphia, PA
Lankford, Joshua	45-H-TE	20-Nov-45	2nd Lt.	San Antonio, TX
Lawrence, Erwin B.	42-F-SE	03-Jul-42	2nd Lt.	Cleveland, OH
Lawrence, Robert W.	44-F-SE	27-Jun-44	2nd Lt.	Bloomfield, NJ
Lawson, Walter E.	42-G-SE	05-Aug-42	2nd Lt.	Newton, VA
Lawson, Herman A.	42-I-SE	09-Oct-42	2nd Lt.	Fresno, CA
Leahr, John H.	43-G-SE	28-Jul-43	2nd Lt.	Cincinnati, OH
Lee, Frank	44-F-TE	27-Jun-44	2nd Lt.	Los Angeles, CA
Leftenant, Samuel G.	44-H-SE	08-Sep-44	2nd Lt.	Amityville, NY
Leftwich, Ivey L.	43-J-SE	03-Nov-43	2nd Lt.	Fairfield, AL
Leonard, Wilmore B.	42-H-SE	06-Sep-42	2nd Lt.	Salisbury, MD
Leslie, William A.	45-G-TE	16-Oct-45	2nd Lt.	Boston, MA
Lester, Clarence D.	43-K-SE	05-Dec-43	2nd Lt.	Chicago, IL
Lewis, Joe A.	43-F-SE	30-Jun-43	2nd Lt.	Denver, CO
Lewis, William R.	43-K-SE	05-Dec-43	2nd Lt.	Boston, MA
Lewis, Herbert J. L.	45-H-SE	20-Nov-45	F/O	South Bend, IN
Lieteau, Albert J.	44-H-SE	08-Sep-44	1st Lt.	New Orleans, LA
Liggins, Wayne V.	43-F-SE	30-Jun-43	2nd Lt.	Springfield, OH
Lindsey, Perry W.	45-G-TE	16-Oct-45	2nd Lt.	Kokomo, IN
Lockett, Claybourne A.	43-G-SE	28-Jul-43	2nd Lt.	Los Angeles, CA
Long, Wilbur F.	44-B-SE	08-Feb-44	2nd Lt.	New Rochelle, NY
Long, Clyde C. Jr.	45-B-SE	15-Apr-45	F/O	Itasca, TX
Love, Thomas W. Jr.	46-A-SE	23-Mar-46	2nd Lt.	Ardmore, PA
Lucas, Wendell M.	44-E-SE	23-May-44	1st Lt.	Fairmont Hgts., MD
Lyle, Payton H.	44-C-TE	12-Mar-44	1st Lt.	Chicago, IL
Lyle, John H.	44-G-SE	04-Aug-44	F/O	Chicago, IL
Lynch, George A.	44-F-SE	27-Jun-44	F/O	Valley Stream, NY

NAME	CLASS	GRAD DATE	RANK	HOMETOWN
Lynch, Lewis	44-F-SE	27-Jun-44	2nd Lt.	Columbus, OH
Lynn, Samuel	43-K-TE	05-Dec-43	2nd Lt.	Jamaica, NY
Macon, Richard D.	44-B-SE	08-Feb-44	2nd Lt.	Birmingham, AL
Manley, Edward E.	44-H-SE	08-Sep-44	F/O	Los Angeles, CA
Mann, Hiram E.	44-F-SE	27-Jun-44	2nd Lt.	Cleveland, OH
Manning, Albert H.	43-E-SE	28-May-43	2nd Lt.	Hartsville, SC
Manning, Walter P.	44-D-SE	15-Apr-44	2nd Lt.	Philadelphia, PA
Maples, Andrew	43-A-SE	14-Jan-43	2nd Lt.	Orange, VA
Maples, Harold B.	45-E-TE	04-Aug-45	F/O	Orange, VA
Marshall, Andrew D.	44-C-SE	12-Mar-44	2nd Lt.	Wadesboro, NC
Martin, Robert L.	44-A-SE	07-Jan-44	2nd Lt.	Dubuque, IA
Martin, August	45-F-SE	08-Sep-45	2nd Lt.	Bronx, NY
Martin, Maceo C.	46-B-SE	14-May-46	UNK	Unknown
Masciana, Andrea P.	44-A-TE	07-Jan-44	2nd Lt.	Washington, DC
Mason, James W.	43-G-SE	28-Jul-43	2nd Lt.	Monroe, LA
Mason, Vincent	43-J-SE	03-Nov-43	2nd Lt.	Orange, NJ
Mason, Theodore O.	44-I-I-TE	16-Oct-44	2nd Lt.	Cadiz, OH
Mason, Ralph W.	45-F-SE	08-Sep-45	2nd Lt.	Detroit, MI
Matthews, George B.	44-B-TE	08-Feb-44	2nd Lt.	Los Angeles, CA
Matthews, Samuel	44-H-SE	08-Sep-44	F/O	Birmingham, AL
Matthews, Charles R.	46-A-TE	23-Mar-46	2nd Lt.	Philadelphia, PA
Mattison, William T.	42-I-SE	09-Oct-42	2nd Lt.	Conway, AR
Maxwell, Charles C.	44-I-I-TE	16-Oct-44	F/O	New York, NY
Maxwell, Robert L.	45-F-TE	08-Sep-45	2nd Lt.	Bronx, NY
May, Cornelius F.	43-I-SE	01-Oct-43	2nd Lt.	Indianapolis, IN
McCarroll, Rixie H.	44-C-SE	12-Mar-44	2nd Lt.	Gary, IN
McClelland, Harvey L.	45-A-TE	11-Mar-45	F/O	Asheville, NC
McClenic, William B. Jr.	43-H-SE	30-Aug-43	2nd Lt.	Akron, OH
McClure, John	42-G-SE	05-Aug-42	2nd Lt.	Kokomo, IN
McCreary, Waiter L.	43-C-SE	25-Mar-43	2nd Lt.	San Antonio, TX
McCrory, Felix M.	44-H-SE	08-Sep-44	2nd Lt.	Yuma, AZ
McCrumby, George T.	43-A-SE	14-Jan-43	2nd Lt.	Fort Worth, TX
McCullin, James L.	42-H-SE	06-Sep-42	2nd Lt.	St. Louis, MO
McDaniel, Armour G.	43-A-SE	14-Jan-43	2nd Lt.	Martinsville, VA
McGarrity, Thomas H.	45-I-SE	29-Jan-46	2nd Lt.	Chicago, IL
McGee, Charles E.	43-F-SE	30-Jun-43	2nd Lt.	Champaign, IL
McGinnis, Faythe A.	42-F-SE	03-Jul-42	2nd Lt.	Muskogee, OK
McIntyre, Clinton E.	45-E-SE	04-Aug-45	2nd Lt.	Bronx, NY
McIntyre, Herbert A.	45-F-SE	08-Sep-45	2nd Lt.	Cleveland, OH
McIver, Frederick D. Jr.	44-A-SE	07-Jan-44	2nd Lt.	Philadelphia, PA
McKeethen, Lloyd B.	45-H-TE	20-Nov-45	2nd Lt.	East Chicago, IL

NAME	CLASS	GRAD DATE	RANK	HOMETOWN
McKenzie, Alfred U.	45-A-TE	11-Mar-45	F/O	Washington, DC
McKnight, James W.	45-C-SE	23-May-45	2nd Lt.	Washington, DC
McLaurin, Eddie A.	43-G-SE	28-Jul-43	2nd Lt.	Jackson, MS
McQuillan, Douglas	44-I-TE	20-Nov-44	F/O	Brooklyn, NY
McRae, Ivan J. Jr.	44-J-TE	28-Dec-44	2nd Lt.	Yonkers, NY
Melton, William R. Jr.	43-G-SE	28-Jul-43	2nd Lt.	Los Angeles, CA
Merriweather, Elbert N.	44-G-SE	04-Aug-44	F/O	Brooklyn, NY
Merriweather, Robert O.	44-K-SE	01-Feb-45	F/O	Birmingham, AL
Merton, Joseph L. Jr.	44-C-SE	12-Mar-44	2nd Lt.	Chicago, IL
Miller, Oliver O.	43-E-SE	28-May-43	2nd Lt.	Battle Creek, MI
Miller, Willard B.	44-G-TE	04-Aug-44	F/O	Portland, OR
Miller, Lawrence I.	44-H-SE	08-Sep-44	2nd Lt.	Los Angeles, CA
Miller, Charles E.	44-I-I-SE	16-Oct-44	2nd Lt.	Plainfield, NJ
Miller, George R.	45-E-TE	04-Aug-45	F/O	Des Moines, IA
Miller, Godfrey C.	45-H-SE	20-Nov-45	2nd Lt.	Bloomington, IL
Millett, Joseph H.	44-I-I-SE	16-Oct-44	2nd Lt.	Los Angeles, CA
Mills, Clinton B.	43-A-SE	14-Jan-43	2nd Lt.	Durham, NC
Mills, Theodore H.	43-J-SE	03-Nov-43	2nd Lt.	New Rochelle, NY
Mitchell, Paul G.	42-F-SE	03-Jul-42	2nd Lt.	Washington, DC
Mitchell, Vincent I.	44-D-SE	15-Apr-44	F/O	Mt.Clemens, MI
Mitchell, James T. Jr.	44-F-SE	27-Jun-44	F/O	Gadsden, AL
Moffett, Wilbur	45-A-SE	11-Mar-45	F/O	Detroit, MI
Moody, Frank H.	44-B-SE	08-Feb-44	2nd Lt.	Los Angeles, CA
Moody, Roland W.	44-D-SE	15-Apr-44	2nd Lt.	Cambridge, MA
Moody, Paul L.	44-D-TE	15-Apr-44	2nd Lt.	Cambridge, MA
Moore, Theopolis D.	43-F-SE	30-Jun-43	2nd Lt.	St. Louis, MO
Moore, Willis E.	44-I-SE	20-Nov-44	2nd Lt.	Chicago, IL
Moore, Flarzell	44-J-TE	28-Dec-44	F/O	Chicago, IL
Moore, Abe B.	46-A-TE	23-Mar-46	F/O	Austin, TX
Moret, Calvin G.	44-I-SE	20-Nov-44	F/O	New Orleans, LA
Morgan, John H.	42-H-SE	06-Sep-42	2nd Lt.	Cartersville, GA
Morgan, Dempsey W.	43-E-SE	28-May-43	2nd Lt.	Detroit, MI
Morgan, Woodrow F.	43-I-SE	01-Oct-43	2nd Lt.	Omaha, NE
Morgan, William B.	45-F-SE	08-Sep-45	F/O	Yukon, PA
Morris, Harold M.	44-D-SE	15-Apr-44	2nd Lt.	Seattle, WA
Morrison, Thomas J. Jr.	45-A-SE	11-Mar-45	2nd Lt.	Roxbury, MA
Moseley, Sidney J.	43-D-SE	29-Apr-43	2nd Lt.	Norfolk, VA
Mosley, John W.	44-G-TE	04-Aug-44	2nd Lt.	Denver, CO
Mosley, Clifford E.	45-E-TE	04-Aug-45	F/O	Boston, MA
Moss, Richard M.	46-B-SE	14-May-46	UNK	Unknown
Mozee, David M. Jr.	45-F-TE	08-Sep-45	F/O	Chicago, IL

NAME	CLASS	GRAD DATE	RANK	HOMETOWN
Mulzac, John I.	44-J-TE	28-Dec-44	F/O	Brooklyn, NY
Murdic, Robert J.	44-F-SE	27-Jun-44	F/O	Franklin, TN
Murphy, David J. Jr.	44-I-I-TE	16-Oct-44	F/O	Whiteville, NC
Murray, Louis U.	45-C-SE	23-May-45	F/O	Gary, IN
Myers, Charles P.	44-I-I-SE	16-Oct-44	2nd Lt.	Indianapolis, IN
Nalle, Russell C. Jr.	44-H-TE	08-Sep-44	F/O	Detroit, MI
Neblett, Nicholas S.	46-C-SE	28-Jun-46	2nd Lt.	Cincinnati, OH
Nelson, Robert H.	43-G-SE	28-Jul-43	2nd Lt.	Pittsburgh, PA
Nelson, Neal V.	43-I-SE	01-Oct-43	2nd Lt.	Chicago, IL
Nelson, Lincoln W.	44-I-SE	20-Nov-44	2nd Lt.	San Diego, CA
Nelson, Dempsey, Jr.	44-J-SE	28-Dec-44	F/O	Philadelphia, PA
Nelson, John W.	45-H-TE	20-Nov-45	F/O	Bronx, NY
Newman, Christopher W.	43-I-SE	01-Oct-43	2nd Lt.	St. Louis, MO
Newsum, Fitzroy	43-K-TE	05-Dec-43	1st Lt.	Brolyn, NY
Nicolas, Pelissier C.	44-B-TE	08-Feb-44	UNK	Port au Prince, Haiti
Nightingale, Elton H.	44-C-SE	12-Mar-44	2nd Lt.	Tuskegee Inst., AL
Noches, R. F.	44-G-TE	04-Aug-44	F/O	Junction City, KS
Norton, George G. Jr.	45-B-TE	15-Apr-45	F/O	St. Louis, MO
Oliphant, Clarence A.	44-E-SE	23-May-44	2nd Lt.	Council Bluffs, IA
Oliver, Luther L.	45-A-TE	11-Mar-45	2nd Lt.	Montgomery, AL
O'Neal, Walter N.	45-E-TE	04-Aug-45	F/O	Cleveland, OH
O'Neil, Robert	44-A-SE	07-Jan-44	2nd Lt.	Detroit, MI
Orduna, Ralph	44-E-SE	23-May-44	2nd Lt.	Omaha, NE
Page, Maurice R.	43-G-SE	28-Jul-43	2nd Lt.	Los Angeles, CA
Palmer, Walter	43-F-SE	30-Jun-43	2nd Lt.	New York, NY
Palmer, Augustus L.	45-F-SE	08-Sep-45	2nd Lt.	Newport News, VA
Parker, Frederick L. Jr.	44-A-TE	07-Jan-44	2nd Lt.	Chicago, IL
Parker, Melvin	44-J-SE	28-Dec-44	F/O	Baltimore, MD
Parker, George	45-C-SE	23-May-45	F/O	Youngstown, OH
Parkey, Robert M.	44-I-TE	20-Nov-44	F/O	Des Moines, IA
Pasquet, Alix	43-H-SE	30-Aug-43	UNK	UNK, Haiti
Patton, Thomas G.	44-B-SE	08-Feb-44	2nd Lt.	South Franklin, TN
Patton, Humphrey C. Jr.	45-B-SE	15-Apr-45	F/O	Washington, DC
Payne, Turner W.	43-J-SE	03-Nov-43	2nd Lt.	Wichita Falls, TX
Payne, Verdell L.	45-B-SE	15-Apr-45	F/O	Mamaroneck, NY
Peirson, Gwynne W.	43-J-SE	03-Nov-43	2nd Lt.	Oakland, CA
Pendleton, Frederick D.	44-J-SE	28-Dec-44	2nd Lt.	Texarkana, TX
Penn, Starling B.	43-H-SE	30-Aug-43	2nd Lt.	New York, NY
Pennington, Leland H.	44-G-SE	04-Aug-44	F/O	Rochester, NY
Pennington, Robert F.	45-B-SE	15-Apr-45	F/O	Little Silver, NJ
Peoples, Henry R.	44-D-SE	15-Apr-44	2nd Lt.	St. Louis, MO

NAME	CLASS	GRAD DATE	RANK	HOMETOWN
Peoples, Francis B.	44-D-SE	15-Apr-44	2nd Lt.	Henderson, NC
Perkins, Sanford M.	44-A-SE	07-Jan-44	2nd Lt.	Denver, CO
Perkins, John R. Jr.	44-F-TE	27-Jun-44	F/O	Seattle, WA
Perkins, Roscoe C. Jr.	45-C-SE	23-May-45	F/O	Canonsburg, PA
Perry, Henry B.	42-H-SE	06-Sep-42	2nd Lt.	Thomasville, GA
Pillow, Robert A. Jr.	44-E-SE	23-May-44	F/O	Nashville, TN
Pinkney, Harvey A.	43-J-SE	03-Nov-43	2nd Lt.	Baltimore, MD
Pokinghome, James R.	43-B-SE	16-Feb-43	2nd Lt.	Pensacola, FL
Pollard, Henry	43-K-SE	05-Dec-43	2nd Lt.	Buffalo, NY
Pompey, Maurice D.	44-G-TE	04-Aug-44	F/O	South Bend, IN
Ponder, Driskell B.	43-I-SE	01-Oct-43	2nd Lt.	Chicago, IL
Porter, John H.	44-C-SE	12-Mar-44	2nd Lt.	Cleveland, OH
Porter, Robert B.	45-B-SE	15-Apr-45	F/O	Los Angeles, CA
Porter, Calvin V.	45-F-TE	08-Sep-45	2nd Lt.	Detroit, MI
Powell, William S. Jr.	45-B-SE	15-Apr-45	F/O	Eggertsville, NY
Prather, George L.	45-D-SE	27-Jun-45	F/O	Atlanta, GA
Prewitt, Mexion O.	45-E-TE	04-Aug-45	F/O	East Berkley, WV
Price, William S. III	44-C-SE	12-Mar-44	2nd Lt.	Topeka, KS
Price, Charles R.	45-G-TE	16-Oct-45	F/O	Garden City, KS
Prince, Joseph A.	45-D-SE	27-Jun-45	F/O	Dayton, OH
Proctor, Oliver W.	45-E-TE	04-Aug-45	F/O	Norfolk, VA
Proctor, Norman E.	45-H-TE	20-Nov-45	F/O	Oberlin, OH
Prowell, John	43-B-SE	16-Feb-43	2nd Lt.	Lewisburg, AL
Pruitt, Wendell O.	42-K-SE	13-Dec-42	2nd Lt.	St. Louis, MO
Pruitt, Harry S.	45-A-SE	11-Mar-45	F/O	Independence, KS
Pullam, Richard C.	42-K-SE	13-Dec-42	2nd Lt.	Kansas City, KS
Pulliam, Glenn W.	44-I-I-SE	16-Oct-44	F/O	Los Angeles, CA
Purchase, Leon	43-H-SE	30-Aug-43	2nd Lt.	New York, NY
Purnell, Louis R.	42-F-SE	03-Jul-42	2nd Lt.	Wilmington, DE
Purnell, George B.	45-B-SE	15-Apr-45	F/O	Philadelphia, PA
Qualles, John P.	44-J-TE	28-Dec-44	F/O	Bronx, NY
Quander, Charles, Jr.	44-G-TE	04-Aug-44	F/O	Washington, DC
Radcliff, Lloyd L.	45-B-SE	15-Apr-45	2nd Lt.	New Haven, CT
Ragsdale, Lincoln	45-H-SE	20-Nov-45	2nd Lt.	Ardmore, OK
Ramsey, James C.	44-E-SE	23-May-44	F/O	Augusta, GA
Ramsey, Pierce T.	45-F-TE	08-Sep-45	F/O	Philadelphia, PA
Rapier, Gordon M.	44-C-SE	12-Mar-44	2nd Lt.	Gary, IN
Rayburg, Nathaniel P.	43-J-SE	03-Nov-43	F/O	Washington, DC
Rayford, Lee	42-E-SE	20-May-42	2nd Lt.	Washington, DC
Raymond, Frank R.	45-D-SE	27-Jun-45	F/O	Martinville, LA
Rayner, Ahmed A. Jr.	44-C-TE	12-Mar-44	2nd Lt.	Chicago, IL

NAME	CLASS	GRAD DATE	RANK	HOMETOWN
Rector, John A.	44-H-TE	08-Sep-44	1st Lt.	Pittsburgh, PA
Reed, Marsille P.	45-A-SE	11-Mar-45	2nd Lt.	Tillar, AR
Reeves, Ronald W.	44-G-SE	04-Aug-44	2nd Lt.	Washington, DC
Reid, Maury M. Jr.	44-G-SE	04-Aug-44	F/O	New York, NY
Reynolds, Clarence E. Jr.	45-E-SE	04-Aug-45	F/O	Ahoskie, NC
Rhodes, George M. Jr.	43-I-SE	01-Oct-43	2nd Lt.	Brolyn, NY
Rice, Price D.	42-I-SE	09-Oct-42	2nd Lt.	Montclair, NJ
Rice, William E.	44-G-SE	04-Aug-44	F/O	Swarthmore, PA
Rice, Clayo C.	45-A-SE	11-Mar-45	2nd Lt.	Bridgetown, NJ
Rich, Daniel L.	44-D-SE	15-Apr-44	2nd Lt.	Rutherford, NJ
Richardson, Virgil J.	43-F-SE	30-Jun-43	2nd Lt.	Bronx, NY
Richardson, Eugene J. Jr.	45-A-SE	11-Mar-45	2nd Lt.	Camden, NJ
Roach, John B.	45-E-TE	04-Aug-45	F/O	Boston, MA
Roach, Charles J.	45-F-TE	08-Sep-45	F/O	Brooklyn, NY
Robbins, Emory L. Jr.	43-J-SE	03-Nov-43	2nd Lt.	Chicago, IL
Roberts, George S.	42-C-SE	06-Mar-42	2nd Lt.	Fairmont, WV
Roberts, Leon C.	42-G-SE	05-Aug-42	2nd Lt.	Prichard, AL
Roberts, Frank E.	44-A-SE	07-Jan-44	2nd Lt.	Boston, MA
Roberts, Leroy, Jr.	44-E-SE	23-May-44	2nd Lt.	Toccoa, GA
Roberts, Lawrence E.	44-J-TE	28-Dec-44	2nd Lt.	Vauxhall, NH
Roberts, Logan	45-E-SE	04-Aug-45	F/O	Philadelphia, PA
Robinson, Curtis C.	43-D-SE	29-Apr-43	2nd Lt.	Orangeburg, SC
Robinson, Carroll H.	44-D-SE	15-Apr-44	2nd Lt.	Atlanta, GA
Robinson, Robert C. Jr.	44-G-SE	04-Aug-44	2nd Lt.	Asheville, NC
Robinson, Spencer M.	45-A-SE	11-Mar-45	2nd Lt.	Monroe, NJ
Robinson, Robert L. Jr.	45-D-SE	27-Jun-45	2nd Lt.	Wilcoe, WV
Robinson, Isaiah E. Jr.	45-H-TE	20-Nov-45	2nd Lt.	Birmingham, AL
Robinson, Theodore W.	45-H-TE	20-Nov-45	2nd Lt.	Chicago, IL
Robnett, Harris H. Jr.	44-G-TE	04-Aug-44	F/O	Denver, CO
Rodgers, Marion R.	44-B-SE	08-Feb-44	2nd Lt.	Elizabeth, NJ
Rogers, John W.	42-G-SE	05-Aug-42	2nd Lt.	Chicago, IL
Rogers, Cornelius G.	43-G-SE	28-Jul-43	2nd Lt.	Chicago, IL
Rogers, Amos A.	43-K-TE	05-Dec-43	F/O	Tuskegee Inst., AL
Rohlsen, Henry E.	44-C-SE	12-Mar-44	2nd Lt.	Christiansted, Vir. Is.
Romine, Roger	43-H-SE	30-Aug-43	2nd Lt.	Oakland, CA
Ross, Mac	42-C-SE	06-Mar-42	2nd Lt.	Dayton, OH
Ross, Washington D.	43-I-SE	01-Oct-43	2nd Lt.	Ashland, KY
Ross, Merrill Ray	45-I-SE	29-Jan-46	2nd Lt.	Pineville, KY
Rowe, Claude A.	46-C-TE	28-Jun-46	2nd Lt.	Detroit, MI
Rucker, William A.	44-A-TE	07-Jan-44	2nd Lt.	Washington, PA
Russell, James C.	45-G-TE	16-Oct-45	F/O	Los Angeles, CA

NAME	CLASS	GRAD DATE	RANK	HOMETOWN
Samuels, Frederick H.	44-H-TE	08-Sep-44	F/O	Philadelphia, PA
Sanderlin, Willis E.	45-C-SE	23-May-45	2nd Lt.	Washington, DC
Satterwhite, Harry J.	45-E-TE	04-Aug-45	2nd Lt.	New York, NY
Saunders, Pearlee E.	43-C-SE	25-Mar-43	2nd Lt.	Bessemer, AL
Saunders, Martin G.	45-E-SE	04-Aug-45	2nd Lt.	Jamaica, NY
Sawyer, Harold E.	43-D-SE	29-Apr-43	2nd Lt.	Columbus, OH
Scales, Norman W.	43-I-SE	01-Oct-43	2nd Lt.	Austin, TX
Schell, Wyrain T.	44-F-SE	27-Jun-44	F/O	Brooklyn, NY
Schwing, Herbert J.	45-A-TE	11-Mar-45	2nd Lt.	New York, NY
Scott, Henry B.	43-I-SE	01-Oct-43	2nd Lt.	Jersey City, NJ
Scott, Joseph P.	45-E-SE	04-Aug-45	2nd Lt.	Chicago, IL
Scott, Floyd R. Jr.	45-F-SE	08-Sep-45	F/O	Asbury Park, NJ
Scott, Wayman E.	45-H-TE	20-Nov-45	F/O	Oberlin, OH
Selden, Wiley W.	43-F-SE	30-Jun-43	2nd Lt.	Norfolk, VA
Sessions, Mansfield L.	45-C-SE	23-May-45	2nd Lt.	Los Angeles, CA
Sheats, George H.	45-B-SE	15-Apr-45	2nd Lt.	New Haven, CT
Shepherd, James H.	44-G-TE	04-Aug-44	F/O	Washington, DC
Sheppard, Harry A.	43-E-SE	28-May-43	2nd Lt.	Jamaica, NY
Sherard, Earl S. Jr.	43-J-SE	03-Nov-43	2nd Lt.	Columbus, OH
Sherman, George	45-G-SE	16-Oct-45	F/O	Albany, IL
Shivers, Clarence L.	44-J-SE	28-Dec-44	F/O	St. Louis, MO
Shults, Lloyd R.	44-D-TE	15-Apr-44	2nd Lt.	N. Plainfield, NJ
Sidat-Singh, Wilmeth W.	43-C-SE	25-Mar-43	2nd Lt.	Washington, DC
Simeon, Albert B. Jr.	45-D-SE	27-Jun-45	F/O	Detroit, MI
Simmons, Alphonso	43-I-SE	01-Oct-43	2nd Lt.	Jacksonville, FL
Simmons, Paul C. Jr.	43-J-SE	03-Nov-43	2nd Lt.	Detroit, MI
Simmons, Donehue	45-I-TE	29-Jan-46	F/O	Chicago, IL
Simons, Richard A.	44-I-I-SE	16-Oct-44	2nd Lt.	White Plains, NY
Simpson, Jesse H.	44-G-TE	04-Aug-44	F/O	Fresno, CA
Singletary, Lloyd G.	43-C-SE	25-Mar-43	2nd Lt.	Jacksonville, FL
Sloan, John S.	43-F-SE	30-Jun-43	2nd Lt.	Louisville, KY
Smith, Graham	42-F-SE	03-Jul-42	2nd Lt.	Ahoskie, NC
Smith, Lewis C.	43-D-SE	29-Apr-43	2nd Lt.	Los Angeles, CA
Smith, Luther H.	43-E-SE	28-May-43	2nd Lt.	Des Moines, IA
Smith, Edward	43-G-SE	28-Jul-43	2nd Lt.	Philadelphia, PA
Smith, Robert H.	43-I-SE	01-Oct-43	2nd Lt.	Baltimore, MD
Smith, Eugene D.	43-J-SE	03-Nov-43	2nd Lt.	Cincinnati, OH
Smith, Harold E. Jr.	44-I-I-TE	16-Oct-44	1st Lt.	Memphis, TN
Smith, Thomas W.	44-J-SE	28-Dec-44	F/O	Lebanon, KY
Smith, Albert H.	45-A-SE	11-Mar-45	F/O	Jersey City, NJ
Smith, Quentin P.	45-A-TE	11-Mar-45	2nd Lt.	East Chicago, IL
Smith, Burl E.	45-B-SE	15-Apr-45	2nd Lt.	Oakland, CA
Smith, Frederick D.	45-C-TE	23-May-45	2nd Lt.	Pasadena, CA
Smith, Robert C.	45-D-SE	27-Jun-45	F/O	Muskogee, OK
Smith, Reginald V.	45-E-SE	04-Aug-45	F/O	Ahoskie, NC
Spann, Calvin	44-G-SE	04-Aug-44	F/O	Rutherford, NJ
Spears, Leon W.	44-F-SE	27-Jun-44	F/O	Pueblo, CO
Spencer, Roy M.	43-B-SE	16-Feb-43	2nd Lt.	Jacksonville, FL
Spicer, Cecil	45-H-TE	20-Nov-45	2nd Lt.	Greenville, OH
Spriggs, Thurman E.	45-H-SE	20-Nov-45	2nd Lt.	Des Moines, IA
Spurlin, Jerome D.	43-J-SE	03-Nov-43	2nd Lt.	Chicago, IL
Squires, John W.	44-H-SE	08-Sep-44	F/O	St. Louis, MO
Stanton, Charles R.	43-A-SE	14-Jan-43	2nd Lt.	Portland, OR
Starks, Arnett W. Jr.	44-E-SE	23-May-44	F/O	Los Angeles, CA
Stephenson, William W.	44-J-SE	28-Dec-44	F/O	Washington, DC
Stevens, Fuchard G.	44-I-I-SE	16-Oct-44	2nd Lt.	Washington, DC
Steward, Lowell C.	43-G-SE	28-Jul-43	2nd Lt.	Los Angeles, CA
Stewart, Nathaniel C.	43-J-SE	03-Nov-43	2nd Lt.	Philadelphia, PA
Stewart, Harry T. Jr.	44-F-SE	27-Jun-44	2nd Lt.	Corona, NY
Stiger, Roosevelt	44-C-SE	12-Mar-44	2nd Lt.	Jackson, MI
Stoudmire, Norvel	43-H-SE	30-Aug-43	2nd Lt.	St. Louis, MO
Stovall, Charles L.	44-I-I-SE	16-Oct-44	2nd Lt.	Wichita, KS
Streat, William A. Jr.	45-H-TE	20-Nov-45	F/O	Lawrenceville, VA
Street, Thomas C.	44-G-SE	04-Aug-44	2nd Lt.	Springfield, NJ
Suggs, John J.	43-E-SE	28-May-43	2nd Lt.	Terre Haute, IN
Surcey, Wayman P.	44-I-TE	20-Nov-44	F/O	Jacksonville, FL
Talton, James E.	45-F-TE	08-Sep-45	F/O	Merchantville, NJ
Tate, Charles W.	43-H-SE	30-Aug-43	2nd Lt.	Pittsburgh, PA
Taylor, Ulysses S.	43-D-SE	29-Apr-43	2nd Lt.	Kaufman, TX
Taylor, Elmer W.	43-G-SE	28-Jul-43	2nd Lt.	Pittsburgh, PA
Taylor, George A.	43-H-SE	30-Aug-43	2nd Lt.	Philadelphia, PA
Taylor, James	45-B-TE	15-Apr-45	F/O	Champaign, IL
Taylor, William H. Jr.	45-E-TE	04-Aug-45	F/O	Inkster, MI
Temple, Alva N.	43-G-SE	28-Jul-43	2nd Lt.	Carrollton, AL
Terry, Roger C.	44-K-TE	01-Feb-45	2nd Lt.	Los Angeles, CA
Terry, Kenneth E.	45-F-TE	08-Sep-45	F/O	Emporia, KS
Theodore, Eugene G.	44-I-SE	20-Nov-44	2nd Lt.	Port of Spain, Trin.
Thomas, William H.	43-J-SE	03-Nov-43	2nd Lt.	Los Angeles, CA
Thomas, Edward M.	43-J-SE	03-Nov-43	2nd Lt.	Chicago, IL
Thomas, Walter H. Jr.	45-D-SE	27-Jun-45	F/O	Redlands, CA
Thompson, Floyd A.	43-H-SE	30-Aug-43	2nd Lt.	London, WV
Thompson, Reid E.	43-K-SE	05-Dec-43	2nd Lt.	New Rochelle, NY

NAME	CLASS	GRAD DATE	RANK	HOMETOWN
Thompson, Donald N. Jr.	44-I-I-SE	16-Oct-44	2nd Lt.	Philadelphia, PA
Thompson, Francis R.	45-A-TE	11-Mar-45	2nd Lt.	Brolyn, NY
Thompson, James A.	45-G-SE	16-Oct-45	F/O	Cleveland, OH
Thorpe, Richard E.	44-I-I-SE	16-Oct-44	2nd Lt.	Brolyn, NY
Thorpe, Herbert C.	45-G-TE	16-Oct-45	2nd Lt.	Brolyn, NY
Tindall, Thomas	45-C-SE	23-May-45	F/O	East Orange, NJ
Toatley, Ephraim E.]r.	44-K-SE	01-Feb-45	2nd Lt.	Philadelphia, PA
Tompkins, William D.	43-J-SE	03-Nov-43	2nd Lt.	Fall River, MA
Toney, Mitchel N.	45-E-TE	04-Aug-45	F/O	Austin, TX
Toppins, Edward L.	42-H-SE	06-Sep-42	2nd Lt.	San Francisco, CA
Tresville, Robert B. Jr.	42-K-SE	13-Dec-42	2nd Lt.	Bay City, TX
Trott, Robert G.	45-D-SE	27-Jun-45	2nd Lt.	Mt. Vernon, NY
Tucker, Paul	45-B-SE	15-Apr-45	F/O	Detroit, MI
Turner, Andrew D.	42-I-SE	09-Oct-42	2nd Lt.	Washington, DC
Turner, Leonard F.	43-F-SE	30-Jun-43	2nd Lt.	Washington, DC
Turner, Leon L.	44-A-TE	07-Jan-44	2nd Lt.	Washington, DC
Turner, Ralph L.	44-D-SE	15-Apr-44	F/O	Los Angeles, CA
Turner, John B.	44-F-TE	27-Jun-44	2nd Lt.	Atlanta, GA
Turner, Allen H.	44-I-I-SE	16-Oct-44	2nd Lt.	Flint MI, MI
Turner, Gordon G.	45-E-SE	04-Aug-45	2nd Lt.	Los Angeles, CA
Twine, Saint M. Jr.	44-A-TE	07-Jan-44	F/O	Los Angeles, CA
Tyler, William A. Jr.	45-C-TE	23-May-45	2nd Lt.	Pittsburgh, PA
Valentine, Cleophus W.	45-A-TE	11-Mar-45	2nd Lt.	Detroit, MI
Vaughan, Leonard O.	44-I-SE	20-Nov-44	F/O	Brooklyn, NY
Velasquez, Frederick B.	44-I-SE	20-Nov-44	F/O	Chicago, IL
Verwayne, Peter C.	42-K-SE	13-Dec-42	2nd Lt.	New York, NY
Waddell, Reginald C. Jr.	44-I-SE	20-Nov-44	F/O	Chicago, IL
Walker, William H.	42-K-SE	13-Dec-42	2nd Lt.	Suffolk, VA
Walker, Quitman C.	43-A-SE	14-Jan-43	2nd Lt.	Indianola, MS
Walker, William H.	43-B-SE	16-Feb-43	2nd Lt.	Carbondale, IL
Walker, James A.	43-E-SE	28-May-43	2nd Lt.	Manning, SC
Walker, Frank D.	43-F-SE	30-Jun-43	2nd Lt.	Richmond, KY
Walker, Charles E.	44-A-TE	07-Jan-44	2nd Lt.	Jackson, MI
Walker, William C. Jr.	44-E-SE	23-May-44	2nd Lt.	Atlantic City, NJ
Walker, John B. Jr.	45-A-SE	11-Mar-45	2nd Lt.	Canton, OH
Wanamaker, George E.	45-C-SE	23-May-45	F/O	Montclair, NJ
Warner, Hugh St. Clair	43-J-SE	03-Nov-43	2nd Lt.	New York, NY
Warren, James W.	44-I-I-SE	16-Oct-44	F/O	Brooklyn, NY
Warrick, Calvin T.	45-A-TE	11-Mar-45	2nd Lt.	Elkton, MD
Washington, Samuel L.	44-F-SE	27-Jun-44	F/O	Cleveland, OH
Washington, Milton	44-H-SE	08-Sep-44	F/O	Willow Grove, PA
Washington, William M.	44-I-SE	20-Nov-44	2nd Lt.	Chicago, IL
Washington, Morris J.	44-I-TE	20-Nov-44	F/O	Atlantic City, NJ
Watkins, Edward Wilson	43-I-SE	01-Oct-43	2nd Lt.	Freeman, WV
Watkins, Edward W.	45-F-SE	08-Sep-45	F/O	Omaha, NE
Watson, Spann	42-F-SE	03-Jul-42	2nd Lt.	Hackensack, NJ
Watson, Dudley M.	43-E-SE	28-May-43	2nd Lt.	Frankfort, KY
Watts, Samuel W. Jr.	44-E-SE	23-May-44	2nd Lt.	New York, NY
Weatherford, Fuchard	45-G-TE	16-Oct-45	F/O	Albion, MI
Weathers, Luke	43-D-SE	29-Apr-43	2nd Lt.	Memphis, TN
Webb, Rhohelia	44-F-TE	27-Jun-44	2nd Lt.	Baltimore, MD
Wells, Johnson C.	43-F-SE	30-Jun-43	2nd Lt.	Buffalo, NY
Wells, Wendell D.	43-K-TE	05-Dec-43	2nd Lt.	Washington, DC
Westbrook, Shelby F.	44-B-SE	08-Feb-44	2nd Lt.	Toledo, OH
Westmoreland, Walter D.	43-G-SE	28-Jul-43	2nd Lt.	Atlanta, GA
Westmoreland, Julius C.	45-F-SE	08-Sep-45	2nd Lt.	Washington, DC
Wheeler, William M.	44-C-SE	12-Mar-44	2nd Lt.	Detroit, MI
Wheeler, Jimmie D.	44-D-SE	15-Apr-44	2nd Lt.	Detroit, MI
White, Sherman W.	42-E-SE	20-May-42	2nd Lt.	Montgomery, AL
White, Cohen M.	44-B-SE	08-Feb-44	2nd Lt.	Detroit, MI
White, Charles L.	44-C-SE	12-Mar-44	2nd Lt.	St. Louis, MO
White, Hugh	44-F-SE	27-Jun-44	2nd Lt.	St. Louis, MO
White, Harold L.	44-G-SE	04-Aug-44	2nd Lt.	Detroit, MI
White, Joseph C.	44-G-SE	04-Aug-44	F/O	Chattanooga, TN
White, Ferrier H.	44-I-I-SE	16-Oct-44	2nd Lt.	Oberlin, OH
White, Raymond M.	44-I-TE	20-Nov-44	F/O	Bronx, NY
White, Haydel	44-K-TE	01-Feb-45	F/O	New Orleans, LA
White, Harry W.	45-C-SE	23-May-45	F/O	Baltimore, MD
White, Marvin C.	45-E-SE	04-Aug-45	F/O	Wichita, KS
White, Vertner, Jr.	45-F-TE	08-Sep-45	2nd Lt.	Cleveland, OH
Whitehead, John L,. Jr.	44-H-SE	08-Sep-44	2nd Lt.	Lawrenceville, VA
Whiten, Joseph	43-K-TE	05-Dec-43	2nd Lt.	New York, NY
Whiteside, Albert	45-E-TE	04-Aug-45	F/O	San Antonio, TX
Whitney, Yenwith K.	44-F-SE	27-Jun-44	F/O	New York, NY
Whittaker, Peter H.	44-C-SE	12-Mar-44	2nd Lt.	Detroit, MI
Whyte, James W., Jr.	44-I-SE	20-Nov-44	2nd Lt.	New Haven, CT
Wiggins, Robert H.	43-G-SE	28-Jul-43	2nd Lt.	New York, NY
Wiggins, Leonard W.	45-E-SE	04-Aug-45	F/O	Detroit, MI
Wilburn, Arthur	44-A-SE	07-Jan-44	2nd Lt.	Asheville, NC
Wiley, James T.	42-F-SE	03-Jul-42	2nd Lt.	Pittsburgh, PA
Wilhite, Emmet	45-D-SE	27-Jun-45	2nd Lt.	Los Angeles, CA
Wilkerson, William G.	43-F-SE	30-Jun-43	2nd Lt.	Camden, NJ

NAME	CLASS	GRAD DATE	RANK	HOMETOWN
Wilkerson, Oscar L. Jr.	45-F-TE	08-Sep-45	2nd Lt.	Chicago Hts., IL
Wilkins, Laurence D.	43-E-SE	28-May-43	2nd Lt.	Los Angeles, CA
Wilkins, Ralph D.	44-I-SE	20-Nov-44	2nd Lt.	Washington, DC
Willette, Leonard R.	44-B-SE	08-Feb-44	F/O	Belleville, NJ
Williams, Romeo M.	42-K-SE	13-Dec-42	2nd Lt.	Marshall, TX
Williams, Charles I.	43-D-SE	29-Apr-43	2nd Lt.	Lima, OH
Williams, Craig H.	43-E-SE	28-May-43	2nd Lt.	Chicago, IL
Williams, William F.	43-F-SE	30-Jun-43	2nd Lt.	Cleveland, OH
Williams, LeRoi S.	43-G-SE	28-Jul-43	2nd Lt.	Roanoke, VA
Williams, Leslie A.	43-J-SE	03-Nov-43	2nd Lt.	San Mateo, CA
Williams, Edward J.	43-K-SE	05-Dec-43	F/O	Columbus, GA
Williams, Clarence	44-A-TE	07-Jan-44	F/O	Fairfield, AL
Williams, Herbert	44-A-TE	07-Jan-44	2nd Lt.	Los Angeles, CA
Williams, Kenneth I.	44-B-SE	08-Feb-44	2nd Lt.	Los Angeles, CA
Williams, Charles T.	44-C-SE	12-Mar-44	2nd Lt.	Los Angeles, CA
Williams, Vincent E.	44-D-SE	15-Apr-44	F/O	Los Angeles, CA
Williams, Robert W.	44-E-SE	23-May-44	2nd Lt.	Ottumwa, IA
Williams, Robert E. Jr.	44-G-SE	04-Aug-44	F/O	Chicago, IL
Williams, Joseph H.	44-I-TE	20-Nov-44	2nd Lt.	Chicago, IL
Williams, Yancey	44-J-SE	28-Dec-44	1st Lt.	Tulsa, OK
Williams, William L. Jr.	44-J-TE	28-Dec-44	F/O	New London, OH
Williams, Raymond L.	45-D-SE	27-Jun-45	F/O	Jersey City, NJ
Williams, Eugene W.	45-E-SE	04-Aug-45	2nd Lt.	Roanoke, VA
Williams, Thomas E.	45-F-SE	08-Sep-45	2nd Lt.	Philadelphia, PA
Williams, James L.	45-F-SE	08-Sep-45	F/O	Philadelphia, PA
Williams, James R.	45-G-TE	16-Oct-45	2nd Lt.	Bryn Mawr, PA
Williams, Andrew B. Jr.	45-H-TE	20-Nov-45	F/O	Los Angeles, CA
Williamson, Willie A.	44-J-SE	28-Dec-44	F/O	Detroit, MI
Wilson, Theodore A.	43-F-SE	30-Jun-43	2nd Lt.	Roanoke, VA
Wilson, Charles E.	44-C-TE	12-Mar-44	F/O	Chicago, IL
Wilson, Myron	44-D-SE	15-Apr-44	F/O	Danville, IL
Wilson, James A.	44-D-SE	15-Apr-44	2nd Lt.	Kokomo, IN
Wilson, Bertram W. Jr.	44-E-SE	23-May-44	2nd Lt.	Brolyn, NY
Wilson, LeRoy J.	45-F-TE	08-Sep-45	2nd Lt.	Independence, KS
Winslow, Eugene	44-A-TE	07-Jan-44	2nd Lt.	Chicago, IL
Winslow, Robert W.	45-B-SE	15-Apr-45	2nd Lt.	East St. Louis, IL
Winston, Harry P.	45-A-SE	11-Mar-45	F/O	Franklin, VA
Winston, Charles H. Jr.	45-B-SE	15-Apr-45	F/O	Seattle, WA
Wise, Henry A.	44-B-SE	08-Feb-44	2nd Lt.	Cheriton, VA
Wofford, Kenneth O.	45-C-SE	23-May-45	2nd Lt.	Springfield, MO
Woods, Carrol S.	43-H-SE	30-Aug-43	2nd Lt.	Valdosta, GA
Woods, Willard L.	43-H-SE	30-Aug-43	2nd Lt.	Memphis, TN
Woods, Carl J.	44-D-SE	15-Apr-44	F/O	Mars, PA
Woods, Isaac R.	45-E-SE	04-Aug-45	F/O	Tulsa, OK
Wooten, Howard A.	44-J-TE	28-Dec-44	F/O	Lovelady, TX
Wright, Hiram	44-E-SE	23-May-44	F/O	Los Angeles, CA
Wright, Kenneth M.	44-E-SE	23-May-44	2nd Lt.	Sheridan, WY
Wright, Frank N.	44-F-SE	27-Jun-44	2nd Lt.	Elmsford, NY
Wright, James W. Jr.	44-F-SE	27-Jun-44	2nd Lt.	Pittsburgh, PA
Wright, Sandy W.	45-F-SE	08-Sep-45	F/O	Berkeley, CA
Wyatt, Beryl	43-G-SE	28-Jul-43	2nd Lt.	Independence, KS
Wynn, Nasby, Jr.	44-J-TE	28-Dec-44	F/O	Mt. Vernon, NY
Yates, Phillip C.	45-D-SE	27-Jun-45	F/O	Washington, DC
York, Oscar H.	44-I-TE	20-Nov-44	2nd Lt.	Los Angeles, CA
Young, Albert L.	44-C-SE	12-Mar-44	2nd Lt.	Memphis, TN
Young, Benjamin, Jr.	45-C-SE	23-May-45	2nd Lt.	Philadelphia, PA
Young, Lee W.	45-D-SE	27-Jun-45	F/O	Litchfield Park, AZ
Young, William W.	45-F-SE	08-Sep-45	F/O	Oberlin, OH
Young, Eddie Lee	46-B-SE	14-May-46	UNK	UNK

Pilots Trained at Tuskegee for Service Pilot Duties

NAME	CLASS	GRAD DATE	RANK	HOMETOWN
Cargill, Gilbert A.	45-BI-1	UNK	F/O	Cleveland, OH
Gordon, Robert A.	UNK	UNK	F/O	Troy, OH
Hutcherson, Fred	45-BI-1	UNK	F/O	Evanston, IL
Moret, Adolph J. Jr.	UNK	UNK	F/O	New Orleans, LA
Pinkett, John R.	45BI-1	UNK	2nd Lt.	Washington, DC
Plinton, James O. Jr.	UNK	UNK	F/O	Westfield, NJ
Stephens, Charles W	UNK	UNK	F/O	Monroeville, AL
Terry, Robert	UNK	UNK	F/O	Unknown
Williams, Archie	UNK	UNK	2nd Lt.	Oakland, CA
Witherspoon, Fred	UNK	UNK	F/O	Houston, TX
Wright, James E.	UNK	UNK	F/O	Savannah, GA

Pilots Trained at Tuskegee (Kennedy Field) for Liaison Duties with 92nd Infantry Division

NAME	CLASS	GRAD DATE	RANK	HOMETOWN
Baker, Lee Arthur	CL-43-3	7-Dec-1943	1st Lt	Unknown
Battle, John D.	CL-43-3	7-Dec-1943	2nd Lt	New York, NY
Bennett, Henry	CL-43-2	22-Oct-1943	2nd Lt	New Orleans, LA
Bishop, Darryl C.	CL-43-1	30-Sep-1943	2nd Lt	Houston?, TX
Bizzell, George F.	CL-43-2	22-Oct-1943	2nd Lt	Dayton, OH
Brice, Edward W.	CL-43-3	7-Dec-1943	2nd Lt	Orangeburg, SC
Brooks, Johnny Y.	CL-43-3	7-Dec-1943	2nd Lt	Calumet City, IL
Brooks, Terry H.	CL-43-2	22-Oct-1943	1st Lt	Unknown
Chatman, Richard C., Jr.	CL-43-2	22-Oct-1943	2nd Lt	Chicago, IL
Cleage, Scott K.	CL-43-3	7-Dec-1943	1st Lt	Chicago, IL
Cleveland, William J.	CL-43-2	22-Oct-1943	2nd Lt	Columbiana Cty, OH
Conquest, George D.	CL-43-3	7-Dec-1943	2nd Lt	New Haven, CT
Cunningham, John O.	CL-43-2	22-Oct-1943	2nd Lt	Delaware Cty, IN
Dudley, John B.	CL-43-2	22-Oct-1943	1st Lt	Brooklyn, NY?
Dungill, Harry W.	CL-43-1	30-Sep-1943	2nd Lt	Chicago, IL
Dunn, Charles G.	CL-43-1	30-Sep-1943	2nd Lt	Cleves, OH
Elam, Charles B.	CL-43-3	7-Dec-1943	2nd Lt	Washington, DC
Eskridge, Chauncey	CL-43-1	30-Sep-1943	1st Lt	Homewood, PA
Farley, Gaines C.	CL-43-2	22-Oct-1943	1st Lt	Paducah, KY
Franklin, John M.	CL-43-2	22-Oct-1943	2nd Lt	Toledo, OH
Goldsborough, Ernest W.	CL-43-3	7-Dec-1943	2nd Lt	Glen Mills, PA
Grant, Arnold D.	CL-43-1	30-Sep-1943	2nd Lt	Coffeyville, KS
Hall, Leander A., Jr.	CL-43-1	30-Sep-1943	2nd Lt	Mobile, AL

NAME	CLASS	GRAD DATE	RANK	HOMETOWN
Hanks, Louis K.	CL-43-2	22-Oct-1943	2nd Lt	Toledo, OH
Honemond, Maxwell	CL-43-3	7-Dec-1943	2nd Lt	Baltimore, MD
Howard, Fred E.	CL-43-2	22-Oct-1943	1st Lt	Chicago, IL
Jackson, Sterling K.	CL-43-3	7-Dec-1943	2nd Lt	Chicago, IL
Johnson, Alvin J.	CL-43-1	30-Sep-1943	2nd Lt	Chicago, IL
Johnson, William H.	CL-43-3	7-Dec-1943	2nd Lt	Franklin County, OH
Jordan, William M.	CL-43-2	22-Oct-1943	2nd Lt	Chicago, IL
Long, Wendell W.	CL-43-3	7-Dec-1943	2nd Lt	Champaign-Urb, IL
Mason, Thurston	CL-43-2	22-Oct-1943	2nd Lt	Chicago, IL
McCode, John E.	CL-43-2	22-Oct-1943	2nd Lt	Houston, TX
Minor, James I., Jr.	CL-43-1	30-Sep-1943	1st Lt	Richmond, VA
Moore, Benjamin F.	CL-43-1	30-Sep-1943	2nd Lt	Ocilla, GA
Norman, Henry A.	CL-43-3	7-Dec-1943	2nd Lt	Gallipolis, OH
Oates, Horace W.	CL-43-3	7-Dec-1943	2nd Lt	Tulsa, OK
Rose, William Y.	CL-43-1	30-Sep-1943	1st Lt	Chicago, IL
Shannon, William H.	CL-43-1	30-Sep 1943	Capt	Chicago, IL
Smith, Elwood A.	CL-43-3	7-Dec-1943	2nd Lt	Unknown
Smith, Sherman W.	CL-43-3	7-Dec-1943	2nd Lt	San Antonio, TX
Stephens, Leroy, Jr.	CL-43-2	22-Oct-1943	1st Lt	Chicago, IL
Taylor, Lloyd R. V.	CL-43-1	30-Sep-1943	2nd Lt	Atlanta, GA
Thomas, Daniel C.	CL-43-2	22-Oct-1943	2nd Lt	Washington City, PA
Tucker, Lemuel L.	CL-43-3	7-Dec-1943	2nd Lt	Philadelphia?, PA
Weathersby, Paul	CL-43-2	22-Oct-1943	2nd Lt	Chicago, IL
Wilburn, Leonard E.	CL-43-1	30-Sep-1943	2nd Lt	Franklin County, OH
Wilson, Aldrick H.	CL-43-1	30-Sep-1943	2nd Lt	Chicago, IL
Woods, George	CL-43-3	7-Dec-1943	2nd Lt	Cleveland, OH
Woodson, James E.	CL-43-1	30-Sep-1943	2nd Lt	Unknown
Wrenn, Robert L.	CL-43-2	22-Oct-1943	1st Lt	Hamilton County, OH

APPENDIX SEVEN
TUSKEGEE AIRMEN - ROLL OF HONOR

The core of this Appendix is from the work of Dr. Daniel L. Haulman, Chief of the Organizational Histories Branch at the Air Force Historical Research Agency. When the question about 150 Distinguished Flying Crosses being awarded to Tuskegee Airmen was posed, he refuted the figure instantly. Dr. Haulman stated that he had personally verified every Awarding Order for the DFCs listed below (those order references are on file) and could confirm that 95 Tuskegee Airmen were awarded DFCs and 96 medals were awarded, one man, Captain William A. Campbell, receiving two – his first in October 1944 and his second in April 1945. To ensure that none were lost from any listing, Dr. Haulman checked every medal awarding order from the summer of 1943, knowing the first was awarded to Captain Charles Hall in January 1944, all the way through to the end of 1945. However, this takes nothing from the still-staggering record of decorations awarded to these men, who remain the most highly decorated Fighter Group in the Mediterranean and Italian Theaters of Operation.

The Distinguished Flying Cross is a decoration awarded to any officer or enlisted member of the United States Armed Forces who distinguishes himself or herself in support of operations by "heroism or extraordinary achievement while participating in an aerial flight, subsequent to November 11, 1918." The decoration may also be given for an act performed prior to that date when the individual has been recommended for, but has not received the Medal of Honor, the Distinguished Service Cross, the Navy Cross, the Air Force Cross or the Distinguished Service Medal.

TUSKEGEE AIRMEN DISTINGUISHED FLYING CROSS AWARDEES, BY DATE

DATE	NAME	SQUADRON
28-Jan-44	Captain Charles B. Hall	99th Fighter Sqn
12-May-44	Captain Howard L. Baugh	99th Fighter Sqn
21-May-44	1st Lieutenant Charles W. Tate	99th Fighter Sqn
27-May-44	1st Lieutenant Clarence W. Dart	99th Fighter Sqn
4-Jun-44	Captain Edward L. Toppins	99th Fighter Sqn
4-Jun-44	Captain Leonard M. Jackson	99th Fighter Sqn
5-Jun-44	Captain Elwood T. Driver	99th Fighter Sqn
9-Jun-44	Colonel Benjamin O. Davis, Jr.	332nd Fighter Grp
12-Jul-44	Captain Joseph D. Elsberry	301st Fighter Sqn
16-Jul-44	Captain Alphonza W. Davis	332nd Fighter Grp
16-Jul-44	1st Lieutenant William W. Green	302nd Fighter Sqn
17-Jul-44	1st Lieutenant Luther H. Smith	302nd Fighter Sqn
17-Jul-44	1st Lieutenant Laurence D. Wilkins	302nd Fighter Sqn

DATE	NAME	SQUADRON
18-Jul-44	2nd Lieutenant Clarence D. Lester	100th Fighter Sqn
18-Jul-44	1st Lieutenant Jack D. Holsclaw	100th Fighter Sqn
18-Jul-44	Captain Andrew D. Turner	100th Fighter Sqn
18-Jul-44	1st Lieutenant Walter J. A. Palmer	100th Fighter Sqn
18-Jul-44	1st Lieutenant Charles P. Bailey	99th Fighter Sqn
20-Jul-44	Captain Henry B. Perry	99th Fighter Sqn
25-Jul-44	Captain Harold E. Sawyer	301st Fighter Sqn
27-Jul-44	1st Lieutenant Edward C. Gleed	332nd Fighter Grp
12-Aug-44	Captain Lee Rayford	301st Fighter Sqn
12-Aug-44	Captain Woodrow W. Crockett	100th Fighter Sqn
12-Aug-44	Captain William T. Mattison	100th Fighter Sqn
12-Aug-44	1st Lieutenant Freddie E. Hutchins	302nd Fighter Sqn
12-Aug-44	1st Lieutenant Lawrence B. Jefferson	301st Fighter Sqn

DATE	NAME	SQUADRON
12-Aug-44	1st Lieutenant Lowell C. Steward	100th Fighter Sqn
14-Aug-44	Captain Melvin T. Jackson	302nd Fighter Sqn
14-Aug-44	1st Lieutenant Gwynne W. Pierson	302nd Fighter Sqn
14-Aug-44	Captain Arnold W. Cisco	301st Fighter Sqn
14-Aug-44	Captain Alton F. Ballard	301st Fighter Sqn
24-Aug-44	1st Lieutenant John F. Briggs	100th Fighter Sqn
24-Aug-44	1st Lieutenant William H. Thomas	302nd Fighter Sqn
27-Aug-44	Captain Wendell O. Pruitt	302nd Fighter Sqn
27-Aug-44	Captain Dudley M. Watson	302nd Fighter Sqn
27-Aug-44	1st Lieutenant Roger Romine	302nd Fighter Sqn
30-Aug-44	Captain Clarence H. Bradford	301st Fighter Sqn
8-Sep-44	Major George S. Roberts	332nd Fighter Grp
8-Sep-44	1st Lieutenant Heber C. Houston	99th Fighter Sqn
4-Oct-44	1st Lieutenant Samuel L. Curtis	100th Fighter Sqn
4-Oct-44	1st Lieutenant Dempsey Morgan	100th Fighter Sqn
4-Oct-44	Captain Claude B. Govan	301st Fighter Sqn
4-Oct-44	1st Lieutenant Herman A. Lawson	99th Fighter Sqn
4-Oct-44	1st Lieutenant Willard L. Woods	100th Fighter Sqn
6-Oct-44	1st Lieutenant Alva N. Temple	99th Fighter Sqn
6-Oct-44	Captain Lawrence E. Dickson	100th Fighter Sqn
6-Oct-44	1st Lieutenant Edward M. Thomas	99th Fighter Sqn
6-Oct-44	1st Lieutenant Robert L. Martin	100th Fighter Sqn
6-Oct-44	Captain Robert J. Friend	301st Fighter Sqn
11-Oct-44	Captain William A. Campbell	99th Fighter Sqn
11-Oct-44	1st Lieutenant George E. Gray	99th Fighter Sqn
11-Oct-44	1st Lieutenant Felix J. Kirkpatrick	302nd Fighter Sqn
11-Oct-44	1st Lieutenant Richard S. Harder	99th Fighter Sqn
12-Oct-44	1st Lieutenant Lee Archer	302nd Fighter Sqn
12-Oct-44	Captain Milton R. Brooks	302nd Fighter Sqn
12-Oct-44	1st Lieutenant Frank E. Roberts	100th Fighter Sqn
12-Oct-44	1st Lieutenant Spurgeon N. Ellington	100th Fighter Sqn
12-Oct-44	1st Lieutenant Leonard F. Turner	301st Fighter Sqn
12-Oct-44	Captain Armour G. McDaniel	301st Fighter Sqn
12-Oct-44	Captain Stanley L. Harris	301st Fighter Sqn
12-Oct-44	1st Lieutenant Marion R. Rodgers	99th Fighter Sqn
12-Oct-44	1st Lieutenant Quitman C. Walker	99th Fighter Sqn
13-Oct-44	1st Lieutenant Milton S. Hays	99th Fighter Sqn

DATE	NAME	SQUADRON
14-Oct-44	1st Lieutenant George M. Rhodes, Jr.	100th Fighter Sqn
21-Oct-44	Captain Vernon V. Haywood	302nd Fighter Sqn
16-Nov-44	Captain Luke J. Weathers	302nd Fighter Sqn
19-Nov-44	Captain Albert H. Manning	99th Fighter Sqn
19-Nov-44	Captain John Daniels	99th Fighter Sqn
19-Nov-44	1st Lieutenant William N. Alsbrook	99th Fighter Sqn
19-Nov-44	1st Lieutenant Norman W. Scales	100th Fighter Sqn
16-Feb-45	Captain Emile G. Clifton	99th Fighter Sqn
17-Feb-45	Captain Louis G. Purnell	301st Fighter Sqn
25-Feb-45	1st Lieutenant Roscoe C. Brown	100th Fighter Sqn
25-Feb-45	1st Lieutenant Reid E. Thompson	100th Fighter Sqn
12-Mar-45	Captain Walter M. Downs	301st Fighter Sqn
14-Mar-45	1st Lieutenant Shelby F. Westbrook	99th Fighter Sqn
14-Mar-45	1st Lieutenant Hannibal M. Cox	99th Fighter Sqn
14-Mar-45	2nd Lieutenant Vincent I. Mitchell	99th Fighter Sqn
14-Mar-45	1st Lieutenant Thomas P. Braswell	99th Fighter Sqn
14-Mar-45	2nd Lieutenant John W. Davis	99th Fighter Sqn
16-Mar-45	1st Lieutenant Roland W. Moody	301st Fighter Sqn
16-Mar-45	1st Lieutenant Henry R. Peoples	301st Fighter Sqn
16-Mar-45	1st Lieutenant William S. Price III	301st Fighter Sqn
24-Mar-45	1st Lieutenant Earl R. Lane	100th Fighter Sqn
24-Mar-45	2nd Lieutenant Charles V. Brantley	100th Fighter Sqn
31-Mar-45	1st Lieutenant Robert W. Williams	100th Fighter Sqn
31-Mar-45	1st Lieutenant Bertram W. Wilson, Jr.	100th Fighter Sqn
1-Apr-45	1st Lieutenant Charles L. White	301st Fighter Sqn
1-Apr-45	1st Lieutenant John E. Edwards	301st Fighter Sqn
1-Apr-45	1st Lieutenant Harry T. Stewart, Jr.	301st Fighter Sqn
1-Apr-45	2nd Lieutenant Carl E. Carey	301st Fighter Sqn
15-Apr-45	Captain Gordon M. Rapier	301st Fighter Sqn
15-Apr-45	1st Lieutenant Gentry E. Barnes	99th Fighter Sqn
15-Apr-45	Captain William A. Campbell	99th Fighter Sqn
15-Apr-45	1st Lieutenant Jimmy Lanham	301st Fighter Sqn
26-Apr-45	1st Lieutenant Thomas W. Jefferson	301st Fighter Sqn

There are three significant "firsts" here: The first DFC awarded to a Tuskegee Airman was to Captain Charles B. Hall in January 1944 for the first Tuskegee Airmen victory, when he shot down a Focke-Wulf Fw-190 on July 2, 1943. The first (and only) Tuskegee Airman to win two DFCs was Captain William A. Campbell and the first DFC to be awarded to a Tuskegee Airman for shooting down a jet fighter (a Messerschmitt Me-262) went to 1st Lieutenant Earl R. Lane in March 1945.

In addition to these medal numbers, it is said that one thousand and thirty-one Air Medals were awarded to Tuskegee Airmen, which is a phenomenal number, though it is a fact that some individuals were awarded as many as ten and many others were awarded multiples of that medal. Then, there were two Silver Stars, one Bronze Star, one Soldier's Medal, eight Purple Hearts and, of course, the Officer Class of the Legion of Merit to Colonel Benjamin O. Davis. In addition to this, some 300 Congressional Gold Medals were awarded to former Tuskegee Airmen on March 27, 2007 in the Rotunda of the Capitol Building in Washington, DC. The ultimate accolade.

AIR-TO-AIR COMBAT RECORD

The Air-to-Air combat record of this remarkable group of men is also worthy of examination.

PILOT AND UNIT	NOTED VICTORIES
Lt. Clarence Allen 99th FS	1 Fw-190 (shared with Capt Baugh 27 Jan 1944 P-40)
Capt. Lee Archer 302nd FS	1 Bf-109 (18 July 1944 P-51) 3 Bf-109s (12 Oct. 12 1944 P-51)
Lt. Willie Ashley, Jr. 99th FS	1 Fw-190 (Damaged 9 June 9 1943 P-40 1 Bf-109 (Probable 18 June 18 1943 P-40) 1 Fw-190 (27 Jan 1944 P-40)
Lt. Charles Bailey 99th FS	1 Fw-190 (27 Jan 1944 P-40) 1 Fw-190 (18 July 18 1944 P-51)
Capt. Howard Baugh 99th FS	1 Fw-190 (shared with Lt. Allen 27 Jan 1944 P-40) 1 Fw-190 (Damaged 27 Jan 1944 P-40)
Lt. Rual Bell 100th FS	1 Fw-190 (31 March 1945 P-51)
F/O Charles Brantley 100th FS	1 Me-262 Jet (24 March 1945 P-51)
Lt. Thomas Braswell 99th FS	1 Fw-190 (31 March 1945 P-51)
Capt. Roscoe Brown 100th FS	1 Me-262 Jet (24 March 1945 P-51) 1 Fw-190 (31 March 1945 P-51)
Lt. John Briggs 100th FS	1 Bf-109 (24 August 1944 P-51)
Lt. Milton Brooks 302nd FS	1 Bf-109 (12 Oct 1944 P-51)
Capt. Charles Bussey 302nd FS	1 Bf-109 (9 June 1944 P-47)

PILOT AND UNIT	NOTED VICTORIES
Maj. William Campbell 99th FS	2 Bf-109s (31 March 1945 P-51) Note: Some records indicate 1 kill
Lt. Carl Carey 301st FS	2 Bf-109s (1 April 1945 P-51)
Capt. Lemuel Custis 99th FS	1 Fw-190 (27 Jan 1944 P-40)
Capt. Alfonso Davis 99th FS	1 Macchi MB-205 (16 July 1944 P-51)
Lt. John Davis 99th FS	1 Bf-109 (31 March 1945 P-51)
Lt. Robert Diez 99th FS	1 Fw-190 27 Jan 1944 P-40) 1 Fw-190 28 Jan 1944 P-40
Capt. Elwood Driver 99th FS	1 Fw-190 (Shared Probable 27 Jan 1944 P-40) 1 Fw-190 (5 Feb 1944 P-40)
Lt. Wilson Eagleson 99th FS	1 Fw-190 (20 July 1944 P-40)
Lt. John Edwards 301st FS	2 Bf-109s (1 April 1945 P-51)
Capt. Joseph Elsberry 301st FS	3 Fw-190s (12 July 1944 P-51) 1 Fw-190 (Probable 12 July 1944 P-51) 1 Bf-109 (20 July 1944 P-51)
F/0 James Fischer 301st FS	1 Fw-190 (1 April 1945 P-51) 2 Fw-190s (1 April 1945 P-51)
Lt. Frederick Funderburg 301st FS	2 Bf-109s (9 June 1944 P-47)

THE TUSKEGEE AIRMEN AND BEYOND

PILOT AND UNIT	NOTED VICTORIES
Maj. Edward Gleed 302nd & 301st FS	2 Fw-190s (27 July 27 1944 P-51) 1 Fw-190 (Damaged 27 July 1944 P-51) Note: Some sources indicates 3 kills 2 Probables
Lt. Alfred Gorham 301st FS	2 Fw-190s (27 July 1944 P-51)
Capt. Claude Govan 301st FS	1 Bf-109 (27 July 1944 P-51)
Capt. George Gray 99th FS	1 Bf-109 (4 Oct 1944 P-51)
Lt. William Green, Jr. 302nd FS	1 Macchi MB-205 (16 July 1944 P-47) 1 Bf-109 (shared with Lt. Groves 26 July 1944 P-51) 1 He-111 (12 Oct 1944 P-51)
Lt. Weldon Groves 302nd FS	1 Ju-88 (17 March 1943 P-39) 1 Bf-109 (shared with Lt. Green 26 July 1944 P-51) 1 Bf-109 (12 Oct 1944 P-51)
Capt. Charles Hall (99th FS)	1 Fw-190 (2 July 1943 P-40) 1 Bf-109 (28 Jan 1944 P-40) 1 Fw-190 (28 Jan 1944 P-40)
Lt. James Hall, Jr. 99th FS	1 Bf-109 (31 March 1945 P-51)
Lt. Richard Hall 100th FS	1 Bf-109 (27 July 1944 P-51)
Lt. Milton Hayes 99th FS	1 Fw-109 (shared with Capt. Perry 4 Oct 1944 P-51)
Lt. Richard Harder 99th FS	2 Me-262 Jets (24 March 1945 P-51)
F/O William Hill 302nd FS	1 Bf-109 (23 August 44 P-51)
Lt. Jack Holsclaw 100th FS	2 Bf-109s (18 July 1944 P-51)
Lt. Heber Houston 99th FS	1 Bf-109s (26 July 1944 P-51)
Capt. Freddie Hutchins 302nd FS	1 Bf-109 (26 July 1944 P-51) 1 Bf-109 (Probable 26 July 1944 P-51)
Capt. Leonard Jackson 99th FS	1 Fw-190 (7 Feb 1944 P-40) 1 Bf-109 (26 July 1944 P-51) 1 Bf-109 (27 July 1944 P-51)
Capt. Melvin Jackson 302nd FS	1 Bf-109 (9 June 1944 P-47)
Lt. Thomas Jefferson 301st FS	2 Bf-109 (26 April 1945 P-51)
Lt. Carl Johnson 100th FS	1 Bf-109 (6 August 1944 P-51) 1 Re-2001 (30 July 1944 P-51)
Lt. Langdon Johnson 100th FS	1 Bf-109 (20 July 1944 P-51)
Lt. Felix Kirkpatrick, Jr. 302nd FS	1 Bf-109 (27 July 1944 P-51)
Lt. Earl Lane 100th FS	1 Me-262 Jet (24 March 1945 P-51) 1 ME 109 (31 March 1945 P-51)
Lt. Jimmie Lanham 301st FS	1 Bf-109 (15 April 1945 P-51) 1 Bf-109 (Probable 15 April 1945 P-51) 1 Bf-109 (26 April 1944 P-51)
Lt. Herman Lawson 99th FS	1 Fw-190 (Probable 8 July 1943 P-40)
Lt. Walter Lawson 99th FS	1 Bf-109 (2 July 1943 P-40) 2 Bf-109s (Both Probables 2 July 1943 P-40)
Capt. Clarence Lester 100th FS	3 Bf-109s (18 July 1944 P-51)
F/O John Lyle 100th FS	1 Bf-109 (31 March 1944 P-51)
Lt. Walter Manning 301st FS	1 Fw-190 (27 July 27 1944 P-51) 1 Bf-109 (1 April 1945 P-51)
Capt. Armour McDaniel 301st FS	1 Bf-109 (20 July 1944 P-51)
Capt. Charles McGee 302nd FS	1 Fw-190 (4 Oct 1944 P-51)
Lt. William Melton 302nd FS	1 Ju-88 (Unclaimed Victory – Damaged later confirm destroyed 28 March 1944 P-39) 2 Fw-190s (Unclaimed Victory - Destroyed around August 1944 P-51)
Lt. Clinton Mills 99th FS	1 Fw-190 (7 Feb 1944 P-40)
Lt. Harold Morris 301st FS	1 Bf-109 (1 April 1945 P-51)
Capt. Walter Palmer 100th FS	1 Bf-109 (18 July 1944 P-51)
Capt. Henry Perry 99th FS	1 Fw-190 (Damaged 27 Feb 1944 P-40) 1 Bf-109 (Damaged 18 July 1944 P-40) 1 Bf-109 (shared with Lt. Milton Hayes 4 Oct 1944 P-51)
Lt. William Price III 301st FS	1 Bf-109 (1 Feb 1945 P-51)
Capt. Wendell Pruitt 302nd FS	1 Bf-109 (9 June 1944) P-47) 1 Bf-109 (12 Oct 1944 P-51) 1 He-111 (12 Oct 1944 P-51)
Lt. George Rhodes, Jr. 100th FS	1 Fw-190 (12 August 1944 P-51) 1 Bf-109 (4 Oct 1944 P-51)
Lt. Daniel Rich 99th FS	1 Bf-109 (31 March 1945 P-51)
Maj. George Roberts 99th FS	1 Fw-190 (Damaged 27 Jan 1944 P-40) Note: Fellow 99th pilots witnessed 2 kills by G. Roberts but never claimed.
Capt. Leon Roberts 99th FS	1 Fw-190 (27 Jan 1944 P-40)
Lt. Roger Romine 302nd FS	1 Bf-109 (18 July 1944 P-51) 1 Bf-109 (26 July 1944 P-51) 1 Bf-109 (12 Oct 1944 P-51) 1 Bf-109 (12 Oct 1944 P-51)
Lt. Harold Sawyer 301st FS	2 Fw-190s (12 July 1944 P-51) Note: This was the first kill using the P-51 for the 332nd FG A hand-me-down olive colored P-51 from the 31st FG 1 Bf-109 (25 July 1944 P-51) 2 Bf-109s (Damaged 25 July 1944 P-51)
Lt. Richard Simons 100th FS	1 Bf-109 (26 April 1945 P-51)
Capt. Lewis Smith 99th FS	1 Bf-109 (27 Jan 1944 P-40)

PILOT AND UNIT	NOTED VICTORIES
Lt. Luther Smith, Jr. 302nd FS	1 Bf-109 (17 July 1944 P-51) 1 He-111 (12 Oct 1944 P-51)
Lt. Robert Smith 302nd FS	1 Bf-109 (17 July 1944 P-51)
Lt. Roy Spenser 302nd FS	1 Ju-88 (Damaged March. 28 1944 P-39)
Lt. Harry Stewart, Jr. 301st FS	3 Bf-109s (1 April 1945 P-51)
Capt. Edward Thomas 99th FS	1 Bf-109 (4 Oct 1944 P-51) 1 Me-262 Jet (shared victory March 24 1945 P-51)
Lt. William Thomas 302nd FS	1 Fw-190 (24 August 1944 P-51)
Capt. Edward Toppins 99th FS	1 Fw-190 (27 Jan 1944 P-51) 1 Fw-190 (18 July 1944 P-51) 1 Bf-109 (20 July 1944 P-51) 1 Bf-109 (26 July 1944 P-51) 1 Bf-109 (Probable 26 July 1944 P-51)
Lt. Hugh Warner 302nd FS	1 Bf-109 18 July 1944 P-51)
Lt. Span Watson 99th FS	2 Bf-109s (16 June 1943 P-40)

PILOT AND UNIT	NOTED VICTORIES
Capt. Luke Weathers 302nd FS	1 Bf-109 (Destroyed shared with Lt. William Hill 23 August 1944 P-51) 2 Bf-109s (16 Nov 1944 P-51)
Lt. Shelby Westbrook 99th FS	1 Bf-109 (4 Oct 1944 P-51)
Capt. Charles White 301st FS	2 Bf-109s (1 April 1945 P-51)
Capt. Hugh White 99th FS	1 Bf-109 (31 March 1945 P-51)
Lt. Robert Wiggins 301st FS	1 Bf-109 (9 June 1945 P-47)
Lt. Lawrence Wilkens 302nd FS	1 Ju-88 (Damaged 14 March 1944 P-39) 1 Bf-109 (17 July 17 1944 P-51)
Lt. Robert W. Williams 100th FS	2 Fw-190s (31 March 1945 P-51) 1 Fw-190 (Damaged 31 March 1945 P-51)
Lt. Bertram Wilson, Jr. 100th FS	1 Fw-109 (31 March 1945 P-51) 1 Bf-109 (Damaged 31 March 1945 P-51)

This total tally reflects a score of 138 victories with 18 Damaged or Probables.

The 1,031 Air Medals were awarded to 265 recipients. Only forty of those awardees received just one Air Medal, two received ten. The overall distribution of the Air Medal to members of the 332nd Fighter Group is shown below:

1st	Oak Leaf Cluster	225
2nd	Oak Leaf Cluster	172
3rd	Oak Leaf Cluster	152
4th	Oak Leaf Cluster	107
5th	Oak Leaf Cluster	62
6th	Oak Leaf Cluster	31
7th	Oak Leaf Cluster	12
8th	Oak Leaf Cluster	3
9th	Oak Leaf Cluster	2

The Air Medal was established by Executive Order 9158, endorsed by President Franklin D. Roosevelt, on May 11, 942. It was awarded retroactively to September 8, 1939. The decoration is awarded to any person who, while serving in any capacity in or with the Armed Forces of the United States of America, shall have distinguished himself or herself by meritorious achievement while participating in aerial flight. Awards may be made to recognize single acts of merit or heroism, or for meritorious service. Award of the Air Medal is primarily intended to recognize those personnel who are on current crew member or non-crew member flying status that requires them to participate in aerial flight on a regular and frequent basis in the performance of their primary duties.

APPENDIX EIGHT
THE ATTEMPT TO DISBAND THE 99TH

The 99th Fighter Squadron's formation and arrival in North Africa was not a blessing in everybody's mind. Having succeeded in its formation and training, there were now much bigger obstacles to face. It's doubtful that Lieutenant-Colonel Davis ever thought his troubles were over with the formation and deployment of his squadron, and especially since he was not there in North Africa at the point of the unit's arrival. The task of the initial location of the squadron and its men on site at Oued Nja fell to Captain George Roberts (who was quickly promoted to temporary Major).

Colonel William Momyer.

As the 99th was about to be assigned to the 33rd Fighter Group and be relocated to Fardjouna, so Lieutenant-Colonel Davis took command. His initial meeting with Colonel Momyer, the 33rd Fighter Group Commander, did not go well, for he received no assistance or guidance in the process of finding accommodation for his men, or a dispersal area for his aircraft. Benjamin Davis never expected the path to be easy, but he was now discovering that he was about to face major problems that went far outside normal military boundaries or etiquette. But he never expected to have to face Colonel Momyer in the battle of wills that ensued, culminating in facing the Senate House Armed Services Committee.

Colonel William Momyer's arrival in the North African Desert campaign was initially as a military observer for air with the US Military Attache in Cairo. While in that post, he acted as technical adviser to the Royal Air Force when it was to equip the first squadron of the Western Desert Air Force with the Curtiss P-40 "Tomahawk" aircraft. His service there was of great value to the British, who became the biggest single user of the P-40 outside the United States. Among the earliest Royal Air Force squadrons to use the P-40 in North Africa were 112 Squadron and 208 Squadron. Ultimately, twenty seven Commonwealth squadrons operated the P-40 in various forms. While with the Royal Air Force, Colonel Momyer was awarded the Distinguished Flying Cross (RAF).

In 1943, Momyer was appointed Group Commander of the 33rd Fighter Group, now under Brigadier-General Jimmy Doolittle's command in the 12th Air Force, still in North Africa, but now at Fardjouna in Tunisia. He certainly was a spirited fighter pilot. But Colonel Momyer ignored cautions from his superiors, Generals Doolittle and Craig, when he decided to commit small detachments of his fighter force far from base and in areas where the Luftwaffe had significant air superiority. Within a month. the 33rd Fighter Group was knocked out of combat by its losses and had to be re-grouped with replacement pilots and aircraft before it could return to action. This is how the 99th Fighter Squadron came to be part of that re-grouping.

In reviewing the situation with Colonel Momyer, General Doolittle was very clear that he did not approve of the foolishness that had taken place, especially since he had personally seen Momyer's plan and warned against the action he took. This had cost more than forty aircraft and it can only be presumed that Momyer escaped a court-martial because of his previous success in introducing the Curtiss P-40 into Britain's Royal Air Force service in the Western Desert and his personal skill as a fighter pilot. But he was now faced with being told that, instead of having the pick of the Army Air Forces' squadrons, the first three fighter squadrons to arrive in North Africa would be allocated to him to re-form the 33rd Fighter Group. Colonel Momyer didn't bargain for what was to come, for among the squadrons allocated to the re-formed 33rd was the 99th Fighter Squadron, the first African American squadron in the Army Air Forces. Colonel Momyer came from Savannah, Georgia, where segregation was life in those days.

Colonel Momyer's involvement with the 99th Fighter Squadron was a distinctly unsavory affair from the very beginning. When the 99th arrived in North Africa, air and ground crews were left to their own devices, to find their own way around the base and to settle themselves in with no outside assistance. They were told that their first mission from Fardjouna would be as bomber escorts for a bombing run on Pantelleria Island just off Sicily in the Mediterranean. When it came to their first vital pre-mission briefing, Lieutenant-Colonel Davis was told quite bluntly by his Group Commander that he would not be allowed to attend the briefing with his pilots, because they were black. Given little guidance from battle-experienced pilots, the 99th's first combat mission was virtually doomed from the beginning. So Lieutenant-Colonel Davis called his own pre-mission briefing. He established the time of take-off for the bomb group and ensured that his pilots would be in the air in readiness to provide escort cover.

Despite no briefing, the 99th was off the ground at the same time as the bombers of the 320th Bombardment Group. They had no knowledge of Pantelleria's air defenses and so ran headlong into a Luftwaffe fighter wing. But they didn't actually reach Pantelleria, because of being "jumped". After this incident, when the 99th pilots received no flight maps, no pre-flight briefing and no

inclusion in the 33rd Fighter Group, Momyer directed them to ground support tasks. Momyer then accused the 99th of being a failure, accusing its pilots of being incompetent and cowardly. Ignoring the fact that they had now been awarded a Distinguished Unit Citation and the fact that he personally had ordered them into a ground attack role, he blamed them for not seeking out air to air combat.

HEADQUARTERS XII AIR SUPPORT COMMAND
APO #766

16 September 1943

SUBJECT: Combat Efficiency of the 99th Fighter Squadron.

TO: Major General J. K. Cannon, USA, Deputy Commander,
     Northwest African Tactical Air Force, APO #509, U. S. Army.

1. On June 12th, 1943, I took command of the XII Air Support Command. With one of the Groups assigned to the Command was the 99th Fighter Squadron, which I visited quite frequently. Their Commanding Officer, Lt. Col. Davis, particularly impressed me. On the day of the 99th's first encounter with enemy aircraft, I happened to be on the airdrome and was very complimentary and encouraging to the personnel I met. At that time one of the colored correspondents asked me if I thought there should be a colored group, and I answered to the effect that I saw no reason why there should not be such a group in the near future. Since that day, I have compared the operating efficiency of the 99th Fighter Squadron with that of a white fighter squadron operating in the same group and with the same type of equipment. I quote from a report by an officer who has been in the best position to observe carefully the work of the 99th Squadron over its entire combat period:

"The ground discipline and ability to accomplish and execute orders promptly are excellent. Air discipline has not been completely satisfactory. The ability to work and fight as a team has not yet been acquired. Their formation flying has been very satisfactory until jumped by enemy aircraft, when the squadron seems to disintegrate. This has repeatedly been brought to the attention of the Squadron, but attempts to correct this deficiency so far have been unfruitful. On one particular occasion, a flight of twelve JU 88's, with an escort of six ME 109's, was observed to be bombing Pantelleria. The 99th Squadron, instead of pressing home the attack against the bombers, allowed themselves to become engaged with the 109's. The unit has shown a lack of aggressive spirit that is necessary for a well-organized fighter squadron. On numerous instances when assigned to dive bomb a specified target in which the anti-aircraft fire was light and inaccurate, they chose the secondary target which was undefended. On one occasion, they were assigned a mission with one squadron of this Group to bomb a target in the toe of Italy; the 99th turned back before the reaching of the target because of the weather. The other squadron went on to the target and pressed home the attack. As later substantiated, the weather was considered operational.

"Up to the present moment, the 99th Squadron averages approximately 28 sorties per man. Their operations since being placed on combat duty have been considerably easier than past operations due to the nature of the tactical situation. However, the Squadron Commander of the 99th requested during the battle of Sicily to be removed from operations for a period of three days, and longer if possible. The reason given was that his pilots

Momyer's complaint was brought before the House Armed Services Committee in Washington and both Colonel Momyer and Lieutenant Colonel Benjamin Davis were summoned to be present. In his submission Momyer observed: *"It is my opinion that they have failed to display appropriate aggressiveness and daring for combat. It may be expected that we will get less work and less operational time out of the 99th FS* *than any squadron in this group."* After hearing Colonel Davis's story of lack of support and lack of inclusion, the House Committee refuted and rejected Momyer's accusations. This first all-black squadron thus survived, despite his recommendation, and became the nucleus of the all-African American Fighter Group, the 332nd.

Colonel Momyer returned to the United States in 1944 and became chief of the combined operations of the Army Air Forces Board. As a member, he played a significant role in the development of Air Force doctrine for air-ground operations. After the Tuskegee incident, it might seem a little surprising that he should be given such a prestigious job and even more surprising, perhaps, that he should ultimately rise to four-star rank. But then, one can reflect on the certain fact that many of his peers echoed his views on racist policies and his political connections would certainly have been helpful to his career advancement. It is interesting to observe that Major-General "Chuck" Yeager reflected in his memoirs that he felt, after a serious difference of opinion with General Momyer, that Momyer had highly prejudiced views, which contrasted greatly with his tactical expertise. The evidence of those prejudiced views was clearly demonstrated by his earlier attitude to the Tuskegee Airmen.

were suffering from pilot's fatigue. The Squadron's Surgeon submitted a medical report stating that the pilots of the 99th should be removed from combat duty because of the strenuous and rigorous conditions under which they have been operating. In comparison, the pilots of this Group had an average of approximately 70 sorties and had been in operations for nine continuous months.

"Based on the performance of the 99th Fighter Squadron to date, it is my opinion that they are not of the fighting caliber of any squadron in this Group. They have failed to display the aggressiveness and desire for combat that are necessary to a first-class fighting organization. It may be expected that we will get less work and less operational time out of the 99th Fighter Squadron than any squadron in this Group."

2. At the present time the 99th Squadron is not in the Naples area because there is insufficient room on the P-40 field on which to place them. It is our intention to bring them into the area as soon as space is available. We also brought forward two Spitfire Groups less squadrons because of lack of space.

3. Shortly before the Naples operation, a radiogram came to me stating that Lt. Col. Davis had been selected to return to the United States to command a colored group. Although with the knowledge that in turning the command of the 99th Squadron over to the next ranking officer who would not approach the standard of Davis, I relieved Davis for his new assignment.

4. On many discussions held with officers of all professions, including medical, the consensus of opinion seems to be that the negro type has not the proper reflexes to make a first-class, fighter pilot. Also, on rapid moves that must be a part of this Command, housing and massing difficulties arise because the time has not yet arrived when the white and colored soldiers will mess at the same table and sleep in the same barracks. No details in this connection have been brought out because it is desired that administrative features not be a part of this report.

5. I believe it would be much better to assign the 99th to the Northwest African Coastal Air Force, equip it with P-39's and make the present P-40's available to this Command as replacements for the active operations still to come in this theater.

6. It is recommended that if and when a colored group is formed in the United States, it be retained for either the eastern or western defense zone and a white fighter group be released for movement overseas.

/s/
EDWIN J. HOUSE
Major General, U. S. A. (by J.H.C.)
Commanding

COPY

One thing has to be said, though, about Colonel Momyer's dealings with the 99th Fighter Squadron in general, and with Colonel Benjamin Davis in particular. It is that Momyer's attitude and handling of the whole affair in such a prejudiced and bigoted way almost guaranteed that, as long as the Tuskegee Airmen performed well after that Senate investigation, their future was assured. So in that respect, Momyer did the cause of African American participation in aviation – and ultimately the cause of desegregation – a great service. Unwittingly, he made a significant contribution to their progress and success, by bringing them to the attention of those who could bring about change.

In his attempts to discredit the 99th Fighter Squadron and its commander, Lieutenant-Colonel Benjamin Davis, Colonel Momyer enlisted the support of an old acquaintance. Major-General Edwin House, now commander of the 12th Air Support Command, an element of the 12th Air Force. He submitted his report to General House, who wrote a supporting letter to Major-General John K. Cannon, Deputy Commander of 12th Air Force.

Major-General John K. Cannon pinning Air Medals to the uniforms of Captains Charles B. Hall, Lemuel Custis and Willie Fuller – the same General Cannon who recommended the repatriation of the 99th Fighter Squadron.

General Cannon congratulating Captain Charles Hall, already a DFC recipient, on the award of his Air Medal.

The letter below was written in September 1943, very shortly after Major General House took command of 12th Air Support Command. It has to be remembered that Colonel William Momyer had already "crossed swords" with Lieutenant-Colonel Benjamin Davis and had launched his vendetta against the 99th Fighter Squadron for little other reason than the crews were black. There is a reference in his letter to the fact that, under the rules of segregation, it was extremely difficult to provide separate messing facilities and accommodation for the 99th Squadron crews. Yet Colonel Bates had found no trouble in accommodating the 99th crews when they were placed under his command. Why? Simply because

he and his squadrons broke, or ignored, the rules.

The pictures on the previous page were taken some time after the letters here were written by Major Generals Edwin House and John Cannon. The letter below, from General Cannon, needs no explanation. It was certainly written after he had read and accepted the report from General House. General House had received and was clearly in sympathy with Colonel William Momyer's view of the 99th Fighter Squadron. But pretty surely, by the time these pictures were taken, General Cannon at least had modified his views and position.

```
                           1st Ind.                      A/lee
HQRS NORTHWEST AFRICAN TACTICAL AIR FORCE, APO #509, U. S. Army, 18 Sept. 1943.

TO:  Commanding General, Northwest African Air Force, APO #650, U. S. Army.


     1.  The pilots of the 99th Fighter Squadron fall well below the standard
of pilots of other fighter squadrons of this Command in the following cate-
gories:

     a.  They are not eager to engage in combat.

     b.  They lack aggressiveness.

     c.  They do not possess and seem unable to acquire the will to win
or to reach the objective.

     d.  They do not possess the stamina or lasting qualities of the
pilots of other fighter squadrons.

     e.  Although excellent pilots they seem unable to fight as a team
under pressure.

     2.  The pilots of the 99th Fighter Squadron have no outstanding
characteristics in which they excel in war the pilots of other squadrons of
this Command.

                              /s/ J. K. Cannon

                                  J. K. CANNON
                              Major General, U. S. Army
                              Deputy Commander
```

APPENDIX NINE
POSTSCRIPT

Steward First Class Carl E. Clark and the USS "Aaron Ward" (DM-34), 1944-1946

The USS "Aaron Ward" was a 2200-ton Robert H. Smith class light minelayer. It was the third US Navy ship to carry the name Aaron Ward and was built by Bethlehem Steel Corporation at San Pedro, California. The ship was originally intended to be a destroyer, but was converted to a minelayer after launching on May 5, 1944 and was commissioned into service in October of that year. Her captain was Commander William H. Sanders, Jr.

The USS "Aaron Ward", DM-34, shortly after her launching in November 1944.

The "Aaron Ward" arrived in the Pacific war zone in February 1945, and in March took part in the invasion of Okinawa. For several weeks, she supported minesweeping operations, performed escorts, patrols and radar picket duties, in addition to helping fight off constant Japanese air raids.

On May 3, 1945, while on picket station west of Okinawa, "Aaron Ward" was the target of intense attacks by Kamikaze suicide planes. She shot down several, but was hit and near-missed by many more. Her crew managed to keep their badly damaged ship afloat, an effort that was recognized by the award of a Presidential Unit Citation, and she was towed to an anchorage the next day.

One incident which was not officially recorded in the ship's log concerned Seaman 2nd Class Carl E. Clark, who was on deck at the time of a 25-aircraft Japanese Kamikaze attack. At dusk, the ship had taken direct hits from six Kamikaze planes and two separate bombs. Carl Clark had a broken collar bone already, yet he alone aimed a fire hose that would normally have taken four men to control at the ship's

The USS "Aaron Ward" after sustaining damage from a massive Kamikaze attack on May 3, 1945.

smoldering ammunition locker. Clark's action prevented a major explosion that would almost certainly have split the ship in two. After putting out the fire, Carl Clark risked his own life once again by exposing himself to incoming fire in order to aid his shipmates. Despite his injury and with no concern for his own safety, he carried his fellow injured sailors to safety and endured fire from the enemy running to and from the aid station. His ship's captain, Commander Sanders told Seaman Clark that he had saved the ship, yet his name was never mentioned in the ship's log or in the damage report.

Following temporary repairs, the "Aaron Ward" was able to steam across the Pacific and through the Panama Canal, to arrive at New York in August 1945. With World War II now nearly at an end, the ship was judged not worth the expense of renovation and was decommissioned in late September 1945 and sold for scrap in July 1946.

Sixty-six years after this sequence of events. Carl Clark was finally given the recognition he deserved for his courageous actions on that May 1945 evening. Thanks to Sheila Dunec's researches and the stringent efforts of Congresswoman Anna Eshoo (the Democrat Representative for California's 14th District), Carl Clark was awarded the Navy and Marine Corps Commendation Medal with Combat Distinguished Device (a gold-colored letter "V" placed on the ribbon of the medal) on January 17, 2012. The circumstances of this event would seem to justify the award of the Navy Cross when compared with other Navy Cross award citations, however, the lack of official records and surviving witnesses made any award to Carl Clark difficult. Anna Eshoo shook the nation's conscience and brought about a just recognition of Carl Clark's courageous action all those years ago. It was she who said: *"It is a singular privilege to be in a position to correct the record for those who have fought to preserve our freedoms."* She went on to say that *"it was good to know that when our nation makes a mistake, it can atone for it and put things right."*

The award was made in a ceremony on January 17, 2012 at the former Naval Air Station Moffett Field. It was a significant event for Chief Petty Officer Carl E. Clark USN (ret), since he finally received recognition for what he did two thirds of a century ago. He was less concerned with the level of the medal – he simply felt that since others had been commended in 1945, and since his ship's captain personally praised him for "saving my ship", he should have received some recognition. Instead, at the time of the incident and while the event was still fresh in people's memories, his actions had been ignored and never formally recorded.

For Congresswoman Eshoo, it was a special day because she saw the culmination of the efforts of several people come to fruition. She felt that a great injustice had been done and was both anxious and determined to put it right. Racism had robbed Carl Clark of the acknowledgement his outstanding courage deserved. Thanks in no small part to the research efforts of Sheila Dunec, his story emerged, and as the facts came to hand, Anna Eshoo made it her business to take this case to Congress and press for the long overdue recognition

An overhead view of the damage sustained by the "Aaron Ward". Carl Clark's action prevented the ship from splitting in half and sinking.

to which Carl Clark was entitled. She pursued it through Navy channels and took it all the way to Secretary of the Navy, Ray Mabus. Her efforts were vindicated.

Navy Secretary Ray Mabus had the honor of pinning that long overdue medal to Carl Clark's chest. In his address, Secretary Mabus said:

"You know, the Defense Department creates a lot of paperwork. I work in the Pentagon, you can trust me on this one.

"One of the most important pieces of paper generated in every service member's record is the "Certificate of Release or Discharge from Active Duty" – DD Form 214

On the left: Congresswoman Anna Eshoo, proudly stands alongside an immaculately turned out Chief Petty Officer Carl E. Clark USN (ret) as they attend the ceremony at which Carl Clark is to receive the Navy and Marine Corps Commendation Medal with Combat Distinguished Device.

Carl Clark addresses the audience at his presentation, while Navy Secretary Mabus and Congresswoman Eshoo observe with pride.

Secretary of the Navy Ray Mabus shakes Carl's hand after pinning the medal to his uniform. Congresswoman Eshoo looks on and applauds.

which is completed at the end of every service person's time in the military and offers a really concise, one-page overview of that person's time in service. I, like everyone else who has served, have one from my time in the Navy and I, like most people, have kept it.

"Carl Clark's DD 214 includes all of his personal information data, including his home address, the same address in San Mateo where he has lived for over 60 years. It also records that Carl's service was honorable. But his DD 214 is missing one entry. And today, we will add that final official entry that has been missing for almost exactly two-thirds of a century. That entry will record that Carl E. Clark has been awarded the Navy and Marine Corps Commendation Medal with Combat V.2"

At that point, Secretary Mabus pinned on to the uniform of an impeccably turned out Chief Petty Officer Carl E. Clark the Navy and Marine Corps Commendation Medal with Combat Distinguished Device. The nation had answered its conscience and a great wrong had been put right. Carl Clark has never considered himself a hero – but his deeds on that day were truly heroic. As Navy Secretary Mabus concluded:

"Your actions were timely. Our recognition of them, sadly, was not".

THE SECRETARY OF THE NAVY

WASHINGTON

The President of the United States takes pleasure in presenting the PRESIDENTIAL UNIT CITATION to the

UNITED STATES SHIP AARON WARD

for service as set forth in the following

CITATION:

"For extraordinary heroism in action as a Picket Ship on Radar Picket Station during a coordinated attack by approximately twenty-five Japanese aircraft near Okinawa on May 3, 1945. Shooting down two Kamikazes which approached in determined suicide dives, the U.S.S. AARON WARD was struck by a bomb from a third suicide plane as she fought to destroy this attacker before it crashed into her superstructure and sprayed the entire area with flaming gasoline. Instantly flooded in her after engine room and fire room, she battled against flames and exploding ammunition on deck and, maneuvering in a tight circle because of damage to her steering gear, countered another coordinated suicide attack and destroyed three Kamikazes in rapid succession. Still smoking heavily and maneuvering radically, she lost all power when her forward fire room flooded under a seventh suicide plane which dropped a bomb close aboard and dived in flames into the main deck. Unable to recover from this blow before an eighth bomber crashed into her superstructure bulkhead only a few seconds later, she attempted to shoot down a ninth Kamikaze diving toward her at high speed and, despite the destruction of nearly all her gun mounts aft when this plane struck her, took under fire the tenth bomb-laden plane, which penetrated the dense smoke to crash on board with a devastating explosion. With fires raging uncontrolled, ammunition exploding and all engine spaces except the forward engine room flooded as she settled in the water and listed to port, she began a night-long battle to remain afloat and, with the assistance of a towing vessel, finally reached port the following morning. By her superb fighting spirit and the courage and determination of her entire company, the AARON WARD upheld the finest traditions of the United States Naval Service."

The Legend Lives On

Seventy years on, the legend of the Tuskegee Airmen is being enthusiastically carried forward. The Squadron and Group numbers are still alive and well. The 99th Fighter Squadron has mutated into the 99th Training Squadron, flying the T-1A "Jayhawk". It operates out of Randolph Air Force Base and is part of the 12th Flying Training Wing.

The 99th Flying Training Squadron carries its heritage with pride. The "Red Tails" badge endures as a red tip on the fin of the "Jayhawks" to remind observers of its illustrious past. The Tuskegee Airmen live on, but with multi-racial members – a consequence of President Harry Truman's courage and foresight to invoke Executive Order 9981, abolishing segregation in the Armed Forces. It is creditable that the modern mixed crews are extremely proud to be a part of this particular Squadron.

All the other squadrons of the 332nd Fighter Group exist today as fighter units. There have been long periods when, after disbandment post-World War II, they were de-activated, but in more recent years, the Tuskegee Airmen have become "fashionable". The revival of interest has come from the activities of authors who have revealed more of their past. In their day nobody was interested, but as America has become more liberal in its attitude to the variety of the human race, so its people have taken more interest in all aspects of social and military history. Filmmakers have played their part by seeing the opportunity at the box office and have promoted interest in the broader aspects of military history in particular and so, slowly, we have moved towards celebrating Black History Month. African Americans can stand with pride and hold their heads high for the actions of their forefathers.

This is a key reason why the United States Air Force has picked up the baton of the Tuskegee Airmen's history and molded it into a major part of Air Force history.

The 332nd Aerospace Expeditionary Wing is located at present at Balad Air Base in Iraq where its job is to preserve the aims and objectives of Operation Iraqi Freedom, and has the task

A "Jayhawk" in the air.

The revised badge of the 99th Squadron, showing its current training role.

Two T-1a "Jayhawks" of the 99th FTS on the apron at Randolph AFB. Randolph Field is one of the oldest US air bases, located where General Jimmy Doolittle once flew in his early career.

Operation Iraqi Freedom in operation. An F-16 shortly after take-off from Balad in a desert sunset.

of keeping Iraqi air space free from intrusion by would-be aggressors. It proudly carries the standard and the streamers of the 332nd Fighter Group of World War II and beyond. Were he alive today, General Benjamin O. Davis would look on with pride.

The 100th Fighter Squadron was revived in September 2007 as a part of the Alabama National Guard, by re-numbering the 160th Fighter Squadron, a component of the 187th Fighter Wing, an appropriate designation since the Tuskegee Airmen have their roots in that state. The 100th is based at Montgomery Regional Airport, just 37 miles from where it all began. Unfortunately, Alabama has not always been proud of its adopted sons. When the Tuskegee Airmen first arrived there, many were made far from welcome despite their contribution to the war effort. They still could not eat in "white" restaurants, they were separated on buses and were excluded from so many things that are taken for granted today. The attitude in Alabama is different now. The population regards the 100th Squadron as "its own" and there was a moving ceremony when the 160th was re-numbered. Once again, a squadron with a proud history flies close to its birthplace.

An F-16 over Iraq releases a flare during Operation Iraqi Freedom. The 332nd AEW is based at Balad Air Base in the Salah Ad Din Province of Iraq. (USAF photo)

The modern flight suit patch of the 332nd AEW.

Colonel Sam Black, Director of Operations of the 100th Fighter Squadron, taxies out from the apron at Pearl Harbor (Hickam Field) in April 2010.

100th Fighter Squadron's F16 and a P51.

100th FS Badge.

The TF-16 above is seen taking off from Luke Air Force Base in Arizona. The tail marking is clear to see, as is the "301 FS" below the Luke AFB tail code. F-16s came to the 301st Fighter Squadron in the year 2000 and served most of that period between then and 2010 at that location, with temporary duties in other locations too. For example, Exercise "Brilliant Arrow" in 2006 saw the F-16 below at Spangdahlem Air Base in Germany.

F-22 "Raptors" of the 301st Fighter Squadron, flying now over a remote region of New Mexico.

The 301st Fighter Squadron also operated F-16 "Fighting Falcons" up to 2010, converting to the F-22 "Raptor" in that year and relocating from Luke AFB in Arizona to Holloman Air Force Base in New Mexico, remote enough to be away from prying eyes, yet within reach of any region essential to preserving the nation's security from the air. Unlike the 100th Fighter Squadron's F-16 "Red Tail" markings, this squadron marked its aircraft in a more subdued fashion, with the red and yellow colors of the 332nd Fighter Group aircraft restricted to a stripe along the top of the fin. The other identifying feature was the characters "301 FS", beneath the tail code "LR", denoting "Luke Reserve" squadron.

The 302nd Fighter Squadron is one of the most charismatic of the modern Tuskegee "successor" squadrons. It also flies the ultimate in modern Air Force fighting equipment – the Lockheed F-22 "Raptor" which is a "state-of-the-art" front-line fighter aircraft and the envy of many a fighter squadron and fighter pilot. The 302nd Fighter Squadron operates its "Raptors" in a forbidding environment, at Elmendorf Air Force Base, to the north of Anchorage. But these aircraft do not carry the bright symbol of the "Red Tails", since they are intended, after all, to be low visibility "stealth" aircraft.

The modern rendering of the 301st Fighter Squadron badge, showing the origins of the Squadron and the Raptor adaptation of the original design.

Many years ago, USAF aircraft operating out of Alaska did carry red markings to give them high visibility in case they were downed, but today, low visibility is the keyword, so the 302nd Fighter Squadron identifies itself on its aircraft with only the characters "302 FS" under the tail code.

Before converting to the F-22, the 302nd Fighter Squadron shared its home with the 301st at Luke Air Force Base. The difference between the two squadrons was that the 302nd made its aircraft instantly identifiable by adopting the striking original red tail decoration of the Tuskegee Airmen. They

The Squadron Commander's F-16 of the 302nd Fighter Squadron flying over Arizona.

The Luke AFB "Gate Guardian", an F-16 standing at the gate of its former home.

The Squadron's modern presentation of its badge.

also used the yellow wing bands on their aircraft and their "Fighting Falcons" were unmistakable.

It is a pity in one respect that these five units are not all located together in one place and operating as a single Wing to represent the original Group of World War II. However, the fact that they are spread out does have a benefit in that the heritage, the name and the image of the Tuskegee Airmen is proclaimed widely and is unlikely to be forgotten. Four of those units are modern fighter operations and the fifth is in a unique position, as a training squadron, to spread the word among the most impressionable of the Air Force's numbers – the young men about to embark on their careers.

The Tuskegee Airmen are not forgotten anyway, for there are many Chapters of the formal organization, Tuskegee Airmen Inc., spread across the United States and there are several post-Tuskegee African American senior officers today associated with them, ensuring public awareness of their existence and deeds. Such organizations as the Du Sable Museum in Chicago ensure that the public is reminded of African

Top, a P-51D marked up in the Tuskegee colors. Above, the Commemorative Air Force P-51C, flying before its terrible fatal accident.

The new 302nd FS aircraft, the F-22 "Raptor" over Alaska.

American contributions to American society down three centuries. Most particularly, that establishment featured in the summer of 2011 the Smithsonian traveling exhibition "Black Wings", a stunning display of the involvement in and the contribution to aviation history over the century of its existence. Black History Month has provided an opportunity to remind the world of the Tuskegee Airmen's contribution too and this author has taken the opportunity to raise public awareness in lectures given during that period.

And then, there are restored and rebuilt aircraft which carry forward the link with the Tuskegee Airmen and their past. The Commemorative Air Force, an organization which exists solely for the preservation of America's military aviation history, bought and restored a North American P-51C to represent a Tuskegee aircraft. It suffered a major crash, killing its pilot and sponsor, Don Hinz, in the process. However, the Commemorative Air Force picked up the challenge and restored it again, so that today it is back in the air. The CAF's example of the P-51 is a tribute to the Tuskegee Airmen and is, even more than that, a symbol of the dogged determination that characterized those men during the dark days of World War II. It takes to the skies regularly to remind us all of the great contribution these men made to the ultimate peace in Europe, to say nothing of their rightful place in aviation history.

In the State of Iowa, the 132nd Fighter Wing of the Iowa National Guard operates its F-16 "Fighting Falcons" out of Des Moines. Two of Iowa's famous flyers of the past are both Tuskegee Airmen. One, the former Captain Robert Williams of the 332nd Fighter Group, wrote the manuscript for the motion picture "The Tuskegee Airmen" produced by HBO in 1995, and the other, Captain Luther Smith, was shot down and captured by the Germans during the war, suffering life-threatening wounds. These two flyers are being commemorated by the recreation of a Tuskegee Airmen P-51D Mustang, to be put on display at the main entrance to the 132nd's building. The aircraft will be known as the Iowa Tuskegee Airmen Memorial.

Taking our Epilogue further back to the beginning of African American involvement in military aviation, in the United

The CAF Mustang in rebuild.

Don Hinz flying the P-51C after its first restoration.

The aircraft after its repair following the Don Hinz crash.

Eugene Bullard memorial.

This elegantly restored North American P-51D "Mustang", marked up as a Tuskegee Airmen aircraft from the 332nd Fighter Group, will stand as the "Gate Guardian" to the 132nd Fighter Wing HQ. Photo by Senior Master Sergeant Tim Day.

Ninety-five Distinguished Flying Crosses, three Distinguished Unit Citations, one Presidential Unit Citation and one thousand and thirty-one Air Medals. This is the heritage of the Tuskegee Airmen.

The RQ-4 "Global Hawk" pilotless reconnaissance aircraft of the 380th Reconnaissance Wing seems an unlikely link to the Tuskegee Airmen. This aircraft, based in South East Asia, was decorated in February 2010 with a memorial to Lieutenant-Colonel Lee Archer who had died in New York the month before. Photo by Master Sergeant Scott Sturkol.

States Air Force Museum at Wright-Patterson Air Force Base, there is a small display commemorating Corporal Eugene Bullard. Enclosed in a cabinet is an effigy of him in uniform, some photographs and fourteen of his fifteen medals.

One recent memorial was the decoration of an RQ-4 pilotless reconnaissance aircraft of the 380th Reconnaissance Wing in South East Asia with a tribute to Lieutenant-Colonel Lee Archer who died in January 2010.

At last, there are live and static memorials to commemorate the great achievements of all the African American participants in American military aviation history. Most important, perhaps, are the living memorials in the form of operational squadrons and wings working in locations in the United States and around the world as they continue to uphold their pride and serve their country.

It is appropriate here to remind ourselves of the courage and dedication of this group of men who not only helped to liberate the world, but set the pace and triggered the action to liberate the African American in his own society. Ninety-five Distinguished Flying Crosses, three Distinguished Unit Citations, one Presidential Unit Citation and one thousand and thirty-one Air Medals. This is the heritage of the Tuskegee Airmen.

Finally, while looking for an illustration of the badge of the 99th Flying Training Squadron, the modern successor to the 99th Fighter Squadron, the author made an interesting discovery. Illustrated below is the badge of 99 Squadron, Royal Air Force. Note the similarity with that of the 332nd Fighter Group of which the 99th was part, and whose emblem also contained a black panther.

99 Squadron badge.

In World War II, 99 Squadron RAF was a bomber unit which, from its base at Digri in India, carried out night bombing raids against Japanese targets in Burma. In September 1944, the Squadron received its first American-manufactured aircraft, the Consolidated Liberator VI (B-24J) long-range bomber. Equipped with this new aircraft, in July 1945 the Squadron deployed from Dhubalia to the Cocos Islands, in preparation for the possible invasion of Malaya. That November, following the Japanese surrender, 99 Squadron was disbanded.

Even the motto of 99 Squadron seems to be prophetic of the 99th Fighter Squadron USAAF, despite the fact that there was never a connection between the two. "Quisque Tenax" translates to "Each One Tenacious". Entirely appropriate to the Tuskegee Airmen.

BIBLIOGRAPHY

Slavery in Colonial America, 1619-1776

Wood, Betty (2005)

The Black Soldier – From the American Revolution to Vietnam

David, Jay; Craner, Elaine (1971)

The Negro's Civil War

McPherson, James M. (2003)

The Unwept – Black American Soldiers and the Spanish-American War

van Zile Scott, Edward (1996)

The Unknown Soldiers

Barbeau, Arthur E; Henri, Florette; Nalty, Bernard C. (1996)

Harlem's Hell Fighters:
The African American 369th Infantry in World War I

Harris, Stephen L. (2005)

Freedom Flyers

Moye, J. Todd (2010)

The Tuskegee Airmen – An Illustrated History

Caver, Joseph; Ennels, Jerome; Haulman, Daniel L. (2011)

Blue Skies Black Wings

Broadnax, Samuel A., Osur, Alan M. (2008)

An American Experience

Johnson, Theopolis (1945)

Americaís First Black General – Benjamin O. Davis, Sr.

Fletcher, Marvin (1999)

Benjamin O. Davis, Jr. – American

Davis, Benjamin O. Jr. (2000)

A-Train – Memoirs of a Tuskegee Airman

Dryden, Charles W; Davis, Benjamin O. Jr. (2002)

Firefight at Yechon – Courage and Racism in the Korean War

Bussey, Charles M. (2002)

Fighting on Two Fronts –
African Americans and the Vietnam War

Jefferson, RF (2002)

My American Journey

Powell, Colin L. (1996)

Dreams From My Father

Obama, Barack H. (2004)

We Were Soldiers Once – And Young

Moore, Harold G. (2004)

Target: Berlin – a paper

Haulman, Daniel L. (2012)

The Tuskegee Airmen and the 'Never Lost a Bomber' Myth

Haulman, Daniel L. (2011)

The files of Dr. Daniel Haulman

The files of Craig Huntly

The files of Andre Swygert

INDEX
PROPER NAMES

Layout & Design Jodi Ellis Graphics
Printer   Toppan LeeFung Printing Limited
Printing   4 color process
Page Size   207mm x 234mm
Text Paper   120 gsm UPM Woodfree Paper
End Papers   140 gsm Woodfree Paper
Dust Jacket   157 gsm Gloss Artpaper, with gloss lamination
Body Text   10/12pt Cheltenham Light
Captions   10/12pt Gotham Condensed Medium